ELECTROMECHANICAL COMPONENTS FOR SERVOMECHANISMS

ELECTROMECHANICAL COMPONENTS FOR SERVOMECHANISMS

SIDNEY A. DAVIS

Consulting Electrical Engineer

BYRON K. LEDGERWOOD

Editor, Control Engineering

McGRAW-HILL BOOK COMPANY, INC.

New York   Toronto   London

1961

ELECTROMECHANICAL COMPONENTS FOR SERVOMECHANISMS

II
15550

THE MAPLE PRESS COMPANY, YORK, PA.

PREFACE

The complexity and accuracy requirements of present-day electro-mechanical servomechanisms call for a more precise knowledge of control component capabilities to permit their satisfactory application in critical systems. The system designer needs to know what the components can do and how best to use them. The component designer must be prepared to supply the systems engineer with specifications of component performance that permit intelligent systems design with a minimum of trial-and-error experimentation. This book attempts to contribute to both the systems and component designer's knowledge in the limited area of electromechanical components for servomechanisms, including potentiometers, synchros, induction potentiometers and resolvers, tachometers, a-c and d-c servomotors, and various miscellaneous components. By devoting an entire book to a subject that is normally relegated to a chapter or two in books on servo theory, it is possible to cover in detail those obscure points that often make the difference between a successful initial design and one that must be completely redesigned in the breadboard stage.

This is intended to be a working book rather than a theoretical one; the emphasis is on the practical application of actual hardware. The intention is not to tell how to design servo components but rather to point out how design features of the various components such as materials, winding distribution, and skew affect the component's performance in a system—in other words, what to look for in the components you buy and how to specify them. Although the treatment is consistently rigorous, the approach is via basic physical principles. The object is to make it easy to visualize and get a feel for even relatively complex phenomena. There are many original results as well as new simple presentations of material that was previously derived by highly mathematical treatments. An example is the examination of velocity errors in synchros from the point of view of the tachometer generator effect.

For all of the a-c components heavy reliance is placed on the equivalent circuit as a useful tool for determining the system characteristics of components. In each case the equivalent circuit is derived and examples are included to show how to obtain the equivalent circuit constants, both

v

from data normally supplied by the component manufacturer and from measurements made on an actual component. The examples then continue to demonstrate how these equivalent circuits can be used to determine shifts in component characteristics caused by changes in temperature, frequency, line voltage, line capacitance, etc. In several cases circuits are developed to compensate for such things as shifts in parameters and nonideal characteristics of components.

In particular, this approach permits the component user to extrapolate from the manufacturer's data, thereby arriving at a more complete knowledge of component parameters than is available from a catalogue sheet. The effects of nonlinearities can be judged, and the true value at some particular operating point can be determined, rather than just taking the theoretical average values from standard reference formulas.

The opening chapter sets the stage for the rest of the book by covering those electrical and mechanical features that are common to all components. Here and in the chapter on potentiometers are the only places where emphasis is placed on the current state of the art. The remaining chapters concentrate on basic principles, so that the material in them will apply just as well in the future, when smaller, more precise, and more efficient components come along, as it does today. The commercially available components used in the numerical examples are there only as typical guides: the techniques will apply as well to new components. Photographs and cutaways of existing components are shown in the first chapter to give the newcomer a feel for equipment, and the existing state of the art is covered for such mechanical details as bearings, lubricants, gearing, and insulation.

It was the authors' feeling that potentiometers had never been thoroughly documented in book form and that up-to-date information was available only in the technical press and in manufacturers' literature. Thus, the chapter on pots includes the authors' experience plus information from technical society papers and magazine articles. Although much of the material is germane to any potentiometer, a substantial portion relates to existing equipment, including tabulations of characteristics of commercial potentiometers.

Much of the material in the book was used in a course in servomechanism components taught by Sidney A. Davis at Polytechnic Institute of Brooklyn. The authors hope that the book itself will prove equally useful for this purpose as well as for a working reference source for control system designers in industry and the military.

Sidney A. Davis
Byron K. Ledgerwood

CONTENTS

Chapter 1

INTRODUCTION TO ROTATING COMPONENTS

1-1. Why Rotating Components? The increased use of precision servomechanisms and computers in both military and industrial automatic control systems has caused a marked increase in the importance of the smaller rotating components. Although no different in basic operating principles from the standard types of electrical machinery, these components excel in precision and in their dynamic characteristics. These properties are musts if the components are to perform satisfactorily in high-accuracy, fast-response, closed-loop control systems.

Most of the development work in this field has been sponsored by the government; beginning during World War II when the feedback techniques long used in communication equipment were adapted to the control of energy and power. Even today it is estimated that 95 per cent of the rotating components that are produced are used in military applications. But this is gradually beginning to change. The trend toward the automatic control of production to reduce labor costs, improve quality, and increase capacity is expanding the use of electromechanical computers and control systems into such fields as machine-tool control, rolling-mill control, process control, and many other industrial areas.

The requirements of industrial systems may cause some changes in the design of these components. Precision and dynamic characteristics will still be the important things, but reliability, environmental features, and cost must be viewed in a different light.

Military specifications speak of reliability in terms of 1,000 hr or at most a few years. But the industrial plant operator is used to a piece of equipment with a life of 20 years. Compromises may have to be made in an attempt to meet industrial reliability standards, and the industrial user must be reeducated.

Military specifications require that these components must withstand wide variations in environmental conditions, such as temperature, humidity, altitude, shock, and more recently, outer space environments. Although there are industrial applications where some of these characteristics are important (nuclear reactors, for example), in general the conditions are less severe, particularly with regard to variations in environment. Reduced requirements in this direction may permit increased reliability and lower costs.

Cost is closely related to standardization and production. Although the high-performance characteristics of these devices will always make them expensive, type standardization and high-quantity production are bound to result in lower costs. Some manufacturers are already producing commercial low-cost components with good performance and life characteristics. While these may not meet military specifications, they are satisfactory for industrial systems.

Most of the transducing, computing, and power elements described in this book are designed around a circular structure. While essentially analog devices, accuracies of 0.05 per cent can be obtained in carefully designed systems. Although most electrical machines are designed to deliver or be driven by rotary power, there are specific reasons associated with accuracy, response, and other control system requirements that dictate this configuration. These reasons are:

1. *Unlimited motion.* This means small physical size and high resolution.

2. *Angular input and output.* Most measured or controlled quantities can be converted into proportional angular positions.

3. *Geared output.* Scaling and inertia matching can be accomplished by selecting the proper gear ratio.

4. *Symmetrical construction.* This inherently results in a sturdy and compact design.

5. *Mass production.* The cylindrical shape of parts lends itself to high-quality and high-quantity production.

6. *Continuous operation.* There are often no limit stops, reversals, or discontinuities such as are encountered in linear-motion devices.

7. *Magnetic structure.* Satisfactory methods have been developed for using circular a-c magnetic structures that can be laminated along the lines of flux. In noncircular a-c devices, fringing difficulties and eddy-current problems are encountered.

For convenience, the various types of electromechanical rotating control components have been classified as follows: potentiometers, synchros, induction components, speed-measuring devices, a-c and d-c servomotors, and miscellaneous control components. Figure 1-1 points out the function of each of these categories in a closed-loop system. Since there is often no distinct line of demarcation, this cannot be a rigid designation but depends on the design.

The characteristics required by the individual components depend on their location and function in a closed control loop. In feedback systems, a reference value of a controlled variable is compared with the measured value of that variable. The difference is the actuating signal, which is amplified and directed to correct the measured value to secure correspondence with the desired reference value. This correction will continue until the actuating signal approaches zero. Components are required that will measure the input (reference) and output (actual)

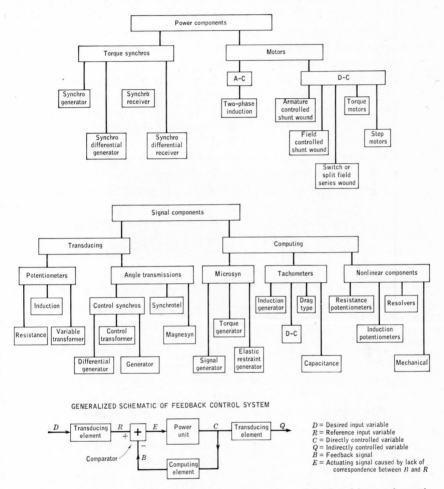

GENERALIZED SCHEMATIC OF FEEDBACK CONTROL SYSTEM

D = Desired input variable
R = Reference input variable
C = Directly controlled variable
Q = Indirectly controlled variable
B = Feedback signal
E = Actuating signal caused by lack of correspondence between B and R

FIG. 1-1. Breakdown of power and signal components, with closed-loop schematic showing usual location of these components.

values and transform them to a common unit of measure for purposes of comparison. The low-power actuating signal is amplified and drives the output to a null position. The output of the amplifier can range from a few milliwatts to many horsepower, depending on the power required to force the controlled variable to rapidly follow the reference.

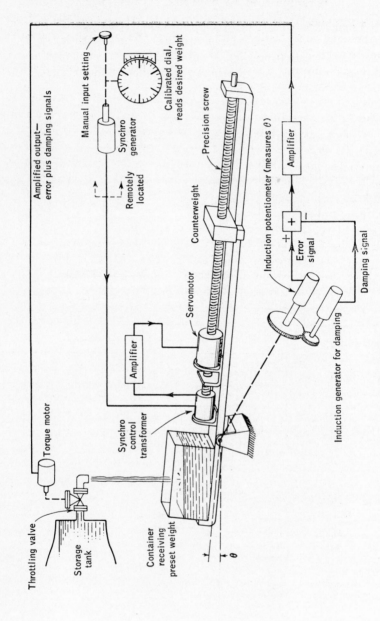

Amplified output—
error plus damping signals

Manual input setting

Calibrated dial,
reads desired weight

Synchro
generator

Precision screw

Remotely
located

Counterweight

Induction potentiometer (measures θ)

Amplifier

Error
signal

Torque motor

Servomotor

Amplifier

Damping signal

Throttling valve

Synchro
control
transformer

Induction generator for damping

Storage
tank

Container
receiving
preset weight

θ

FIG. 1-2. See opposite page for descriptive legend.

4

Thus, a feedback system consists of a set of precise, low-power transducing and computing devices, and a high-power controlled prime mover that converts the amplified actuating signal into a correcting force. This distinction is important; it is difficult to obtain both high power level and precision in the same component.

In closed-loop systems, any time lag between a change in input and the application of a correcting force to the output tends to introduce instability. With a varying input, this delay can cause the correction to be applied at the wrong time or in the wrong direction, either of which can result in an oscillatory response of the output. Thus, a special requirement of these components is a high speed of response. Energy-storage elements, such as springs, inertias, capacitors, and inductors, should be reduced to a minimum.

The selection of the low-power elements is based on the most convenient over-all arrangement for converting all signals to a common denominator with a minimum number of transducers. Accuracy, dynamic response, and stability are also important factors. Loading of these signal components should be kept to an absolute minimum to reduce loading errors.

High-power-component selection involves a study of the power requirements of the load, the rate of change and acceleration of the input variable, the allowable error in correspondence, and system dynamics.

Figures 1-2 and 1-3 show two examples of typical control systems using these components. Many similar problems can be solved by combining standard components in various ways with both electrical and mechanical connections.

The power components discussed in the following chapters are limited to outputs of under 100 watts. The precision signal components are applicable to systems of any size.

1-2. Characteristics of Electrical Machines. An electrical machine consists of an arrangement of coils having mutual inductance. By applying excitation to one or more of the coils, and by varying the mutual

---

FIG. 1-2. Automatic weighing system. Circuit for accurately metering a specified weight of a liquid. The desired weight can be set at a remote location. Two servo loops control the weighing and metering equipment.

One servo is a conventional synchro-transmission system that converts the set position of the remotely calibrated dial to an accurately corresponding position of the counterweight along the drive screw. The dial is calibrated to read the weight of liquid required to balance the counterweight.

When the counterweight is moved, the horizontal null setting of the beam is unbalanced and an error voltage is developed by the induction potentiometer. The error, plus the induction-generator damping voltage, is amplified and energizes the torque motor to regulate the flow of material into the container. The system must be critically damped to prevent overshoot, since it is impossible to remove liquid automatically if the quantity in the container is allowed to exceed that required to balance the beam.

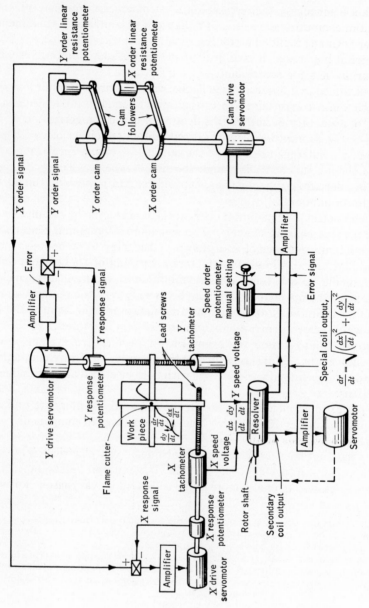

Fig. 1-3. See opposite page for descriptive legend.

inductance, torques can be developed and voltages can be induced. In conventional motors and generators, inductance is varied by rotating one member with respect to the other.

Electrical machinery is designed to ensure efficient coupling between the coils, so that a minimum magnetizing force can generate a field of the required strength. Thus, efficient flux transmission can be obtained with the familiar cylindrical rotor inside a cylindrical shell or stator.

The permeability of the iron path is also closely associated with the efficiency of flux transmission. High permeability is desirable, and most analyses of electrical machinery assume it to be infinite. To minimize eddy currents, the magnetic structure should be designed so that the flux flows through laminated-iron paths. This can be accomplished with the cylindrical configuration, since both the rotor and stator can be built up of laminated sections. Also very small airgaps can be obtained with the cylindrical construction by using conventional grinding procedures. This minimizes the magnetic reluctance of the gap.

There are several disadvantages to the cylindrical configuration, but no satisfactory alternate has been found. For example, on small motors it is difficult to install windings on the inner surface of the stator. In addition, multipolar windings give a minimum number of linkages per pole. This causes a reduction in the entire exciting reactance, thereby increasing the required exciting current.

1-3. Electrical and Mechanical Design Features. Although the many different components discussed in this book vary radically in their end use, the cylindrical type of construction is a common denominator which results in many similar electrical and mechanical design features. For

---

FIG. 1-3. Flame-cutting control. Arrangement for automatically cutting preset contours with a flame cutter. The system provides for cutting the proper contour, and for maintaining constant cutting speed regardless of the shape of the contour. The control system can be divided into two parts in accordance with these functions.

The contour-shaping system is controlled by two cams that contain the proper coordinate information. The cam followers drive X- and Y-order linear resistance potentiometers which transmit signals to the X and Y lead-screw drives. Each drive consists of a closed loop, which positions the lead screw and response potentiometer until the response signal equals the order signal.

In the cutting-speed regulating circuit, the tachometers attached to the lead screws develop outputs proportional to the angular velocity of the screws or to dx/dt and dy/dt in the coordinate system. These rate-of-change voltages are applied to the primary coils of a resolver. The output of the secondary resolver coils is amplified and used to drive a servomotor which positions the rotor to reduce the resolver output to zero. A special coil, with its axis perpendicular to the secondary coils, is wound on the rotor of the resolver. A voltage is induced in this special coil proportional to the vector sum of dx/dt and dy/dt, so that this voltage dr/dt is proportional to the instantaneous tangential cutting speed at any point on the contour. The signal dr/dt is compared with the voltage from a manually set speed-order potentiometer, and the difference is amplified and used to energize the motor driving the X- and Y-order cams.

example, the dielectric strength of the insulation, type of bearing, lubrication, and resistance to environmental conditions are common problems that are encountered in the design of any precision rotating component.

Insulation Requirements. With many of the components covered in this book, there are no particular electrical or mechanical strains imposed on the insulation materials, since the components are intended for the precise transformation of signals rather than for the generation of power. However, those components that develop mechanical energy require dielectrics that can reliably insulate the wires from one another and from the frame under severe conditions. Military applications in particular have increased the requirements on dielectrics because of such factors as:

1. Miniaturization, with higher outputs per unit of component volume, and per unit area of radiating surface.

2. High-altitude operation, where the air density is too low for efficient cooling.

3. High ambient temperatures such as caused by the proximity of electronic equipments that generate large quantities of heat.

Ordinary class A insulation, when used for military purposes, has been rated as high as possible over the normal commercial standards. Commercially, class A insulation can be used up to a maximum temperature of 105°C; military specifications permit a maximum of 135°C, MIL-E-5400. This variation results from the difference in life requirements. As mentioned before, military life requirements are usually several thousand hours, while commercial requirements go up to 20 years.

Enamel insulations such as Formvar are normally used on the windings of most signal components. These are class A coatings. Where higher temperatures are encountered, Teflon, silicone, and epoxy dielectrics have proved satisfactory. Silicone insulated wire will withstand temperatures up to 180°C and can be easily impregnated by silicone bonding agents and other compounds. On the other hand, Teflon is not easily impregnated, and it is difficult to adhere to its smooth surface. Also Teflon seems to do poorly under severe nuclear radiation.

Often servomotors are driven directly from the plate circuit of a pair of tubes in push-pull, without an isolating transformer. This imposes the additional burden of the B+ plate voltage on the insulation of the motor. Also various circuits have been developed where raw alternating current is used as the plate voltage instead of direct current. While this permits efficient power dissipation, the peak values developed during transients in the a-c circuit can cause a voltage surge on the motor windings that is three or four times the normal voltage. The high voltage stress plus high ambient temperatures lead to difficult insulation problems.

A novel requirement has been imposed on epoxy and other resins when they are used to encapsulate or "pot" the stators of very small servomotors. These motors have airgaps of approximately 0.001 in. and as a result the resin impregnant is required to maintain stator rigidity so that the closely held gap does not close up during the life of the unit. Unfortunately, epoxy resins are only reliable up to temperatures of about 140 to 150°C. This is in contrast to a good class H insulation which can be used up to 200°C.

Table 1-1 lists the classes of insulation.

TABLE 1-1. TEMPERATURE CLASSIFICATIONS OF INSULATING MATERIALS

Class	Hot-spot temperature, °C	Description
Y	90	Insulation consists of cotton, silk, paper, and materials such as synthetic fibers, plastics, and resins with similar thermal stability
A	105	Insulation consists of cotton, silk, and paper, when impregnated or immersed in oil, and materials such as plastics, resins, and impregnated synthetic fibers with similar thermal stability
E	120	Insulation consists of materials or combinations of materials which can be shown by experience or test to possess a degree of thermal stability which will allow them to be operated at temperatures at least 15°C higher than the materials in class A
B	130	Insulation consists of inorganic materials (mica, glass fiber, asbestos, etc.) with bonding substances (e.g., shellac) and other materials or combinations of materials with similar thermal stability
F	155	Insulation consists of materials or combinations of materials which can be shown by experience or test to possess a degree of thermal stability which will allow them to be operated at temperatures at least 25°C higher than the materials in class B
H	180	Insulation consists of: 1. Mica, asbestos, glass fiber, and similar inorganic materials in built-up form with bonding substances composed of selected silicone compounds or materials with similar thermal stability 2. Selected silicone compounds in rubbery or resinous form, and materials with similar thermal stability
C	Greater than 180	Insulation consists of mica without bonding substances, porcelain, glass, quartz, and other materials of similar thermal stability

Guided-missile applications have imposed temperatures of 205 to 260°C and higher on component insulation. While these temperatures have caused very high dielectric strains, they are not as serious as might be expected since life requirements are not more than a few hundred hours.

Fan cooling is often used in military equipment to reduce high-temperature strains on the insulation. In some servo and actuator motors, the temperature rise has been cut in half by using this technique. But the effectiveness of fan cooling is reduced when the components are operated at high altitudes, since air density is low and the fan cannot move a sufficient mass of air to carry the heat away.

Bearings. All precision signal and power components must have good bearings. For example, to maintain low starting voltage and maximum sensitivity to error signals, servomotors must be equipped with bearings of absolutely minimum friction. Besides, in servomotors with airgaps as small as 0.001 in., bearings with a sideshake of even several ten-thousandths of an inch may be excessive. Spring loading to prevent sideshake is no final solution in these motors, since this technique increases the bearing friction. Class 5 and even class 7 bearings are the accepted standard in high-quality units (see Table 1-2).

TABLE 1-2. BEARING CLASSES AND TOLERANCES*

ABEC class	Bore, +0.0000 in. to minus	OD, +0.0000 in. to minus	Eccentricity, TIR	
			Inner race	Outer race
1	0.0003	0.0004	0.0004	0.0006
3	0.0002	0.0003	0.0003	0.0004
5	0.0002	0.0002	0.0002	0.0002
7	0.00015	0.0002	0.0001	0.0002

* From ¼ in. bore (⅝ in. OD) to ½ in. bore (1⅛ in. OD). Class 1 is standard SAE tolerance. Antifriction Bearing Manufacturers Association (ABEC).

Low-torque bearings are even more important in synchros used for angular-position transmission. A typical synchro receiver may develop a torque of several hundredths of an ounce-inch per degree misalignment with transmitter. Thus, where accuracies on the order of minutes are required, maximum bearing torques of thousandths of an ounce-inch are often unsatisfactory. Special bearings have been developed that have spring positioners between the balls to maintain very low starting torques. Although the running torque of these bearings is higher than when standard retainers are used, over-all accuracies are better. Plastic retainers have been used, but they have dropped from the picture because of difficulties encountered with fungus, high temperatures, and other environmental factors.

To ensure precision alignment, some component manufacturers make their own bearings. These are usually of the separable variety. The inner race is fitted on the component rotor shaft, while the outer race is pressed into a stator bearing seat. The balls and the retainers are separate, and the bearing is not assembled until the rotor is placed in the stator. A slight amount of end thrust is applied to secure accurate alignment with no sideshake.

In many applications, military requirements have forced the use of stainless-steel bearings in place of ordinary hardened steel. This has resulted in increased friction, but usually there is no choice but to make this compromise. In certain missile applications, where ambient temperatures are as high as 260°C, ball bearings have been run dry. Stainless-steel bearings must be used here, since there is no lubricant to form a protective film against the environment.

The problem of loading bearings to a satisfactory safe limit is a difficult one in small rotating components. Since these bearings, the bearing housings, and rotor shaft of the component are held within very close tolerances, temperature variations can cause excessive changes in loading because of expansion and contraction. Also at high speeds, unbalance in the rotating members can cause excessive bearing wear. But by far the biggest problem results from environmental conditions, where particles of dirt, condensed moisture, or impurities in the lubricant cause high spots and wearing away of the bearing with ultimate component failure.

Noise generation is a bearing selection factor that is more or less peculiar to these types of components. Bearings are to some extent magnetic, and their rotation in the magnetic field of a motor can sometimes generate interference. This has caused problems in some types of communication equipment. Class 7 bearings are often recommended to minimize this effect.

Lubrication. No discussion of bearings is complete without a consideration of the accompanying lubrication problems. Like dielectrics, lubricants are being forced to their maximum capabilities by military requirements (Table 1-3). Components and their bearing lubricants must be able to operate over extreme temperature ranges. In the past, specific lubricants have been operated satisfactorily at 150°C; however, these same lubricants were not considered for use at -48 to -57°C. A high-viscosity lubricant is required at high temperatures, and a low-viscosity lubricant at low temperatures. For wide temperature range operation, a lubricant must have a low temperature-viscosity coefficient, or in other words, its viscosity must not vary too greatly with temperature. At the present time, silicone-based greases are the best lubricant for use over extreme temperature ranges.

TABLE 1-3. MILITARY SPECIFICATIONS FOR BALL-BEARING LUBRICANTS

Former designation	Now designated	Application and performance characteristics
AN-G-3	(Superseded)	Low-temperature petroleum greases ($-65°F$)
AN-G-5a	MIL-L-3545	High-temperature (0 to 300°F) grease, soda soap, petroleum oil
AN-G15a	MIL-L-7711	-40 to 250°F; 1,000 hr, 250°F, 10,000 rpm; 250 hr, 300°F, 10,000 rpm
AN-G-25	MIL-G-3278	Synthetic oil grease, -67 to 250°F, and 300°F for short periods of time; 1,000 hr, 10,000 rpm, 250°F bleeding 5 per cent
	MIL-G-7421 (USAF)	Low-starting torque ($-100°F$) 650 hr, 250°F, 10,000 rpm; diester oils, lithium base
	MIL-G-15719 (Ships)	Grease, high-temperature, electric motor, ball bearing (silicone)
AN-O-6a	MIL-L-7870	Lubricating oil, general-purpose, low-temperature
AN-O-11	MIL-L-6085A	Low-volatility instrument oil; galvanic corrosion a central requirement; diester oil

These greases can be used over a range from $-60°C$ to about 200 or 230°C. There are various types of silicone greases depending on whether the area of application is the high or low end of the temperature extremes, for although they have a relatively low coefficient, the viscosity variation is still too great for completely satisfactory operation at both ends of the spectrum. Thus, there are lubricants that are most useful in the low-temperature range while others are superior at high temperatures.

Even with these improved silicone greases there is still much to be desired in the currently available lubricants, and it is usually found that they limit the temperatures that can be imposed on rotating equipment. That is, the new electrical insulations and the satisfactory properties of the elements that make up a rotating component are still way ahead of the greases in their operating capabilities over large temperature ranges. For this reason, dry lubricants such as Molykote have been tried. This particular lubricant is a combination of graphite and molybdenum. Unfortunately, although these dry lubricants are not limited by temperature, under certain environmental conditions they tend to form hard little cakes that can ruin the bearing in a short time. Recent developments in dry lubricants may ultimately make these suitable for very high-temperature applications.

A common difficulty is the tendency for a lubricant to "run" at high temperatures. The RMB Filmoseal bearing incorporates an interesting solution to this problem. It has a nonrubbing capillary seal that compensates for the effects of temperature changes. For example, when internal bearing temperatures increase or decrease, pressure against the capillary film is exerted or reduced, causing it to move until the pressures are equalized. Three-eighth-inch-diameter bearings of this type have been run for several thousand hours at 165°C and 24,000 rpm.

Gearing. For convenience, gearing is often built integrally with a motor (Fig. 1-4). Lubrication problems occur not only in the bearings that support the gear shafts but also in the gears themselves. But usually the selection factors for gear lubricants in this application pretty well parallel those for the bearing lubricants since temperature is often the primary consideration. Many gear trains use sleeve bearings, particularly in the higher-torque stages. Increased temperature rise of the motor may be an indirect consequence of using an integral gear train when the combined unit is supported by the gear-train housing. The gear train increases the resistance to conductive heat flow from the motor stator to the mounting surface.

Fig. 1-4. Servomotor with integral universal gearhead. (*Courtesy of Servomechanisms, Inc.*)

Where environmental conditions dictate the use of steel gear housings, the increased resistance to heat flow can double the normal temperature rise of a motor. With more conductive aluminum housings, the effect is not nearly so pronounced.

Further Environmental Considerations. As mentioned previously, there are two basic types of environmental situations that are encountered. These result primarily from the application, military vs. industrial. In the former, extremes of temperature and other environmental conditions are encountered. Shock mounting is common and special care must be taken to make sure that lock washers, lock nuts, springs, and the like are properly used to maintain rigidity under conditions of vibration and shock. This is particularly true with flange-mounted units, where strains must be prevented at the mountings points and where the flange joins the body. These are common points of failure. Close-gap units must be sturdy enough to prevent binding of the airgap. Many motors and generators fail because the rotor strikes the stator when the units are subjected to vibration.

Special paints are required to prevent corrosion under salt-spray conditions (Table 1-4). Also dissimilar metals, such as brass and aluminum, must be protected from one another to prevent galvanic action. The aluminum bars in a squirrel-cage motor are particularly susceptible to corrosion. Often small particles of iron from the finishing tool become embedded in the aluminum. Even though coated with the correct paint, these particles can generate galvanic corrosion that will ultimately close up a small airgap.

On the other hand, in industrial applications size and the consequent problems of miniaturization are usually not important, nor are shock and vibration and extremes in temperature. Successful long-term reliability

TABLE 1-4. PROTECTIVE COATINGS

Application	Coating
Stainless steel.........	Clear or black passivate
Aluminum	Clear, black, or colored anodize
Paints...............	Sealac, Black Paladin, or Red Synthite

is the major problem. Occasionally shock and vibration are considerations, such as when the control equipment is mounted on a punch press or rolling mill. But these are the exception rather than the rule. Special industrial problems are caused by dust, lint, and other particles in the air, together with caustic fluids and vapors, sometimes capable of causing explosions. Often industrial equipment must operate under thick layers of dust.

1-4. Variety of Mechanical Configurations. A variety of rotor and stator configurations are common to the components discussed in this book. Thus many of the signal and power components look alike, although their design is based on substantially different principles.

FIG. 1-5. Miniature size 08 high-performance squirrel-cage servomotor. (*Courtesy of Ketay Dept., Norden Div., United Aircraft Corp.*)

The most common servomotor uses squirrel-cage construction and differs from a conventional squirrel-cage unit in its ratio of rotor to frame diameter (Figs. 1-5 and 1-6). In a control motor this ratio must be small to give low inertia and the high rotor resistance required for servo operation.

The drag-cup motor is similar to a basic squirrel-cage motor with the squirrel-cage windings removed from the rotor slots and formed into a drag cup of conducting material rotating in the airgap (Fig. 1-6). The slotted rotor laminations are replaced by a set of stationary iron-ring laminations that provide the required low-reluctance path for the magnetic flux.

To secure a maximum ratio of torque to inertia, motor-rotor diameter must be small. This makes it difficult to install the stator coils. For this reason some manufacturers use special stator laminations that can be wound by machine from the outside, reducing winding costs and coil size. Since winding and installing the coils are the most expensive operations in component manufacture, a gain is realized even though the two-piece stator construction is more complex than the conventional type.

Several other more or less specialized motor configurations are also available. These include motors with solid rotors of pure unlaminated iron that offer a compromise between the high performance of squirrel-

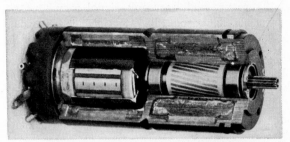

Fig. 1-6. Squirrel-cage servomotor and integral drag-cup tachometer. Construction of drag-cup motor is similar to that of tachometer. (*Courtesy of Ketay Dept., Norden Div., United Aircraft Corp.*)

Fig. 1-7. Complete servo in instrument case using miniature components. (*Courtesy of Servomechanisms, Inc.*)

cage motors and the uniformity of drag-cup units; motors with separate rotors and stators that can be designed into a user's equipment; and inverted motors in which the wound stator is mounted on a fixed shaft, while the rotor assembly rotates around the outer diameter of the stator. For damping purposes, motors can be obtained that have adjustable eddy-current or mechanical dampers, or stabilizing tachometers on the same shaft.

Components ¾ in. or less in diameter are finding wide application in instrumentation systems. With these units, the mechanical hardware of an entire servomechanism can be installed in a meter case (Fig. 1-7).

Although signal-type components are generally similar in construction, there are variations because of the different functions of these types of components. To secure high accuracy, signal components usually have a larger airgap; a gap that would be intolerable in a motor in which efficiency of torque generation is important. With a large gap the effect of the iron is less important and slight irregularities in the gap are insignificant on a percentage basis. However, this does not imply relaxed tolerances on precision grinding, runout, and bearing quality.

FIG. 1-8. Differential synchro, size 16. Stator is bearing mounted permitting angular mechanical inputs via exposed gear. (*Courtesy of Ketay Dept., Norden Div., United Aircraft Corp.*)

FIG. 1-9. Through-bore synchro. (*Courtesy of Ketay Dept., Norden Div., United Aircraft Corp.*)

Synchros look much like motors except that wound rotors are used (Figs. 1-8 and 1-9). Externally connected windings are installed on the rotor, in contrast to the squirrel-cage or drag-cup type of construction in which slip rings and brushes are not required. Synchros use dumbbell or salient-pole rotor construction. In synchros designed to transmit torque directly without the use of a servomotor, mechanical oscillation dampers are built into the receiver unit to prevent oscillation during transient positioning. Although slip rings are required, they are usually of a minimum diameter with a very light brush pressure to avoid introducing excessive frictional loads.

The rotors of other synchros and the rotors of induction potentiometers and resolvers resemble the rotor of an ordinary wound-rotor induction motor (Fig. 1-10). Windings are distributed in the slots and the terminals are brought out through slip rings.

Units of the reluctance variety, for example, a microsyn (Fig. 1-11), use ordinary laminated structures of iron as a rotor. No slip rings or windings are required. These units usually operate by varying the reluctance and coupling between input and output coils, both of which are distributed on the stator.

When used as components in automatic control systems, precision potentiometers require the same care in design and construction as do

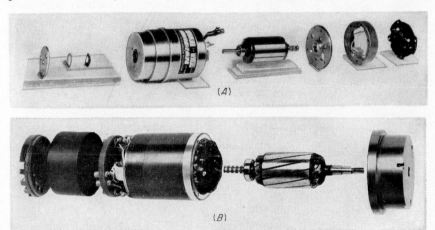

(A)

(B)

Fig. 1-10. (A) Exploded view of 400-cycle induction potentiometer. (*Courtesy of Arma Div., American Bosch Arma Corp.*) (B) Exploded view of size 23 resolver. (*Courtesy of Ford Instrument Co.*)

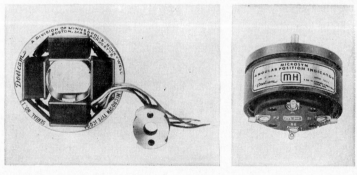

Fig. 1-11. Microsyn position indicator. (*Courtesy of Boston Div. of Minncapolis-Honeywell.*)

the other components (Fig. 1-12). Thus they are available with synchro-type mountings, ball bearings, and rigid steel housings. In some applications, potentiometer torque cannot be permitted to exceed several thousandths of an inch including the mounting bearings and wiper friction. This has forced the use of jewel bearings.

Units containing a motor, gear train, control transformer, resistance potentiometer, and other components are available as packaged assem-

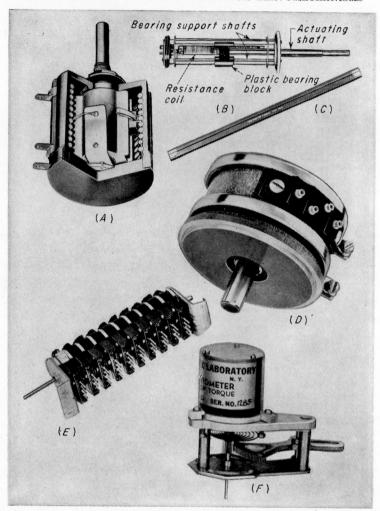

FIG. 1-12. Variety of potentiometer configurations.   (A) Cutaway of 10-turn pot; (B) linear-motion wire-wound pot; (C) linear-motion pot with conducting plastic resistance element; (D) single-turn wire-wound with synchro-type mounting; (E) ten-ganged pot assembly designed for plug-in service; (F) low-torque pot in pressure-gage linkage subassembly.   (*Courtesy of The Helipot Corp., G. M. Giannini & Company, Inc., Markite Corp., Fairchild Camera and Instrument Corp., Potentiometer Div., Fairchild Camera and Instrument Corp., Potentiometer Div., Electro-Mec Laboratory.*)

blies (Fig. 1-13).   Designs are varied and flexible to meet the requirements of the user.   Plug-in connectors are used wherever possible. These packaged elements simplify design and reduce control-system assembly and maintenance costs.

1-5. Equivalent Circuits of Rotating Machines.   The equivalent circuit of most electrical machines is derived from the basic equivalent circuit of the ordinary transformer (Fig. 1-14). The elements in this equivalent circuit correspond to a convenient breakdown of the resistances and inductances in an actual transformer, as visualized by a transformer designer.

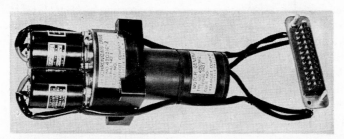

FIG. 1-13. Packaged servo synchronizing drive. Includes two synchro-control transformers and a motor-generator unit driving through a gear train. (*Courtesy of Kearfott Company, Inc.*)

It is possible that this transformer network might be converted to a variety of equivalent forms. But while the external performance characteristics remain unchanged in these equivalent forms, it is impossible to maintain the identity of the individual resistances and inductances

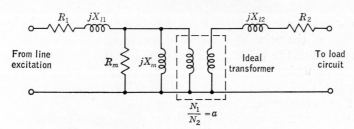

FIG. 1-14. Equivalent circuit of ordinary transformer.

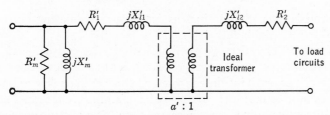

FIG. 1-15. Equivalent circuit of ordinary transformer. Primed values denote small differences in parameters as compared with Fig. 1-14.

observed by the designer. This point can be clarified by defining the separate elements of the equivalent circuit shown in Fig. 1-14.

First consider the simplified transformer sketch of Fig. 1-15. Essentially, the impedance of the primary winding (ignoring all nonlinearities) appears as a resistive element in series with a reactive element. But as remarked above, the circuit cannot be simplified this far if the identity of the various design constants is to be preserved.

In accordance with the laws of electromagnetic theory, the flux field generated by the primary when it is carrying current is distributed through all space. However, for convenience assume that this field is divided into two parts: one part that links the secondary winding turns and therefore is capable of inducing a voltage in the secondary, and a second part that does not link the turns of the secondary. The first part is called mutual inductance, and the second part leakage inductance. Since those flux lines that link the secondary, and those that do not, play entirely different roles in the performance of electrical machinery, this separation is a convenient one. This is notwithstanding the fact that both fields together actually constitute a single flux field, inducing a reactive magnetomotive force in the primary winding.

Where only a partial linkage occurs between the primary flux and the secondary turns (only some turns of the secondary are linked), then an equivalent figure for leakage must be determined.

As a fairly accurate approximation, it can be assumed that the mutual flux travels through the iron portion of the magnetic circuit, while the leakage flux predominantly travels through air. As a result, the reluctance of the leakage flux is relatively constant and is independent of the magnitude of the primary current, while the reluctance of the mutual flux varies with the primary current. This latter relationship is nonlinear. Harmonics are generated because of this nonlinearity and the hysteresis of the iron, and a saturation effect is experienced as the density of the flux in the iron approaches a saturating field.

The choice of iron-core material directly influences the magnitude and variation of the mutual inductance, but has little effect on the leakage inductance.

Since iron is a conductor just as is copper, circulating currents are generated by a variable flux field. These circulating currents are called eddy currents. They can be minimized by using a steel with a high electrical resistivity, such as silicon steel, and by laminating the steel into thin sections, each insulated from one another in such a manner as to impede the flow of current. If the leakage and mutual inductances are represented as two inductances in series, then the eddy-current losses can be represented as a resistance across the mutual inductance since this corresponds to the flux in the iron core. Although the eddy currents can have inductive characteristics of their own, the mutual inductance and the eddy-current resistance can be approximately represented as an inductance and a resistance in parallel. From another point of view, the eddy-current losses might be represented by a short-circuited high-resistance turn, absorbing power from the primary because it is linked with the mutual inductance.

Unlike eddy currents, hysteresis losses are nonlinear and vary in a nonlinear manner with the flux density in the iron. Therefore, strictly speaking, hysteresis losses cannot be represented by a constant resistance in an equivalent circuit. However, such an approximation is fairly accurate, and it is almost universal practice to include hysteresis losses as a modification to the value of the eddy-current resistance.

An examination of the resistance and losses of the secondary of a transformer shows an analogous set of parameters. Since the mutual inductance must be common to both windings, the equivalent circuits for the individual windings can be joined as shown in Fig. 1-14. An ideal transformation is required to correlate the differences in turns and impedance levels between the two windings.

When applied to a rotating machine, the equivalent circuit has certain basic similarities to the transformer equivalent circuit described above. Regardless of the number of windings, each winding has its own primary resistance, its own leakage impedance, its own airgap inductance, and its own core-loss figure. The principal difference in the rotating machinery equivalent circuit is the load that appears across the airgap inductance. This load includes the coupling of the rotor and also the mutual coupling to any other winding in the system.

A three-terminal network can be used to represent the coupling between any pair of windings on a rotating machine. Since a considerable portion of the coupling is caused by actual rotation, the elements of the network must include terms that vary with speed. Then, in general, rotating machines having one or more windings can be represented by the usual input circuits at each of these windings, inter-connected on their secondary sides by three-terminal networks having speed sensitive elements.

A balanced rotating machine with symmetrical coupling balancing out to zero presents a special case of the general equivalent circuit. It is only necessary to show one phase. Since

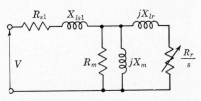

Fig. 1-16. Equivalent circuit of balanced servomotor.

the reaction of the rotor is a function of speed even under the symmetrical conditions of a balanced machine, a speed-sensitive load will appear across the airgap mutual inductance of the equivalent circuit.

Figure 1-16 shows the equivalent circuit of an ordinary balanced servomotor. The primary circuit is self-explanatory in terms of the above discussion. The secondary circuit shows the resistive term R_r/s, where s is the slip of the rotor with respect to the rotating field. The variation of this term with speed shows the effect of speed on the input impedance. The total power transmitted to the rotor must appear in the equivalent circuit as dissipation in this resistor. Output power and rotor losses are parts of this total rotor power. This division of power will be discussed in more detail in the chapter on servomotors.

Figure 1-17 shows the equivalent circuit of a general two-phase machine. Notice that under balanced operating conditions there is no coupling between the two windings; that is, there is no current flowing in the resistor $R_r[(1-s)/s]$. Under balanced conditions of a general nature, there would be coupling and it would be a function of speed. This circuit can be applied to the two-phase motor with unbalanced operation, or to the two-phase induction generator which is operated with its output winding open.

The equivalent-circuit technique can also be applied to any stationary network such as found in a resolver or synchro. By selecting some

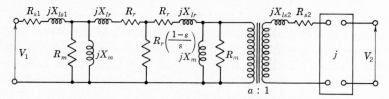

FIG. 1-17. Equivalent circuit of general two-phase machine.

arbitrary zero position, the transmitter and receiver can be converted to two-winding transformers, having a single pair of input and output terminals. By replacing each synchro with its transformer-type equivalent circuit, the system can be represented by Fig. 1-18. The equivalent-circuit constants can be measured or they can be estimated by applying transformer theory to the data supplied by the synchro manufacturer. This technique will be covered in detail in the following chapters.

1-6. Performance Factors in Signal Units. Induction-type signal units are designed to achieve a precise variation of mutual inductance as a function of shaft angle. Whether the object is to transmit angles (as in a synchro) or to generate linear or sinusoidal output functions, this fundamental purpose still applies.

The accuracy of performance is intimately related to the accuracy of the mutual inductance function. Thus there are two principal types of errors:

Type A errors—inherent in the design, independent of manufacturing errors

Type B errors—caused by departure of manufacturing from the ideal, and by imperfect materials

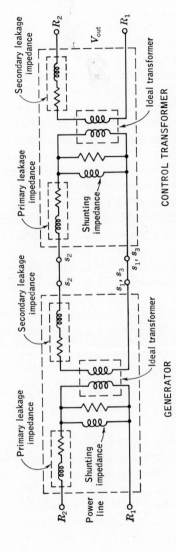

Fig. 1-18. Equivalent circuit of synchro generator-control transformer system.

The performance specifications for a given signal component spell out the nature of the variation of the mutual inductance. Coils must then be distributed on the rotor and stator members so as to approximate most closely this required mutual-inductance variation. Most situations require approximations since the finite number of slots limit the possible coil distribution. These approximations cause type A errors.

To reduce cost, it is usually desirable to use the same number of turns per coil in a given coil grouping. This reduces the refinement possible in the approximation of the desired inductance function, and consequently reduces accuracy. However, good accuracies are possible by the suitable selection of the number of coils and their span. Where absolutely minimum type A errors are desired, the number of turns in each coil is individually optimized.

Skewing of the primary or secondary structure is an additional variable in the synthesis of an ideal mutual-inductance function. Skewing gives an important measure of control by modifying the distribution of the flux. From the point of view of accuracy, it is immaterial whether the primary or secondary is skewed, since it is the relative skew that counts.

Included among the type A errors are those resulting from the non-smooth nature of the airgap caused by the slot openings. While the openings distort the flux field generated by the primary windings, these errors are themselves minimized by suitable design, primarily by adjustment of the skew. Additional type A errors often occur in high-accuracy low-voltage units where it is impossible to achieve an ideal number of turns (as determined by computation) because it is impossible to install arbitrary fractional numbers of turns.

Type B errors break down into two principal categories: those caused by manufacturing imperfections and those caused by nonideal material qualities. Most type B errors fall into the first category.

Coil layout and skew are selected to achieve a desired magnetomotive-force distribution, which should generate a corresponding flux field. The pickup winding is distributed so as to derive the desired variation of coupling with this flux field. The airgap, which is in the order of 0.003 to 0.015 in., constitutes the principal reluctance of the magnetic circuit and thus determines the flux distribution. For this reason, manufacturing errors that effect the gap are serious when fractional per cent accuracies are required. Fortunately, absolute accuracy of the airgap dimension is relatively unimportant, since variations here merely change the scale factor. However, ellipticity and eccentricity can severely influence accuracy. Gap variations in the order of 50 millionths of an inch are serious in high-precision units.

Similarly, the magnetic steels contribute a substantial and difficult-to-control group of type B errors. Errors caused by nonideal materials include:

1. Generation of residual voltages
2. Introduction of nonlinearities
3. Errors caused by grain effects

Residual voltage can be divided into two components: fundamental frequency and harmonic frequency. Fundamental-frequency voltage is in quadrature time phase with the output signal. If it were not in time quadrature, it could be canceled out by reorienting the rotor and then would be manifested as an error and not as residual.

Fundamental-frequency residual or quadrature can be described in terms of purely linear phenomena. In induction-type signal units a pulsating-line-frequency single-phase flux exists in the airgap of the machine. As long as the flux field is absolutely on a time basis, and if every flux tube is pulsating in exact phase correspondence, then it is impossible to generate an out-of-phase quadrature component. Thus quadrature must be derived from factors tending to produce localized phase shifts.

One of these factors is localized eddy currents that occur between laminations, especially where a conducting-surface smear is generated during grinding. These local eddy currents generate an out-of-phase field component that produces flux in the output coil. In general, this flux will continue to act even when the in-phase component is nulled out. Shorted turns in a winding can generate quadrature in a similar manner.

The usual iron loss in an iron structure is another source of quadrature. These iron losses tend to introduce phase shift. This phase is sometimes nonuniform because of uneven interlaminar resistance, local flux concentrations caused by airgap irregularities, and the difference in phase generated in the air region around the end turns. Skew at times also tends to introduce quadrature by generating an uneven gap density.

Several sources generate harmonics in electrical machines. Assuming perfect sinusoidal line voltage, the hysteresis characteristics of a magnetic material can cause harmonic variations. Harmonics from this source can be predicted from the hysteresis loop of the material, just as in regular transformers. However, the airgap tends to minimize these harmonics.

The basic nonlinearity of the permeability curve causes harmonic generation in the local flux fields of an electrical machine. However, these cancel in a perfectly symmetrical geometry. Unfortunately, the directional tendency caused by the grain orientation in each lamination causes residual harmonics to be generated as a result of dissymmetry.

The flux density in signal units is kept low to avoid operating on the nonlinear portion of the iron curve. Thus, signal units generate a negligible amount of heat. This facilitates temperature compensation, but results in high output impedance.

To minimize harmonic generation, accurate units are often made with the individual laminations rotated one slot at a time to ensure uniform characteristics in all directions. Manufacturers often provide a notch on the outer diameter of the laminations to facilitate grain orientation and to simplify inspection.

Nonlinear iron causes an additional source of error since the mutual inductance varies with the voltage level. Thus the coupling between the primary and secondary coils changes with voltage. In very precise units the tendency has been to use special grades of steel such as Permalloy, with initial permeabilities of about 30,000, and Supermalloy, with initial permeabilities of over 100,000.

These new steels require careful hydrogen annealing, and impurities must be controlled to within hundredths of a per cent. They are very difficult to handle since they are quite soft after annealing. Excessive handling tends to cause local work hardening and changes in the magnetic characteristics. These introduce the same kinds of errors as do unbalanced grain effects.

On the positive side, these materials have high initial permeabilities and are extremely resistant to corrosion. On the negative side, their softness makes them extremely hard to grind without smearing, and smearing causes eddy currents and quadrature. Interlamination insulation is very important in the reduction of eddy currents.

These high-permeability materials tend to minimize the variation in mutual inductance with voltage. A figure of merit would be:

1. High initial permeability
2. Minimum ratio of maximum to minimum permeability

These two factors must be optimized in selecting the best steel for a given unit. The former is most important.

Note that decreasing the airgap will not reduce scaling errors caused by variations in mutual inductance. A reduction in the airgap tends to increase the relative proportion of leakage impedance which is actually the basic source of scaling error.

Errors caused by grain effects are similar to airgap variations, since they result in an uneven flux distribution. The permeability can vary as much as two to one in the direction of the grain and perpendicular to the grain.

Signal units usually operate under very light loads so that the principal magnetomotive force in the airgap is derived from the primary. They generally feed into some high-impedance source, such as an amplifier. Complicated compensation, sometimes including electronic equipment, is often required to maintain precise scaling of signal units in the presence of variations in line voltage, frequency, and temperature.

In general, the components discussed in this book all operate together in closed-loop arrangements, and the voltages are eventually added up and nulled to zero. The output of each component is basically related to line voltage, and except for the nonlinearities discussed above, line voltage variations do not cause errors in an over-all system. Thus the null setting of an output shaft will not change as the line voltage makes ordinary variations. This means that a regulated supply is not required. However, excessive variations in line voltage affect the stiffness and stability of a precision servo so that in precise systems a reference supply accurate to several hundredths of 1 per cent might be required.

In general, the airgap in signal units is larger than in torque units since maximum accuracy and uniformity are required. This results in larger phase shifts and increased problems of compensation. In torque-type signal units (torque synchros) the gap is reduced to a minimum consistent with the required accuracy. But in general these are not as accurate as the pure signal units.

1-7. Performance Factors in Torque Units. There are a number of varieties of torque components, for example, servomotors and torque synchros. An error in a servomotor means a departure from the ideal form visualized by the servo designer. Included in these departures are friction and slot effect or cogging. These tend to increase the required starting voltage. The usual time delays in figures of merit can also be classified as errors in servomotors, since they are easily predicted and calculated design factors.

In torque synchros errors are introduced by slot effect, finite winding distribution compared with the infinitesimally distributed sine wave, and friction which is increased by side pull resulting from eccentricities in the rotor. Brush friction is also a factor in torque synchros. As mentioned previously, torque synchros are not as accurate as control synchros since they operate at high flux densities to secure high torques. The high flux density causes low iron permeability and the generation of harmonics, each producing its own residual torque. Low iron permeability means that the iron becomes an important reluctance in the magnetic circuit. The imperfections in the iron, in contrast to air, result in nonideal and nonsinusoidal flux distribution. Flux waves tend to become flat because of the high saturation of the iron.

Chapter 2

POTENTIOMETERS

2-1. Introduction. Potentiometers are electromechanical devices that develop an electrical output signal proportional to the product of an input electrical signal and some function of shaft angle. In the special but highly important case where the shaft-angle function is a straight line, a potentiometer is called linear.

Of the types that are available, the resistance potentiometer is the most versatile and widely used. It develops a shaft-responsive electrical signal by the sliding of a contactor or wiper along an energized resistance element. The resistance potentiometer is the most important type because it is:

1. Functionally flexible; used in innumerable diverse applications
2. Easily integrated with other elements of analog computers and electromechanical control systems
3. Reliable, and capable of withstanding the most severe environmental conditions
4. Economically available to very high accuracies and in compact sizes
5. Representable by fixed parameters with predictable system characteristics

Although the major portion of this chapter will be devoted to resistance pots, some discussion is included of the less familiar types, occasionally employed to satisfy unusual application requirements.

But even within the confines of resistance-pot types, there are many different varieties. The following points out the characteristics of some of the most popular kinds.[1,*]

Single-turn Wire-wound Potentiometers. This is the most common variety, available in small sizes to linearities within 0.1 per cent. Resistance wire is wrapped around a core, and then coated (except on the contact surface) with an insulating material that also anchors it in place.

---

* References, indicated in the text by superscript figures, are listed at the end of the chapter.

Three types of cores are used: copper mandrels (insulated copper magnet wire), cards (insulated metal or plastic strips formed into a cylindrical shape), and toroids (a short length of plastic or insulated metal tubing). The mandrel type offers ease of manufacture, low cost, close control of the winding process, and high resolution, while the card type permits higher resistances in the same diameter because of the width of the card. The closed toroid type is hard to wind accurately. In all cases a rotating wiper rides on the bare contact surface. The majority of present-day single-turn pots provide for continuous mechanical travel with electrical travel varying from about 320 to 360°. Potentiometers with mechanical travel limited to about 320 to 340° are also available. In the latter case, electrical travel is often equal to mechanical travel.

Because of limitations on wire size, the resolution of single-turn potentiometers cannot exceed 1 part in 2,500 per inch of diameter. Life is longer than with higher-speed multiturn units, and the small angular motion of single-turn potentiometers allows them to be operated heavily geared down, thereby reflecting negligible friction and inertia to a servomotor. Large diameters of 3 or 4 in. are not uncommon where high accuracies are required. This type is readily adaptable to ganging. The maximum resistance values that are easily obtainable with stable, low-temperature-coefficient wire range from 25K in $\frac{7}{8}$-in.-diameter pots to 200K in 3-in.-diameter units. Higher values are obtainable in special cases. Table 2-1 lists mechanical and electrical characteristics of typical commercially available single-turn and multiturn pots.

Multiturn Wire-wound Potentiometers. Multiturn wire-wound potentiometers are usually wound on a mandrel which is then formed into a helix. The rotary wiper is driven axially along the helix by means of a lead screw, and stops are required to limit servomechanism travel. Units are available to about 60 turns.

Multiturn potentiometers are inherently capable of delivering better accuracies and resolution than single-turn units. Gain in quality, however, is not in the same ratio as the number of turns, since many of the geometric errors become difficult to control in the more complex multiturn structure. Such errors as eccentricity of the wiper and the coils of the resistance element and ellipticity in the shape of the resistance element are diminished in proportion to the total number of potentiometer turns for given manufacturing tolerances. Errors from these sources appear as periodic variations over the angular travel of a potentiometer, repeating for successive turns. But all in all, for a given size, especially where small diameter is to be desired, the multiturn potentiometer is superior to the single-turn pot. Accuracies and resolutions of better than one-hundredth of 1 per cent can be achieved in a 10-turn unit, thousandths of 1 per cent in large-diameter units.

Thus, the principal advantage of the multiturn potentiometer is greater accuracy in miniature size. Subsidiary advantages include: much finer resolution for a given size of resistance-element wire (roughly, resolution improves proportionally to total angular travel), much higher resistance values where necessary, large total angular travel requiring much less precision in the gearing and associated mechanical hardware, less critical installation since mechanical mounting tolerances may be reduced, ease of shaft zeroing due to large angular range, improved stability of performance, and much closer tolerances percentagewise on total angular travel. For example, total electrical angle for a typical 10-turn potentiometer is defined as 3,600 plus 2 minus 0°, a total spread of 1 part in 1,800, or 0.055 per cent. This simplifies or may even eliminate the need for trimming in many applications. Similarly, the location of taps within ±1° in a 10-turn unit roughly corresponds in accuracy to ±0.1° in single-turn units, an extremely tight specification.

TABLE 2-1. CHARACTERISTICS OF PRECISION WIRE-WOUND

Diameter, in.	0.5	0.625	0.875	0.875	0.875	1	1	1.125	1.438
No. of turns	1	1	1	10	10	1	10	1	1
Manufacturers*	Ace	Pre	Osb	Hel	Cla	Gia	Hub	Fai	Tec
Model No.	X500	R6	09	AJ	....	85111	101	741 C	LT15
Length, in.	0.571	0.656	0.625	1.5	1.568	1.31	1.297	0.685	1.090
Length add'l cups, in.	....	....	0.478	....	....	....	.....	.....	0.520
Weight, oz	¼	....	0.6	1	1.1	0.6	1.43	0.77	1.0
Mount (Servo or Bushing)	S or B	S	S or B	S or B	S or B	....	.....	S or B	S
Housing material	alum.	alum.	alum.	....	....	mold. plas.	.....	alum.	....
Shaft diameter, in.	⅛	⅛	0.1248	⅛	....	0.031	0.1248	⅛	....
Starting friction, oz-in.	....	....	0.05	1	0.6	....	1	0.25	0.15
Mech. travel (total), deg	cont.	320	cont.	3,600	3,600	cont.	3,600	cont.	....
Mech. travel (tolerance), deg	...	....	....	+10-0	+5-1	....	±5	....	....
Elec. travel (total), deg	325	320	354	3,600	3,600	360	3,600	350	350
Elec. travel (tolerance), deg	±2	±3	+0-2	+10-0	+5-1	±5	±5	....	±0.4
Moment of inertia, g-cm²	....	....	0.15	0.3	1.7	0.035	.....	.....	....
Maximum taps	....	.....	9	32	20	....	.....	13	17
Overtravel, deg	....	.....	....	....	....	....	.....	.....	....
Ind. linearity (conformity) stand., %	±0.3	±0.5	±0.5	±0.5	±0.25	±0.5	±0.5	±0.5	±0.4
Ind. linearity (conformity) spec., %	....	±0.2	.....	±0.1	±0.05	....	±0.05	±0.25	0.2
Resolution (max.), %	....	....	......	....	0.005	0.05	0.007	0.05	....
Resistance min., ohms	10	100	10	25	....	100	25	300	50
Resistance max., K	250	30	20	100	100	100	100	150	250
Ambient temp. (max.) stand., °C	50	85	125	80	125	100	85	150	150
Ambient temp. (max.) spec., °C	....	125	......	....	....	150	.....	.....	....
Resistance tolerance stand., %	±2	±5	±3	±5	±5	....	±5	±5	±5
Resistance tolerance spec., %	....	.....	......	±2.5	.....	....	.....	.....	±2
Power at °C, watts	2/60 rise	1/80	1.25/25	2.8/40	3/40	1.63/25	3 40	2/40	....

*Ace Electronics Associates
Analogue Controls, Inc.
Circuit Instruments, Inc.
Clarostat Mfg. Co.

DeJur-Amsco Corp.
Fairchild Controls Corp.
G. H. Giannini & Co., Inc.
Helipot Corp.

In many applications, the multiturn unit provides improved reliability with its use of heavier wire for a given resolution and resistance specification. Heat generated in a multiturn unit is distributed over a much longer resistance element, providing greater thermal capacity through increased heat-transfer area and better contact to the housing, with a reduction in hot-spot problems.

The higher speed of the multiturn potentiometer results in much lower motor torques on the shaft, and much less chance of severe impact on the limit stops. This is an important safety feature in the gear-reduction portion of an instrument servo.

But the multiturn units have limitations and disadvantages also. For example, the multiturn potentiometer is not as suitable for lower resistance values, and it is not as readily adaptable to the generation of nonlinear functions, except through the use of external shunt resistors. In some applications where it is desirable to avoid gearing, the single-turn

POTENTIOMETERS (CLASSIFIED BY DIAMETER)

1.505	1.750	1.758	1.758	1.875	2	2	2	3	3	3.313
10	1	3	10	1	1	15	20	1	10	15
Voa	Cir	Hel	Spe	Kin	Tec	Ana	Lit	DeJ	Lit	Hel
RV	2800	......	800	1000C	LT20	N1815	MD20-20	C 300	MA30-10	......
1.83	0.890	1.141	1.984	0.889	1.090	$2\frac{33}{64}$	$2\frac{9}{16}$	1¼	2.266	2⅞
......	0.468	......	1.997	0.562	0.520	....	....	......	....	......
2.6	3	2.5	4.5	1.5	2	....	8	......	14	13
B	S	B	S or B	S	S	....	S	S or B	S	S or B
alum.	phenolic	......	phenolic	alum.	....	....	....	alum.	....	......
¼	¼	¼	0.2497	¼	....	....	¼	0.2499	0.250	¼
0.7	0.40	1.8	1.2	0.25	0.18	0.75	1.5	......	2.0	2.75
3,600	cont.	1,080	3,600	cont.	....	5,580	7,385	cont.	3,785	5,400
+3-0	....	+4-0	+3-0	....	....	±4	+5-4	......	....	+4-0
3,600	350	1,080	3,600	358	350	5,400	7,200	cont.	3,600	5,400
+2-0	±2	+4-0	+3-0	±1	±0.25	+1-0	+1-0	......	+1-0	+4-0
....	3.8	7	15	....	....	30	40	......	60	200
....	avail.	14	111	12	17	....	....	......	....	80
....	....	......	....	....	....	....	....	......	....	......
±0.3	±0.5	±0.5	±0.3	±0.1	±0.2	±0.01	±0.05	±1	±0.0075	0.5
±0.025	0.1	±0.1	±0.020	....	±0.1	±0.1	0.0075	......	....	0.025
....	....	......	....	0.04	....	....	....	......	....	......
100	....	5	50	20	100	....	1,000	......	2,000	40
300	330	130	1,000	200	355	400	600	......	300	1,000
150	150	80	105	....	150	150	85	......	85	80
avail.	....	......	125	225	....	....	125	......	....	......
0.5	±5	±5	....	±5	±5	±5	±5	±10	±5	±5
....	....	±1	....	±2	±1	±1	±1	±5	±1	±1
5/90	3/100	4.1	6.9/25	2.5/160	......	4.5/100	4/85	4/25	8/40	13.8

Hubbard Potentiometers, Inc.
Kintronic Div.
Litton Industries
Osborne Electric Corp.

Precision Line, Inc.
Spectrol
Technology Instrument Corp.
Voak Engineering Corp.

potentiometer is more sensitive to small mechanical inputs. This is especially true where a sensitive transducer provides an output displacement to actuate directly a precise resistance potentiometer. When a servomechanism has a duty cycle requiring frequent slewing, or operation with rapidly changing inputs, the slider of the multiturn potentiometer must go much faster, resulting in increased noise and slider wear and eventually in reduced life.

It should not be inferred that because a multiturn potentiometer can be made to very high-resistance values, loading problems can be handled simply by specifying indefinitely higher resistances in consecutive stages of a potentiometer chain. In high-resistance circuits, particularly at 400 cps and higher frequencies, errors due to stray capacitance, both within and external to a potentiometer, become pronounced. These result in phase shifts and quadrature voltages which seriously impair the operation of precision servomechanism loops.

Slide-wire Potentiometers. In this type a single slide wire serves as the resistance element, the principal advantage being very high resolution in small sizes. The resistance in a given frame is limited by the length of the wire, while the fineness of the wire needed for high resistance results in wear and reduced life. Slide-wire construction is often used in multiturn potentiometers where the additional active length permits practical resistance values. A typical 1.8-in.-diameter unit has a resistance of 250 ohms/turn; larger diameters are often used where higher resistances are needed.

Low-torque Potentiometers. Low-torque units are useful where the output of a transducer can drive a potentiometer directly, often eliminating a servomechanism. Low contact pressure causes high contact resistance (up to several hundred ohms) and sensitivity to vibration. In the lowest-torque units, with sensitivities under a few thousandths of an ounce-inch, jewel bearings must be used. Very low-torque units are of the single-turn variety, and maximum available resistance values correspond to the values for that category. These types of potentiometers are often packaged directly with the transducer; mechanical dial indicators, pressure transducers, and accelerometers with a direct electrical signal output from an integral low-torque potentiometer are typical examples.

Linear-motion Potentiometers. Where the displacement to be measured is linear, the rack and pinion required for converting to a rotary motion can often be eliminated by using this type of potentiometer. Linear-motion units are available in wire-wound, slide-wire, and deposited-film types. As in the case of the rotary pot, the resolution and accuracy of the wire-wound linear-motion type are limited by the length of the resistance element. Thus a linear-motion potentiometer $2\frac{1}{2}$ in.

long performs approximately the same as a 1-in.-diameter rotary pot. Linear units require careful mechanical design to achieve good rigidity and repeatability with minimum friction. And they are often considered as space wasters, since the shaft must extend a distance almost equal to the length of the potentiometer body. Some varieties permit substantial coupling misalignment without sacrificing accuracy or increasing friction loading.

Nonlinear Potentiometers. These are used where a nonlinear function of shaft rotation is required. They may be considered as electrical cams. Because of their importance and the many ways of achieving nonlinearity, nonlinear potentiometers are covered in detail in a later section.

Deposited-film Potentiometers. Varieties of high-resolution potentiometers have been developed using deposited metal, carbon, or conducting-plastic films. Resolution is ten to one hundred times better than that of the best wire-wound pots (excepting the slide-wire type) and is only limited by the granularity of the deposited film. These units offer promise in applications requiring good resolution, potentiometers capable of operating at high temperatures, and high accuracy in small size.

Carbon-film precision potentiometers provide exceptional resolution, delivering a continuously varying stepless voltage. Manufacturers claim a theoretical resolution of 5μin.; however, in practical production, this performance is reduced by mechanical limitations such as bearing play and brush adjustment to the values shown in Table 2-2. This high resolution is excellent for sector-pot applications and is essentially independent of resistance. Field experience indicates that linearity accuracies of ±0.02 per cent can be maintained in a 5-in.-diameter carbon-film pot under all conditions of environment called for by military specifications and over a life in excess of 10 million revolutions.

The smooth unbroken surface of the element permits high-speed operation and ensures long life (1 million cycles at rotational speeds up to 1,000 rpm). Separately available carbon resistance elements are especially useful where a potentiometer must be built into a mechanical component (such as a gyro or accelerometer) because of space or torque limitations. When tapped for the addition of other circuit elements, the effective tap width is zero, as long as no current is drawn from the tap. Standard carbon-film potentiometers are good to 150°C, and special units have been built that are capable of continuous operation at 500°C with a required life of 5 million revolutions. Failure of these units is gradual, and can be detected at any point in the failure cycle.

By control of film properties—thickness, width, and resistivity—very high linearities or nonlinear conformities can be achieved. By a contour milling technique, the carbon film can be "trimmed" with servo control to achieve high accuracy. Highly nonlinear functions can be generated

TABLE 2-2. PERFORMANCE CHARACTERISTICS OF
PRECISION CARBON-FILM POTENTIOMETERS[a]

Characteristic	Linear and nonlinear models			Sine-cosine models[b]	
	78	105	305	106	506
Diameter, in.................	$\frac{7}{8}$	$1\frac{3}{32}$	3	$1\frac{3}{32}$	5
Case length, in...............	0.575	0.635	1.100	0.635	1.675
Additional length per gang, in...	0.240	0.240	0.690	0.635	1.675
Shaft diameter, in............	0.1250	0.1250	0.2500	0.1250	0.2500
Mechanical rotation, deg.......	360 continuous				
Electrical function angle, deg...	320	350	350	360	360
Resistance range..............	1K to 250K ± 10%			20K	50K
Best linearity or conformity....	0.3%	0.2%	0.025%	Quad. max. 0.3PP	Quad. max. 0.025PP
Virtual resolution[c]...........	$\frac{1}{40,000}$	$\frac{1}{75,000}$	$\frac{1}{300,000}$	$\frac{1}{75,000}$	$\frac{1}{500,000}$
Wattage[d]...................	2	2	4	2	6
Temperature range, °C[e].......	−55 to 85				
Taps, maximum No.[f].........	4	7	18		
Starting torque, in.-oz.........	0.06	0.08	0.15	0.1	0.35
Guaranteed life..............	In excess of 2 million cycles at 100 rpm				

[a] Courtesy of Computer Instruments Corp.

[b] Sine-cosine types available with two wipers (sine, cosine, minus sine, minus cosine) and with ground taps (at 0 and 180°).

[c] This resolution caused mainly by wiper spring and other mechanical effects.

[d] For single cup at 25°C.

[e] All units are available for operation to 150°C on special order.

[f] Available both with infinite- and zero-series resistance types.

with carbon-film pots since the obtainable resistance range is much greater than for comparable wire-wound potentiometers.

In effect, the carbon film may be regarded as a surface across which a potential difference is applied. A family of orthogonal equipotential current-flow lines exists in the film, uniformly spaced for the linear case. The wiper serves as a pickoff, indicating the potential at its contact point with the film. Wear, which occurs along a current flow line, does not disturb the field or impair accuracy. It does, however, manifest itself in an increasingly erratic output voltage, ultimately showing intermittent opens. Relocating the wiper path restores potentiometer output to its original quality. The very gradual deterioration in performance is an important reliability feature in equipment where a sudden failure, such as an open in the resistance element, could have serious consequences.

By its nature the carbon-film potentiometer is flexible. This is a consequence of the ease with which the "resolutionless" film can be deposited in narrow or irregular paths. For example, a special step-function potentiometer has a total travel of 3° coupled with a sensitivity approximately 100 times that of a conventional one-turn pot. A great variety of other specialized types, including units with built-in resistors formed out of carbon film (to be used in conjunction with potentiometer portion), pulse generators that provide as many as 36 sinusoidal oscillations per shaft revolution, and units with switching and commutation functions, are available.

Carbon-film potentiometers exhibit certain peculiarities that must be understood if the units are to be properly applied. Inherently they are intended for use principally as voltage dividers and not as rheostats, and specifications must be on a voltage output vs. rotation basis and not on a resistance basis. The reason for this is that the slider is a potential pickoff having high resistance rather than a conventional low-resistance contact. Thus slider current must be limited to a few milliamps.

These units exhibit significant end resistance as well as resistance from a tap to the film, but if properly applied this does not impair accuracy. In addition, total resistance varies with temperature and humidity, an important factor when a carbon-film potentiometer is used in a resistive attenuation network.

Metal-film Potentiometers. Although engineers have been working for some years on precision potentiometers with metal-film resistance elements, only recently have manufacturers promoted them commercially. Problems of achieving a stable metal film and low contact noise have been difficult to solve, and there is still room for improvement. Nevertheless, there is a feeling that metal-film pots could provide an answer to extremely high-temperature requirements anticipated for the near future, and the current models are being stressed to broaden the knowledge of both the system designer and the user. A recent development is based upon a hermetically sealed resistance element brought into contact by "dimpling" a thin conducting diaphragm on the resistance element.

The problem areas in metal-film potentiometers are stability of total resistance under various environmental conditions and resistance noise at the wiper, especially with rotational wear. Table 2-3 lists the characteristics of typical commercial units.

Conducting-plastic-film Potentiometers. The Markite Corp. has developed a variety of both linear-motion and rotary plastic-film potentiometers, incorporating the infinite resolution and other important characteristics of film-type units. The conductive plastic track provides inherent toughness and extreme resistance to wear and corrosion. Like other film units, the resistive element is not subject to failure by sudden open circuiting. Standard accuracies of miniature single-turn units are of the order of 1 per cent, with closer tolerances available on special order. Recent developments have vastly increased accuracy and extended upper-temperature limits to several hundred degrees centigrade.

Trimming Potentiometers. Trimming potentiometers are widely used where precise settings or occasional readjustments are necessary. Usually used as voltage dividers (less often as variable resistors), their principal requirements are compactness, stability of setting under shock and vibration, reliability at very high temperatures, and good resolution and low backlash for ease of setting. A large electrical angle simplifies adjustment. Factors such as linearity are usually not important. Categories of trimming potentiometers include single-turn rotary vs. multiturn screw-actuated types, carbon- or metal-film vs. wire-wound types, and an impressive variety of convenient mechanical types for compact packaging of one or more units. Since electrical requirements of these pots are not stringent, selection should be made on the basis of suitable mechanical configuration, resistance to anticipated environmental extremes, reliability of source, and price.

TABLE 2-3. PERFORMANCE CHARACTERISTICS OF PRECISION
METAL-FILM POTENTIOMETERS

Servomechanisms, Inc. (Single-turn)

Diameter. $1\frac{1}{16}$ in.

Independent Linearity. ± 1 per cent; ± 0.5 per cent in values less than 2K. Substantially no change of linearity with mechanical life.

High-temperature Test. Load life tests have been conducted at 100°C with 2 watts dissipation for 1,000 hr with resistance change less than 3 per cent. Load-life tests have been satisfactorily conducted for 1,000 hr at 200°C, but insufficient data are available to give specific guarantees.

Resistance Stability. Less at higher ohmic values.

Resolution. Angular resolution is less than 0.01°, but tests have not yet measured the true values.

Construction. Resistance element, taps, terminals, all applied by vacuum deposition to give rugged unitized construction.

End and Tap Resistance. Order of few ohms. When tap or end resistances of less than 20 to 50 ohms are required, a flat spot of a degree or so may occur in the output characteristic.

Electrical Angle. 350° maximum in present models. Can be readily made for continuous electrical rotation with multiple taps.

Resistance Range. 50 ohms–10K. High resolution is present regardless of resistance.

Torque. 0.01 oz-in. is normal without sacrifice of life or noise.

Vibration. 2,000 cps at 10g is standard without resonance; 2,000 cps at 200g without damage.

Environmental. Manufacturer states "a modification from standard construction makes our pot capable of withstanding humidity, salt spray and fungus tests. In such pots the shaft torque is under 1 oz-in." Environmental requirements usually are taken from MIL-E-5272 and MIL-Std-202.

Resistance Tolerance. ±5 per cent; ±10 per cent above 10K.

Power Rating. 2 watts.

Future Goals. Ultrahigh temperature, 500°C and above. Also, wiper that does not physically contact the resistance element, but uses a sealed film resistance element to give greatly improved life.

Technology Instrument Corp. (Single-turn)

Standard Resistance Range

MFR-1—1K, 25K (1¼₆ in. diam.)

MFR-2—1K, 50K (2 in. diam.)

Equivalent Noise Resistance. Less than 100 ohms.

Linearity. Less than 0.5 per cent, independent.

Resolution. Essentially infinite.

Dielectric Strength. Will withstand a 60-cps 900-volt rms signal for 1-min duration at atmospheric pressure; a 60-cps 450-volt rms signal for 1 min at 3.4 in. of mercury pressure.

Electrical Angle. 350°, ±3° max.

Temperature Coefficient of Resistance Element. Less than 0.0003 ohm/ohm/°C.

Insulation Resistance. Greater than 10 megohms.

Torque. Less than 1 oz-in. (std); less than 0.5 oz-in. special.

Rotation. Continuous or as desired.

Mounting. Servo mount standard; other mounting special.

Mounting Hardware. Noncorrosive type used exclusively, per U.S. Army 72-53.

Shaft. Centerless-ground stainless-steel type.

Shaft Play. Not more than 0.001 in.

Concentricity. Within 0.001 in.

Perpendicularity. Within 0.001 in.

Rotating Contact. Rotating contact electrically insulated from shaft.

Resistance Element. Metallic film protected against mechanical damage and is substantially dustproof and moistureproof.

Construction of these units provides full hermetic sealing while maintaining moderately low torque and zero backlash. Seal provides a dust- and humidity-free enclosure.

One company is starting production on a wire-wound trimming potentiometer with a maximum operative temperature of 225°C. Standard load life at rated power for this pot is 1,000 hr, but test data suggest a 2,000-hr life at slightly lower ratings and from 5,000 to 10,000 hr reliable life at negligible dissipation. Specified linearity is less than ±5 per cent; however, actual linearity averages 1 per cent or less in units with a resistance of 1,000 ohms and above. After 200 cycles, total resistance shift is less than 2 per cent.

Carbon-type trimming potentiometers are characterized by a higher temperature coefficient, lower power rating, and increased contact resistance when compared with wire-wound units. Usually carbon types are not suited to humid environments because of their sensitivity to moisture.

Table 2-4 lists characteristics of typical wire-wound and carbon-film trimming potentiometers.

TABLE 2-4. CHARACTERISTICS OF TRIMMING POTENTIOMETERS[a]

Type, class, and model	Terminals[b]	Resistance[c], ohms	End settings, %	Power rating, watts	Maximum operating temp, °C	Humidity-proof MIL specs[d]	Size, in. H	Size, in. W	Size, in. L	Standard resistances, ohms
Wire-wound pots:										
Trimpot 200.............	L, S, P	10-50K	0-0.7[e]	0.25	105	No	5/16	1/4	1 1/4	10-10K, 20K, 50K
Hi-R Trimpot 207[f].........	L	100-100K	0-7.5	2.0	175	No[f]	13/16	9/32	1 1/4	100-50K, 100K
Trimpot 260 (high temp.)...	L, S, P	10-50K	0-0.1[e]	1.0	175	No	5/16	1/4	1 1/4	10-10K, 20K, 50K
Wire-wound variable resistors:										
TrimR 201.............	L	20K-100K	0-0.7[e]	0.25	105	No	5/16	1/4	1 1/4	20K, 25K, 50K, 100K
TrimR 261 (high temp).....	L	20K-100K	0-0.1[e]	1.0	175	No	5/16	1/4	1 1/4	20K, 25K, 50K, 100K
Carbon pots:										
Trimpot 213 (general purpose).............	P	20K-1 meg	0-7.5	0.2	95	No	5/16	1/4	1 1/4	20K-1 meg
Trimpot Resiston 215......	L, S, P	20K-1 meg	0-1.0	0.25	125	Yes	5/16	1/4	1 1/4	20K-1 meg

[a] Courtesy of Bourns Laboratories, Inc.

[b] S, Solder lugs; L, stranded insulated leads; P, printed-circuit pins; W, solid wire.

[c] Standard resistance (ohms): 10, 20, 50, 100, 200, 500, 1K, 2K, 5K, 10K, 20K, 50K, 100K, 200K, 500K, 1 meg. Units are available in these resistances within resistance limits shown in chart. Other resistances on special order.

[d] All military models listed are sealed against sand and dust and are splash-proof.

[e] Or 0 to 0.5 ohms, whichever is greater.

[f] Consult manufacturer for humidity-proof model.

Mechanical Variations. A great number of mechanical variations based on such factors as type of mounting, output shaft, provision for ganging, inclusion of switching circuits within the potentiometer, etc., are available or can be specially designed. In addition, unusual environmental features can be obtained by design tricks such as sealing, filling with oil, dynamically balancing the wiper assembly for greater vibration and shock resistance, etc.

2-2. System Functions of Potentiometers. Establishing optimum potentiometer specifications is a complex task because of the great range of possible applications and the great variety of potentiometer types that are available to fill these applications. Selection factors that are relatively unimportant in some applications become primary in others. Figure 2-1 shows eight basic potentiometer system functions, each requiring its own distinctive potentiometer characteristics. These eight are comparable to the large majority of complex potentiometer applications in industrial and military equipment. By becoming familiar with the important performance specifications for these eight basic functions, the system designer can quickly assign specifications to pots based on the function they perform.

Data Conversion. The importance of the electromechanical computer for analog computation and automatic control has established the potentiometer in a leading role as a converter between shaft angle and electrical signal. Figure 2-1A shows the mechanical to electrical and electrical to mechanical conversion. In both cases the accuracy of the potentiometer must be sufficient to meet the requirements of the application. In the electrical to mechanical conversion, pot resolution must be consistent with the stability requirements of the closed loop. Note also the possibility of multiplying or dividing with line excitation as one variable.

Angle Transmission. Here a continuous-winding potentiometer with three equally spaced taps is used as the transmitter in a direct-angle transmission system (Fig. 2-1B). As in a torque synchro system, the transmitter pot must provide the energy for positioning the d-c synchro, and must, therefore, be capable of continuously dissipating a large amount of heat. Inherently, open-loop systems of this type are not highly accurate. Potentiometer-shaft frictional torque is apt to be appreciable since heavy contacts are required for current conduction. However, in an open-loop system, resolution is important only as it affects accuracy.

Function Generation. As pointed out elsewhere, a potentiometer can develop a nonlinear function of a mechanical or electrical input in addition to the normal straight-line characteristic. Figure 2-1C shows the nonlinear mechanical to electrical and electrical to mechanical conversions.

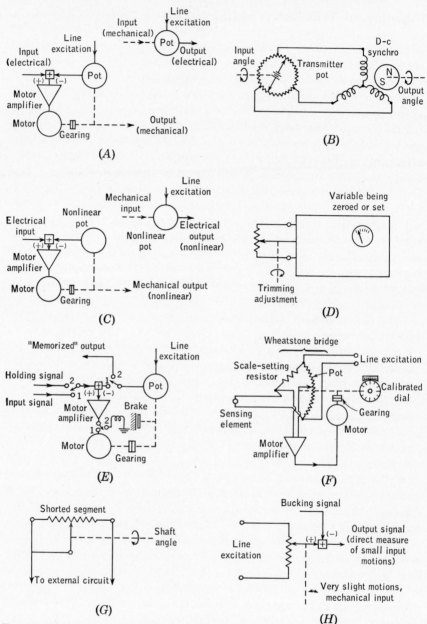

FIG. 2-1. Basic system functions of potentiometers. (*A*) Data conversion; (*B*) angle transmission; (*C*) function generation; (*D*) trimming; (*E*) nulling; (*F*) balancing; (*G*) varying resistance; (*H*) detecting small motions.

The requirements are similar to those for data conversion. Depending on the way the nonlinearity is developed, resolution may be a function of shaft position, in which case stability must be investigated under the worst conditions. In the electrical to mechanical conversion circuit, servomechanism stiffness can vary according to potentiometer gradient. Adequate stiffness must be achieved under the sloppiest conditions, while at the same time stability must be maintained at the other high-gain extreme. Nonlinear servo techniques, such as automatic gain control, ease the design problem.

Trimming. Potentiometers can be used to make adjustments in a circuit where normal system variations cause shifts in calibration (Fig. 2-1D). Principal trimmer characteristics are precise maintenance of setting and adequate resolution to permit the finest adjustments required in an application. Where these units are used as variable-resistance elements, rather than as straight voltage dividers, low-temperature coefficient and low contact resistance are also required characteristics. Since trimmers are often used in electronic equipment, they are designed to operate at temperatures up to 350°F. Locking features are required to maintain the initial setting. Since accuracy is not a factor, they can be designed extremely small. Recent designs use metal films as the resistance element.

Nulling. In nulling circuits, a servomechanism positions a potentiometer so that it bucks out an input signal. Since precise nulling is important in a high-gain servo, resolution must be adequate if oscillation is to be avoided. Figure 2-1E shows a potentiometer as a nulling device in a "memory" circuit. After the potentiometer is positioned to balance the input signal, it may be locked in that position by a brake. Then the "memorized" output voltage may be switched to another circuit.

Balancing. When used as a balancing device, potentiometer accuracy must be consistent with the requirements of the application. High resolution is also necessary because of the closed loop. In the circuit of Fig. 2-1F, balancing-potentiometer shaft position is an indication of the quantity being measured.

Varying Resistance. When used as a variable resistance, constancy of total resistance and low contact resistance are important (Fig. 2-1G). Resolution affects only the fineness of the adjustment, and accuracy is usually unimportant.

Detecting Small Motions. Potentiometers can be used to detect small motions in open- and closed-loop systems, as shown in Fig. 2-1H. Typical examples are pressure pickups, gyro pickups, accelerometers, and strain gages. Resolution and low noise level are principal factors, while total resistance and accuracy are less important.

2-3. Selecting and Applying Potentiometers. Figure 2-2 shows 10 typical potentiometer application circuits that emphasize the purpose of the over-all system rather than the potentiometer function. They are included to show how the basic potentiometer function can be recognized in relatively complex circuits. Once the basic function is determined, the key specifications will be apparent following the approach outlined in Sec. 2-2.

Circuit for Determining Tangential Cutting Speed. The table of a milling machine shown in Fig. 2-2A is being oriented by the motion of X and Y lead screws to permit cutting a nonlinear contour, such as a plate cam. The assembly of components delivers an output voltage proportional to the tangential speed of the cam-cutting operation. In a complete contouring system this voltage could be used to maintain constant cutting speed. The squaring pots on the lead screws are function generators, with accuracy important but resolution not a problem. The potentiometer in the feedback loop is both a function generator and balancing device. Both high accuracy and high resolution are required. The servo has variable stiffness as noted in the preceding section on system functions of potentiometers.

Alternate Circuit for Determining Tangential Cutting Speed. In the alternate computational scheme of Fig. 2-2B, two trigonometric-function-generating potentiometers supply the nonlinear functions in lieu of the three squaring pots in the previous circuit. Since they are both in the loop, resolution and accuracy are problems. Again, variable servo gain (depending on the magnitude of X and Y) is characteristic of this type system. An additional linear potentiometer is also required to convert the electrical signal R into a shaft rotation.

Table-position Indication. Linear-motion potentiometers convert mechanical displacement to a proportional electrical signal in Fig. 2-2C. For this data-converting function, accuracy is the problem, not resolution.

Torque Amplifier. In Fig. 2-2D, a differential potentiometer is used for torque amplification. The motion of the low-torque input (wiper) shaft produces an output signal which, when amplified, actuates the worm drive and delivers a high torque output. The potentiometer performs a nulling function so that pot accuracy and total resistance are unimportant, while resolution is critical.

Revolution Counter. Figure 2-2E shows an unusual use of potentiometers for data conversion. The voltages from the four potentiometers indicate corresponding digits. In this application, the digital nature of the output minimizes potentiometer requirements in general.

Liquid-level Indication. The remote transmission of liquid level by means of a potentiometer and a d-c synchro is shown in Fig. 2-2F. The basic function is angle transmission. Resolution is unimportant, and

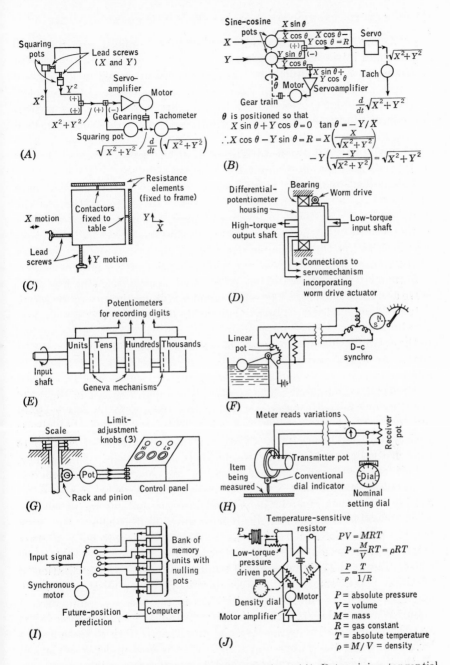

FIG. 2-2. Typical potentiometer application circuits. (A) Determining tangential cutting speeds; (B) alternate way to determine cutting speeds; (C) table-position indication; (D) torque amplifier; (E) digital revolution counter; (F) liquid-level indication; (G) high-low weight indicator; (H) thickness gage; (I) memory units; (J) air-density computer.

43

accuracy better than a few tenths of a per cent is unnecessary because of friction and intrinsic system errors.

High-low Weight Indicator.   The arrangement shown in Fig. 2-2G is useful in repetitive industrial weighing operations.   The potentiometers in the control panel, preset to the required limits, buck the transmitting pot coupled to the scale.   The basic function is detecting small motions, so that the transmitting potentiometer must have sufficiently good resolution to detect small variations from the preset nominal weight. Total resistance and accuracy are less important.

Thickness Gage.   The potentiometer on the conventional dial indicator of Fig. 2-2H simultaneously detects small motion variations and remotely transmits them to an output meter.   The transmitter potentiometer must be of the low-torque variety and must have high accuracy. The accuracy of the meter reading depends completely on the accuracy of the transmitting pot.   The receiving potentiometer is not critical.

Memory Units.   Potentiometers, used as memory units in Fig. 2-2I, serve as nulling devices.   The input signal is switched in turn to the servo-actuated bucking pots.   These bucking potentiometers thus "remember" a uniformly time-spaced sequence of input signals, which, when applied to the computer, permit prediction of the input signal at some given future time.   Accuracy and total resistance are unimportant, but resolution must be adequate to avoid servo instability.

Air-density Computer.   The air-density computer shown in Fig. 2-2J operates on the perfect-gas law, using two potentiometers as variable resistors.   The bellows-driven potentiometer must be of the low-torque variety and highly accurate.   The balancing potentiometer coupled to the density dial must have good resolution to avoid closed-loop instability.

Besides the gross application factors that are obvious once the function of a potentiometer in a system is recognized, there are many other specific items that must be considered in every potentiometer system. These selection factors, while dealt with generally throughout the chapter, are summarized in Table 2-5.   Careful attention to each of these areas should ensure a successful system design.

2-4. Standard Definitions and Terminology.   The standardization of precision potentiometer definitions, terminology, sampling, inspection, and test procedures has been undertaken in the past by committees of manufacturers and users such as the Aircraft Industries Association (AIA) and the Electronic Industries Association (EIA).   Both of these groups have completed their work and a MIL spec is now under formulation. By the time this book is published the MIL specifications will undoubtedly be finished, based primarily on the standard specifications of these two industry groups.

Table 2-5. Check List of Potentiometer Selection Factors

Type of Potentiometer. Check against the available varieties of resistance potentiometers as covered in Sec. 2-1. In the case where special system requirements indicate that a nonresistive potentiometer is needed, consider those potentiometric devices described in Sec. 2-19.

Linearity, Zero Location, and Trimming. These relate to the problem of fitting the best straight line to the actual output curve of a potentiometer. The best straight line is that which gives minimum error. Trimming resistors in series (and also in parallel) with the potentiometer and arbitrary choice of zero location make this optimum fit possible. Tolerances for accomplishing this adjustment must be specified in the potentiometer-circuit design.

Total Resistance and Tolerance. Total resistance is related to heating and also to loading, since high-resistance potentiometers can only be loaded by even higher-resistance potentiometers. Unless the resistance of the loading pot exceeds the resistance of the loaded pot by at least a factor of 10, there is apt to be significant loading error. Thus, minimizing the resistance of the first potentiometers in a chain is normal practice. Minimum resistance is, however, limited by heating effects, and by the poor resolution of low-resistance units with their fewer turns of wire. Another significant factor is the frequency error resulting from stray capacitance that becomes effective in high-resistance circuits. In several-thousand-ohm pots, errors due to stray capacitance can amount to several tenths of a per cent at 400 cps.

Contact Resistance and Noise Generation. Noise at the contact behaves like an additional voltage source and a variable resistance in series with the output lead. When a potentiometer is loaded for use as a variable resistor, contact resistance may be extremely important. When a pot is feeding a high-impedance vacuum-tube circuit, noise is less important but still significant, in that it may saturate the amplifier. Also, excessive noise may generate radio interference.

Resolution. In wire-wound potentiometers (not slide-wire types), the output varies in a steplike fashion with shaft position as the wiper arm moves from one wire to the next. This steplike behavior corresponds to infinite slopes at discrete points, which means infinite gain in a servo. These points of infinite slope may become points of oscillation when the unit is used in closed-loop systems. Resolution should be kept to a fraction of the allowable error.

Granularity. This applies only to film-type potentiometers, and corresponds roughly to resolution in wire-wound units. It relates to the film's crystalline structure.

Temperature Coefficient of Resistance. This is related to the tolerance imposed on total resistance, since high-temperature coefficients cause total resistance to vary widely with temperature.

Accuracy of Tap Location. Where taps are used to increase potentiometer flexibility (as in the generation of nonlinear functions), tap location accuracy may be significant. This must be tied to a specific application.

Cost. The cost of resistance potentiometers is related primarily to degree of standardization and volume of production. For general-purpose medium-precision work, 10-turn potentiometers of approximately $1^{13}\!/_{16}$ in. diameter, and single-turn units of 2 to 3 in. diameter are most economical. Less popular units, such as zero-resolution or very low-torque types, or special designs, can easily cost five to ten times the price of the general-purpose ones. Trimmer units cost roughly one-fourth the price of the low-priced potentiometers.

TABLE 2-5. CHECK LIST OF POTENTIOMETER SELECTION FACTORS (*Continued*)

Availability and Performance Experience. To the engineering specifications must be added the ability of a manufacturer to deliver in production quantities, according to specification, the availability of additional sources, and the previous successful application of the selected potentiometer type.

Miscellaneous Mechanical Characteristics. Permissible environmental conditions; aging; life under required duty cycle; sensitivity to shock and vibration; required driving torque; physical suitability (size, mounting dimensions, shaft requirements, etc.); useful angle of rotation; shorting or nonshorting characteristics of terminals.

The AIA specifications were issued by the National Aircraft Standards Committee as specification NAS710. The following is adapted from these standards.

2-5. Electrical and Mechanical Angular Relationships. Figure 2-3 shows the terms that are to be defined. The *mechanical angle* is the total angle through which the shaft can be rotated. When no stops are specified, the mechanical angle is understood to be unlimited or continuous. The *mechanical overtravel* is the angle of shaft rotation between an end point and the near mechanical stop. When no stops are specified, this angle is 360° minus the actual electrical angle.

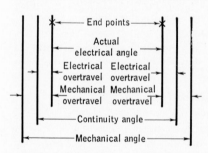

FIG. 2-3. Definitions of electrical and mechanical angular relationships.

The *actual electrical angle* is the actual angle between the end points, while the *theoretical electrical angle* is the angular motion specified by the user, effective in producing useful electrical output. The *continuity angle* is the total angle of shaft rotation over which electrical continuity is maintained. It is the sum of the actual electrical angle and the electrical overtravel at each end. In turn, the *electrical overtravel* is defined as the angle of shaft rotation over which there is continuity between the contact and the resistance element beyond each end of the actual electrical angle.

The *end point* is the point of sudden variation in the rate of change of resistance as the wiper moves from the overtravel region toward the variable-resistance element. When the mechanical angle is less than the angle encompassed by the winding, the end points are at the mechanical stop positions. *Backlash* is the maximum difference in shaft angular position in degrees which is obtained when the shaft is rotated to any prescribed electrical output from opposite directions. The *end resistance from the end point* is the resistance between the wiper terminal and an end terminal when the wiper is positioned at the corresponding end point.

The *index point* is that point in a function that is intended to serve as a reference, either for phasing purposes (with ganged pots) or to place the electrical function in step with the drive shaft. Then *phasing* is the alignment of the respective tolerance bands of the individual ganged potentiometers with the tolerance band of the cup at the driven end. This automatically prescribes that the voltage ratios of all ganged potentiometers fall within their respective tolerance bands at any angle of shaft rotation, when referred to the index point on the pot nearest the driven end.

2-6. Basic Electrical Relationships. The *resolution* of a potentiometer is a measure of the precision to which the input and output can be set; however, to be completely restrictive, both electrical and angular relationships must be specified. *Electrical resolution* is a measure of the accuracy to which a potentiometer can be set with reference to the input. (The wiper is moved through the smallest finite angular displacement that will produce a single change in resistance or voltage.) The maximum incremental change in resistance or voltage output thus produced, observed anywhere in the total mechanical rotation of the potentiometer shaft, when multiplied by 100 and divided by the total variable resistance or voltage is the percentage electrical resolution. The *angular resolution* is a measure of the precision to which the input of the potentiometer can be set with reference to the output. (The wiper is moved through the largest angular displacement that will produce no change in resistance or voltage.) The maximum incremental change in shaft rotation thus produced, in degrees, is the angular resolution.

Noise is defined quantitatively in terms of an equivalent parasitic, transient, contact resistance in ohms, appearing between the wiper and the resistance element when the shaft is rotated. The equivalent noise resistance is defined independently of the total resistance, resolution, functional characteristics, and total angle. The magnitude of the equivalent noise resistance is taken as the peak-to-peak value that is obtained. The wiper arm must be excited by a specified current and rotated at a specified speed.

A *built-in resistor* is an internal or external resistor connected to the variable resistance element for the purpose of modifying the potentiometer to obtain a desired characteristic. It should form an integral part of the potentiometer assembly. A *test point* is an additional terminal used to obtain electrical access to the variable resistance element. It is often used where built-in resistors are employed.

The *total variable resistance* is the resistance between the end points, while the *total resistance* of a potentiometer is the resistance across the input terminals with the wiper positioned to give a maximum resistance value.

Deviation is defined as the difference between the actual electrical output and that specified by the function at any shaft angle. As a special case, the *end error* is the actual deviation that exists at either angular extreme of the idealized characteristic from which the deviations are measured.

A *tap* is an electrical connection made to the variable-resistance element at any point between the end points. Tap location is defined as being the mechanical center of the effective tap width. The *effective tap width* is the angle of mechanical rotation during which there is no change in voltage or resistance as the wiper is moved past the tap in any one direction.

2-7. Basic Mechanical Relationships. *Lateral runout* is the total maximum difference between the high and low readings of a dial indicator suitably arranged to denote the out-of-squareness relation of the mounting surface with respect to the rotational axis of the shaft. *Shaft runout* is the maximum difference between the high and low readings of a dial indicator arranged to measure the eccentricity of the shaft at any point on its exposed length, when the shaft is rotated on its own bearings with the body held stationary.

Radial play is the maximum difference between the high and low readings of a dial indicator arranged to measure the total radial travel (sum of both directions) of the shaft in its own bearings. It should be measured as closely as possible to the front-plate bearing with a 0.5-lb radial load on the shaft at a distance 0.5 in. from the mounting surface. *End play* is the maximum difference between the high and low readings of a dial indicator arranged to measure the total axial travel of the shaft in its own bearings with a 0.5-lb axial load on the shaft applied alternately in each direction.

2-8. Potentiometer Accuracy Definitions. *Independent linearity* is the maximum deviation (in per cent of the input reference voltage E_r) of the actual measured electrical output E_O at any point from the best straight line drawn through the actual output vs. rotation curve for the extent of the actual electrical angle. The slope and position of the straight line from which the linearity deviations are measured must be adjusted to minimize these deviations. As shown in Fig. 2-4, this permits the use of resistance (or voltage) adjustment at both ends of the resistance element to minimize end errors. Center-tapped trimmers are shown as they might be used to obtain maximum precision from a potentiometer.

Independent conformity is the maximum deviation (in per cent of the input reference voltage E_r) of the actual measured electrical output E_O at any point from the best specified function curve drawn through the output vs. rotation curve for the theoretical electrical angle. Independent conformity allows the average slope and the rotational axis intercept to be adjusted to minimize the conformity deviations. Again Fig. 2-5 shows the use of trimmers to obtain maximum precision. This definition

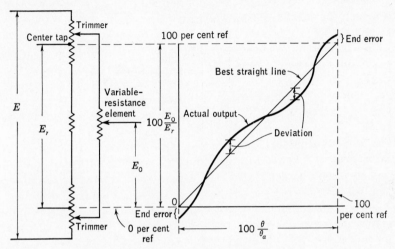

FIG. 2-4. Independent linearity.

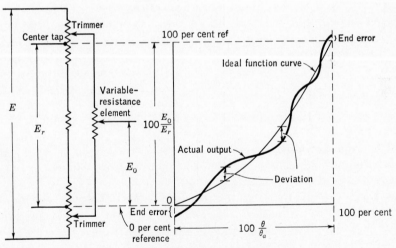

FIG. 2-5. Independent conformity.

is a perfectly general one, since it can be applied to any potentiometer (whether the function is nonlinear or linear).

Terminal conformity is the deviation (in per cent of the total measured electrical input E) of the actual electrical output at any point, from the specified functional curve drawn through the following theoretical points:

(1) zero output at zero rotation and (2) maximum output at the specified function angle of rotation. Terminal conformity specifies the idealized characteristic curve to be drawn through points determined by the total output of the unit and the function angle. It does not require the error

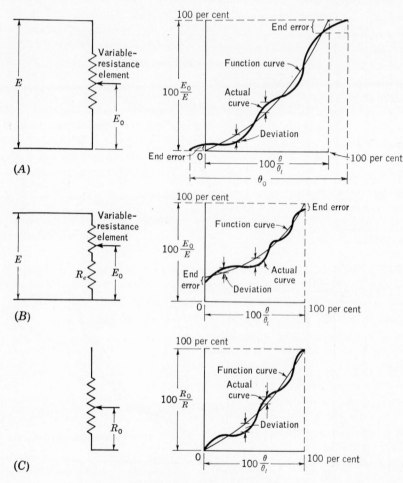

Fig. 2-6. Terminal conformity.

at these points to be zero. Three applications of terminal conformity are discussed.

In Fig. 2-6A, no adjustment is provided to compensate for end errors to the ideal zero or 100 per cent output points. Units must be completely interchangeable. This criterion may be used to specify a linear function where desired.

In Fig. 2-6B, an end resistor is required at either end to fill out the function. Note that the addition of the end resistor R_e fills out the specified resistance R while providing an electrical offset from the zero per cent intercept.

Figure 2-6C shows the case where the potentiometer is connected as a rheostat and applies to both linear and nonlinear functions. The electrical output is in ohms and the deviation is a percentage of the specified total resistance. There is no need for a tolerance on either the minimum total angle of rotation or the minimum total resistance, since these are included in the conformity criterion.

2-9. Performance Characteristics—Accuracy. The most important single performance characteristic of a resistance potentiometer is its accuracy. Linearity is a measure of this accuracy, indicating a potentiometer's ability to produce a slider output voltage that is directly proportional to the angular rotation of the shaft. When this voltage definition of linearity is used, it is normally presumed that no current is drawn through the slider. For purposes of generality, it is often convenient to represent potentiometer output voltage as a per cent of total excitation voltage. Then per cent voltage is plotted against the per cent of total shaft rotation, yielding a nondimensional plot of potentiometer performance.[2]

Potentiometer performance can also be defined in terms of the resistance between the slider and the zero end of the resistance element. This resistance value, divided by the total resistance of the resistance element, yields a per cent resistance to be plotted against per cent shaft rotation. Figure 2-7 shows the per cent voltage or per cent resistance of a typical linear potentiometer. Deviations from the desired linear output are usually in the form of a somewhat periodic variation (shown exaggerated for purposes of illustration). The per cent deviation for any position of the slider is the difference between the two curves at that point.

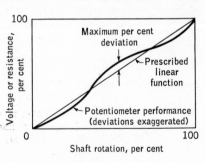

Fig. 2-7. Periodic nature of typical potentiometer deviations from prescribed linear function.

Potentiometer linearity is normally defined in terms of the maximum per cent deviation.

The linearity capability of a given potentiometer is not determined solely by the accuracy (or linearity) of the resistance element, since, in many cases, voltages or resistances are introduced at one or both ends of the resistance element to make the total voltage or resistance function conform more closely to the prescribed function. Thus, the linearity of a potentiometer can be defined in several ways, depending on the freedom or constraints of the particular application. Section 2-8 summarizes the accepted linearity definitions as abstracted from National Aircraft Standards Committee's specification NAS710.

Uniform wire composition and diameter and accurate winding techniques in wire-wound potentiometers, and accurate film deposition in film pots are not the only prerequisites for good linearity; backlash, shaft perpendicularity, bearing runout, concentric construction, and other mechanical variables are also important factors. However, the inherent high linearity that is built into a potentiometer can be nullified by poor application engineering. For example, excessive uncompensated electrical loading, or poor mounting or driving mechanism design can introduce nonlinearities when a potentiometer is incorporated in a system.

Linearity in commercially available potentiometers ranges from about ±0.01 per cent to several per cent, depending on the size and quality of the potentiometer. A survey of manufacturers to determine the highest accuracies available in single and multiturn wire-wound potentiometers yielded the data listed in Table 2-6. There is some disagreement as to whether an accuracy of better than ±0.01 per cent can be maintained in service. The manufacturers who claim the practicality of these accuracies usually add the requirements of reduced shock and vibration specifications, as well as restrictions on wire size, brush pressures, resolution, safety factors, and noise specifications. But most manufacturers claim that these superhigh accuracies cannot be held in practical military and commercial applications during the life of the units, primarily because of aging of the parts resulting in minute dimensional instability, plus wear of the contacting surfaces.

TABLE 2-6. HIGHEST LINEARITIES OF COMMERCIALLY AVAILABLE WIRE-WOUND POTS

Diameter, in.	Linear pots independent linearity, ± per cent		Sine-cosine pots independent conformity, ± per cent
	Single-turn	Multiturn	
$\frac{1}{2}$	0.5–1.0		
$\frac{7}{8}$	0.2–0.25	0.025–0.05	
$1\frac{1}{16}$	0.2		
$1\frac{1}{2}$	0.15	0.02–0.025	
$1\frac{7}{8}$			0.25
2	0.1	0.02–0.025	
3	0.05–0.10		
8	0.01		0.05
10		0.002	

Resolution. Resolution in a wire-wound resistance potentiometer is due to the stepwise voltage variations occurring as the slide moves across the discrete turns of the resistance winding (Fig. 2-8). Resolution is measured as the reciprocal of the total number of turns in the resistance element, although usually where the slider simultaneously contacts two or more wires the resolution phenomenon is more complex.

A direct relationship exists between achievable resolution and the total winding resistance of a potentiometer. The factors include dimensions and resistivity of the resistance wire (Table 2-7 lists common wire materials), size of card or mandrel, number of turns required to achieve the desired total resistance, and the resultant spacing of successive turns of the winding. Wire size is limited on one extreme by the fineness that

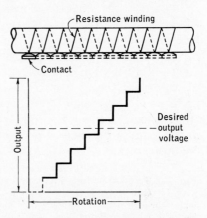

FIG. 2-8. Stepped voltage characteristic caused by discrete turns.

can be wound without damage, still maintaining an adequate expected life, and on the other hand by the bulk, which results in poor resolution. As resistance is increased, finer wire is used and resolution improves. When the limit of fineness is reached, a grade of material having a higher resistivity is required, resulting in a heavier wire with poorer resolution.

TABLE 2-7. COMMON RESISTANCE WIRE MATERIALS*

Resistivity, ohms/cir mil-ft	Nominal temp. coeff. of resistance, 20–100°C	Trade name	Manufacturer
800	0.00002	Karma	Driver-Harris
800	0.00002	Evanohm	W. B. Driver
550	0.00002	L.T.C.	Sigmund Cohn
650	0.00011	Nichrome V	Driver-Harris
650	0.0001	Tophet A	W. B. Driver
294	0.00002	Advance	Driver-Harris
294	0.00004	Cupron	W. B. Driver
400	0.00024 max	Alloy No. 479	Sigmund Cohn
180	0.0006 max	Alloy No. 851	Sigmund Cohn
80	0.00067	Ney-Oro G	J. M. Ney

* Courtesy of George Rattray and Co.

Figure 2-9 shows the resolution range for single-turn potentiometers for various diameters and total winding resistances. As expected, resolution improves with increasing total resistance and with increasing diameter. The specific case of a 3-in.-diameter potentiometer is shown in Fig. 2-10. Here optimum wire type and wire size is used for the various total resistance values, and type and size are changed as the wire becomes either too bulky or too fragile.

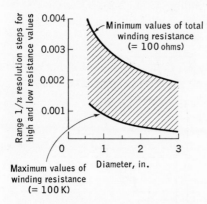

FIG. 2-9. Trend in $1/n$ resolution limits with increase in potentiometer diameter. Curves pertain principally to wound-card aluminum-base precision pots. (*Courtesy of Technology Instrument Corp.*)

Resolution places an upper limit on the accuracy of a potentiometer; the maximum possible accuracy is equal to one-half the resolution. Thus, if a potentiometer has a resolution of 0.2 per cent, the best accuracy obtainable with everything else perfect is 0.1 per cent. Good resolution is particularly important in high-gain closed-loop systems, since there is a tendency for the actuator to hunt, driving the receiving potentiometer back and forth between

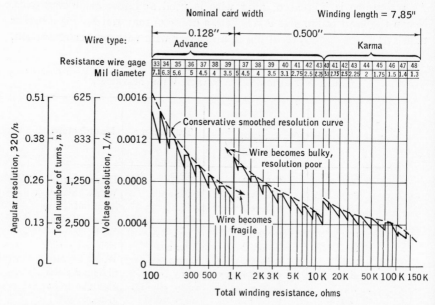

FIG. 2-10. Resolution vs. total winding resistance for optimum wire size in a 3-in. diameter wound-card potentiometer. (*Courtesy of Technology Instrument Corp.*)

adjacent turns of wire, seeking a voltage level that does not exist. This condition is shown by the voltage level indicated by the dashed line on Fig. 2-8. The system would hunt between the voltage levels corresponding to the steps above and below this line.

Current practice limits minimum wire spacing in wire-wound potentiometers to about 500 to 1,000 turns/in. Greater packing results in reduced life and reliability and in manufacturing difficulties. The best resolution obtainable in practical commercially available pots with a 1-in. wiper radius is therefore about 0.035 to 0.065 per cent.

If better resolution characteristics are required, it is necessary to go to one of the so-called "resolutionless" pots. High-quality slide wires give essentially continuous resistance variation, and the newer film-type potentiometers have more or less continuous characteristics, although the granularity encountered in the latter units gives a discontinuous effect.

Noise.[3,4] Noise, in a precision potentiometer, may be defined as any fluctuating distortion of output that is not due to linearity (or conformity) deviation. Of the many ways that have been used to classify noise, one of the most logical appears to be to divide the noise sources into those that stem from mechanical environmental factors, and those that result from the inherent design, construction, and electrical application of a potentiometer. The first class includes vibrational or microphonic noise, and residual noise from foreign particles.

Vibrational noise, while electrical in effect, is purely mechanical in cause. It is produced by the contact jumping away from the winding, thereby opening the contact circuit. Proper design of the contact arms, carefully calculated pressures, and close control of all structural resonances will practically eliminate this type of noise. High-velocity noise is another type of distortion that has application effects similar to vibrational noise. Too high rotational speed causes the slider to bounce along the coil, resulting in a series of momentary open circuits. Such factors as winding pitch, uniformity of wire and winding, slider design, and contact force determine the critical speed beyond which high-velocity noise will result.

Residual noise is caused by foreign material such as dirty windings and wear products that intrude between the contact surface and the winding. Contact resistance fluctuations arising from this type of contamination are characteristically large, relatively stationary with respect to time, and independent of slider velocities. This type of noise can be guarded against by maintaining clean assembly conditions and by using long-wearing and electromechanically compatible wire and contact materials.

Noise resulting from the inherent design and application of a potentiometer includes loading noise, shorting noise, resolution noise, and various types of generated noise. Figure 2-11 shows oscilloscope patterns of noise from three of these sources, while Table 2-8 summarizes the inherent types of noise with regard to origin and possible modes of expression.

Loading noise occurs only when current is drawn through the slider to

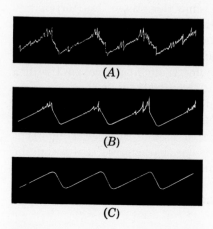

(A)

(B)

(C)

Fig. 2-11. Oscilloscope patterns of electrical noise. (A) Loading noise; (B) shorting noise; (C) resolution noise. (*Courtesy of Helipot.*)

an output circuit. It is due to fluctuating contact resistance at the interface between the slider and the coil, and at the interface between the slip ring and the slip-ring contact. Closely similar to particle noise, loading distortion can be caused by foreign material, metal oxidation, or by spot contact. At any metallic interface, current is carried through spot contacts, with the size, number, and position of the spots varying from contact surface to contact surface.

Shorting noise is present in wire-wound potentiometers even when no current is drawn through the slider to an output circuit. As the slider travels over the coil, it may short out adjacent turns of resistance wire. A portion of the current will then flow through the slider from one turn to the next, and the output will be distorted.

Resolution noise is a stepping voltage variation caused by the contact traveling across discrete turns of resistance wire. It is inversely pro-

Table 2-8. Potentiometer Noise*

Noise type	Origin	Expression (noise figure)
Loading noise.................	Load current flowing through fluctuating contact resistance	Ohms (peak-to-peak variation in contact resistance)
Shorting noise...............	Winding current flowing through fluctuating contact resistance	Equivalent ohms peak-to-peak (calculated from an observed winding current and noise voltage)
Resolution noise (due to winding current)	Stepped nature of wire-wound resistance element	Per cent (reciprocal of number of turns of resistance wire)
Resolution noise (due to load current)	Stepped nature of wire-wound resistance element	Ohms (resistance per turn of resistance wire)
Generated noise..............	Tribo effect	Millivolts or microvolts

* Abstracted from I. T. Hogen, Electrical Noise in Wire Wound Potentiometers, Helipot Corp., paper presented at 1952 Western Electronics Conference.

portional to the resolution of a given pot. Two types of resolution noise can be distinguished, that due to winding current, and that due to load current.

Sources of generated noise are not simply analyzed, but fortunately, the resultant electrical disturbance rarely exceeds a small fraction of a millivolt. Self-generated noise voltages occur under three principal sets of conditions: galvanic or chemical action at the point of contact between slider and wiper; thermoconjunctive effects, which depend on frictional or external heat; and triboelectrical phenomena, small voltages generated by abrasion of the contact on the wire. Here again, noise is minimized by using compatible materials, proved welding techniques, and optimum contact pressures.

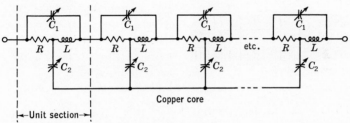

Fig. 2-12. Equivalent internal circuit of a multiturn copper-mandrel potentiometer. (*Courtesy of Helipot.*)

Noise tolerances are most commonly expressed as an equivalent resistance, although some users appraise noise voltagewise. In either case, unless otherwise specifically noted, evaluations are made with a constant current of 1 ma. This noise figure is a quantitative measure of total noise and is defined as the total noise peak voltage divided by the source current, the source current and angular velocity always being specified.

Frequency Characteristics. The widely used Kohlrausch wound resistance element acts as a pure resistive load from direct current to operating frequencies of about 400 cps for most potentiometers. At higher frequencies, the distributed inductance and capacitance plus the winding resistance assume a complex characteristic. An inductive effect is produced by the many turns of wire on the metal mandrel. Capacitive effects arise from turn to turn of the winding, turn to turn of the helix, and between these and other parts of the unit, particularly the copper mandrel. The resistance element supplies the resistance parameter of a complex transmission line with R, L, and C distributed throughout its length (Fig. 2-12).

In single-turn potentiometers, frequency does not affect impedance until it reaches several thousand cycles per second. In multiturn models, no change of impedance is likely to be noted at 60 cps. At 400 cps, no change is likely in 3-turn or 10-turn models, except perhaps in units having high total resistance.   In 15-, 25-, and 40-turn units, impedance change is likely to occur above 400 cps; the higher the resistance, the greater the change in impedance.   Low-resistance pots with many turns

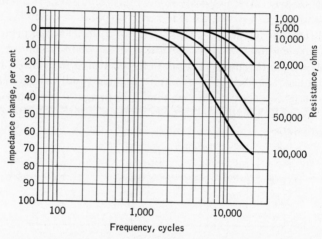

will probably not incur an impedance change except at frequencies well above 400 cps.

Figure 2-13 shows the frequency characteristic of Borg 10-turn potentiometers.   Note that the impedance change becomes more pronounced as total resistance increases.   Schneider, Hiraoka, and Gaudlin discuss the subject of phase shift in potentiometers in great detail and suggest methods of compensation.[5]

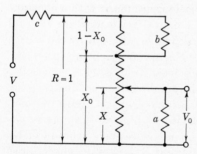

FIG. 2-14. Single-tap compensated loaded linear potentiometer.

2-10. Compensation of Potentiometer Loading Errors.   When a linear potentiometer is resistance-loaded, the output voltage is no longer a linear function of shaft position.   There are two ways to counteract this finite-load-impedance generated error: (1) specify a winding-compensated function pot specifically designed to operate into the required load, and (2) add shunt resistors to a tapped linear potentiometer in a manner that will recreate the desired linear function when the pot is operated into the required load.   The first method has the disadvantages of inflexibility, long delivery, and high cost: the load impedance must be finalized in the early design stages and cannot be satisfactorily changed during the experimental period unless a new winding-compensated pot is specified, designed to match the new load impedance. In contrast, the shunt-resistor-compensated potentiometer can be matched to new load impedances simply by changing the shunt values. And besides, in many cases the tapped potentiometer can be more accurately compensated.

Straightforward techniques for selecting tap location and shunt value were described in Refs. 6 to 9. These are summarized below.*

2-11. Load Compensating Linear Potentiometers with One Tap. Figure 2-14 shows a loaded linear potentiometer with a dropping resistor and shunting resistor added to minimize loading errors. Optimum selection of these resistors and tap location can reduce loading error to the order of potentiometer resolution for single-turn potentiometers (a reduction factor of 6 to 9 over the uncompensated case) for load ratios varying from unity to infinity. The symbols in Fig. 2-14 are defined as follows:

a = load resistance or load ratio (ratio of load resistance to potentiometer resistance)

b = compensating shunt resistor

c = dropping resistor

X_0 = tap location of compensating resistor

X = wiper location

R = potentiometer resistance

V = input voltage to potentiometer circuit

To simplify the approach, potentiometer resistance is normalized, or R equals 1.

First analyze the circuit of Fig. 2-14 with the dropping resistor equal to zero and the compensating resistor open-circuited to determine the uncompensated loading error. By inspection it can be shown that the error caused by load ratio a is

$$\epsilon = \frac{X^2(1 - X)}{a - X - X^2} \tag{2-1}$$

or for a greater than 10 the following approximate relation applies

$$a\epsilon \cong X^2(1 - X) \tag{2-2}$$

The maximum error ϵ_m from Eq. (2-2) occurs when X_m is equal to $\frac{2}{3}$, where X_m is the wiper position for maximum error. This error will then be

$$\epsilon_m \cong \frac{0.148}{a} \tag{2-3}$$

Equation (2-2) indicates that a single error curve can be drawn for large

* The authors would like to thank Jack Gilbert of Norden Laboratories Div., Norden-Ketay Corp., for permission to reproduce his techniques.

values of a.   This is shown as the heavy curve in Fig. 2-15: it consists of a plot of potentiometer error $a\epsilon$ against shaft rotation X.

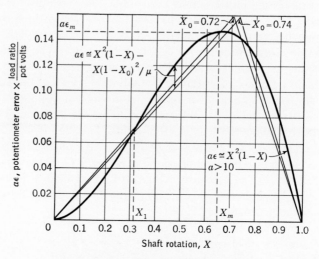

FIG. 2-15. Error plot for single-tap design.

Now consider the case where the dropping resistor c has a finite value, but the compensating resistor b is still open-circuited.   Then the error expression as a function of a, c, and X is

$$\epsilon = \frac{X(X - c)(1 - X)}{a(c + 1) + cX + X - X^2} \qquad (2\text{-}4)$$

When c equals zero, this expression reduces to Eq. (2-1).   For values of a greater than 10, Eq. (2-4) can be simplified to give the following approximate relationship

$$a\epsilon \cong \frac{X(1 - X)(X - c)}{c + 1} \qquad (2\text{-}5)$$

Figure 2-16 shows this equation plotted for various values of c.   For c equal to 0.5, the maximum error reduces to $a\epsilon_m = 0.032$.   Thus the maximum loading error for a equals 100 is only 0.032 per cent when c equals 0.5.   This design minimizes errors without using the compensating resistor.   But for large c the errors increase to minus $0.25/a$.   Therefore it is desirable to limit c to a maximum of about 2.5 to restrict loading errors to less than $0.15/a$.

Note that the maximum errors can be halved for all curves where the errors are essentially in one direction only.   However, the resulting error curve will not pass through zero at zero shaft rotation.   It is necessary to offset the voltage zero by the proper amount in the direction of maximum error. Thus the maximum error can be reduced to $0.125/a$ for large c and to $0.036/a$ for c equals 1.

To obtain these results, either the shaft must be displaced from zero by the proper amount, or a suitable end resistor must be supplied with the potentiometer assembly.

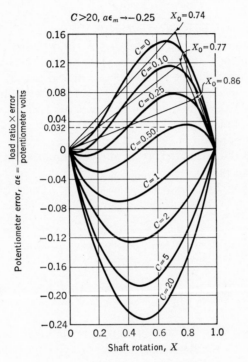

FIG. 2-16. Error curves for finite c.

When the compensating resistor has a finite value, and the dropping resistor is zero and the load ratio greater than 10, the approximate error expression is as follows, where $u = b/a$. Expressions are required for three locations of the wiper contact X in relation to the compensating resistor X_0.

Below the tap, $\quad 0 < X < X_0$

$$a\epsilon \cong X\left[X(1 - X) - \frac{(1 - X_0)^2}{u} \right] \tag{2-6}$$

At the tap, $\quad X = X_0$

$$a\epsilon_0 \cong X_0(1 - X_0)\left(X_0 - \frac{1 - X_0}{u} \right) \tag{2-7}$$

Above the tap, $X_0 < X < 1$

$$a\epsilon \cong (1 - X) \left[X^2 - \frac{X_0(1 - x_0)}{u} \right] \tag{2-8}$$

For convenience, Eq. (2-6) can be written as follows

$$a\epsilon = X^2(1 - X) - \frac{X(1 - X_0)^2}{u} \tag{2-9}$$

This equation can be interpreted as the difference of two curves. The first is the original error curve of Eq. (2-2) and the second is a straight line with a slope of $(1 - X_0)^2/u$. A similar interpretation holds for Eq. (2-8), except that the slope is $X_0(1 - X_0)/u$ and is negative.

This analysis leads to a graphical method for determining the optimum position of tap X_0. This is shown in Fig. 2-15. The location of X_0 and the slope of the line can be altered so that the error at the tap is equal in magnitude but opposite in sign to the maximum errors above and below the tap. Both the estimated errors and the tap location X_0 can be read directly from the curve.

The value of u can be calculated as follows. Let X_1 be the point at which the straight line intersects the original error curve. Then in Eq. (2-6),

$$a\epsilon_1 = 0 \text{ at } X = X_1$$

or

$$u = \frac{(1 - X_0)^2}{X_1(1 - X_1)} = \frac{b}{a} \tag{2-10}$$

From Fig. 2-15, when X_0 equals 0.74, X_1 equals 0.324. Therefore

$$u = \frac{(0.26)^2}{(0.324)(0.676)} \cong 0.31$$
$$b \cong 0.31a$$

Checks on this method show a decreasing accuracy with decreasing load ratio. This means that the straight lines of Fig. 2-15 are really curved, but that the difference is negligible for large a.

To obtain particular characteristics, the slope of the lines and the position of the tap can be altered. For example, if X_0 is chosen equal to 0.72, the errors at and below the tap can be reduced to about $0.015/a$, while the maximum error above the tap increases to about $0.023/a$. This might be desired where greater errors are permitted for large values of X, but smaller errors are required for small X.

When the design constants are fixed, a given potentiometer can be used for any load ratio greater than 10 by switching in an appropriate resistor at the tap. This permits interchangeability and flexibility in a given setup.

The same procedure for locating X_0 can be used for values of the dropping resistor c between 0 and 0.5, again, with a load ratio greater than 10. An approximate error expression below the tap is equated to zero, resulting in an expression for u similar to Eq. (2-10). This results in

$$u = \frac{(c+1)(1-X_0)^2}{(X_1-c)(1-X_1)} = \frac{b}{a} \tag{2-11}$$

Typical minimum error designs show improvements of 7 to 9 over the uncompensated curves. Two examples are plotted on Fig. 2-16.

Unfortunately, the use of the resistor b increases the linearity error for c greater than 0.5. This is because the original error curves change sign at this point, but the compensating effect of b does not.

When the dropping resistor is zero and the load ratio less than 10 there is no straight-line justification for plotting the values of u and X_0. However, experiments show that the optimum position of the tap X_0 varies only from 0.74 for very large a to 0.73 for a equals 1. It is probable, therefore, that the tap X_0 could remain at 0.735 for all values of a greater than 1, provided the value of b is altered for the best fit.

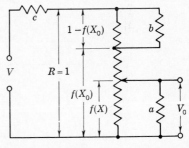

2-12. Load Compensating Nonlinear-function Potentiometers. Nonlinear potentiometers suffer from load-induced errors just as do linear

FIG. 2-17. Single-tap compensated loaded function potentiometer.

pots, and similar techniques can be used to achieve load compensation. Figure 2-17 shows a loaded function potentiometer with identical nomenclature to that used in Fig. 2-14 except that

$f(X_0)$ = resistance at tap for compensating resistor
$f(X)$ = resistance at wiper of function potentiometer

Referring back to the linear analysis, it is apparent that an expression can be derived for the error below the tap of the function pot that is similar to Eq. (2-9). This is

$$a\epsilon \cong f^2(1-f) - \frac{f(1-f_0)^2}{u} \tag{2-12}$$

And in turn a similar graphical interpretation holds for Eq. (2-12). Using the linear analysis, let

$$f = f(X) = X' \tag{2-13}$$
$$f_0 = f(X_0) = X_0' \tag{2-13a}$$
$$u = u' \tag{2-14}$$

where the primes refer to the parameters of the equivalent linear potentiometer circuit.

From experience gained in the linear case substitute X_0' equals 0.74 and u' equals 0.31 in Eq. (2-12).

$$a\epsilon = f^2(1 - f) - 0.218f \qquad (2\text{-}15)$$

As in the linear method, Eqs. (2-12) and (2-15) can be interpreted as the difference of two curves, one the uncompensated error curve and the other a replica of the original function whose scale factor is the same slope as that in the linear example.

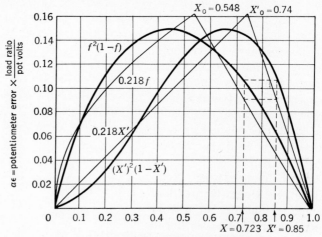

Function potentiometer shaft rotation, X
Linear potentiometer shaft rotation, X'

Fɪɢ. 2-18. Graphical determination of loading compensation. Compensated function potentiometer $f = \sqrt{X} = X'$; $f_0 = \sqrt{X_0} = X_0'$; $(1 - f_0)^2/\mu = 0.218$; $c = 0, a > 10$.

Equations (2-13) and (2-14) are valid because the loading effect is essentially resistive. Therefore, an identical error should be obtained when the tap X_0 for the function potentiometer is located where its resistance $f(X_0)$ is equal to the resistance at the tap X_0' of the linear potentiometer. Similarly, the compensating resistor ratio u must be the same for both cases.

The resultant errors for the loaded function potentiometer can be obtained by plotting Eq. (2-15) directly or by interpreting the plot of a linear unit in terms of Eqs. (2-13) and (2-14). The latter procedure is followed in Fig. 2-18 for the function

$$f(X) = \sqrt{X}$$

Then, from Eq. (2-13),

$$X = (X')^2$$
$$X_0 = (X'_0)^2 = 0.548$$

A typical construction is shown by the dashed lines for X' equals 0.85 and X equals 0.723. The graph shows that the maximum errors are the same as for the linear case, but occur where the corresponding abscissas are squared.

Once the optimum design for the equivalent linear case is fixed, there is no need to plot the loading errors. The designs are given by Eqs.

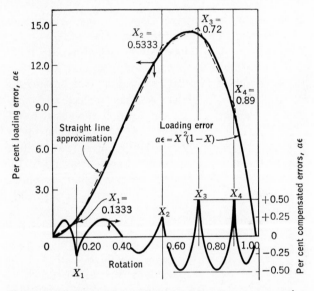

Fig. 2-19. Graphical determination of four-tap compensation.

(2-13) and (2-14) directly. It can be shown that the compensated linear designs apply to all loaded function potentiometers as well. But the transformations must be made from the equivalent linear circuit.

2-13. Multiple-tap Compensation of Loaded Potentiometers. If the single-tap compensating technique does not reduce the loading error sufficiently, then the use of more taps must be considered. By using four taps and shunt resistors, the maximum loading error can be limited to about $0.005/a$ for a load ratio of 20: even better compensation can be achieved with a five-tap design.

Figure 2-19 shows an expanded plot of the familiar error function. To determine the required number of taps, draw several straight lines through this plot, such that the maximum difference between each straight line and the curve is the desired tolerance. The number of straight lines required to approximate this curve and still stay within tolerance determines the number of taps, and the intersections of the straight lines give the desired tap locations. Figure 2-20 shows a typical multiple-tapped pot and indicates nomenclature.

It can be shown that the following relationship gives the approximate values of the shunting resistors:

$$\frac{b_i}{a} = \frac{X_j - X_i}{a(S - S_{ji})} \tag{2-16}$$

where X_j, X_i = adjacent tap locations

S = maximum positive slope of any straight line drawn through the error function curve

S_{ji} = straight-line slope between adjacent taps X_j and X_i

b_i = shunting resistor across taps X_j and X_i

The graphical results of Fig. 2-19 show that it is possible to limit the loading error to $0.0025/a$ for values of X between 0 and 0.55, provided the error is increased to $0.0050/a$ for the second half of potentiometer travel. For a load ratio of 20 these errors range from 50 to 100 per cent of potentiometer resolution, where this resolution is taken as 0.025 per cent.

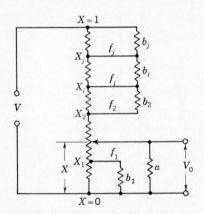

FIG. 2-20. Generalized multiple-tap design.

Since the assumed expression for the error function is more nearly exact for high load ratios, the design values for b_i should be calculated using a load ratio of 100. Then as a check, the actual voltage ratios existing at the taps can be calculated from the resulting multiple-tap network. If the difference is excessive at a tap, the resistor value can be reestimated to bring the error inside the allowable tolerance. When a is less than 100, the resistor values must be reestimated, but this is simple starting with the b_i/a values for a equals 100.

If a maximum loading error of $0.0050/a$ cannot be tolerated, then a five-tap design must be used. This will limit the error to less than $0.0025/a$ at any point in the travel. The design techniques are identical to those used for the four-tap pot discussed above. The five-tap design yields a loading-error reduction of about 60 to 1 from an uncompensated condition, and should be considered for use in multiturn potentiometers with load ratios of 10 or higher.

2-14. Phase Compensation of Loaded Potentiometers. When a linear potentiometer excited by an a-c voltage drives a resistive load through shielded wire or cable, the output voltage consists of in-phase and quadrature components, both of which can influence electronic computation. Quadrature errors can be reduced by using taps and shunting capacitors in a technique similar to that described above. Quadrature reduction factors vary from 6 to 60, depending on the tap design.

It can be shown that the linearity errors and the quadrature voltage are identically dependent on shaft rotation. Hence, the analytical expressions for linearity error in the presence of tap X_0 and compensating resistor b should apply to the quadrature error in the presence of tap X_0 and capacitor C_b (Fig. 2-21). As shown

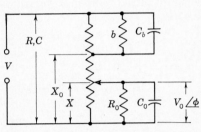

Fig. 2-21. Single-tap quadrature compensation for capacitive loading.

earlier by Eq. (2-9), the linearity error after loading compensation has been applied is equal to the original error minus the corrective effect of the compensating resistor, or

$$\epsilon = \frac{X^2(1-X)}{R_0/R} - \frac{X(1-X_0)^2}{b/R} \qquad (2\text{-}17)$$

where $0 < X < X_0$. Substitute in this expression to include the effect of the compensating capacitor as follows:

Replace b by
$$Z_b = \frac{b}{1 + j\omega b C_b}$$

Replace R_0/R by
$$\frac{Z_0}{R} = \frac{R_0}{R(1 + j\omega R_0 C_0)}$$

and let
$$R_0 C_0 = b C_b$$

Then

$$\epsilon = \epsilon_i - j\epsilon_q = \left[\frac{X^2(1-X)}{R_0/R} - \frac{X(1-X_0)^2}{b/R} \right](1 + j\omega R_0 C_0) \qquad (2\text{-}18)$$

where ϵ_i = in-phase linearity error
ϵ_q = quadrature error
R_0 = load resistance
C_0 = load capacitance
C_b = compensating capacitance

Separating the in-phase and quadrature errors, and letting $u = b/R_0$,

$$a\epsilon_i = X^2(1-X) - \frac{X(1-X_0)^2}{u} \qquad (2\text{-}19)$$

and

$$a\epsilon_q = \omega R_0 C_0 \left[X^2(1-X) - \frac{X(1-X_0)^2}{u} \right] \qquad (2\text{-}20)$$

Therefore the quadrature-voltage error is

$$V_q = \omega R C_0 V \left[X^2(1-X) - \frac{X(1-X_0)^2}{u} \right] \tag{2-21}$$

Equations (2-19) and (2-21) describe the in-phase and quadrature errors of a compensated potentiometer with small phase shift, where the time constant of the compensating network bC_b equals the time constant of the load R_0C_0.

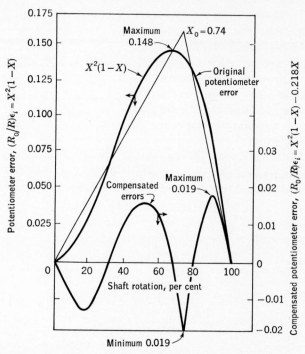

Fig. 2-22. Quadrature-compensated and linearity-compensated error curves are identical if potentiometer has negligible phase shift.

It was shown previously that the optimum values of X_0 and the shunting resistor b for the resistive-compensated single-tap design are 0.74 and $0.31R_0$, respectively.   And since

$$bC_b = R_0C_0 = 0.31R_0C_b \tag{2-22}$$

then
$$\frac{C_b}{C_0} = \frac{1}{0.31} = 3.22 \tag{2-23}$$

Experiment showed that the compensated quadrature plot as well as the original quadrature plot are practically identical to the in-phase plot in Fig. 2-22.   An uncompensated maximum quadrature figure of 80 mv was reduced to about 11 mv.

Thus, all the compensated designs for high load ratio discussed in the section on single-tap compensation of linear pots can be extended to include the capacity-load condition if $bC_b = R_0C_0$. (If there is a dropping resistor c in the circuit, a shunt capacitor C_s must be added such that $cC_s = RC_0$. This ensures zero phase error at the upper end of the potentiometer.)

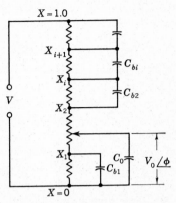

Where single-tap capacitive compensation will not reduce the quadrature error sufficiently, a multiple-tap compensating technique can be used that is similar to multiple-tap resistive compensation. Figure 2-23 shows the general case. It can be shown that a relationship similar to Eq. (2-16) holds for values of shunting capacitors C_{bi} in terms

Fig. 2-23. Multiple-tap design for capacitive-compensated pots.

of the tap points and straight-line slopes drawn on the quadrature plot. This relationship is

$$C_{bi} = \frac{S_i - S}{(\Delta X_i)RV} \qquad (2\text{-}24)$$

where C_{bi} = desired value of shunt capacitor

S_i = slope of given straight line drawn on measured or theoretical quadrature voltage plot

S = maximum negative slope of any line drawn on plot

ΔX_i = per cent rotation difference between adjacent taps X_i and X_{i+1}

V = low impedance exciting voltage

For cases of high load ratio and potentiometers with negligible phase shift, the same quadrature voltage reduction can be obtained as was previously found for the analogous resistive loading case. For this condition, $R_iC_{bi} = R_0C_0$, or the time constant of each compensation network equals the time constant of the load.

If the quadrature plots differ functionally from the linearity curves (for example, where a potentiometer has substantial phase shift), the taps must be chosen separately for each type error. However, the equal time-constant criterion quite often gives sufficient quadrature reduction.

2-15. How Potentiometers Generate Nonlinear Functions. Although the large majority of resistance potentiometers generate an output voltage that is directly proportional to mechanical input motion, this is a chosen rather than necessary relationship, and there are many ways of building and applying potentiometers that will cause them to yield an output voltage that is some desired nonlinear function of input motion. These nonlinear potentiometer function generators are useful in a-c and d-c computers and in servomechanisms for such things as transducer signal conditioning and simulating the known nonlinear relationship between two variables.

The many ways of obtaining a nonlinear function from a potentiometer divide into two general classes: (1) those cases where a specific nonlinear function is designed and built into a potentiometer, and (2) those cases where the desired nonlinear function is developed by suitably interconnecting one or several standard linear potentiometers. The first class includes nonlinear pots that use variable wire spacing, variable wire resistance, variable-width cards, and special arrangements of wire on forms. The second class takes in cases where a linear potentiometer is driven by a nonlinear linkage or cam, where linear cams are ganged, and where the nonlinear function is obtained by applying a substantial load to the potentiometer. Shunting a tapped potentiometer with resistors is a method that does not clearly fit into either class: a standard tapped linear pot may be used, or the system designer may specify a potentiometer with taps at desired points. And, of course, some potentiometers use two or three of the above methods.

Variable Wire Spacing. Here the resistance wire is wound on the card or mandrel with continuously varying pitch, as shown in Fig. 2-24. Coils wound in this manner are called "space-wound." Manufacturing difficulties are encountered with this technique, since the winding machine must be equipped with a special cam that accurately varies the wire spacing to achieve the desired nonlinear function. Servo-controlled winding machines are sometimes used, which accurately measure w nding resistance versus displacement and compare it with a nonlinear master. This winding method gives direct, rather than inferential, control of the desired

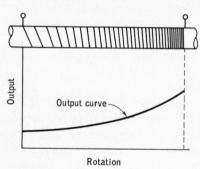

Fig. 2-24. Varying wire pitch to obtain nonlinear function.

function and also compensates for variations in card width and wire resistance. In fact, space winding is often used to achieve precise linear potentiometers by compensating for other uncontrollable factors.

A slope ratio of about 3:1 is the maximum that can be obtained by space winding alone, and this method has the disadvantage that resolution varies with spacing.

Variable Wire Resistance. Changing wire size or the resistivity of the wire permits the approximation of a nonlinear function by a series of straight lines. Figure 2-25 shows the result of changing wire size. There is almost no limit to the slope ratio, and nonlinear functions having abrupt changes can be approximated by this method. The individual wire segments can be joined together by splices or knots, or they may be fuse-welded. The better potentiometers use the latter method. Some

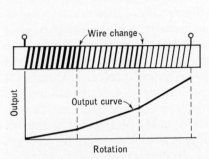

FIG. 2-25. Changing wire resistivity yields nonlinear function.

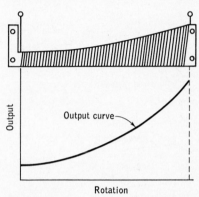

FIG. 2-26. Nonlinear pot using variable width card.

attempts have been made actually to vary wire resistivity in accordance with the nonlinear function. Controlled chemical or electrolytic etching, or special plating techniques, are useful for this purpose.

Variable-width Cards. One of the most common ways to achieve nonlinearity of potentiometer output is to place the winding on a card of varying width, as shown in Fig. 2-26. Here the length of wire for the individual turns (and therefore the resistance per turn) varies continuously: the rate of change of output will vary similarly. The maximum practical slope ratio of a card's contour is about 5:1: the wire slips down the card if this ratio is exceeded.

Special Arrangements of Wire on Forms. In this type of potentiometer, a contact moves across the flat surface of a specially shaped element to develop the required nonlinear function. The element can either be

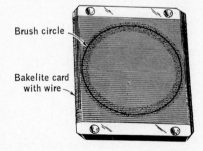

FIG. 2-27. Flat surface sine-cosine pot.

wire-wound or coated with a resistive film. In addition to the special shaped element (similar to a variable-width card except that the wiper moves over a plane instead of around the inside of a cylinder), it is also possible to force the wiper to follow special paths.

Figure 2-27 shows a wire-wound sine-cosine pot of this variety originally developed at the MIT Radiation Laboratory. With four brushes located accurately at the corners of a square and tracking on the brush circle, the voltage differences between diametrically opposite brushes will be proportional to the sine and cosine of rotation. Using the difference voltages as the output (rather than the output of two individual brushes) cancels out errors that would result if the axis of rotation does not correspond exactly to the geometrical center of the square formed by the brushes.

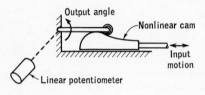

Nonlinear Mechanical Input to a Linear Pot. Almost any type of nonlinear function can be generated by using some type of nonlinear mechanical mechanism to drive a linear potentiometer. Figure 2-28 shows rotary linear potentiometers driven by a nonlinear rectilinear-motion cam and by a special linkage. In the latter case the output from the potentiometer is a function of two input variables. Rectilinear-motion potentiometers can also be used as the output element; for example, in transducing the mechanical displacement output of a three-dimensional barrel cam. Where applicable, this method of nonlinearizing potentiometers permits the system designer to modify the nonlinear function without incurring the added expense or excessive lead time of special potentiometers.

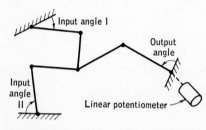

FIG. 2-28. Cam-driven nonlinear potentiometers.

FIG. 2-29. Mechanically-ganged pots for nonlinear function generation.

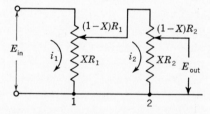

FIG. 2-30. Squaring circuit using two ganged pots.

Ganging Linear Potentiometers. Mechanically ganged potentiometers (Fig. 2-29) feeding into one another in cascade can be used to develop certain limited functions. Most precision potentiometers are available in forms suitable for ganging and angular orientation so that this is a convenient technique.

Figure 2-30 shows a typical double-ganged circuit, where the output voltage is approximately proportional to the square of the input angular motion. Expressed mathematically:

$$\frac{E_{\text{out}}}{E_{\text{in}}} = \frac{X^2}{1 + XR_1/R_2 - X^2R_1/R_2} \tag{2-25}$$

The accuracy of this relationship depends on how much potentiometer 2 loads potentiometer 1. If the ratio R_1/R_2 is very small, and potentiometer 2 feeds a very high impedance load, then the circuit will adhere very closely to a square-law relationship.

Substantial Loading of a Linear Potentiometer. A limited but useful variety of nonlinear functions can be developed by loading a linear potentiometer with a specific network of fixed resistors. Figure 2-31 shows two of the more common arrangements. In Fig. 2-31A, the output voltage E_O is proportional to the tangent of the input angle X, while in Fig. 2-31B, E_O varies as the secant of X. An excellent summary of the types of functions that can be generated in this manner is given by Greenwood, Holdam, and MacRae.*

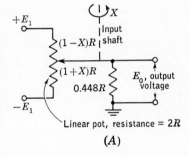

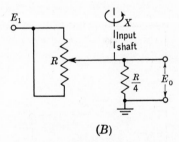

(A)

(B)

Fig. 2-31. Nonlinear functions obtained by loading linear potentiometers.

Tapped Potentiometers with Shunt Resistors. This technique is similar to that of using different resistance wire in different segments of a potentiometer, since again the nonlinear function is approximated by a series of straight lines. The crudest form of this would be to connect fixed resistors between the successive poles of a multipole selector switch: this would yield a stepped approximation to the nonlinear function. The usual method is to connect fixed resistors across the taps on a linear-resistance potentiometer as shown in Fig. 2-32. Specially placed taps can be specified by the systems designer, or standard multitapped potentiometers can be used. A wide variety of functions can be developed in this manner.

---

* I. A. Greenwood, J. V. Holdam, Jr., and D. MacRae, Jr., "Electronic Instruments," chap. 5, MIT Radiation Laboratory Series, McGraw-Hill Book Company, Inc., New York, 1948.

Figure 2-33 shows how to determine the tap locations. First plot the desired nonlinear function on a normalized plot of output voltage E vs. shaft rotation X. Then sketch in the conformity tolerance limits, making sure that these limits are tight enough to leave some room for manufac-

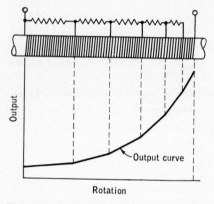

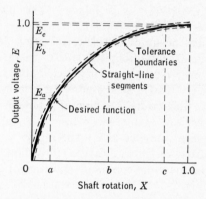

FIG. 2-32. Shunting resistors nonlinearize linear pots.

FIG. 2-33. Method of determining tap locations for shunting resistors.

turing imperfections. To determine tap locations, start at the origin and draw the maximum possible length straight lines to approximate the curve while staying within the tolerance band. This gives both the taps $(a, b,$ etc.) and the desired normalized voltage at these taps (E_a, E_b, etc.).

The normalized values of the shunting resistors R_1, R_2, and R_3 can be calculated using the following relationships. Here, E_l is the normalized voltage at the last tap and l is the unit position of the last tap. Figure 2-34 shows the circuit.

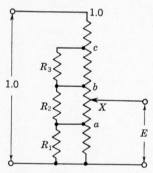

FIG. 2-34. Shunting resistor circuit. Total resistance $= R$.

$$k = \frac{1 - E_l}{1 - l} \tag{2-26}$$

$$R_1 = \frac{k_1(a - 0)(E_a - E_O)}{k_1(a - 0) - (E_a - E_O)} \tag{2-27}$$

$$R_2 = \frac{k_2(b - a)(E_b - E_a)}{k_2(b - a) - (E_b - E_a)} \tag{2-28}$$

$$R_3 = \frac{k_3(c - b)(E_c - E_b)}{k_3(c - b) - (E_c - E_b)} \tag{2-29}$$

The actual values of the shunting resistors are arrived at by multiplying the above normalized values by the desired total resistance R. Narrowing the conformity tolerance zone increases the required number of taps and yields a better approximation of the actual nonlinear function. Errors in tap location can occur during the manufacturing process, but this can be at least partially corrected for by measuring the resistance across the taps before the shunt resistors are attached and modifying the value of the shunt resistors to suit.

Combining Methods. Often two or more of the above techniques can be combined to give high accuracy or a specially high degree of non-linearity. Figure 2-35 shows two examples. In the upper one, shunting resistors are combined with a space-wound card to give the high rate of change obtainable with the shunt-ing technique with the smooth curve characteristic of space wind-ing. The lower example shows a variable-width card combined with changing wire size that achieves essentially the same end. Most precision potentiometer manufac-turers either include items such as these in their standard line, or are willing to make them up on special order.

2-16. A Typical Problem in Potentiometer Selection. Select the potentiometers in a system that must develop an output control voltage proportional to tempera-ture in the range 20 to 80°C. The circuit uses a self-balancing Wheat-stone bridge with a thermistor

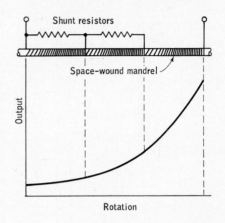

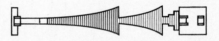

Fig. 2-35. Combining methods of non-linearizing pots.

temperature-sensing element. Figure 2-36 shows the resistance variation with temperature for the selected thermistor. Since the temperature characteristic of the thermistor can be defined mathematically, this relationship (noted in Fig. 2-36) can be used in the analysis of the system.

Because of the highly nonlinear character of the thermistor bridge, sensitivity will tend to vary with temperature. To counteract this, the self-balancing bridge must be designed to maintain uniform servo stability at any temperature in the operating range. The output voltage is to be zero at 20°C and 100 volts at 80°C. Temperature measurement must be accurate within ± 1°C, corresponding to $1\frac{2}{3}$ volts at the output. In terms of output accuracy, this is a relatively crude $1\frac{2}{3}$ per cent.

A schematic diagram of the proposed self-balancing bridge is shown in Fig. 2-37. This bridge contains three potentiometers, P_1, P_2, and P_3, that must be specified. Neglecting the loading of the bridge by P_2, then, by inspection,

$$\frac{R_1}{R_1 + R} - \frac{R_2}{R_2 + R} = \frac{E}{V} \qquad (2\text{-}30)$$

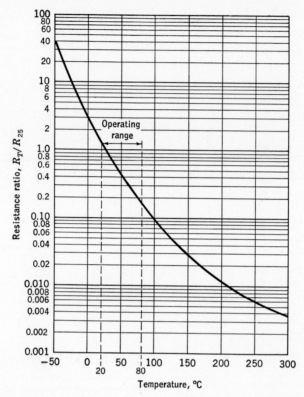

Fig. 2-36. Temperature characteristic of thermistor expressed graphically and mathematically.

$$R_T = R_O e^{\beta(1/T - 1/T_o)}$$

where T_O = reference temperature, deg abs (corresponds here to 25°C); R_O = reference resistance at temperature T_O; T = actual temperature, deg abs; R_T = actual resistance at temperature T; β = constant (depends on thermistor material); β = 3,545 ± 80 for this material (G.E. No. 2).

For approximately balanced conditions, where $R_1 = R_2$

$$\frac{E}{V} = \frac{R(R_1 - R_2)}{2(R_1 + R)} = k \tag{2-31}$$

As R increases, it can be seen that E/V (sensitivity) increases to a limiting value of $(R_1 - R_2)/2$. Thus, at high temperatures where sensitivity tends to fall, it is advisable to specify $R \gg R_1, R_2$.

R_1 is the resistance of the thermistor, which, as shown in Fig. 2-36, is related to temperature as follows:

$$R_1 = R_T = R_0 e^{\beta(1/T - 1/T_0)} \tag{2-32}$$

To determine bridge sensitivity to temperature change, differentiate R_T with respect to T.

$$\frac{dR_T}{dT} = -\frac{\beta}{T_2} R_0 e^{\beta(1/T - 1/T_0)} = -\frac{\beta R_T}{T^2} \qquad (2\text{-}33)$$

To determine the output for a small change dT in temperature, rewrite the expression for k as follows:

$$dk = d\left(\frac{E}{V}\right) = \frac{R\, dR_1}{2(R_1 - R)} \qquad dR_1 = \frac{\beta R_1}{T^2}\, dT$$

and therefore

$$\frac{dk}{dT} = \frac{-R\beta R_1}{2(R_1 - R)T^2} \qquad (2\text{-}34)$$

This shows the variation of output voltage with temperature change, and is a measure of sensitivity. Sensitivity decreases continually with increasing temperature, as noted above. The gain-control poten-tiometer must vary its attenuation as a function of temperature (or shaft angle c) in a reciprocal man-ner, to ensure uniform tempera-ture-insensitive loop gain. Thus, the ratio of electrical output to mechanical input for P_2 must vary as

$$\frac{2(R_1 - R)T^2}{\beta R_1} \qquad (2\text{-}35)$$

where $R_1 = f(T) = f(c)$; R and β are constants.

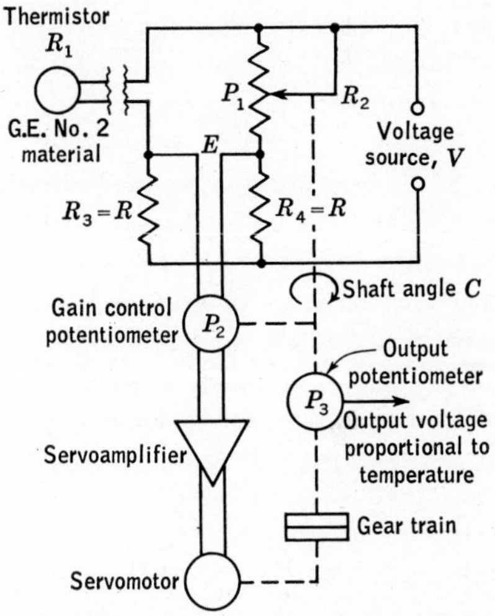

At very low temperatures where R_1 approaches infinity, the output impedance of the bridge as seen at P_2 approaches 250 ohms. Loading

Fig. 2-37. Schematic of self-balancing bridge.

will be no problem if P_2 is assigned the convenient value of 5,000 ohms.

For good bridge sensitivity with low voltage dissipation in the bridge elements, the general properties of a bridge suggest that

$$R_3 = R_4 = R$$
$$R_1 = R_2 \qquad \text{at bridge balance}$$
$$R \gg R_1, R_2$$

As indicated by the above analysis, the nature of the resistance-tempera-ture variation of the thermistor shows that bridge sensitivity tends to decrease with increasing temperature. Thus, potentiometer P_2, whose setting is a function of temperature, is included to compensate for this change in sensitivity and maintain constant gain as temperature varies. This constant gain will approximate the lower gain encountered at the maximum temperature extreme, since P_2 cannot amplify, but can only attenuate. If R is much greater than R_1 and R_2 at the higher temperature limit, then the uncontrolled gain at this point will be increased. The reduction in gain at low temperatures resulting from a reduction in the inequality simply means less attenuation will be required of P_2 in this region. Thus, if R_1 is 156 ohms at 80°C, a suitable value for R would be 500 ohms.

The system is simplest if P_1 is a nonlinear potentiometer with exact correspondence to R_1 (the thermistor resistance) as a function of temperature. Thus, shaft angle c will be a linear function of temperature, and P_3, the output potentiometer, will be linear. There are advantages to selecting P_1 with the proper nonlinear function. Since output shaft angle and temperature are proportional, servo stiffness (the error per unit displacement of the controlled shaft) and temperature sensitivity (the error per unit temperature change) are equal and (with the help of P_2) constant.

2-17. Selecting Specific Potentiometers. The balancing potentiometer P_1 has as its system functions balancing, resistance variation, and function generation. Its total resistance should be 964 ohms, and it must be capable of matching the thermistor resistance characteristic to within a fraction of the ohmic equivalent of 1°C at all temperatures in the range 20 to 80°C. Contact resistance must not exceed a few ohms, since the unit is used as a variable resistor. A single-turn nonminiature pot should provide adequate resolution for this medium-precision application. Because of the nonlinearity, resolution can be poorer at the higher temperatures where the rate of change of resistance with shaft angle is minimum, but the resolution at maximum temperature must exceed the accuracy requirement by at least a factor of 2. The total resistance of the purchased potentiometer, and the required precision, must be related to the method of achieving the nonlinearity and the techniques for trimming.

A commercially available potentiometer—TIC Model No. RVC2—can be modified to meet these requirements. This is a 2-in. precision potentiometer, modified with three equally spaced taps so that shunting resistors can be added to approximate the nonlinear function. Figure 2-38 shows that the optimum adjustment of shunt resistors gives equal plus and minus errors. This unit has uniform resolution, and since loop gain is kept constant by P_2, stability is no problem. The servo-mount construction is well suited for integration in the closed-loop assembly. If greater accuracy were required, a slight intrinsic nonlinearity could be designed into the pot.

The gain-control potentiometer P_2 is used as a function generator. The resistance characteristic of this potentiometer is selected to maintain loop gain constant, independent of shaft angle; however, the degree of nonlinearity is less than that of P_1. A 5,000-ohm wire-wound pot with a conformity of ± 5 per cent should be adequate. A 2-in. general-purpose pot with a shaped card for achieving the nonlinear function—TIC Model No. RV2—with the manufacturer's standard tolerance of ± 5 per cent on total resistance satisfies requirements.

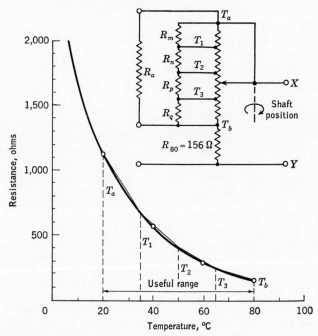

FIG. 2-38. Nonlinear potentiometer curve obtained from tap-shunted pot matches thermistor characteristic by a series of straight lines. Total resistance $P_1 - P_2 =$ $1,120 - 156 = 964$ ohms. Variable-resistor terminals are X and Y. R_m, R_n, R_p, and R_q are adjusted for optimum fit. Required accuracy is $\pm 1°C$ or equivalent in shaft angle.

The output potentiometer P_3 is used for linear-data conversion. In this application, resolution must be merely adequate to ensure accuracy, since there is no loop closed around the mechanical to electrical data conversion. Over-all accuracy is $\pm 1°C$, so that potentiometer accuracy of $\pm \frac{1}{4}°C$ is satisfactory (corresponds to about 0.4 per cent). Since the unit must be capable of dissipating heat corresponding to 100 volts, the lower limit of permissible resistance is established by the power rating. A standard 2-in. general-purpose precision potentiometer—TIC Model No. RV2—with $\frac{1}{2}$ per cent linear output will meet requirements.

2-18. Environmental Influences on Potentiometer Characteristics. *
The environment in which a potentiometer operates affects such secondary potentiometer characteristics as insulation resistance, temperature coefficient of resistance, life, and shaft play, which, in turn, affect the primary characteristics of linearity or conformity, resistance stability, physical dimensions, torque, electrical noise, and dielectric strength. Table 2-9 summarizes the environmental conditions that are commonly encountered, and the effect of these conditions on the listed characteristics. More detail on these problems is given below.

TABLE 2-9. ENVIRONMENTAL EFFECTS ON PRECISION
WIRE-WOUND POTENTIOMETERS

Environment	Affected potentiometer characteristics	Cause
High temperature.....	Noise, life	Oxidation of contacting surfaces, resin vapors, spring relaxation
	Resistance	Wire-temperature coefficient and strain-gage effect
	Torque	Unequal expansion, shrinkage, gummed lubricants
	Voltage breakdown, life	Dielectric deterioration, excess wattage, exceeding temperature life of material
Low temperature......	Torque	Unequal expansion, viscosity increase of lubricants
	Noise	Viscosity increase of lubricants
	Resistance	Wire-temperature coefficient, strain gage effect
Vibration and shock...	Noise	Contact bounce, dither
Humidity............	Linearity, resistance, torque	Low and unequal insulation resistance, growth of hygroscopic materials
	Noise	Electrolytic corrosion
Altitude..............	Dielectric strength	Lower breakdown of air
	Power dissipation	Lower convection
Acceleration..........	Torque	Unbalanced rotor

High Temperature. Elevated ambient temperatures cause increased electrical noise, dielectric degradation and breakdown, reduced accuracy, higher torque requirements, reduced power-handling capabilities, and resistance instability.

* The effect of environment on precision potentiometers is excellently covered by A. W. Green and K. S. Schulz of Helipot.[13] The material in this section is abstracted from that source.

Prolonged exposure to high ambient temperatures increases electrical noise by more rapid oxidation of resistance wire and sliprings, by vaporization and subsequent deposit on contact surfaces of partially cured plastics and bonding resins, and by contact spring relaxation.

Dielectric strength reduction occurs because of the inherent time-temperature degradation of insulations, and because of moisture and gases absorbed in the insulation. Electrical insulating materials including organic compounds gradually lose their dielectric properties with time, with the rate of reduction proportional to ambient temperature. High temperatures drive the moisture absorbed in plastic insulating materials to the surface, reducing the dielectric strength. The latter problem can be overcome by applying a sealant to the insulation after it has been completely cured.

Many things affect the accuracy of a potentiometer operating at a high temperature. Decreasing insulation resistance in the wiper circuit appears as a loading error, and if the insulation resistance from coil to ground varies over the length of the coil, linearity is adversely affected. Mechanical problems can be caused by shrinking or softening of the mandrel or card, or by hardening of the bonding resins. These can result in loose turns of resistance wire and subsequent shorting of adjacent turns as the wiper moves over them.

Torque increase at a high temperature results from wiper indentation into soft thermoplastic coil-core materials, from unmatched expansion coefficients where tolerances are critical, and from gumming of bearing lubricants.

The power-handling capability of a potentiometer is reduced in accordance with the increase in temperature of the potentiometer coil, this increase being the total resulting from both applied electrical power and ambient temperature. The potentiometer manufacturer generally determines the power rating of a given model in still air at a certain ambient temperature, with no other heat-producing components within a certain distance, and with a specified radiating surface conductively attached to the potentiometer, usually at the mounting end. Permissible power input may vary in practice, depending on such things as air flow across the unit, the presence of other heat-producing components, and the ability of the mounting panel to conduct heat away from the potentiometer.

Potentiometer total resistance changes at high temperatures because of the temperature coefficient of resistance of the wire, the strain-gage effect if the mandrel or card expands more than the metal wire, and the relief of stresses created in the resistance wire during the winding process.

Low Temperature and Temperature Cycling. These factors have little effect on potentiometer performance. Slight torque increases may result from differential contraction and expansion of close tolerance parts, and from the increase in lubricant viscosity at low temperatures.   Resistance instability effects are similar to those encountered under high-temperature conditions.

Vibration.   Vibration affects performance by creating electrical noise in the form of an equivalent parasitic, transient contact resistance. Noise can be caused by contact bounce (accentuated at the resonant frequency of the contact-spring assembly) or by movement of the contact along a noisy part of the coil or slip ring (caused by flexing of the contact spring).

Contact bounce and dither are further aggravated during vibration by free play between the potentiometer rotor and its support.   This allows relative movement between the two, rich in harmonics, which takes place within the confines of the static shaft play of the potentiometer and any resulting deformation of the bearings.   At the vibration frequency coincident with the resonant frequency of the spring-mass system formed by the mass of the rotor and the elastic contacting surfaces, a resonance magnification occurs, with resulting acceleration many times the applied acceleration.

In addition to noise, this chattering of the rotor can also produce serious brinneling of bearings (indenting of the races by the balls) if the vibration is severe enough.

Measures can be taken to make a potentiometer vibration insensitive; however, these modifications do affect other performance characteristics. For example, increased contact force will generally reduce life through increased wear, and will increase torque.   The use of O rings as damping agents, or of spring loading will, of necessity, increase torque.   A compromise is almost always necessary.

Humidity.   Prolonged exposure to a humid atmosphere lowers the insulation resistance which degrades linearity because of wiper electrical loading and shunting of the coil.   This decrease in insulation resistance will also decrease the total resistance of the potentiometer, depending on the relative magnitudes of the two.

Total resistance can also be increased by expansion or swelling due to moisture absorption of the materials on which the resistance wire is wound.   In this case the resistance wire is actually being stretched. Another cause of resistance increase is electrolytic corrosion, resulting in metal being removed from the resistance wire.   When fine wire is used, it can corrode through in a relatively short time.   Corrosion of the coil due to the combination of increased temperature and humidity will also increase the noise level.

When a potentiometer that is not hermetically sealed is subjected to humidity-cycling conditions, temperature variations cause the potentiometer to breathe the atmosphere.   Moisture will then condense on interior insulating surfaces. One way out of these difficulties is to use sealed potentiometers. But again compromises in other performance characteristics result from the sealing procedure. If the system designer cannot accept these changes in performance, he has the alternative of mounting the potentiometer and its associated equipment in a sealed enclosure.

Altitude. Only two potentiometer characteristics are greatly affected by operation at high altitudes: dielectric strength and power rating. Dielectric breakdown will occur either across a surface or across an airgap. The point of breakdown will often occur across a surface below a certain altitude, and through an airgap above this altitude. Breakdown across a surface is greatly affected by the presence of moisture, dirt, or wear particles.

Since a large portion of the heat generated in a potentiometer is carried away by convection (according to the normal rating method of potentiometers), an appreciable derating is necessary when a unit is operated in rarefied air at high altitudes. However, the principle of the thermal sink can be used to increase the wattage rating. In the idealized case (when a potentiometer is mounted on what might effectively be a thermal sink of infinite capacity, and when not influenced by radiation from other heat-producing components) a well-designed assembly can be operated at up to 100 per cent increase in wattage at sea level and with as little as 10 per cent derating from this increased figure at an altitude of 50,000 ft.

Shock. As in vibration, the major difficulty encountered in shock is increased noise or loss of continuity because of contact bounce or dither. This is aggravated by free play between the rotor and its support. Repeated shocks can cause severe brinneling of the bearings and a further increase in shaft play. Torque can also be a problem during shock, when a potentiometer has an unbalanced rotor.

Acceleration. Acceleration is generally not considered a serious problem with potentiometers. The only important point is that under high-acceleration forces, rotor unbalance can cause the unit to transmit a shaft torque, equal to the amount of unbalance times the acceleration at the worst condition.

Combined Effects. As pointed out, modifications that are made to improve performance in a particular environment can affect other characteristics and can improve or degrade potentiometer performance in other environments.

On the beneficial side, the compressed shaft seal used in high humidity also damps the rotor in vibration and shock. In most instances the substitution of a material with improved humidity characteristics results in a material that also performs better at high temperatures.

On the undesirable side, increased contact forces for more satisfactory performance under vibration conditions may relax during high-temperature exposure, and hygroscopic materials depending on dimensional stability for secure mounting may shrink at high temperatures (with resulting failure during shock and vibration) unless properly cured and sealed. Coil-winding practice to improve life may prove detrimental to resistance stability.

2-19. Other Types of Potentiometers. In addition to the resistance potentiometer, there are several other types of pots that yield an output voltage that is a linear function of input motion. These include induction pots, inductive pots, reluctance pots, capacitive pots, dielectric pots, and pots that operate on a combination of these principles. These types are normally used where their particular characteristics exactly satisfy a specific system requirement: none is anywhere near as common as the resistance potentiometer.

Induction Potentiometers. Potentiometer action is obtained by varying the mutual inductance between a primary coil and an output or secondary coil, as shown in Fig. 2-39. The instrument is distinguished by exceptionally long life (hundreds of millions of cycles at speeds up to several thousand rpm). Resolution is infinite, and accuracies are comparable to resistance potentiometers. By its nature, it provides plus and minus outputs and isolation between input and output. Its principal limitations are its restricted angular travel (it is linear over a maximum range of only about $\pm 80°$) and its expensive and bulky electronic auxiliary equipment required for phase correction and temperature and non-linearity compensation. The induction pot has a low ratio of output to input impedance, and is not as load-sensitive as the resistance potentiometer. This type of potentiometer is covered in detail in Chap. 4 on induction components.

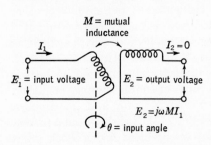

FIG. 2-39. Induction potentiometer.

Inductive Potentiometers. By varying tap position, an autotransformer can be used as an inductive potentiometer. Two types are available; one has fixed taps with selector-switch selection of tap (and possibly with resistance potentiometer interpolation between taps), while the other has a roller contact to vary tap location, with the roller interpolating between taps. The latter has been widely used abroad, but in spite of its advantages has found little application in this country.

The magnetic circuit of a precision roller-type-pickup precision variable transformer consists of a toroid, built up of circular laminations of high-permeability nickel steel. Figure 2-40 shows the construction. As many turns as possible are wound on the iron stack, in keeping with mechanical strength and life requirements. Figure 2-40C illustrates how the windings are placed in engraved grooves in the wire guide. A wiper arm, rotating about a centered axial shaft, contacts the various turns

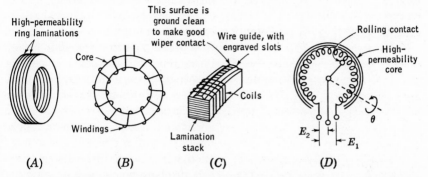

(A) (B) (C) (D)

Fig. 2-40. Inductive potentiometer using carbon roller wiper. θ = input angle. E_1 = input voltage. E_2 = output voltage. $E_2 = K\theta E_1$.

picking off an output potential that varies linearly with shaft angular position.

The wiper is a self-aligning carbon roller. It is this feature that makes this device superior to resistance potentiometers in certain applications. The advantages are as follows:

1. The carbon roller interpolates between turns so that infinite resolution is obtained. As shown in Fig. 2-41, there are no discontinuities in the smoothed curve, and the amplitude of the ripple is only about 20 per cent that of the uninterpolated steps.

2. This type of construction improves contact life. As the roller wears, its diameter merely reduces.

3. Radio interference generation is reduced by the smooth action of the carbon roller in making and breaking contact points.

4. The conducting shaft of the carbon roller turns in a pair of grooves in the wiper arm. This gives a self-wiping action from the roller to the external circuit.

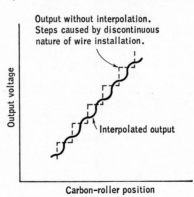

Fig. 2-41. Smoothing effect of roller wiper.

Because of its toroidal construction, the inductive potentiometer has negligible resistance and leakage reactance in many applications. Thus, its performance approaches that of an ideal transformer and it can be heavily loaded without regulation, has a high input impedance, and exhibits negligible phase shift. A typical variable transformer marketed under the trade name Ipot by Muirhead operates on 50 cps with an accuracy of 0.1 per cent.

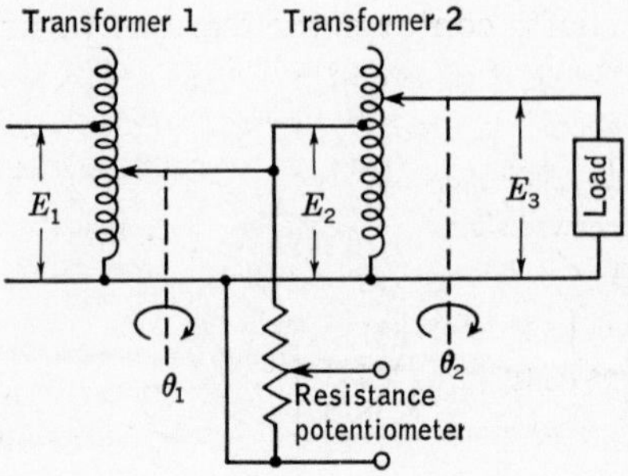

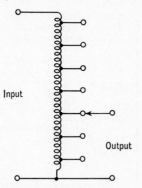

Fig. 2-42. Cascaded inductive potentiometers.

$$E_2 = K\theta_1 E_1. \quad E_3 = K\theta_2 E_2 = K^2\theta_1\theta_2 E_1.$$

Figure 2-42 shows a typical application of an inductive potentiometer in a series chain. The high input impedance and low output impedance permit these units to be loaded directly on one another without an isolating booster amplifier. Also, additional heavy loads (such as a resistance potentiometer) can be connected in the circuit. These units can also be used for voltage step-up in calibrating circuits, an application that cannot be handled by resistance potentiometers.

A straight tapped autotransformer is shown in Fig. 2-43. This can be used as an inductive potentiometer, but has the distinct disadvantage of a stepped output. As discussed below under combined types, resistance potentiometers are often used to interpolate between taps.

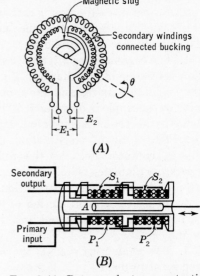

(A)

(B)

Fig. 2-43. Tapped autotransformer as an inductive potentiometer has disadvantage of stepped output.

Fig. 2-44. Rotary reluctance potentiometer A and linear version B. Latter is commonly known as linear differential transformer. θ = input angle. $E_2 = k\theta E_1$.

Reluctance Potentiometers. The reluctance potentiometer varies the mutual inductance by moving a magnetic slug. Figure 2-44A shows a rotary version in which the primary winding is connected to an a-c source, and the split secondary winding is connected series bucking. Secondary output varies in phase and magnitude with the direction and amount of angular displacement from a null. The rectilinear-motion linear differential transformer is a special, and widely used, version of the reluctance potentiometer.

In the typical linear differential transformer shown in Fig. 2-44B, motion of the armature toward the secondary coil S_1 results in an increased output of one phase, and motion toward S_2 results in an increased output of the opposite phase. If the secondary coils are identical and the armature is located so that each receives an equal amount of flux, the voltages induced in the secondary coils will be equal and out of phase and a theoretical output of zero will result.

This winding design gives equal and stable electrostatic coupling between the primary and secondary windings and minimizes changes in this coupling from temperature drift. Uniform magnetic coupling also makes it possible to maintain reasonable linearity without a large number of turns. Thus the coils have a relatively low impedance, adequately matching standard audio-frequency transformers, and allow the use of long transmission lines (up to 5,000 ft) without danger from stray pickup or phase shift due to line capacity.

Transformers with various armature motions (over the linear range) can be produced by redistributing the windings over a longer or shorter form. The characteristics of three types of transformers manufactured by the Automatic Temperature Control Co., Inc., are as follows:

1. Full linear travel, ± 0.15 in.; output with 60 cps input, 0.25 mv/volt input/0.001 in.

2. Full linear travel, ± 0.5 in.; output with 60 cps input, 0.0385 mv/volt input/0.001 in.

3. Full linear travel, ± 2.5 in.; output with 60 cps input, 6.36 mv/volt input/1.0 in.

This type unit is characterized by a high degree of linearity and reproducibility of output with respect to armature displacement. A linearity of better than ± 0.05 per cent can be expected from commercial units and they will match each other within 0.5 per cent without compensation. Since transformer inductance change is negligible for normal armature movements, servos operating with these units need not be compensated for phase shift throughout the operating range. With the input isolated from the output, the units can be combined in a variety of ways and used to perform many useful mathematical functions. Magnetic pull on the armature is low throughout the operating range. On the units listed above, null-balance-point output remains below 0.001 volt up to 5,000 cps, and never exceeds 0.0017 volt.

To obtain a low null signal and good reproducibility, the armature must be carefully constructed and connected. If a cylindrical steel armature is used, it must be slotted along its length to limit eddy currents. These currents affect the null balance of differential transformers.

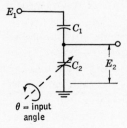

Internal material stresses should also be avoided for the same reason. Care must be taken that large masses of aluminum, copper, brass, or other nonmagnetic materials are not located too close to the unit since they can cause phase shifts. In this connection, the transformers are more sensitive to end effects than to side effects.

θ = input angle

FIG. 2-45. Capacitive potentiometer. E_2/E_1 = $C_1/(C_1 + C_2)$.

Capacitive Potentiometers. The common open-construction audio tuning capacitor can be thought of as a simple capacitive transducer. Combining a variable capacitor like this with a fixed capacitor, as shown in Fig. 2-45, forms a capacitive potentiometer in which output voltage is some function of input shaft displacement. This function can be controlled by the shape of the plates so that both linear and nonlinear (such

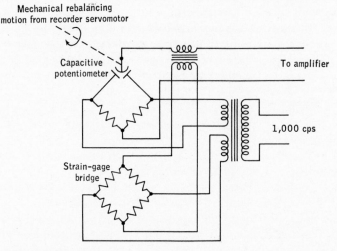

FIG. 2-46. Commercially available self-balancing recorder uses capacitive potentiometer as balancing element.

as sine-cosine) capacitive pots have been used. These devices exhibit infinite resolution and produce very low reaction forces on the input member, but output impedance is inherently high except at very high frequencies. For this reason they are sometimes used as control elements in high-frequency circuits and for function generation in computers.

Major application problems are associated with the effect of output-lead shunt capacitance and stray coupling with the potentiometer itself, so that careful shielding of both the output cables and the active element are prerequisites to successful operation.

Figure 2-46 shows the use of a capacitive potentiometer in a self-balancing recorder manufactured by The Foxboro Co. This type of potentiometer uses a split-stator variable-airgap capacitor, with one-half of the stator in each of two legs of a bridge circuit. Note the 1,000-cps high-frequency supply. The use of a capacitive potentiometer in this instance improves instrument performance and reliability: resolution is infinite and there is no wear from sliding contacts as in a resistance potentiometer.

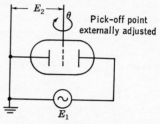

Fig. 2-47. Elementary dielectric potentiometer. $E_2/E_1 = k\theta$.

Dielectric Potentiometers. In dielectric units, potentiometer action is obtained by varying the position point or tap in a current-carrying field. They are primarily used on alternating current because of ionization problems. The total resistance of a dielectric pot varies considerably with temperature; however, the accuracy of the tap voltage as a percentage of applied voltage can be held to very close tolerances. A simple unit is shown in Fig. 2-47. Infinite resolution and unlimited life are its two major features.

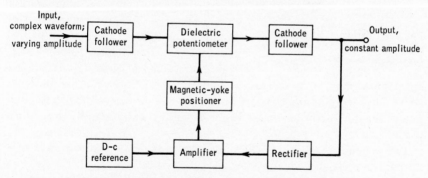

Fig. 2-48. Dielectric potentiometer in compressor amplifier.

The Technology Instrument Corp. has developed a special dielectric potentiometer for use in their Model 501-A compressor amplifier. The input to this amplifier consists of a complex waveform with widely varying amplitude, while the output exhibits the same waveform but at almost constant amplitude. Figure 2-48 shows a block diagram of this instrument.

The dielectric potentiometer works on the theory that the parallel network of resistance and capacitance between two electrodes submerged in an organic fluid having considerable loss has a constant RC product. This product depends only on the specific liquid that is used, and is equal to the product of the dielectric constant and resistivity of this liquid. The pot used in the instrument shown in Fig. 2-48 consists of a grounded metallic housing to which is attached a fixed input electrode, a second fixed input electrode insulated from the housing, and a movable vane-shaped output electrode. Since the RC product between the two fixed electrodes is independent of configuration, spacing, and frequency, the output voltage from the movable electrode has the same waveshape as the input but at a constant amplitude. Of course, the housing is filled with the electrolyte.

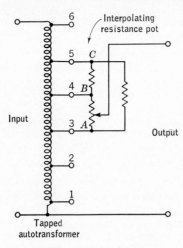

FIG. 2-49. Vernistat uses resistance potentiometer to interpolate between taps on autotransformer.

The rotating-vane electrode is positioned by energizing one or the other of a pair of magnetic yokes. By comparing the output of the instrument with a fixed d-c reference, the closed-loop system minimizes the difference between these two voltages, tending to maintain a constant amplitude output.

Combination Potentiometers. Although several types of combination potentiometers have been used, one of the most common is the Vernistat manufactured by the Perkin-Elmer Corp. This potentiometer consists of a tapped autotransformer with resistance potentiometer interpolation between steps, thus combining the low-impedance advantage of the inductive potentiometer with the high linear accuracy exhibited by resistance potentiometers.

The schematic of Fig. 2-49 shows six taps of a Vernistat, which is normally a 31-tap device. A planetary-type gearing arrangement synchronizes the resistance potentiometer ABC in turn with the tapped sections of the autotransformer. The resistance pot is traversed in 1 turn of the shaft, while 10 turns are required to cover the entire voltage range of the autotransformer. Briefly, this is how it works: The resistance pot is connected as shown while the wiper moves from A to B. But once B is reached, the resistance pot is automatically reconnected so that A contacts tap 6. This leapfrogging effect continues so that a linear output is available for the entire 10-turn travel of the potentiometer.

Linearity accuracies of better than ±0.05 per cent can be achieved in this manner. Special nonlinear functions can be generated also by changing tap spacing.

REFERENCES

1. Gray, H. L., Jr.: A Guide to Applying Resistance Pots, *Control Eng.*, July, 1956, pp. 80–93.
2. "Potentiometer Handbook," Technology Instrument Corp., Acton, Mass.
3. A Symposium of Technical Articles, Borg Equipment Div., The George W. Borg Corp., Janesville, Wis.
4. Hogen, I. T.: Electrical Noise in Wire Wound Potentiometers, Helipot Corp., paper presented at Western Electronics Conference, 1952.
5. Schneider, S., F. Hiraoka, and C. Gaudlin: Measurement and Correction of Phase Shift in Copper-mandrel Precision Potentiometers, Helipot Corp., 1957.
6. Gilbert, J.: Here's a Shortcut in Compensating Pots for Loading Errors, *Control Eng.*, February, 1955, pp. 36–40.
7. Gilbert, J.: Compensating Function Pots for Loading Errors, *Control Eng.*, March, 1955, pp. 70–71.
8. Gilbert, J.: Use Taps to Compensate for Loading Errors, *Control Eng.*, August, 1956, pp. 78–82.
9. Gilbert, J.: How to Phase-compensate Loaded Potentiometers, *Control Eng.*, January, 1957, pp. 82–87.
10. Greenwood, I. A., J. V. Holdam, Jr., and D. MacRae, Jr.: "Electronic Instruments," MIT Radiation Laboratory Series, McGraw-Hill Book Company, Inc., New York, 1948.
11. Blackburn, J. F.: "Components Handbook," vol. 17, MIT Radiation Laboratory Series, McGraw-Hill Book Company, Inc., New York, 1948.
12. Helipot Catalog 540, Helipot Corp., 1954.
13. Green, A. W., and K. S. Schulz: Environmental Effects on Precision Potentiometers, presented at Western Electronics Conference, 1956.

Chapter 3

SYNCHROS

3-1. Introduction. Synchros are small motorlike components, widely used for the remote transmission of shaft position in a-c servomechanisms. The basic electromagnetic structure consists of a wound rotor and a wound stator, concentrically arranged to give adjustable mutual coupling between the windings on the two members. The windings and magnetic circuit are designed to give a substantially sinusoidal variation in magnetic coupling as a function of shaft position. Although similar in appearance and construction to a wound-rotor induction motor, synchros differ in the quality of their materials and the care taken in their fabrication.

As induction-type components, synchros exhibit the good reliability characteristic of that class of device. They are inherently balanced, capable of continuous rotation, and are relatively insensitive to line voltage and frequency fluctuations and temperature variations. Models are available for operation at 1,500 rpm and faster, high speeds for precision components.

Synchros divide into two basic groups: torque units and signal-transmission units. Torque synchros do not amplify torque; therefore, the energy delivered to a mechanical load at the output shaft of a receiving synchro must be supplied by the driving member at the input shaft of the transmitting synchro. This type of transmission is analogous to mechanically driving a load through a flexible shaft having considerable torsional resilience. Being open-loop, torque-synchro angle transmissions suffer the reduced accuracy and sensitivity to load characteristic of this type of system.

In contrast, signal-transmission units develop an output error voltage proportional to the misalignment between the shaft of the receiving (or output) component and the shaft of the transmitting (or input) component. This error voltage is amplified and used to drive a motor that restores input-output correspondence by properly positioning the output-unit shaft. Output torque can be as high as desired, depending on the capacity of the driving motor, since this torque is not reflected back to the input shaft. Although torque synchros will be treated briefly, the greater

92

part of this chapter will be devoted to signal-transmission or control synchros.

. Within the basic classes of torque and control synchros, there are further subdivisions of synchro types depending on the individual functions in angle-transmission systems. In the torque group there are torque transmitters or generators (TX), torque differential transmitters or generators (TDX), and torque receivers (TR); while in an analogous way there are control transmitters or generators (CS), control differential generators or transmitters (CDX), and control transformers or receivers (CT).* These will be treated later.

Before investigating the details of synchro operation, a few observations can be made relating to the unusual performance and consequent widespread popularity of synchro systems. Perhaps maximum insight can be obtained by comparing a control-synchro transmission system (Fig. 3-1A) with a near competitor, a potentiometer transmission system (Fig. 3-1B). This comparison shows that the synchro system has the following advantages:

1. No resolution error. There is no step effect or irregularity in synchro signal transmission.

2. No wear from rotation, except for the slight noncritical wear at the slip rings. Synchro systems operate at much higher speeds for much longer periods than do potentiometer systems.

3. Relative insensitivity to stray cabling capacitance. Because of the symmetrical arrangement of three-legged synchro leads, a "twisted three" or a symmetrical three-wire cable can be used for angle transmission over very long distances with a minimum of sensitivity to stray cabling capacitance or pickup from external sources.

4. The accuracy of a synchro system is high compared to the performance of even the best potentiometer. A typical inexpensive massproduced 400-cps synchro with an accuracy of 7' of angle corresponds to a potentiometer accuracy of 0.032 per cent.

5. A synchro has a useful operating angle of 360° and is capable of continuous rotation.

Other miscellaneous advantages include the high reliability of the synchro, and its adaptability to multispeed operation. With the latter technique, it is possible to achieve accuracies of better than 0.005 per cent, or 1' of angle, by using standard production-line components. And this accuracy persists through long hard usage under extreme military conditions.

The popularity of synchros, particularly in military servomechanisms, has led to the standardization of synchro types by certain government

* Notation is according to Bureau of Ordnance specifications, the numbers of which are given later in text.

agencies.   The BuOrd standards for 60-cps units (MIL-S-17245) and for 400-cps units (MIL-S-16892) apply to synchros for military applications. The SAE is currently preparing a parallel series of specifications for synchros aimed at nonmilitary applications.   Because synchro requirements do not vary much from one application to another, and because of

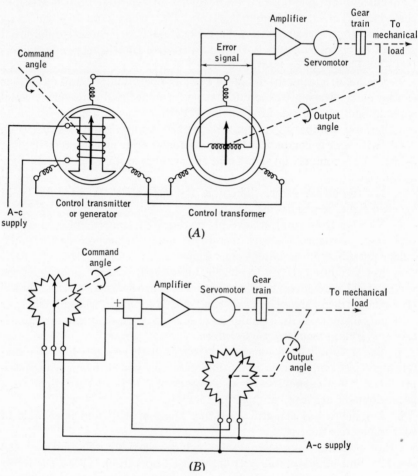

Fig. 3-1. Synchro and potentiometer angle-transmission systems.

general acceptance of the government standards by industry, these standard units fill almost every need.   The important details of these standards are covered later.

3-2. Fundamental Relationships.   Figure 3-2 shows the magnetic circuit of a typical synchro transmitter.   The rotor is usually (but not always) a salient-pole or dumbbell type.   Exciting the rotor winding causes a magnetic field to be generated in the airgap between the rotor and the stator. The flux density around the airgap is distributed as shown in the developed view of Fig. 3-3. The instantaneous magnitude of the whole curve is proportional (assuming constant permeability and negligible hysteresis in the iron) to the instantaneous current, which is varying sinusoidally at line frequency.

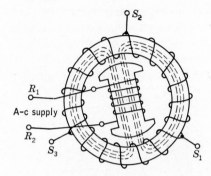

Fig. 3-2. Magnetic circuit of typical synchro transmitter.

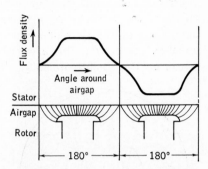

Fig. 3-3. Developed view of instantaneous flux distribution around airgap of salient-pole-rotor synchro generator.

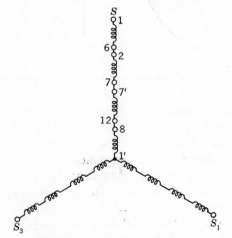

Fig. 3-4. Y stator winding.

The stator is wound with three groups of coils connected in a Y, having one common terminal inside the synchro and three external terminals (Fig. 3-4). Although this figure represents each stator leg as a single coil, the legs actually consist of a number of interconnected coils distributed in the stator slots as shown typically in Fig. 3-5. The resultant axes, or center lines, of the three groups of coils are at 120° angles in space around the periphery of the stator. Correct synchro-transmitter operation requires that as rotor position is varied, the fluxes generated by the varying magnetic field of the rotor induce voltages in the stator coil groups by transformer action, these latter voltages reaching their peak rms values at 120° intervals, as shown in Fig. 3-6.   Note that the voltages shown here are the envelopes of the rms values of line-frequency-varying voltages as rotor position is varied.

For accurate angle transmission, it is not only necessary that the peak values of the voltage envelopes occur at the appropriate 120° intervals, but also that the envelopes themselves be as accurately sinusoidal as possible.   Achieving this accurate sinusoidal variation is the principal concern of the synchro designer.   There are two principal factors affecting

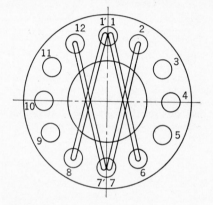

Fig. 3-5. Distribution of coils in stator slots.

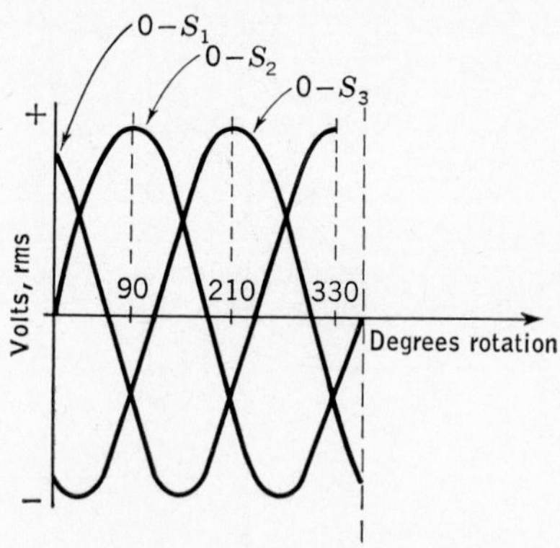

Fig. 3-6. Induced stator voltages as rotor position is varied.

accuracy: first, the shape of the flux distribution curve in the airgap must be made as sinusoidal as possible, and second, the stator winding coils must be distributed so that they are relatively insensitive to the harmonics in the flux density curve.   (The harmonics in the flux density curve are called *space harmonics* since they correspond to a nonsinusoidality in the flux distribution around the airgap.   In contrast, *time harmonics* would correspond to a nonsinusoidality in the variation of the instantaneous flux density with time at any point in the airgap.)

Although a later section will cover the factors influencing the magnitude of the harmonics, assume for the present the ideal situation of a perfectly sinusoidal variation of the stator terminal voltages with shaft position. Under these conditions, the voltages generated from the neutral point O to the external leads can be expressed by the following functions of shaft angle:

$$V_{O\text{-}S1} = V_M \sin \theta \qquad (3\text{-}1)$$
$$V_{O\text{-}S2} = V_M \sin (\theta - 120) \qquad (3\text{-}2)$$
$$V_{O\text{-}S3} = V_M \sin (\theta - 240) \qquad (3\text{-}3)$$

where V_M is the maximum rms voltage that is induced from the stator neutral to any of the external connections.

The voltages across the external stator legs are

$$V_{S1\text{-}S2} = V_{S1\text{-}0} + V_{0\text{-}S2} = V_{0\text{-}S1} + V_{0\text{-}S2}$$
$$= -V_M \sin \theta + V_M \sin (\theta - 120)$$
$$= \sqrt{3} \, V_M \sin (\theta - 150) \tag{3-4}$$

and similarly

$$V_{S2\text{-}S3} = \sqrt{3} \, V_M \sin (\theta + 90) \tag{3-5}$$
$$V_{S3\text{-}S1} = \sqrt{3} \, V_M \sin (\theta - 30) \tag{3-6}$$

These line-to-line voltages are related to the phase voltages by the vectors shown in Fig. 3-7. A common maximum line-to-line voltage for

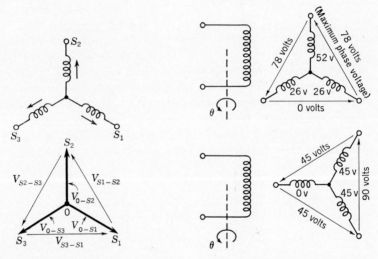

FIG. 3-7. Vector relationship between synchro phase and line voltages. All voltages are in time phase. Vector angles refer to shaft-angle displacements between sinusoidally varying induced rms voltages.

FIG. 3-8. Voltages developed in a standard military synchro for two different rotor positions.

certain standard synchros is 90 volts. Figure 3-8 shows the synchro voltages for some specific shaft positions. Note that the maximum phase voltage is $90/\sqrt{3}$, or 52 volts.

Now assume that some arbitrary balanced three-phase load is placed across the synchro output terminals (Fig. 3-9). It can be shown that the current in each leg of the secondary winding is proportional to the open-circuit voltage induced in the leg. The sum of the voltages (and currents) is zero. Thus the current diagram and voltage diagram are similar. Since the voltage diagram corresponds to components of the rotor flux along the axes of the three stator coils, the current vectors can also be combined to give a resultant current vector that coincides with the rotor axis. Figure 3-10 shows the sets of voltages and currents for a specific setting of the transmitter shaft. Note that the resultant current vector has a constant magnitude and always lies along the rotor axis.

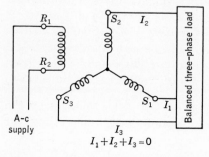

It is now possible to visualize the impedance and power relationships in the synchro rotor. For a perfectly symmetrical transmitter feeding a balanced load, there is effectively a constant-load reaction on the primary, exactly as is encountered when an ordinary static transformer has a fixed load. Thus the input impedance on the primary and primary power are independent

FIG. 3-9. Arbitrary balanced three-phase load across synchro output terminals.

of shaft angle. The group of three stator coils feeding the load behaves (with respect to the primary) as a single equivalent secondary directly coupled to the primary along its flux axis. Thus, the resultant flux field due to the primary lies directly along the primary axis.

Now substitute a perfect control transformer for the balanced load. The control transformer will behave as an exactly balanced load; therefore

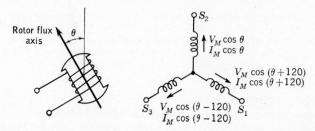

FIG. 3-10. With synchro generator terminated in a balanced load, corresponding voltage and current vectors vary together.

transmitter behavior will be as described above. Assume that the stator of the control transformer incorporates three identical coil groups, each generating only sinusoidally distributed flux fields when excited, and that the coils and magnetic structure of the control transformer are ideally symmetrical. The currents in the stator coils of the control transformer are identical to the transmitter secondary currents. As a result, there is a definite angular correspondence between the resultant flux axes caused by stator currents in the transmitter and control transformer. This correspondence is pointed out in the typical system of Fig. 3-11. In a sense, the flux field in the control transformer can be regarded as a "mirror image" of the transmitter stator field.

To apply synchros systematically, it is necessary to define a zero position. Synchro-generator zero is defined later in this chapter in terms of secondary voltages. The zero (or null) position of a control transformer is defined in terms of rotor position, where the rotor is at a 90° angle with the flux axis with the generator in zero position. Displacing the control transmitter either clockwise or counterclockwise causes a corresponding output voltage in the control transformer. If the control transformer null is maintained (as it is when driven in a servomechanism), transmitter and receiver angles are equal (for a suitably defined zero).

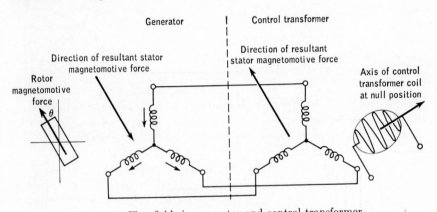

FIG. 3-11. Flux fields in generator and control transformer.
Notes: (1) Resultant generator magnetomotive force tends to buck out rotor magnetomotive force. (2) Magnetomotive force in control-transformer stator is parallel to generator stator magnetomotive force but acts in opposing direction. (3) Control-transformer rotor is at 90° to stator magnetomotive force.

3-3. Other Synchro-system Configurations. In the synchro-control-transmitter/synchro-control-transformer system discussed above, the output signal from the control transformer rotor may be amplified and used to drive its rotor into angular correspondence with the transmitter rotor. As pointed out previously, there is another class of components—torque synchros—which do not depend on external amplification to provide the power required to establish input-output correspondence, but rather on the internal torque-gradient characteristics of the transmitter-receiver combination. These systems, and other more complex control- and torque-synchro-system configurations involving differentials as well as transmitters and receivers, are similar in physical appearance and identical in basic concepts, so that brief descriptions will suffice.

Figure 3-12 schematically shows a pair of interconnected torque synchros. When the rotors are aligned and excited with equal voltages, the generated voltages in the polyphase secondaries exactly cancel and no stator current flows. Notice that in contrast to the control-synchro transmission system discussed above, the transmitter and receiver rotors are both connected to the same single-phase a-c source. In general, transmitter and receiver are very similar in construction. When the rotors are misaligned, a resultant voltage develops that causes current to flow through the leakage impedances of the two components. A stator flux is generated and a torque is exerted on the two rotors tending to align them. If the torque-transmitter synchro and torque-receiver synchro are identical units, the torque per degree misalignment is defined as the synchro torque gradient. With the transmitter shaft rigidly driven,

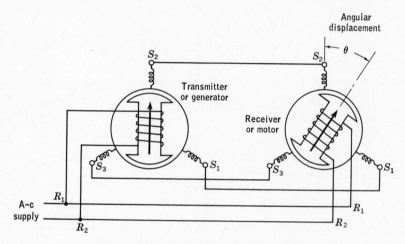

Fig. 3-12. Interconnected torque synchros.

the developed torque acts on the receiver rotor, forcing it to follow the input.

It is feasible to have two or more torque receivers with their stators connected in parallel and driven by one transmitter, with some loss in accuracy. Misalignment due to excessive load on one receiver reflects back into the system and affects the accuracy of other receivers. Mutual interference can be reduced by using as large a transmitter as is permissible. To minimize transmitter loading, Δ-connected tuning capacitors can be connected across the receiver windings. These must be accurately matched to avoid loss of accuracy.

The resilient nature of torque-synchro coupling can cause serious oscillations unless suitable damping devices are incorporated in the receiver. A common damper consists of an inertia wheel coupled to the receiver shaft through a friction element. Not only does this cause smoother following, but it also prevents the receiver synchro from running as a single-phase motor after a transient swing.

Receiver following accuracy is restricted by shaft friction, since the torque required to overcome this friction can only result from a lag or error angle. For this reason, low-friction bearings and slip rings are used. Standard torque units are usually not accurate enough for computer applications, and their use is more or less restricted to presenting display information, such as driving dials and pointers.

Another useful torque-synchro-system component is the differential synchro, available as both motor and generator. Differential units have three-legged Y windings (on both stator and rotor) and can be identified

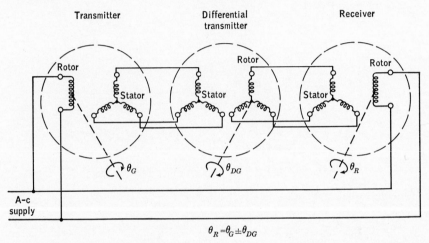

$$\theta_R = \theta_G \pm \theta_{DG}$$

Fig. 3-13. Differential generator between transmitter and receiver.

by the three rotor slip rings. They are similar in behavior to mechanical differentials, but are especially suited to remote indication. Differential generators can be connected between a transmitter and receiver (Fig. 3-13) and used to modify the electrical angle output of the transmitter. The receiver output corresponds to the sum or difference of the input angles applied to the transmitter and differential generator.

Differential motors (Fig. 3-14) are used to indicate the sum or difference of the signals from two generators. Like torque receivers, they are designed for low friction and are equipped with damping devices to prevent hunting and single phasing.

Control differential synchro transmitters are also available (Fig. 3-15) and are used in an identical manner to the torque units.

3-4. Synchro Calculations. Although a synchro is actually a rotating machine, when used in positioning systems at zero speed it can be regarded as a static multiwinding transformer. From this point of view,

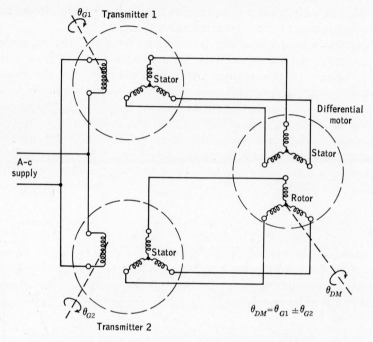

FIG. 3-14. Differential motor (or receiver) and two generators.

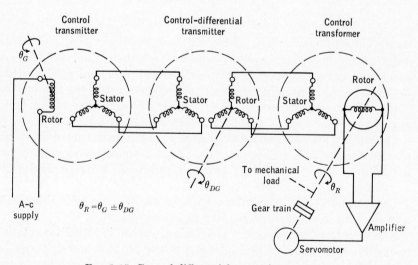

FIG. 3-15. Control-differential-transmitter system.

a synchro can be analyzed using elementary a-c circuit theory, the principal assumptions being linear conditions and a sinusoidal variation of the self- and mutual inductances of the stator coil with shaft position.

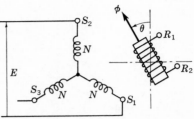

When operated correctly under balanced conditions, the complex circuit equations of an ideal synchro reduce to exceptionally simple forms. These forms permit the system designer to perform synchro-system calculations very readily, without the necessity of referring back into the synchros. This concept is car-

FIG. 3-16. Synchro with salient-pole rotor.

ried to its conclusion in a later section on the synchro equivalent circuit.

3-5. Calculating Synchro-system Impedances. Assuming sinusoidal distribution of the stator coils and magnetic fields of the synchro shown in Fig. 3-16, the self-impedance Z_2 of stator phase 2 consists of resistance R, leakage reactance X_l, and a component of the inductance X which varies with angular position. Neglecting core losses,

$$Z_2 = R + jX_l + j\frac{X_{max} + X_{min}}{2} + j\frac{X_{max} - X_{min}}{2}\cos 2\theta \quad (3\text{-}7)$$

where as shown in Fig. 3-17 $(X_{max} + X_{min})/2$ is the average portion of the angular-dependent component of inductance and $[(X_{max} - X_{min})/2]\cos$

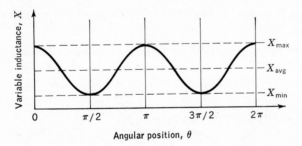

FIG. 3-17. Variable component of inductance vs. angular position.

2θ is the variable portion of this component. Similarly, by symmetry, but taking into account the 120° spacing of the stator windings, the impedances of phases 1 and 3 are

$$Z_1 = R + jX_l + j\frac{X_{max} + X_{min}}{2} + j\frac{X_{max} - X_{min}}{2}\cos 2(\theta + 120) \quad (3\text{-}8)$$

$$Z_3 = R + jX_l + j\frac{X_{max} - X_{min}}{2} + j\frac{X_{max} - X_{min}}{2}\cos 2(\theta - 120) \quad (3\text{-}9)$$

In addition to the self-impedances, the stator legs possess mutual impedances because of the coupling resulting from the 120° spacing and because of the disymmetry of the salient-pole rotor. To determine the mutual impedances of phase 2, it is necessary to resolve the current I_2 into its direct- and quadrature-axis components I_{D2} and I_{Q2} (Fig. 3-18).

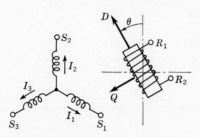

$$I_{D2} = I_2 \cos \theta$$

$$I_{Q2} = I_2 \cos \left(\theta + \frac{\pi}{2} \right) = -I_2 \sin \theta$$

FIG. 3-18. Direct- and quadrature-axis components of I_2.

In turn, the current components determine the ampere-turns of magnetomotive force, so that the following relationships yield the direct and quadrature axis components of the flux for phase 2.*

$$\phi_{D2} = NP_D I_2 \cos \theta$$
$$\phi_{Q2} = -NP_Q I_2 \sin \theta$$

where N = turns per phase
P_D = permeance factor for direct axis
P_Q = permeance factor for quadrature axis

Now find the linkages λ_{32} between ϕ_{D2}, ϕ_{Q2}, and phase 3.

$$\lambda_{32} = N\phi_{D2} \cos (120 - \theta) + N\phi_{Q2} \cos \left(120 - \frac{\pi}{2} - \theta \right)$$

where λ_{32} = linkages with phase 3 due to current in phase 2

And since inductance is defined in terms of linkages per unit current, then the mutual inductance between coils 2 and 3 is

$$M_{32} = \frac{\lambda_{32}}{I_2} = (P_D \cos \theta)N^2 \cos (120 - \theta)$$

$$+ (-P_Q \sin \theta)N^2 \cos \left(120 - \frac{\pi}{2} - \theta \right)$$

and $X_{32} = [P_D \cos \theta \cos (120 - \theta) - P_Q \sin \theta \sin (120 - \theta)]N^2 \omega$

where X_{32} = mutual reactance of phase 3 with respect to phase 2
ω = angular frequency

---

* In the above, currents essentially signify magnetomotive force, which when multiplied by permeance factors, yield flux. Consistent sets of units are required.

This expression can be further simplified. By trigonometry,

$$X_{32} = \left[-\frac{P_D + P_Q}{4} - \frac{1}{4}(P_D - P_Q)(\cos 2\theta - \sqrt{3}\sin 2\theta) \right] \omega N^2$$

since $\qquad\qquad \omega N^2 P_D = X_{max}$

and $\qquad\qquad \omega N^2 P_Q = X_{min}$

then $\quad X_{32} = -\frac{1}{2}\frac{X_{max} + X_{min}}{2} + \frac{X_{max} - X_{min}}{2}\sin(2\theta - 30)$ $\qquad$ (3-10)

Figure 3-19 shows a typical plot of this function. It is all negative and has the expected appearance. By symmetry, the other mutual reactances, X_{21} and X_{31}, can be determined.

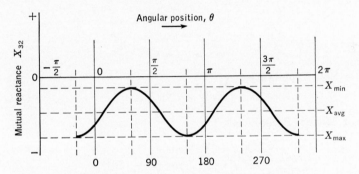

FIG. 3-19. Mutual inductance vs. angular position.

To complete the calculation of the various synchro impedances, it is also necessary to determine the rotor self-impedance Z_r and the mutual impedances resulting from rotor/stator-phase coupling. The self-impedance can be expressed by

$$Z_r = Z_{lr} + X_{max} \qquad\qquad (3\text{-}11)$$

and the mutual impedance caused by the coupling between the rotor and phase 2 by

$$X_{r2} = X_{max}\cos\theta \qquad\qquad (3\text{-}12)$$

where Z_{lr} = rotor leakage impedance

The mutual impedances resulting from the coupling of the rotor with phases 1 and 3, X_{r1} and X_{r3}, can be derived by symmetry. In deriving the rotor-stator impedances it is assumed that the rotor and a single stator phase have the same number of effective airgap turns.

Summarizing the results of the above impedance derivations, there are four self-impedances and six mutual impedances as defined by the following relationships:

Stator Self-impedances

$$Z_1 = Z_{ls} + jX_{avg} + jX_{var} \cos 2(\theta + 120) \qquad (3\text{-}7)$$
$$Z_2 = Z_{ls} + jX_{avg} + jX_{var} \cos 2\theta \qquad (3\text{-}8)$$
$$Z_3 = Z_{ls} + jX_{avg} + jX_{var} \cos 2(\theta - 120) \qquad (3\text{-}9)$$

where Z_{ls} = stator phase leakage impedance

$$X_{avg} = \frac{X_{max} + X_{min}}{2} = \text{average component}$$

$$X_{var} = \frac{X_{max} - X_{min}}{2} = \text{variable component}$$

Stator Mutual Reactances

$$X_{12} = -\tfrac{1}{2}X_{avg} - X_{var} \sin (2\theta + 30) \qquad (3\text{-}13)$$
$$X_{23} = -\tfrac{1}{2}X_{avg} + X_{var} \sin (2\theta - 30) \qquad (3\text{-}10)$$
$$X_{31} = -\tfrac{1}{2}X_{avg} + X_{var} \sin (2\theta + 90) \qquad (3\text{-}14)$$

Rotor Self-impedance

$$Z_r = Z_{lr} + X_{max} \qquad (3\text{-}11)$$

Rotor Mutual Reactances

$$X_{r2} = X_{max} \cos \theta \qquad (3\text{-}12)$$
$$X_{r3} = X_{max} \cos (\theta - 120) \qquad (3\text{-}15)$$
$$X_{r1} = X_{max} \cos (\theta + 120) \qquad (3\text{-}16)$$

3-6. System Calculations Using Synchro Impedances.   First find the voltage induced in phase 2, where the currents are as defined in Fig. 3-20.

$$E_2 = jI_R X_{max} \cos \theta - jI_3 X_{32} - jI_1 X_{12}$$

Substitute the values of X_{32} and X_{12} from Eqs. (3-10) and (3-13), and simplify.

$$E_2 = jI_R X_{max} \cos \theta - jI_3[-\tfrac{1}{2}X_{avg} + X_{var} \sin (2\theta - 30)]$$
$$- jI_1[-\tfrac{1}{2}X_{avg} - X_{var} \sin (2\theta + 30)]$$
$$E_2 = jI_R X_{max} \cos \theta - \tfrac{1}{2}jX_{avg}I_2 - jI_3 X_{var} \sin (2\theta - 30)$$
$$+ jI_1 X_{var} \sin (2\theta + 30) \qquad (3\text{-}17)$$

and by symmetry, the voltages induced in phases 1 and 3 can be expressed by

$$E_1 = jI_R X_{max} \cos (\theta + 120) - \tfrac{1}{2}jI_1 X_{avg} + jI_2 X_{var} \sin (2\theta + 30)$$
$$- jI_3 X_{var} \sin (2\theta + 90) \qquad (3\text{-}18)$$
$$E_3 = jI_R X_{max} \cos (\theta - 120) - \tfrac{1}{2}jI_3 X_{avg} - jI_2 X_{var} \sin (2\theta - 30)$$
$$- jI_1 X_{var} \sin (2\theta + 90) \qquad (3\text{-}19)$$

These equations are perfectly general since there has been no assumption made regarding the load being balanced.

Now analyze the synchro system of Fig. 3-21 assuming a balanced load. In this analysis Z_1, Z_2, Z_3 are the self-impedances of each respective

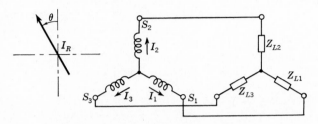

FIG. 3-20. Loads and currents defined.

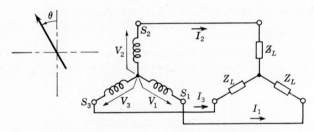

FIG. 3-21. Synchro system with balanced load.

phase, E_1, E_2, E_3 are the induced voltages from the rotor and the remaining phases, and V_1, V_2, V_3 are the terminal voltages. Then

$$V_2 = E_2 - Z_2 I_2 \qquad (3\text{-}20)$$
$$V_1 = E_1 - Z_1 I_1 \qquad (3\text{-}21)$$
$$V_3 = E_3 - Z_3 I_3 \qquad (3\text{-}22)$$
$$I_1 + I_2 + I_3 = 0$$
$$I_2 = \frac{V_2}{Z_L}$$
$$I_1 = \frac{V_1}{Z_L}$$
$$I_3 = \frac{V_3}{Z_L}$$

Find the currents flowing in the three stator phases. For phase 2, substitute Eqs. (3-8) and (3-17) for E_2 and Z_2 in Eq. (3-20). The terminal voltage V_2 is equal to the current flowing in phase 2, I_2, times the load

Z_L. This gives

$$jI_RX_{max} \cos \theta - \tfrac{1}{2}jI_2X_{avg} - jI_3X_{var} \sin (2\theta - 30)$$
$$+ jI_1X_{var} \sin (2\theta + 30)$$
$$= I_2Z_L + I_2Z_{ls} + I_2jX_{avg} + jI_2X_{var} \cos 2\theta$$
$$jI_RX_{max} \cos \theta = I_2Z_S + jX_{var}[-I_1 \sin (2\theta + 30)$$
$$+ I_2 \sin (2\theta + 90) + I_3 \sin (2\theta - 30)] \quad (3\text{-}23)$$

where $Z_S = Z_L + Z_{ls} + (\tfrac{3}{2})jX_{avg}$
In a similar manner, substitute in Eqs. (3-21) and (3-22).
For phase 1

$$jI_RX_{max} \cos (\theta + 120) = I_1Z_S + jX_{var}[I_1 \sin (2\theta - 30)$$
$$- I_2 \sin (2\theta + 30) - I_3 \sin (2\theta - 90)] \quad (3\text{-}24)$$

and for phase 3

$$jI_RX_{max} \cos (\theta - 120) = I_3Z_S + jX_{var}[-I_1 \sin (2\theta - 90)$$
$$- I_2 \sin (2\theta + 150) + I_3 \sin (2\theta + 210)] \quad (3\text{-}25)$$

By proper substitution and manipulation, it is now possible to solve for the three stator currents as expressed by the following relationships:

$$I_1 = \frac{jI_RX_{max} \cos (\theta + 120)}{Z_S + j(\tfrac{3}{2})X_{var}} \quad (3\text{-}26)$$

$$I_2 = \frac{jI_RX_{max} \cos \theta}{Z_S + j(\tfrac{3}{2})X_{var}} \quad (3\text{-}27)$$

$$I_3 = \frac{jI_RX_{max} \cos (\theta - 120)}{Z_S + j(\tfrac{3}{2})X_{var}} \quad (3\text{-}28)$$

In each of the above three equations the numerator represents the induced voltage and the denominator the *equivalent* phase impedance, or

$$Z_{equiv} = Z_S + j(\tfrac{3}{2})X_{var}^*$$

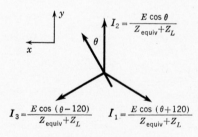

3-7. Measuring the Equivalent Phase Impedance. To develop a means of measuring the equivalent phase impedance, first determine the direction and magnitude of the resultant stator current vector.

Fig. 3-22. Resolve phase currents.

Resolve the phase currents as shown in Fig. 3-22 into their x and y components.

---

* Although Z_S was assumed to *include* the load impedance, Z_L, it is more convenient to assume from here on that it does not. Therefore, when required, Z_L will have to be added to Z_S.

$$I_y = \frac{E \cos \theta}{Z_{equiv} + Z_L} - \frac{E \cos (\theta - 120)}{2(Z_{equiv} + Z_L)} - \frac{E \cos (\theta + 120)}{2(Z_{equiv} + Z_L)}$$

$$= \frac{E}{Z_{equiv} + Z_L} [\cos \theta - \tfrac{1}{2} \cos (\theta + 180)]$$

$$= \frac{E}{Z_{equiv} + Z_L} [\cos \theta + \tfrac{1}{2} \cos \theta]$$

$$= \frac{3E \cos \theta}{2(Z_{equiv} + Z_L)} \tag{3-29}$$

$$I_x = \frac{\sqrt{3}\, E \cos (\theta - 120)}{2(Z_{equiv} + Z_L)} - \frac{\sqrt{3}\, E \cos (\theta + 120)}{2(Z_{equiv} + Z_L)}$$

$$= \frac{\sqrt{3}\,\sqrt{3}\, E \cos (\theta - 90)}{2(Z_{equiv} + Z_L)} = \frac{3E \cos (\theta - 90)}{2(Z_{equiv} + Z_L)}$$

$$= \frac{3E \sin \theta}{2(Z_{equiv} + Z_L)} \tag{3-30}$$

Equations (3-29) and (3-30) yield the resultant magnetomotive-force vector shown in Fig. 3-23; it is always directed along the rotor and always has an amplitude that is constant at $(3E/2)/(Z_{equiv} + Z_L)$. Thus, if the rotor is excited, there is a uniform magnetomotive-force vector of flux directed along the rotor axis in transformerlike manner. The rotor therefore sees a *uniform input impedance* under balanced conditions, regardless of its shaft orientation.

This can be looked at in another way. When a balanced set of currents exists in the stator with the resultant of these currents directed along the rotor axis, the group of stator coils having mutual inductance can be replaced with a fixed set of coils having no mutual inductance. In the previous analysis, a constant rotor current I_R was applied as if from an infinite impedance source. The balanced voltages induced in the stator generated the balanced currents whose resultant lay along the rotor axis. This provided the necessary condition for constant, nonmutual, phase impedances.

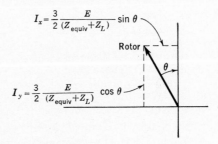

FIG. 3-23. Resultant magnetomotive-force vector.

For the purpose of measuring Z_{equiv} it is also possible to apply these voltages to the stator phases externally rather than obtaining them by induction from the rotor current. The applied voltages, however, must constitute a balanced set corresponding to a particular rotor position. Figures 3-24 and 3-25 show two balanced-set conditions that can be used for measuring Z_{equiv}. Figure 3-24 corresponds to the condition where the current in one leg is zero during normal operation, and the equivalent phase impedance can be expressed by

$$Z_{equiv} = \frac{E}{2I} \tag{3-31}$$

Figure 3-25 corresponds to the condition where the potential across two legs is zero during normal operation, so that

$$Z_{equiv} = \frac{2E}{3I} \tag{3-32}$$

These measurements assume a uniform flux vector in a uniform permeance magnetic path.

3-8. Synchro Equivalent Circuits.   Complex synchro systems using many cascaded and paralleled units often develop problems that may seem

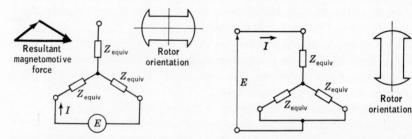

FIG. 3-24. Balanced condition where current in one leg is zero.

FIG. 3-25. Balanced condition where potential across two legs is zero.

out of harmony with the simple nature of the basic synchro.   Among these problems are those relating to the effects of loading and attenuation in the chains, unbalance caused by stray capacitance, pickup problems, tuning, etc.   Most of these problems can be understood with the aid of an equivalent circuit.

As in the case of the other induction components, the synchro equivalent circuit is a four-terminal passive network whose transmission characteristics correspond to those of the synchro.   Thus, having established its parameters, system analysis can be carried out on the network with little additional reference to the complex rotating machine which it represents.   The approximations incurred in transferring from network characteristics to actual machine performance are caused by the assumption of certain ideal conditions.   But in almost all cases, these assumed idealized conditions are sufficiently accurate to yield a clear picture of machine performance.

In synchro equivalent circuits, the following assumptions are usually made:

1. Linear magnetic circuitry, generating no harmonics and incurring no saturation.

2. Perfectly symmetrical construction, i.e., the rotor and stator are perfectly concentric, and the three stator windings are exactly 120° apart.

3. Current flow through any of the windings generates a sinusoidal flux distribution pattern in the airgap. This effectively states that a synchro is perfectly accurate when operated correctly. However, there are actually certain inherent errors peculiar to any particular design which are independent of the quality of construction or method of operation, and occur consistently in all units of a given type. These errors result from the inability to generate a perfect sinusoid. They are discussed in another section of this chapter.

3-9. Equivalent-circuit Applications. Before proceeding to the derivation of the synchro equivalent circuit and to the means of determining network parameters, it is interesting to note some of the information that can be obtained from such a network. As pointed out above, many aspects of synchro system performance can be deduced from simple calculations of network behavior. The following is a partial list of synchro system characteristics that can be deduced in this manner:

1. Voltage gradient and phase shift at any control transformer in a given synchro system. These items are important to establishing the gain and phase adjustments of a servomechanism.

2. The effects of temperature variation on synchro performance can be studied. This is a significant factor as the operating temperature range of electromechanical systems increases. For example, a simple equivalent-circuit analysis will reveal the changes in phase and gradient for a control transformer operating at 500°F.

3. Synchro-system errors and residual voltages due to the method of application can be estimated. Residual voltage may be generated by slight unbalances in the synchro interconnecting lines.

4. Estimates can be made of the loading effects on individual control transformers, and the interaction between loaded transformers, some of which are not synchronized.

5. In torque-transmitting synchro systems, torque gradients can be calculated under various conditions of loading, out-of-synchronism receivers, etc.

6. Velocity errors in constant-speed synchro systems can be determined. This is not to be confused with servomechanism-generated errors.

In addition to these, any other synchro performance characteristic that is not obscured by the assumptions listed in the previous section can be determined from the equivalent circuit. As such, the equivalent circuit is a particularly useful tool to the synchro-system designer who wants to use a component under conditions of temperature, frequency, etc., that are significantly different from manufacturer's ratings.

3-10. Obtaining Equivalent-circuit Parameters. There are several ways to establish the equivalent circuit. One way is to calculate the parameters directly from the electromagnetic structure of the synchro. This method is of greatest utility to the synchro designer who has established the basic dimensions and material characteristics. Frequently it is possible, given certain simplifications, to deduce the equivalent-circuit parameters directly from data normally provided by the manufacturer. This approach is of optimum value to the systems engineer who is interested in an approximate representation that will enable him to estimate system performance. Of course, the most accurate way to determine circuit parameters is by direct measurement, the most agreeable and rapid approach for the engineer who must "debug" subsystems, both servomechanisms and synchros. Synchro design is outside the scope of this book; the remainder of this section explores ways to determine network parameters either by calculation from manufacturer's data or by direct measurement.

By applying simple network theory to manufacturer's data, the equivalent-circuit parameters can often be deduced. The accuracy of these deductions depends on the amount of data supplied by the manufacturer (some provide much more than others), and the accuracy of the data. Depending on the completeness of the data, the systems engineer can usually make the necessary assumptions and calculate network parameters. Equivalent-circuit calculations are usually satisfactory if they are within 10 or 20 per cent of the true value, since the final adjustment of the servomechanism is normally accomplished after the system is assembled. The purpose of the equivalent-circuit analysis is to permit the system designer to approximate actual performance and then to specify an adequate adjustment band. If sufficient data are furnished by the manufacturer, equivalent circuits are not usually more than 5 per cent inaccurate. This topic is covered in more detail later, including the calculation of an equivalent circuit from typical manufacturer's data.

The most accurate technique is to measure the equivalent-circuit parameters directly on the component. In this way it is possible for the systems designer to accumulate a file of very accurate equivalent circuits for the most used synchro models. These equivalent circuits can then be arranged in any manner, depending on system requirements, and no further information is required to describe synchro performance completely.

Synchro equivalent-circuit measurements are made at the synchro terminals that correspond to the terminals of the equivalent network (see Sec. 3-11). The most direct approach is to follow the methods specified in textbooks on transformer theory for measuring the equivalent circuit of a transformer. These methods can be carried over directly to synchro systems. Since a synchro would correspond to a very small transformer, synchro core losses are usually low, not playing the important part in the equivalent circuit that they do for the larger units. However, the small size reduces the accuracy of some of the approximations used for the larger units. For example, in synchros the leakage reactances and winding resistances constitute a much larger percentage of the winding impedances than they do in a fair-sized transformer.

The usual method for measuring equivalent circuits is based on making open-circuit and short-circuit tests on the primary winding, that is, measuring the primary impedance, first with the secondary open, and then with it short-circuited. By additionally measuring the secondary open-circuit voltage and the d-c resistances, and assuming equal primary

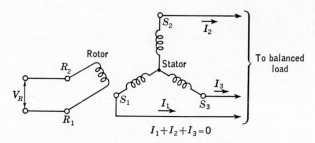

FIG. 3-26. Synchro-generator configuration.

and secondary leakage reactances (corrected for turns ratio), it is possible to determine the equivalent-circuit parameters. (In synchros, the d-c resistance of the windings very closely approximates the a-c resistance, the additional stray load losses being negligible.) Actually these tests provide more information than is necessary, permitting a check on the consistency of the results.

3-11. Deriving the Equivalent Circuit. In the synchro generator of Fig. 3-26, voltage V_R applied to rotor terminals R_1-R_2 generates a magnetic field which induces a set of voltages across the three secondary terminals S_1, S_2, S_3. A corresponding set of currents, I_1, I_2, I_3, is generated in the secondary windings feeding the balanced load, which might be a control transformer or differential synchro. These secondary currents flowing through the balanced load develop self-inductive flux fields within the synchro generator. It has been shown that the resultant flux field (due to the sum of I_1, I_2, I_3) lies directly along the axis of the excited rotor, and tends transformerwise, to buck the rotor flux. Except for certain small errors, the reaction of the resultant stator field has a constant (independent of rotor shaft angle) amplitude. Thus, the impedance seen at the rotor primary is independent of shaft position for a given balanced system.

The parallel between the synchro system and the loaded transformer is very exact, and constitutes the basis for the equivalent-circuit approach. A primary flux field is developed, which, under load, is countered by a

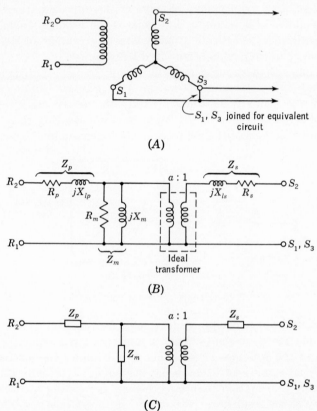

(A)

(B)

(C)

FIG. 3-27. A shows rotor-stator orientation to achieve effect of a two-terminal stator. B shows equivalent circuit based on orientation of A. C lumps parameters. $R_p =$ rotor d-c resistance; $X_{lp} =$ rotor leakage reactance; $R_m =$ equivalent core-loss resistance; $X_m =$ airgap mutual reactance; $a =$ primary-to-secondary turns ratio; $X_{ls} =$ equivalent secondary leakage reactance; $R_s =$ equivalent secondary d-c resistance.

colinear secondary field. The secondary voltages are established by the resultant flux field.

Since the secondary winding has three output terminals, it is necessary to effect a simplification before achieving the equivalent circuit. This can be done by arbitrarily assuming that the rotor is so oriented that S_1, S_3 are at the same potential. Thus, those terminals may be tied together without affecting the circuit, and the common, in conjunction with S_2, constitute the desired *pair* of secondary terminals. A little reflection should convince the reader that the arbitrary choice of rotor position means no loss of generality. Since the synchro flux field is not variant in magnitude or phase, and is always colinear with the rotor axis, any calculations of attenuation, phase, loading, impedance, etc., may as well be made in the simple arbitrary position.

Thus, the synchro generator has been replaced by a four-terminal transformerlike electromagnetic component, and all the theory of the transformer equivalent circuit can be adopted. Figure 3-27 shows the

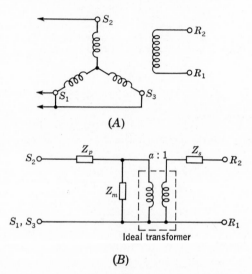

(A)

(B)

Fig. 3-28. Control-transformer equivalent circuit. Note that Z_p, the primary leakage impedance, is now on the stator side, while Z_s is on the primary or rotor side. The rotor is assumed to be of the nonsalient variety (magnetically round).

equivalent-circuit schematic. If the rotor is excited, the calculated voltage across the secondary (under any load condition) is equal to the maximum voltage which would be measured across (S_1, S_3)-S_2.

The equivalent circuit is reciprocal, that is, if the stator windings are excited, the voltage across the rotor can be calculated. Thus, the above concepts can be applied to a control transformer (Fig. 3-28). In this diagram the ideal transformer is shifted to the rotor side. The output voltage calculated across R_1-R_2 represents the maximum voltage across the control-transformer output. The control-transformer gradient in volts per degree would be that output times sin 1°. The extension to a differential transformer is clearly explained in Fig. 3-29.

The problem now is to determine a technique for calculating the equivalent-circuit parameters from readily available (from the manufacturer) or

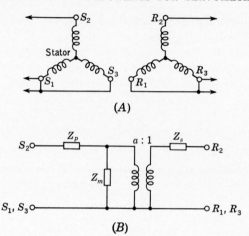

FIG. 3-29. Differential-transformer equivalent circuit.

easily measurable quantities.   The following three independent equations
can be derived by simple network theory from the equivalent circuit of
Fig. 3-27C.

$$Z_{ocp} = Z_p + Z_m \tag{3-33}$$

$$Z_{scp} = Z_p + Z_m \| a^2 Z_s \tag{3-34}$$

$$Z_{ocs} = Z_s + \frac{Z_m}{a^2} \tag{3-35}$$

where Z_{ocp} = open-circuit primary impedance
    Z_{scp} = short-circuit primary impedance
    Z_{ocs} = open-circuit secondary impedance
Simplify by combining Eqs. (3-33) and (3-34), eliminating Z_p.

$$Z_{ocp} - Z_{scp} = Z_m - \frac{Z_m(a^2 Z_s)}{Z_m + a^2 Z_s} = \frac{Z_m^2}{Z_m + a^2 Z_s} \tag{3-36}$$

And from Eq. (3-35),

$$Z_{ocs} = \frac{Z_s a^2 + Z_m}{a^2} \tag{3-37}$$

Multiplying Eq. (3-36) by Eq. (3-37) and taking the square root gives

$$\sqrt{(Z_{ocp} - Z_{scp})Z_{ocs}} = \frac{Z_m}{a} \tag{3-38}$$

and by exact symmetry

$$\sqrt{(Z_{ocs} - Z_{scs})Z_{ocp}} = \frac{Z_m}{a} \tag{3-39}$$

where Z_{scs} = short-circuit secondary impedance.

And the transformation ratios from primary to secondary, K_{ps}, and from secondary to primary, K_{sp}, are

$$K_{ps} = \frac{Z_m}{Z_p + Z_m}\frac{1}{a} = \frac{Z_m/a}{Z_{ocp}} \tag{3-40}$$

$$K_{sp} = \frac{Z_m/a^2}{Z_s + Z_m/a^2}\frac{a}{1} = \frac{Z_m/a}{Z_{ocs}} \tag{3-41}$$

Thus by measuring three out of the four impedances (Z_{ocp}, Z_{scp}, Z_{ocs}, Z_{scs}) it is possible to calculate the fourth and also Z_m/a. Figure 3-30 summarizes the important relationships.

However, since only three of the vector parameters are independent (corresponding to six scalar parameters), and since there are seven unknowns, one additional piece of data is required to determine the real and imaginary parts of the equivalent-circuit parameters. For convenience the primary (or secondary) resistance is chosen as the additional item. (In synchros, the effective a-c and d-c resistance is essentially equal.) This is not a critical item, and whatever reasonable value is used leads to a consistent

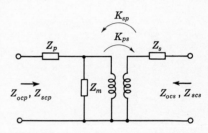

Fig. 3-30. Key equivalent-circuit parameters.

set of parameters that should be satisfactory for system calculations.

Knowing one of the resistances in addition to the measured impedances, it is possible to determine the unknowns by means of the vector diagram shown in Fig. 3-31. The magnitude $|Z_{ocp}|$ and phase angle θ_{ocp} of the open-circuit primary impedance are known and can be plotted as shown. The primary resistance R_p and the phase angle of Z_m, θ_m, are known. Dropping a vertical vector from the end of vector Z_{ocp} until it intersects vector Z_m, gives the magnitude of the primary leakage reactance X_{lp} and the magnitude of Z_m. If a graphical solution is not sufficiently accurate, it is possible to solve for $|Z_m|$ and Z_p by means of the following equations.

$$|Z_m| = \frac{|Z_{ocp}|\cos\theta_{ocp} - R_p}{\cos\theta_m} \tag{3-42}$$

$$Z_p = Z_{ocp} - Z_m$$

The value of a can be determined from Z_m/a and Z_m. The secondary impedance Z_s can be calculated from Eq. (3-37). This method of calculating the equivalent-circuit parameters works equally well from both measured laboratory data and manufacturer's data, presuming the latter is available and is sufficiently accurate.

3-12. Calculating Equivalent Circuit for Typical Unit. To show how to calculate equivalent network parameters using the above method, determine the equivalent-circuit parameters for a Kearfott size 11 R512 synchro transmitter from data supplied by the manufacturer. This is a

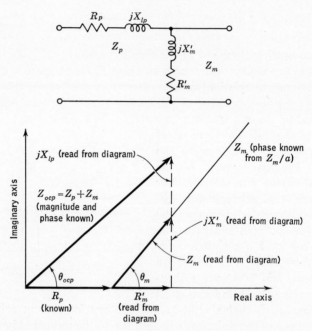

FIG. 3-31. Vector diagram for calculating equivalent circuit parameters. *Note:* Z_m is shown here as an equivalent-series impedance. It may readily be transformed to the parallel form of Fig. 3-27 by elementary circuit theory.

26-volt 400-cps unit. The following is a partial list of the electrical specifications supplied by Kearfott.

$$Z_{ocp} = 32.4 + j219 \text{ ohms}$$
$$Z_{scp} = 36.3 + j17.0 \text{ ohms}$$
$$Z_{ocs} = 5.6 + j37.5 \text{ ohms}$$
$$R_p = 18.25 \text{ ohms}$$
$$K_{ps} = 0.454\underline{/4.9°}$$
$$R_s = 4.26 \text{ ohms (measured line to line)}$$

Actually the first four of the above specifications furnish sufficient data to determine the required parameters. The other items are redundant and can be used for parallel calculations that check the accuracy of the data and of the method.

First determine Z_m/a, using Eq. (3-38).

$$Z_{ocp} - Z_{scp} = (32.4 + j219) - (36.3 + j17.0) = -3.9 + j202$$
$$= 202\underline{/91.1°}$$
$$Z_{ocs} = 5.6 + j37.5 = 37.9\underline{/81.5°}$$

$$\frac{Z_m}{a} = \sqrt{(Z_{ocp} - Z_{scp})Z_{ocs}} = \sqrt{202(37.9)\underline{/172.6}} = 87.4\underline{/86.3°}$$

Knowing the phase angle and magnitude of Z_{ocp}, the phase angle of Z_m (from phase angle of Z_m/a) and the primary resistance R_p, it is possible

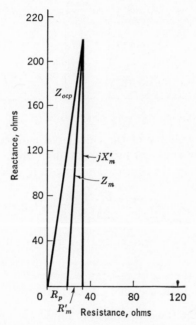

FIG. 3-32. Vector diagram for typical commercial synchro. *Note:* For this particular unit $jX_{l_p} \cong 0$.

to plot the vector diagram of Fig. 3-32. From this it can be noted that X_{lp} is approximately zero, and

$$Z_m = 219\underline{/86.3°} = 14.15 + j219$$
so that
$$X'_m = j219$$
$$R'_m = 14.15$$
and
$$a = \frac{Z_m}{Z_m/a} = (219\underline{/86.3})/(87.4\underline{/86.3}) = 2.5$$

The secondary impedance Z_s can be calculated by subtracting Z_m (reflected to secondary) from the secondary open-circuit impedance Z_{ocs}, or

$$Z_{m(\text{reflected to secondary})} = \frac{Z_m}{a^2} = \frac{14.15 + j219}{2.5^2}$$

$$= 2.26 + j35$$

$$Z_s = (5.6 - 2.26) + j(37.5 - 35) = 3.34 + j2.5$$

so that $X_{ls} = j2.5$

and $R_s = 3.34$

This gives all the parameters required to complete the equivalent circuit of Fig. 3-33. All these results apply entirely to the direct axis of the synchro.

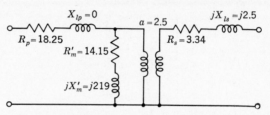

FIG. 3-33. Complete equivalent circuit for typical synchro.

Now check the validity of the calculated equivalent circuit by using the redundant data supplied by the manufacturer. First determine the primary to secondary transformation ratio K_{ps}, using Eq. (3-40).

$$K_{ps} = \frac{Z_m/a}{Z_{ocp}} = \frac{87.4\underline{/86.3}}{221\underline{/81.6}} = 0.396\underline{/4.7°}$$

This compares with the transformation ratio of $0.454\underline{/4.9°}$ specified by the manufacturer.

Now determine the stator resistance (corrected for method of connection used in the equivalent circuit) directly from the manufacturer's data.

$R_s = 4.26$ ohms (measured line to line)

$R_{s(\text{corrected})} = (\frac{3}{4})4.26 = 3.2$ ohms

This compares with a computed resistance of 3.34 as shown on the equivalent circuit.

The equivalent appears quite reasonable; however, as a final check, calculate Z_m/a using another set of parameters and Eq. (3-40).

$$\frac{Z_m}{a} = K_{ps}Z_{ocp}$$

$$\frac{Z_m}{a} = (0.454\underline{/4.9})(221\underline{/81.6}) = 100.4\underline{/86.5°}$$

This compares with the value $Z_m/a = 87.4\underline{/86.3°}$ calculated previously from the first set of data. Although inconsistencies in measured data cause inconsistencies in equivalent-circuit parameters, all values are satisfactory for use in estimating system performance.

Occasionally inaccuracies in the data presented by a manufacturer make it impossible to obtain suitable exact answers to the equivalent-circuit problem. In this case, it is feasible to use the secondary and primary d-c resistance data supplied by the manufacturer, and to assume that X_{lp} and $a^2 X_{ls}$ are equal. From the circuit configuration and the assumed data, it is then possible to solve for the unknown parameters.

3-13. Torque Synchros. Effective torque gradients, accuracy, and interaction are the principal points of interest in multiple torque-synchro systems. Since these are power instead of signal components, they are subject to greater errors than control synchros. High saturation, considerable self-heating, and the emphasis on designing for efficient power transfer instead of accuracy all lead to increased errors. For example, a minimum airgap boosts power efficiency at the expense of angular accuracy, while the use of salient-pole construction yields higher torques but does not give the accuracy of a well-distributed winding.

In addition there are the problems of friction in the driven member and oscillation of the driven member during transients. Coulomb friction reduces static accuracy, while undesirable oscillation impairs dynamic accuracy. Careful bearing and slip-ring design reduces receiver friction, while simple oscillation dampers improve the transient response.

3-14. Synchro-torque Calculations. To calculate the torque gradient of a torque receiver assume that the receiver is excited by a perfect synchro generator which has zero internal impedance. This excitation is such that under balanced conditions there is no current flowing in the synchro lines, since the voltages generated across the torque-receiver terminals by the voltage applied to its own rotor exactly match the voltages from the generator. However, when the system is unbalanced by displacing the torque-receiver rotor from its position of natural alignment with the generator flux field, current will flow in the lines. These currents react with the receiver-rotor currents, resulting in a torque that tends to align the rotor with the flux axis of the stator. The problem is to calculate this torque gradient.

It has been previously pointed out that the torque gradient does not vary with the angular position of the rotor. Therefore, the torque gradient calculated for an arbitrary position that simplifies calculations will also apply for all other positions. This arbitrary position is electrical zero as defined on Fig. 3-34.

With the rotor at null ($\theta = 0$) and under a balanced condition of operation, there will be no current flowing in any of the receiver stator legs. But now consider how the receiver impedance and voltages change if the rotor is deflected by a small angle θ. With only E_S applied, the three sinusoidally distributed coils can be considered equivalent to one sinusoidally distributed coil whose impedance varies as cos 2θ and therefore changes little for small rotor deflections. Thus, the impedance seen across the entire unit (from terminal S_2 to terminals S_1, S_3) can be

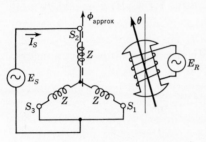

assumed constant. Similarly, the voltage generated across these same terminals as a result of the current flowing in the receiver rotor varies as cos θ and can also be considered constant for small angular deflections. With the impedance and voltage essentially constant for small deflections from null there will be no

FIG. 3-34. Electrical-zero orientation used for torque gradient calculations.

change in the line current I_S. The line current in the S_2 leg remains zero, but there will be a circulating current in the loop consisting of the two lower legs S_1 and S_3.

The previously derived theorem, which stated that the legs of a synchro system can be replaced by fixed impedances having no mutual inductance, can be used to calculate this current since this situation corresponds to a balanced condition with no current flowing in one of the legs. However, the quadrature-axis impedance is used rather than the direct-axis impedance, so that X_{max} is replaced by X_{min} in the formulas for leg impedance. However, X_{max} must still be used in conjunction with the rotor current, since I_R always acts along the direct axis.

With all secondary windings open-circuited, the voltages induced in the S_1 and S_3 legs by the rotor are:

$$E_1 = jI_RX_{max} \cos (\theta + 120) \qquad (3\text{-}43)$$
$$E_3 = jI_RX_{max} \cos (\theta - 120) \qquad (3\text{-}44)$$

where I_R = rotor current
Actually, the short circuit across S_1-S_3 shown in Fig. 3-35 will cause a circulating current which results in a horizontal magnetomotive-force vector directed toward the left (Fig. 3-36). Because the horizontal magnetomotive-force vector acts essentially perpendicularly to the rotor axis, the quadrature-axis stator impedances determine the current flow. The reaction on the rotor direct axis is negligible.

Assuming that the stator impedances are very closely equal to the quadrature-axis impedance Z_q, determine the current in the quadrature axis.

$$E = E_3 - E_1 = jI_RX_{max}[\cos (\theta - 120) - \cos (\theta + 120)]$$
$$E = jI_RX_{max} \sqrt{3} \cos (\theta - 90) = jI_RX_{max} \sqrt{3} \sin \theta \qquad (3\text{-}45)$$

where E = net stator voltage on the quadrature axis. Then

$$I_q = \frac{jI_R X_{max}}{2Z_q} \sqrt{3} \sin \theta$$

where I_q = resultant stator magnetomotive force along quadrature axis yielding a simple expression for I_q

$$I_q = j \frac{I_R X_{max}}{Z_q} \frac{\sqrt{3}}{2} \theta \qquad (3-46)$$

for small rotor displacements.

Knowing the quadrature-axis magnetomotive force, it is now possible to determine the receiver-torque gradient. Because synchro torque is caused by the interaction of rotor (or stator) flux (or magnetomotive

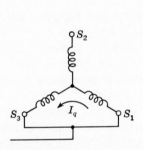

FIG. 3-35. Circulating current caused by short circuit.

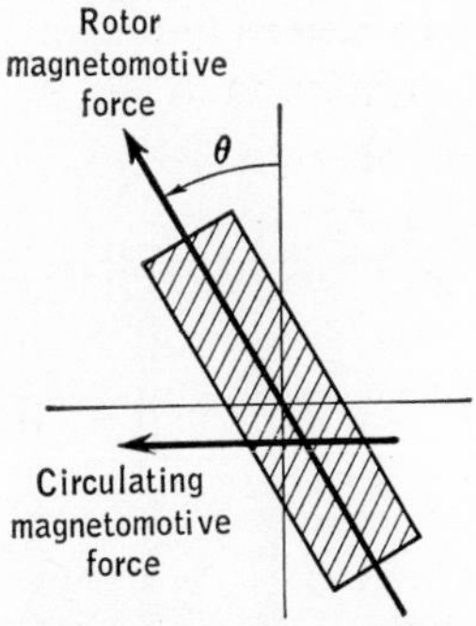

FIG. 3-36. Circulating current causes quadrature-axis magnetomotive force.

force) with stator (or rotor) magnetomotive force (or flux), and since the stator direct-axis magnetomotive force is zero in this situation, torque varies as the product of the main field flux and the quadrature-axis magnetomotive force. The time phase of the interacting components must also be considered. Thus,

$$T = kI_{dr}I_{qs} {\Large \diagdown} \begin{matrix} I_{dr} \\[2pt] I_{qs} \end{matrix}$$

where I_{dr} = rotor magnetomotive force (along its own direct axis)
I_{qs} = stator quadrature-axis magnetomotive force
k = constant of proportionality
Substitution and simplification yield

$$T = \left(k \frac{I_R{}^2 X_{max}}{Z_q} \sin \theta_q \right) \theta \qquad (3-47)$$

where all quantities are scalar and θ_q = phase angle between I_{dr} and I_{qs}. Equation (3-47) is the basic expression for synchro torque. Note that this torque is inversely proportional to the quadrature-axis reactance. This is reasonable, since the circulating current is largest when the quadrature-axis reactance is small. Some synchro designers add a low-impedance shorted coil to the receiver rotor, aligned with the quadrature axis in such a manner that it does not couple with the main field and lead to additional losses. For small displacements from null, the coil has the effect of reducing Z_q with a consequent increase in torque gradient. At the same time this shorted coil increases internal damping and reduces synchro oscillations.

3-15. Torque Gradients in Multiple-synchro Systems. If a unit torque gradient T_u is defined as the gradient of a synchro receiver when it is combined with an identical synchro generator, then the receiver discussed in the previous section has a torque gradient of $2T_u$ since it was driven by a zero impedance source. Equation (3-47) can be applied to a system of two matched synchros simply by replacing Z_q by $(Z_{qa} + Z_{qb})$,

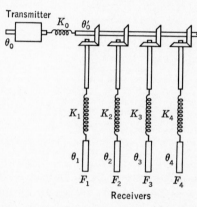

where Z_{qa} and Z_{qb} are the quadrature-axis impedances of the respective synchros. Actually, this same equation can be used with systems that include any number of synchros by adding to Z_q the sum of the quadrature-axis impedances of all the remaining synchros in parallel.

Mechanical and electrical equivalent circuits are convenient for approximately determining the torque gradient in multiple-synchro systems, and at the same time yield a clear physical picture of the problem. The only assumption that is necessary is that the equivalent circuits of the synchros are similar and are related to each other by a simple

FIG. 3-37. Mechanical equivalent circuit. The F terms include "friction" due to effective internal electrical damping, as well as the external shaft friction component.

real numerical proportionality factor. Thus the mechanical equivalent circuit of Fig. 3-37 can be used directly, where

$K_0, K_1, K_2, \ldots$ = spring constants, in ounce-inches per degree, for example

$F_1, F_2, F_3, \ldots$ = friction

$\theta_1, \theta_2, \theta_3, \ldots$ = output shaft angles

In this case it is assumed that all displacements from null are small and, to improve the analogy and distinguish certain classes of errors, it can be visualized that the gearing itself introduces fixed inherent as well as random manufacturing errors.

Now by using simple mechanics, it is possible to write the steady-state equations for a typical problem based on Fig. 3-37.

$$F_1 + F_2 + F_3 + F_4 = \text{torque at generator}$$
$$F_1 + F_2 + F_3 + F_4 = (\theta_0 - \theta_0')K_0$$
$$F_1 = (\theta_0' - \theta_1)K_1$$
$$F_2 = (\theta_0' - \theta_2)K_2$$
$$F_3 = (\theta_0' - \theta_3)K_3$$
$$F_4 = (\theta_0' - \theta_4)K_4$$

The unknowns are θ_0', θ_1, θ_2, θ_3, and θ_4 which can be solved since there are five equations.

$$\theta_0' = \theta_0 - \frac{F_1 + F_2 + F_3 + F_4}{K_0}$$

$$\theta_1 = \theta_0' - \frac{F_1}{K_1}$$

$$\theta_2 = \theta_0' - \frac{F_2}{K_2}$$

$$\theta_3 = \theta_0' - \frac{F_3}{K_3}$$

$$\theta_4 = \theta_0' - \frac{F_4}{K_4}$$

In turn, the mechanical equivalent of two synchros shown in Fig. 3-38 can be useful in estimating the solution to dynamic problems:

θ_1 and θ_2 = input and output angles of generator and receiver, respectively

K_1 and K_2 = spring constants of generator and receiver, respectively

J_1 and J_2 = inertia of generator and receiver rotors, respectively

D_1 and D_2 = viscous friction of generator and receiver, respectively

Actually, it is easier for engineers who are used to thinking in terms of electrical circuit theory to visualize these relationships if the mechanical

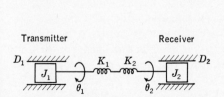
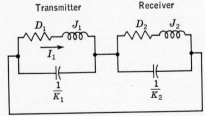

FIG. 3-38. Mechanical equivalent circuit for two synchros.

FIG. 3-39. Electrical equivalent of Fig. 3-38.

equivalent circuit of Fig. 3-38 is itself represented by the electrical equivalent circuit of Fig. 3-39. In this case, the current I_1 flowing through the D_1, J_1 branch is analogous to an input velocity to the transmitter. This equivalent circuit can be generalized to yield the circuit shown in Fig. 3-40, which represents any system (within the limitations mentioned previously) in which one transmitter drives several receivers.

Considering Fig. 3-40, assume that the system is suddenly subjected to a step displacement equivalent to q_0. (q_0 is an electric charge analogous to a mechanical displacement.) The transmitter, being driven, can be regarded as having infinite inertia and viscous friction, so that the

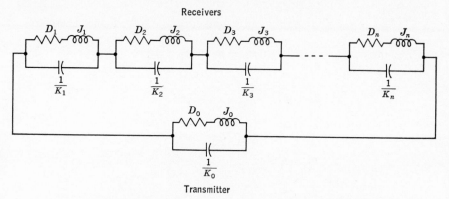

FIG. 3-40. Electrical equivalent circuit of multiple-synchro system.

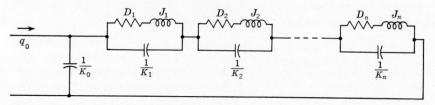

FIG. 3-41. Equivalent circuit assuming transmitter has infinite inertia and viscous friction.

equivalent circuit simplifies to Fig. 3-41. Also, the equivalent circuit of Fig. 3-40 can be simplified to permit the study of torque gradients under steady-state zero-velocity conditions. Assume that all synchro shafts except the one in question are locked, making the effective values of D and J infinite. Then consider the single movable synchro as the transmitter. This yields the effective spring constant, or capacitance, shown in Fig. 3-42, where the spring constant $1/K_m$ of the synchro under test is omitted from the series sequence.

With this background, consider a simple calculation. If a synchro transmitter drives n identical receivers, all following with a given lag angle, what is the torque gradient? Assume that the unit torque gradient is T_u.

The equivalent circuit of the whole group of synchros in parallel simplifies to Fig. 3-43, and the gradient can be calculated as follows:

$$\text{Equivalent capacitance} = \frac{1}{K} + \frac{n}{K} = \frac{1}{K}(1 + n)$$

$$\text{Spring constant} = \frac{K}{1 + n}$$

$$K = 2T_u$$

Therefore $\quad\quad \text{Torque gradient} = \dfrac{2T_u}{1 + n} \quad\quad\quad\quad (3\text{-}48)$

If a control transformer is to be connected to a group of synchros, there will be an effective output angle that differs from the actual angle. This effective angle corresponds to θ_0' in Fig. 3-37 and is the angle that the control transformer will indicate. Since θ_0' can be calculated, this is one way of estimating control-transformer error.

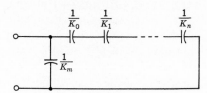

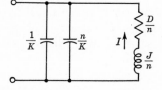

FIG. 3-42. All synchros except mth one are locked.

FIG. 3-43. Simplified equivalent circuit of synchros in parallel.

For accurate equivalence, the internal damping associated with each synchro must be added to the F terms in the mechanical equivalent circuit. This damping effect is approximated by the resistor in series with the inductor in the equivalent circuit of each component. It occurs whenever there is relative synchro motion between the rotor and stator with either one excited. It is inserted only as an approximation, although it can be measured for the various synchros. The equivalent circuit then permits a simple analysis of synchro dynamics, damping, transient response, etc.

3-16. Synchro Errors. The preceding discussion assumed that all synchros are perfect, with ideal materials and flux distribution and perfectly symmetrical construction. But actually every synchro is subject to two types of errors. The first type, inherent electrical errors, is caused by design limitations (such as winding distribution) and is uniform for synchros of the same design. The second type, errors due to manufacturing inaccuracies, is random in nature and varies from synchro to synchro. Elliptical rotors and stators and eccentrically ground rotors yield random errors.

3-17. Inherent Electrical Errors. Even in a geometrically perfect synchro using ideal materials, there is an error resulting from the non-sinusoidal character of the winding distribution. This causes the magnetic flux wave in the airgap to deviate more or less from an ideal sinusoid so that the net effect is to generate a series of superimposed flux waves having different numbers of poles.

Although Fourier analysis is necessary to determine the specific nature of these waves, the general characteristics of the nonsinusoidal components of the flux can be pointed out without reference to the mathematics. Assuming that the windings are symmetrical, three-phase, and balanced, then:

1. The airgap flux wave will include higher harmonics of the two-pole field for which the synchro is designed.

2. There will be no even harmonics.

3. The net effect of all third-order harmonics, or of any harmonic that is an integral multiple of three, is zero.

4. The harmonic flux waves in a control transformer or receiver rotate around the periphery of the machine in an alternating direction sequence. That is, if the direction of the fundamental two-pole wave is considered to be positive, then the next significant harmonic (the fifth) will rotate in a negative direction, while the seventh rotates positively, the eleventh negatively, etc. However, in a transmitter or generator, the rotor is the source of generated harmonics. These maintain a fixed angular relation to the rotor shaft and generate the higher-frequency errors described below.

5. The rate of rotation of a harmonic flux wave generated by a three-phase stator is inversely proportional to the order of the harmonic. Thus, the fifth harmonic rotates at one-fifth the rate of the fundamental, and in the opposite direction as indicated above.

With the aid of these rules it is possible to predict the effect of the harmonic flux waves on synchro-system performance. This reasoning will first be applied to synchro generators and synchro-control transformers, and then extended to cover synchro differential generators.

3-18. Errors Caused by Harmonic Flux Waves. Figure 3-44 shows the general electromagnetic structure of a synchro generator and the instantaneous nature of the airgap flux distribution. While the amplitude of the flux distribution wave will be alternating with the input current, in the absence of saturation the space distribution of the wave will remain unchanged. Thus at a given instant, the rotor will generate a two-pole fundamental wave plus an infinite series of odd harmonics. Because of the symmetry between the two-pole fluxes it can be shown by Fourier analysis that no even harmonics exist: there is no four-pole, six-pole, etc., wave around the airgap of the machine. Physical reasoning will serve to point out the effects of the existing harmonics on the electrical accuracy of a synchro generator.

First consider the two-pole flux wave—the useful fundamental wave of the machine. This introduces an alternating voltage in each stator winding in accordance with the fundamental operating principles of a synchro. The rms values of these alternating voltages vary sinusoidally with the angular rotation of the rotor. The sinusoids are separated by 120°, the electrical separation between the legs of the stator winding.

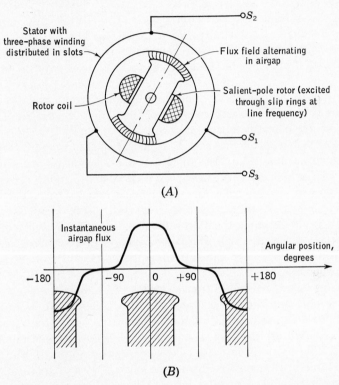

FIG. 3-44. (A) Synchro electromagnetic structure; (B) airgap flux distribution.

Now for a moment examine the effect of the third harmonic flux in the distribution wave. This can be considered equivalent to a superimposed six-pole flux wave distributed around the machine. From the point of view of a six-pole wave having six times 180 or 1080° of electrical angle around the periphery of the machine, the three stator windings are separated by three times 120, or 360 electrical degrees, rather than by 120° as in the case of the two-pole fundamental wave. Thus, the third harmonic induces identical voltages in each of the stator legs at each instant of time and for any angular position of the rotor. Since a three-phase winding without a neutral cannot carry current when identical voltages are applied in each of the three legs, the net effect of the third-harmonic induced voltages across the S_1, S_2, S_3 terminals is zero. Figure 3-45 helps to clarify this point. With identical voltages induced in the three legs, the third-harmonic synchro terminal voltages are as follows:

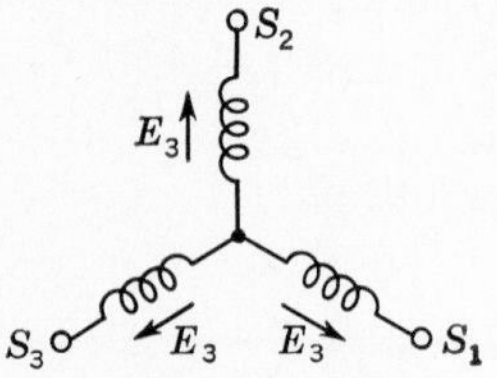

$$V_{S_1-S_2} = -E_3 + E_3 = 0$$
$$V_{S_2-S_3} = -E_3 + E_3 = 0$$
$$V_{S_3-S_1} = -E_3 + E_3 = 0$$

so that no line current can flow.

FIG. 3-45. Three-phase winding carries identical voltages.

Similar reasoning shows that harmonics of the order of 9, 15, 21, and all other multiples of the third are also canceled. As indicated previously, even harmonics do not exist. The cancellation of the harmonics of the order three or multiples of three is one of the major advantages of three-phase synchros over two-phase synchros.

The above conclusions indicate that in three-phase synchros the only troublesome harmonics are the fifth, seventh, eleventh, thirteenth, or, in general, harmonics of the order $6K \pm 1$, where K equals 1, 2, 3, etc.

As a general rule, Fourier analysis reveals that as the order of the harmonics increases, the amplitude decreases. Thus, the lower-order harmonics generally cause the most difficulty. For this reason, a detailed examination of the fifth and seventh harmonics in a synchro generator should also permit a clear understanding of the behavior of the higher-order harmonic groups.

The same line of reasoning that was used to examine the effect of the third harmonic on synchro accuracy can also be used in examining the fifth and seventh harmonics. The fifth harmonic, for example, has ten poles distributed around the machine, while the seventh harmonic has fourteen. The axis of symmetry of these poles coincides with that of the two-pole fundamental wave, and the two harmonic waves and the fundamental move in a fixed angular orientation as the rotor rotates. The condition is thus equivalent to having ten- and fourteen-pole machines superimposed on the fundamental two-pole machine. The three-phase windings of the stator are no longer separated by 120 electrical degrees, as was the case for the two-pole wave; instead, the angular separation is five times 120, or 600 electrical degrees, for the fifth harmonic, and seven times 120, or 840 electrical degrees, for the seventh harmonic. Figure 3-46 shows the relative displacement of the induced voltages in each of the phases.

As mentioned previously (and shown in Fig. 3-46), the voltages induced in the stator as a result of the fifth harmonic flux wave in a synchro-

generator airgap have a phase rotation
opposite to that of the fundamental.
That is, if the voltages reach their positive maximum in the order S_1, S_2, S_3 for
the fundamental, then they will reach the
positive maximum in the order S_1, S_3, S_2
for the fifth harmonic.

In turn, it can be shown that the
seventh harmonic behaves like a separate
fourteen-pole machine, inducing voltages
in the stator legs of the same phase order
as the fundamental. Extending this
analysis to the higher harmonic groups,
the eleventh harmonic induced voltages
are of the opposite phase sequence as the
fundamental, the thirteenth have fundamental phase sequence, etc.

Another way to visualize the effect of
harmonics is to imagine that they are
caused by a sequence of separate ideal,
identical machines. One machine corresponds to each harmonic, with each

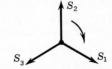

Fundamental sequence of voltages

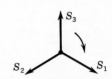

Fifth-harmonic sequence of voltages

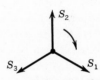

Seventh-harmonic sequence of voltages

FIG. 3-46. Relative displacement
of induced voltages.

geared to operate at a speed proportional to the order of the harmonic.
Figure 3-47 shows such a sequence. The harmonic generators all have
two poles. The stators and rotors are initially aligned so that the

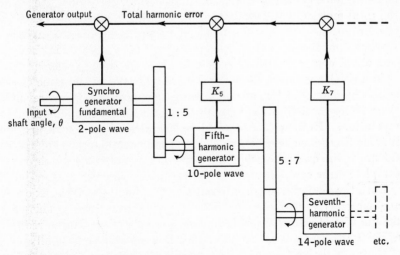

FIG. 3-47. Mechanical harmonic generator. K_5, K_7, . . . are attenuators to set the
relative proportions of the corresponding harmonic.

harmonic flux waves are oriented in the same manner as in the actual machine. The outputs of all the generators, after attenuation to the correct proportions for the harmonic, are summed to yield total generator output. The reversals in phase sequence are caused by the single-stage gearing between machines. All significant harmonics can be shown in this arrangement.

Consider the effect of this harmonic content in the generator output on the transmission accuracy of a synchro generator coupled to an ideal control transformer. Assume that the control transformer is always electrically nulled with respect to the *fundamental* synchro-generator output; for example, the control transformer could be directly coupled to the generator shaft. As the shaft is rotated (turning both units together), the two-pole fundamental wave is continually nulled and the voltage output of the control transformer is due to the individual harmonics in the generator. This voltage is a measure of the error that would result if the synchros were used in a servomechanism.

The next step is to examine the harmonics individually, neglecting the fundamental which is continually nulled in the above arrangement. The first effective harmonic, the fifth, behaves like a ten-pole synchro going at one-fifth shaft speed in a direction opposite to that of the shaft. Thus, for one revolution of the control transformer (and fundamental generator), the relative movement of the fifth-harmonic generator is $\%$ revolutions in the opposite direction. But the relative electrical angle of a fifth-harmonic generator is five times the fundamental electrical angle for a given mechanical angle, so that the total relative electrical rotation of the fifth-harmonic generator to the control generator corresponds to six times the total motion of the fundamental. Thus, the apparent relative electrical rotation of the fifth-harmonic wave and the control transformer is six revolutions, and six complete error cycles are generated in one revolution of the control transformer as a result of the fifth harmonic.

In a similar manner, the seventh harmonic goes in the same direction as the fundamental but at one-seventh the speed. For one revolution, the relative motion of the seventh harmonic and the fundamental is $\%$ revolution. However, since the electrical angle of the seventh harmonic is seven times the electrical angle of the fundamental for a given mechanical angle, in one revolution the control transformer goes through six complete error cycles because of the seventh harmonic.

Both the fifth and seventh harmonic, therefore, introduce six cycles of angular error per revolution of the control transformer. This characteristic of certain synchros, known as six-cycle error, can be recognized as being due to these harmonics and will occur uniformly in all synchros of the same design.

Similarly, it can be shown that the eleventh and thirteenth harmonics produce a twelve-cycle error, the seventh and nineteenth harmonics an eighteen-cycle error, etc.

3-19. Harmonic Errors in Control Transformers. It can be shown that all of the conclusions reached in the last two sections for a synchro generator apply identically to a control transformer with a three-phase primary and a wound-nonsalient rotor excited from an ideal generator. Thus, within the control transformer, as within the generator, errors in the flux waveform due to the nonsinusoidal character of the flux distribution yield undesirable characteristics that affect synchro-system accuracy. Again, in the control transformer, the fifth and seventh harmonics cause six-cycle errors, the eleventh and thirteenth harmonics twelve-cycle errors, etc., very much the same as the errors caused by nonsinusoidality in the generator waveform.

3-20. Harmonic Errors in Differential Generators. The differential generator combines the characteristics of a generator and a control transformer. A differential generator with its three-phase primary coupled to the output of a transmitter behaves exactly like a control transformer. With its rotor held in a fixed position, the differential transformer behaves like a static transformer. The only effect of adjustable shaft pos tion is to vary the relative angular orientation of the output signals of the differential transformer. Nonsinusoidality of the differential generator windings causes harmonics to be generated just as in a control transformer with similar errors resulting. Thus, a differential generator does not affect the basic performance errors described in the previous sections, but merely contributes similar error components.

3-21. Minimizing Winding Errors. It has been pointed out in the previous sections that harmonics cause errors because of the nonsinusoidal character of the flux waves generated in the airgap. The synchro designer tries to minimize these errors by designing the windings and pole structures to give most nearly sinusoidal waveforms within practical economic and manufacturing limitations. It is not the intention to delve deeply into synchro design here, but rather to cover broadly the different techniques. The reader is referred to standard books on electrical machine design for further details.

Perfect sinusoidal flux distribution cannot be obtained with electrical machine windings, but such techniques as using a maximum number of slots, shaping salient-pole structures, selecting proper pole width, skewing the rotor or stator, and using one of a variety of specialized windings all help the designer to approach the ideal waveshape. Table 3-1 gives a detailed summary of the methods used in minimizing electrical errors.

3-22. Errors Caused by Manufacturing Inaccuracies. Besides the errors described above that result from the nonsinusoidality of the airgap flux wave, there are additional errors arising from manufacturing inaccu-

TABLE 3-1. METHODS OF MINIMIZING ELECTRICAL ERRORS IN SYNCHROS

Winding Distribution. Instead of using a single concentrated coil to generate the magnetic flux for a pole, a number of coils is distributed in many slots. While this reduces the effective magnetic flux at the pole, at the same time it reduces the ratio of harmonics to fundamental, improving the waveform. Distributed windings are not used on salient-pole structures.

Chording. Instead of a coil that completely spans 180 electrical degrees, a coil of somewhat shorter span or pitch (called a chorded coil) may be used. The per cent harmonic in the waveform of the flux generated by a chorded coil is usually much lower than in the flux generated by a full-pitch coil. Best results are obtained by properly selecting the pitch; for example, a pitch of about 0.8 is effective in minimizing the fifth and seventh harmonics.

Fractional Slot Windings. This is a convenient way of obtaining the beneficial effects of a winding having a great many slots per pole per phase without requiring an impractical number of slots in the magnetic structure. This equivalent distribution results in considerable harmonic reduction and good waveform.

Skew. Either the rotor or stator slots may be skewed. In skewing, the slot is twisted so that instead of being parallel to the shaft axis it describes a helical path around this axis. Skewing either the rotor or stator is exactly equivalent to a type of winding distribution, and its effect is similar, in particular, sharply reducing the higher harmonics. Skewing has little effect on the fundamental and low-order harmonics and should be aimed at harmonics that cannot be readily canceled by other winding distribution techniques. In particular, skew can be used to cancel slot harmonics. In a synchro these are of the order $KS \pm 1$, where K is any integer and S is the number of slots.

Sinusoidal Windings. Here the distribution of turns per coil varies in a sinusoidal manner with the position of the coil around the periphery of the machine. This eliminates all harmonics except the slot harmonics. While it is a more expensive form of winding, it is used where the most accurate results are required.

Pole Shaping. When a salient pole is used, the flux tends to assume a square shape with a large harmonic content. There are two ways to improve the waveform: (1) pole-span selection and (2) pole shaping. Pole-span selection is equivalent to shortening the winding pitch as described above. The optimum pole pitch minimizes the fifth and seventh harmonics, the most troublesome in synchros. In pole shaping, the pole is tapered so that the airgap is a minimum at the center of the pole and increases symmetrically toward each edge. This results in considerable fringing at the pole ends, and a gradual reduction in flux density. The flux wave is much closer to sinusoidal than it would be with a uniform airgap.

Miscellaneous Items. There are many natural combinations of the above items that result in good over-all performance. For example, chording, winding distribution, and skewing are almost universally applied simultaneously. A somewhat more sophisticated approach is to design the rotor and stator of a synchro to eliminate different harmonics, so that the harmonics generated by one will not be picked up by the other. As a result, only the lowest common harmonic presents a significant source of error.

---

racies. This section examines the latter type of error from a physical viewpoint, without attempting to be mathematically rigorous. It is assumed that ideal materials are used and that the flux distribution is perfectly sinusoidal, so that all errors are due to incorrect synchro geometry caused by manufacturing inaccuracies.

One of the most significant sources of errors is airgap inaccuracies. Although the airgap is very small (several mils), it comprises the major reluctance in the magnetic circuit. Thus, even minor airgap irregularities cause marked distortion of the flux distribution pattern. One of the most common geometric irregularities that affects the airgap is ellipticity of the stator structure (Fig. 3-48). Although this ellipticity may only be of the order of 0.1 mil, this is a significant percentage in a 3-mil gap (3 per cent) where fractional per cent error limits are specified.

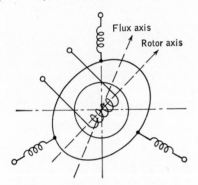

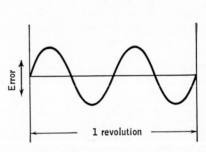

Fig. 3-48. Elliptical stator structure.   Fig. 3-49. Two-cycle error caused by elliptical stator.

If Fig. 3-48 represents a synchro generator, then the rotor magnetic flux will tend to concentrate in the vicinity of the narrower gap. The effect will be a net shift in the flux axis, the magnitude of the shift depending on the relative orientation of the rotor-flux axis and the axes of the ellipse. There will be no flux-shift error when the rotor is aligned with any of the ellipticity axes. In addition, the error reverses in sign when it passes through the zero points since the flux always tends to point to a minor axis. Figure 3-49 shows the error cycle for one complete revolution of the rotor. This two-cycle error is a common system characteristic.

No error is introduced by an elliptical rotor other than a fixed shift in the flux axis. This is automatically canceled as a source of inaccuracy by properly setting the synchro zero.

Now consider the effect of a control-transformer elliptical stator (Fig. 3-50). Under ideal conditions the flux rotates uniformly with the shaft angle of the transmitting generator. However, the elliptical stator causes the flux axis to shift, always tending to favor the direction of the minor axis.   The result is a two-cycle error, identical to that generated by a transmitter with an elliptical stator.

It is also possible for the rotor to be eccentrically located with respect to the stator.   In a synchro generator this causes a one-cycle error, as shown in Fig. 3-51.   The amplitude of the rotor flux varies nonsinusoidally around the airgap, yielding the apparent flux distribution shown by the solid curve in Fig. 3-51.

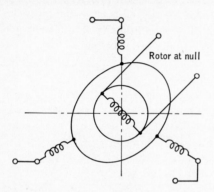

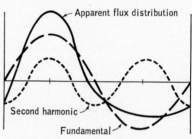

FIG. 3-50. Control transmitter with elliptical stator.

FIG. 3-51. Apparent flux distribution resulting from eccentric synchro-generator rotor.

3-23. Errors Caused by Winding Unbalance.   Another type of manufacturing error is introduced by unbalancing the stator-winding impedances, for example, by winding too many turns on one of the stator legs. The net effect (of any unbalance) is a nonuniformity in flux amplitude. When the flux is lined up with the axis of a high-impedance low-current stator leg, the flux-field strength is lower than it would be in a position 90° away.   The effect is similar to that of stator ellipticity, i.e., more flux on one axis than the other, with the characteristic two-cycle error.   It does not matter whether the unbalance occurs in the generator or in the control transformer, since the unbalanced impedances are in series.   Similar two-cycle errors are introduced by unbalanced stray capacitances or unbalanced impedances in long interconnecting lines.

Some additional conclusions can be reached based on the preceding analysis.   The various unbalances and dissymmetries tend to introduce general two-cycle errors of somewhat varied phase angle, that is, two-cycle quadrature as well as two-cycle angular inaccuracies are encountered.   Although there are no accurate general rules for the type of inaccuracy resulting from a given error, the following usually apply:

airgap dissymmetry and inductive winding unbalance introduce angular inaccuracies, while resistive unbalance produces predominantly quadrature. These rules are most accurate when applied to large synchros operating at high frequencies.

The resultant error in any system of synchros therefore consists of a series of harmonic components: one-cycle due to eccentricity between the rotor and stator; two-cycle due to ellipticity or electrical unbalance in the windings; and higher-order components of the order $6K \pm 1$ (where K equals 1, 2, 3, . . .) due to nonsinusoidal windings. These errors occur similarly in any member of a synchro chain and appear in the final total error.

3-24. Synchro Residual Voltages. Residual voltage occurs at a synchro null when ideally there should be no voltage present. This voltage is made up of three components: (1) in-phase fundamental, (2) quadrature fundamental, and (3) harmonic frequencies.

The first is simply an angular inaccuracy that is canceled out by renulling the controlled shaft, thereby introducing an error. Quadrature voltage is 90° out of time phase with the in-phase component and cannot be nulled by shaft rotation. Quadrature appears as a fundamental component minimum when trying to null a synchro. The most important source of quadrature is stray eddy currents in the magnetic steel, particularly in the vicinity of the airgap. Smearing of the lamination-stack airgap surfaces during grinding is a principal cause of eddy currents and therefore quadrature.

Harmonics, on the other hand, are caused by dissymmetry of the magnetic structure, resulting either from grain effects in the steel or unsymmetrical strains during fabrication. These affect magnetic properties. Careful handling of the material, hydrogen annealing, the use of high-permeability nickel alloys, and operation at low flux densities help to minimize harmonics.

In a servomechanism, quadrature and harmonics, as well as ordinary pickup, act to saturate high-gain control amplifiers. For this reason, residual voltage from these sources must be limited to the same order of magnitude as the true system error signal.

3-25. Synchro-system Velocity Errors. Velocity errors in synchro systems are most easily visualized by assuming that the rotors of a synchro-control transmitter and a synchro-control transformer are directly coupled together, and that both units are ideal to the extent that the generated output voltages are perfectly sinusoidal and angular position errors are zero. The units should be aligned so that the output of the control transformer is nulled, and the stator should be connected so that the control transformer will remain in a nulled condition for any angular setting of the rotors, at least within the accuracy limits of the system.

This is essentially a zero-speed steady-state null condition, in which all voltages are generated by mutual induction just as in an ordinary transformer.   Actually, however, rotation causes additional voltages to be generated in the transmitter and control transformer as a result of conductors moving through a magnetic field in much the same manner as any rotating generator develops an output voltage.   These rotationally generated voltages are in addition to the normal voltages that are developed in synchro systems in static angular-positioning applications, and as such can frequently introduce serious velocity errors.   When the transmitter/control-transformer combination is given an angular velocity, error voltages will be induced at the output of the control transformer as a

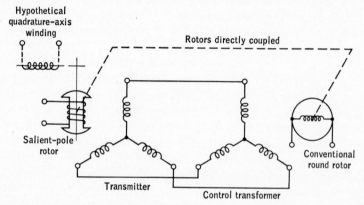

FIG. 3-52. Similarity to induction generator permits calculation of velocity error.

direct result of this rotation.   These voltages introduce servo positional errors that increase with increasing speed.

The actual calculation of these speed errors is a rather difficult task which has been thoroughly worked out.[1,2,*]   However, by making certain simplifying approximations and using the information developed in Chap. 5 (induction generators) a relatively easy technique can be derived for estimating velocity error.   Although this approach can be extended to cover synchro systems of any complexity, the following initial analysis is based on the simple transmitter/control-transformer combination described above.

Figure 3-52 shows a normally connected transmitter and control transformer.   The transmitter has a salient-pole rotor, and the control transformer a conventional round rotor.   A round rotor transmitter would make no change in the analysis except for possible simplification.

This approach is based on the straightforward parallel between the

* References, indicated in the text by superscript figures, are listed at the end of the chapter.

above system and an ordinary induction generator, which permits induction-generator theory to be applied to the problem of velocity errors in synchro systems. Visualize a hypothetical winding on the transmitter of Fig. 3-52, at right angles to the actual primary wound on the dumbbell rotor, and imagine that this actual primary is the primary of an induction generator and that the hypothetical winding is the induction-generator secondary (see Fig. 5-4 for the configuration of an actual induction generator). Then the three-phase synchro-transmitter stator winding, terminated in the balanced three-phase control-transformer stator winding, appears to the transmitter primary as a balanced polyphase winding. This stator winding can be compared to a uniform drag-cup or induction-type squirrel-cage rotor. Thus the situation is exactly that which exists in an induction generator: a primary winding produces the excitation, a quadrature winding serves as the output, and the opposing member has balanced polyphase characteristics. By visualizing the stators rotating while the dumbbell rotor is stationary, the parallel becomes even more exact. The principal difference here is that the equivalent to the squirrel cage is not a drag-cup type construction, such as used in most tachometers, but rather a wound polyphase winding inserted in slots.

Rotating this system (or an induction generator) causes an output voltage to be developed across the hypothetical quadrature winding. This output voltage must result from currents flowing in the three-phase stator, since the quadrature and primary windings are at right angles to each other and currents flowing in one have no effect on the other. In addition, the currents flowing in the transmitter stator are identical to the currents in the control-transformer stator, and the rotor-shaft interconnection means that the control-transformer output winding bears exactly the same alignment to its field as the hypothetical transmitter-rotor winding does to its field. In other words, the two windings are at static null. Therefore, the rotationally generated voltage in the output winding of the control transformer is proportional to the corresponding voltage in the rotor winding of the transmitter. Thus, the first step is to calculate the output voltage in the hypothetical generator winding, and the second step is to determine the proportionality factor.

Figure 3-53 shows the equivalent circuit of the induction generator which corresponds to the synchro system described above. The voltage out of this equivalent circuit with an ideal 1:1 output transformer corresponds to the developed voltage in the hypothetical output winding on the quadrature axis of the generator, having the same number of turns as the main generator winding. This output voltage is generated by stator-coil currents acting along the quadrature axis, as shown in Fig. 3-54. Thus, the speed voltages are generated in the two lower synchro coils.

The voltage across the control-transformer quadrature axis is determined by the ratio of its quadrature-axis impedance to that of the generator. Similarly, the output voltage from the control transformer

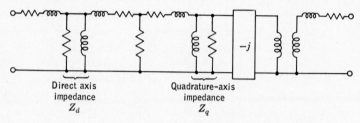

Direct axis
impedance
Z_d

Quadrature-axis
impedance
Z_q

FIG. 3-53. Equivalent circuit.

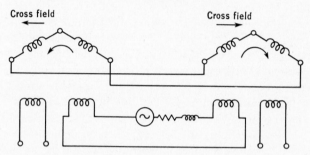

FIG. 3-54. Quadrature-axis fields.

depends on the ratio of control-transformer secondary turns to generator-rotor turns. Therefore

$$\text{Speed voltage} = \frac{Z_{q(\text{ct})}}{Z_{q(\text{gen})}} \frac{a_{\text{gen}}}{a_{ct}}$$

$$\times \text{ calculated voltage from equivalent circuit} \quad (3\text{-}49)$$

where $Z_{q(\text{ct})}$ = quadrature-axis control-transformer impedance

$Z_{q(\text{gen})}$ = quadrature-axis generator impedance

a_{gen} = step-down ratio to generator rotor

a_{ct} = step-down ratio to control-transformer rotor

The velocity error voltage calculated by this method consists of both in-phase and quadrature components. The in-phase component causes the control-transformer axis to be displaced from its null position since the entire servo moves toward a null, and the presence of an in-phase error results in a shift in control-transformer position. The quadrature component, which is caused by phase shift through the synchro system, as usual has a tendency to saturate the servo amplifier with a consequent increase in system sluggishness.

The velocity error problem is most serious in two-speed synchro systems operating at a low supply frequency. System supply frequency is an important factor because the magnitude of the velocity error depends to a large extent on the ratio of running speed to synchronous speed. Synchronous speed for a 60-cycle synchro is 3,600 rpm, whereas synchronous speed for a 400-cycle synchro is 24,000 rpm. It is entirely possible then, that in a two-speed 60-cycle synchro system, the high-speed control transformer might have an angular velocity that is a significant fraction of 3,600 rpm. Speeds above a quarter or a third of synchronous speed can cause serious velocity errors. Fortunately, however, the high-speed error is divided by the gear ratio of the two-speed system.

Now this principle must be extended to systems that have a differential generator between the transmitter and the control transformer. This addition has the effect of changing the leakage and resistance of the rotor of the equivalent induction generator. Take the equivalent circuit for the synchro transmitter, insert the equivalent circuit for the synchro differential generator, and connect to the equivalent circuit of the control transformer. Then the transmitter and control transformer can be combined in such a way that their equivalent impedance includes the impedance of the differential generator. Thus there is no change in the analysis but only in the actual numbers used for the rotor impedance in the equivalent circuit of the equivalent induction generator. These results can be extended to any system.

. **3-26. Multispeed Synchro Systems.** The accuracy of conventional generator/control-transformer synchro systems is limited by inherent electrical errors and by manufacturing inaccuracies. For example, such a system may be electrically nulled and still exhibit a mechanical error as an angular difference between the positions of the input and output shafts. This error appears directly in the servomechanism output, and cannot normally be reduced by increasing amplifier gain, but only by either using more accurate synchros or by using the same synchros in a manner that reduces the effective error.

One way to reduce this effective error is to introduce gearing between the synchros and the command and controlled shafts, so that the transmitter makes, for example, ten revolutions for every revolution of the command shaft, and the control transformer ten revolutions for every revolution of the controlled shaft. Then if the basic error of the original system was 10′, the effective error is reduced to 1′ because of the 10:1 gear ratio. The problem here, however, is that the gearing creates nine false nulls. For example, if at start-up the controlled shaft is more than 18° from the true null, the system will settle on one of the nine false nulls and the controlled shaft will be some multiple of 36° from the correct null.

Of course, such a situation is intolerable, and to prevent it a two-speed system such as shown in Fig. 3-55 is used. Here, two sets of synchros are used; one set, the coarse synchros, operating at the speed of the command and controlled shafts (shown in heavy lines) to make sure that the geared-up fine-speed synchro does not settle on a false null. During normal following operation, the fine-speed synchros are under control, reducing system error by a factor equivalent to the gear ratio. But once the angular error exceeds a predetermined value (either during start-up or under rapid slewing of the command shaft), the coarse synchro takes over and maintains control until the error is again small enough to prevent ambiguity when control is switched back to the fine-speed synchros.

It is immediately evident that this system requires a synchronizing or speed-selector circuit to decide whether the coarse or fine synchro should be in command. The simplest such circuit is a relay operated by the

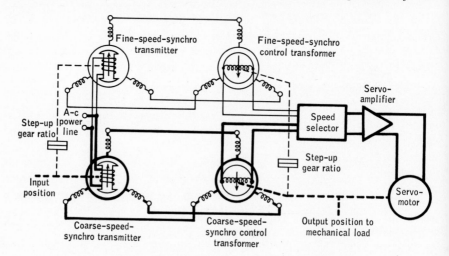

FIG. 3-55. Basic two-speed synchro system.

coarse synchro error signal. When the coarse error signal is less than a certain predetermined value, the relay is open and the fine-speed synchro is in control: when this value of the coarse error signal is exceeded, the relay closes and the coarse-speed synchros assume control. The practical relay limitations of poor sensitivity, low operating speed, and low input impedance, however, usually prevent the use of such a simple synchronizing circuit, and more sensitive and complex switching networks are required. A few of these circuits are described in a later section.

It is now possible to summarize some of the effects of two-speed synchro operation on system performance. With a fixed mechanical error in a synchro transmission system, the accuracy of the system is increased by a factor equivalent to the gear ratio. Also the voltage sensitivity of the system is increased by the same factor; for example, if a synchro has a gradient of 1 volt/deg, then with a gear ratio of 10:1 the effective fine-speed gradient becomes 10 volts/deg. Under this condition it might be possible to reduce servo-amplifier gain by a factor of 10.

Care must be taken to make sure that the geared-up fine-speed synchros are not called upon to operate above rated speed. Since synchro speed can be a large multiple of command shaft speed, this is always a possibility. This high operating speed causes synchro velocity error to increase, but this has little influence on system performance since this larger error is divided by the gear ratio before it becomes effective. The inertial contribution of the high-speed synchros should not be overlooked, since it is often a sizable factor, particularly when low-power servomotors are used.

3-27. Switching-zone Determination. The operation of a two-speed system is clearly shown by referring to the superimposed output waveforms for the coarse- and fine-speed synchros (Fig. 3-56). This shows a system with a 5:1 gear ratio, the fine-speed synchro making five revolutions for every revolution of the coarse-speed synchro. Theoretically, in this arrangement, control could be switched to the fine-speed synchro anywhere within the angular switching zone consisting of 180° revolution of the fine-speed synchro on either side of the true null. Actually, though, it is not desirable to switch to the fine-speed synchro immediately inside this zone because the low-level error signal available from this synchro might result in sluggish system operation. In prac-

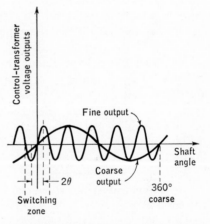

Fig. 3-56. Superimposed output waveforms for coarse- and fine-speed synchros.

tice, the switch-over point is taken at about 90 fine-speed-synchro degrees from the true null, or in other words, at the point of maximum fine-synchro output. In terms of coarse-speed synchro angle, the proper switching point is about

$$\theta = \frac{90}{N} \qquad (3-50)$$

Switching at this point has several advantages. There is little chance of a sufficient shift in parameters to cause the servo to oscillate, and, at the same time, the coarse synchro is still far enough from its null so that at the instant of switch-over the coarse error signal is still large enough to saturate the servo amplifier. This means that since the fine error signal will also be large enough to saturate the amplifier, there will be no sudden change in over-all system gain at the switch-over point. Normally no compensation is necessary even though the effective voltage gradient of the synchro in control changes by a factor equal to the gear ratio, and amplifier gain is selected for proper operation with the fine-speed error signal.

In a typical two-speed system using a 36:1 gear ratio, the switching point should be about 90/36, or 2.5° from the null. If the coarse-speed synchro has a 1 volt/deg gradient, the switching voltage is about 2.5 volts.

There are limits to the use of this technique for increasing system accuracy. The three critical factors are coarse-synchro accuracy, gear-train precision, and synchronizing network sensitivity and repeatability. The gear ratio cannot be so large that the switching zone becomes small enough to approach the magnitude of the coarse-synchro error or of gear-train inaccuracy or backlash. If either of these happen, or if the switching circuit changes its switching point or is too slow, there is a good possibility of the system oscillating.

3-28. Gear Ratio, Even versus Odd. Some of the common gear ratios are 15:1, 20:1, 25:1, and 36:1. One of the most popular, particularly in military systems, is the 36:1 system since it is convenient for operator observation and setting. The coarse-speed dial can be calibrated for 360° of controlled shaft rotation in 10° divisions, while the fine-speed dial can be calibrated in 1° or smaller divisions for 10° of controlled shaft rotation. In any case, system performance differs depending on whether the gear ratio is even or odd.

The output waveforms shown in Fig. 3-56 are typical of those obtained with an odd gear ratio. As in every synchro system, the coarse synchro has two nulls, the true stable null and an unstable null 180° away. In a single-speed system, the slightest motion away from the unstable null will generate an error signal of the correct phase to drive the system to the true null. This same condition still applies in a two-speed system with an odd gear ratio, even though it is possible for the control to switch to the fine-speed synchro at the unstable null.

For example, assume that with the power off the coarse synchro is turned to its unstable null. Now when the power is turned on, the control will switch to the fine-speed synchro since the coarse-speed signal is smaller than the switchover value. But as shown in Fig. 3-56, the phase of the fine-speed signal is the same as the polarity of the coarse-speed signal on both sides of the unstable null, and the fine-speed signal will drive the system away from the unstable null toward the true null. Therefore, the fine signal will increase until the coarse signal again assumes command and the system returns normally to the true null.

But if the gear ratio is even, then the situation about the unstable null is as shown in Fig. 3-57. As before, if the servo is turned on while sitting near the normally unstable 180° null, then the coarse error signal will again be small enough to cause com- mand to switch to the fine-speed synchro. But because of the even gear ratio, the polarity of the fine- speed signal is such as to cause the servo to drive toward the false null, and the system will settle at the un- stable null. This situation is rarely acceptable, except in those systems where total angular rotation of the controlled shaft is restricted by limit stops.

The problem is solved by adding a so-called "stick-off" voltage in series with the coarse synchro signal, with this voltage magnitude such that it changes the phase orientation at the 180° null so that both the coarse and fine signals are of the proper phase to drive the system to the true null.

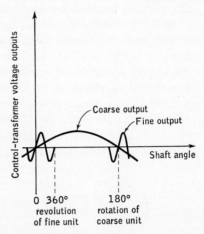

FIG. 3-57. Waveforms about unstable null with even gear ratio.

Figure 3-58 shows the waveforms. The stick-off voltage to be added is just enough to shift the coarse-synchro null 90° of fine-shaft angle at the 0 and 180° null points. For proper system operation after this voltage

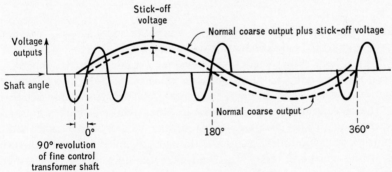

FIG. 3-58. Stick-off voltage added.

has been added, the coarse synchro must be rezeroed, or in other words, shifted relative to the fine synchro by an angle corresponding to a quarter of a revolution of the fine synchro. After this shift, the conditions about the true null are exactly the same as they were before, but the phase relationships of the fine and coarse synchros at the unstable null have been changed to correspond to those encountered with an odd gear ratio. The fine signal at the unstable null is of the proper polarity to drive the system to the true null.   It is apparent that the stick-off voltage should be about the same as the switch-over voltage.

3-29. Switching Circuits.   As pointed out previously, simple relay switching circuits are usually not satisfactory because of poor sensitivity, low operating speed, or low input impedance (and consequent synchro loading).   Many of these problems can be overcome by first amplifying the output of the coarse control transformer.   Figure 3-59 shows such a circuit.   The coarse signal voltage is rectified and fed to the biased grid of the tube.   As long as the coarse signal is small, the relay is closed and the fine-speed control transformer remains in control.   But when the coarse control-transformer error voltage increases, the tube current falls

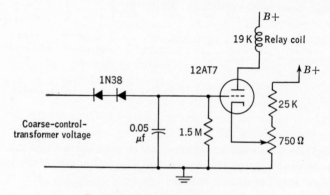

Fig. 3-59. Relay switching circuit.

below the current flow required to keep the relay closed, and control switches to the coarse control transformer.

Figure 3-60 shows a two-speed system used in radar tracking.[3]   The gear ratio is odd, 15:1, so that no stick-off voltage is required.   To equalize over-all system gain, the coarse synchro error signal is delivered to the servo amplifier through an additional amplifier with a gain (15:1) equivalent to the gear ratio.   According to the rule established previously, the switch-over point should be at about 90/15, or 6°.   Actually a switch-over point of 10° was used, near the limit of the 12° permissible switching zone.

Because of the limitations of relays, many of the newer synchronizing circuits use nonlinear elements.   These have the advantages of rapid switching action, high accuracy and sensitivity, small switching transients, and over-all simplicity.   Two types of nonlinear switching circuits are being used: continuous and discontinuous.   In the continuous circuits, the selective properties are based on resistors in which resistance is a nonlinear function of applied voltage.   A network of linear and non-

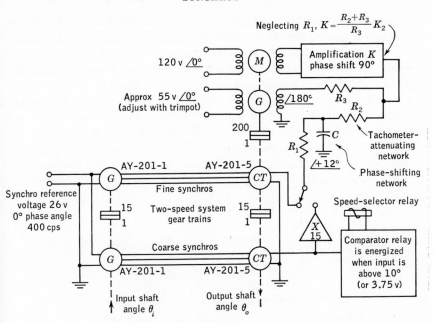

FIG. 3-60. Complete two-speed system used in radar tracking.

linear resistors is connected across the output of the fine and coarse synchros, so that the effective total output is from the fine synchro at small errors and the coarse synchro at large errors. In the discontinuous circuits, the switching point from coarse to fine speed is made to coincide with the firing point of a neon lamp. The high-impedance ratio between the conducting and nonconducting states of the neon lamp is used in voltage-divider fashion to bypass one synchro output to ground while the other is channeled to the servo amplifier.

Figure 3-61 shows a speed-switching circuit of the continuous type using crystal diodes.[4] The crystals in each pair of dividers are connected back-to-back and present a conducting path for both

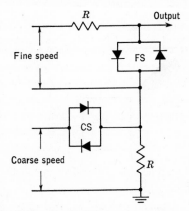

FIG. 3-61. Continuous-type switching circuit using crystal diodes.

directions of the applied alternating voltage. At low error levels the crystals have a high resistance level and with the series resistors form a high bleeder for the fine output and a low bleeder for the coarse-speed output. The switch output will be essentially the fine synchro output.

At high error levels, the crystals have a low resistance value and the process reverses, giving an output dominated by the coarse output. The degree of amplitude discrimination inherent in this circuit depends on the variation of crystal internal resistance with applied voltage. Using the

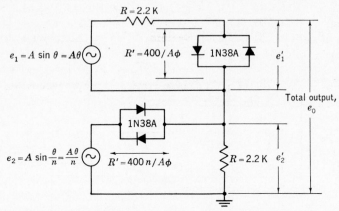

FIG. 3-62. Equivalent circuit of synchronizing network.

1N38A crystal diodes shown in the equivalent circuit of Fig. 3-62 ensures an effective amplitude attenuation of at least 20 db between the fine and coarse synchro outputs near the zero region of the system.

Temperatures ranging from 0 to 75°C do not affect this selector. As the temperature decreases, fine synchro output increases while coarse synchro output decreases—a condition that could result in false nulls at very low temperatures. On the other hand, high temperatures tend to accentuate the effect of the nonlinearities in the system. The output is substantially free from harmonic distortion down to 20 mv. The crystal time lag is a few microseconds, so that no phase shift occurs when the selector is used with carrier frequencies up to 10 kc.

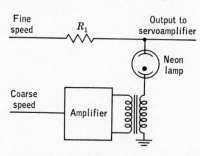

FIG. 3-63. Discontinuous synchronizing circuit.

Figure 3-63 shows the basic circuit elements of a discontinuous synchronizing circuit.[5] At low values of the error signal the neon lamp will not conduct, and the servo system operates at the fine speed. When the error becomes excessive, the coarse error signal, stepped up through the amplifier and transformer, causes the neon lamp to conduct. Since resistor R_1 has a high value compared to the impedance of the transformer secondary impedance, it acts as a voltage divider. The fine error signal bypasses to ground through the shorted neon lamp, while the coarse error signal is channeled through the neon lamp to the servo amplifier. This method has the advantages of maximum sensitivity at low signal levels, very long life, fast response, and an accurate switching zone. In addition, since the neon lamp is on only when the servo is operating on coarse speed, a lighted lamp indicates excessive error.

3-30. Extended Multispeed Systems. Where very high orders of accuracy are required, for example, in positioning a machine tool table within ±0.0001 in. in 50 in., as many as four or five sets of synchros are geared together. In this particular case, if four synchros are geared 10:1 to each other, then one revolution of the coarse-speed unit would be equivalent to 50 in. of table travel, one revolution of the next synchro to 5 in. of travel, one revolution of the next to 0.5 in. of travel, and one revolution of the fine-speed unit to 0.05 in. of travel. Then the fine-speed synchro would have to resolve only 1 part in 500 or a little less than a degree to achieve required accuracy. There are many similar applications.

It is apparent that these need complex mixer and discriminator circuits to provide the information required to put the correct synchro in command. In some cases, the transmitter synchros have been replaced by special tapped transformers, so that the command information specifying final position can be put into the circuit by switching transformer taps rather than by actually setting angular synchro positions for the various stages.

3-31. Synchro Standards. Until a few years ago there were no widely accepted synchro standards, and the different military establishments had their separate standards to which the various manufacturers complied. But these separate standards were primarily performance standards rather than basic design standards, so that there were a great variety of designs, each developed by a different manufacturer, and each meeting the standards of government acceptance. While these standards were certainly useful, often a system that worked satisfactorily with components supplied by one manufacturer would not work when "equivalent components" from other sources were substituted.

Fortunately the picture has changed, and uniform military specifications have been established for both 60- and 400-cycle components, even to the extent of using standard drawings and specifying production processes. This has led to uniformity throughout the industry, with a sharp reduction in costs, standardization of tooling, test methods, nomenclature, etc., and a simplified replacement part situation.

The principal military specifications are MIL-S-16892 (BuOrd) for 115-volt and 26-volt 400-cycle synchros, and MIL-S-17245 (BuOrd) for 115-volt 60-cycle synchros. The Society of Automotive Engineers is currently attempting to broaden these standards to cover more frame sizes and nonmilitary types.   Much of the material in the succeeding sections covering synchro zeroing and synchro testing is based upon the BuOrd standards.

3-32. Synchro Electrical Zero.   When synchros are used for angle transmission, it is important to define an angular reference point so that individual synchros can be properly synchronized in a system, even with considerable distances between them.   This is especially important when the synchro is coupled to some other datum element, such as a potentiometer.   Fortunately, synchros have an inherent angular reference known as *electrical zero*, which can be easily and precisely located for any synchro as described below.   Thus in a synchro angle-transmission system, if the control transformer coupled to the controlled shaft is adjusted to electrical zero when the shaft is at a known reference point (for example, the horizontal position in a gun elevation control system), and the input dial on the synchro transmitter is set so that it reads horizontal when the transmitter is at electrical zero, then the system will operate properly when it is started up without further synchro adjustment.   All angles are defined in a counterclockwise manner from electrical zero.   The following gives the procedure for zeroing the various types of synchros.

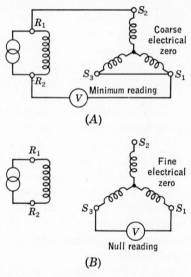

(A)

(B)

Null reading

Fig. 3-64. Locating electrical zero on a synchro transmitter.

Synchro Transmitters.   Since synchro output on any winding has two nulls, 180° apart, it is first necessary to define a correct unambiguous null point.   This definition is in terms of the standard rotor and stator terminal designations—R_1, R_2 and S_1, S_2, S_3—which are used uniformly on the various standard-type synchros.   The method for approximately locating electrical zero is shown in Fig. 3-64A.   With the synchro transmitter connected as in the figure, rotate the rotor until the voltmeter reads a minimum, giving the approximate electrical zero position.   Reconnect the meter as shown in Fig. 3-64B. Electrical zero can be accurately located by turning the rotor clockwise until the null meter reads zero.

In some cases the electrical zero is roughly located on the synchro, by an arrow stamped on the housing and an index mark on the shaft.   In this case, the first step above can be omitted and only the fine zeroing technique used.

Control Transformers. The problem is similar to that of finding electrical zero of a transmitter. The control transformer is connected as shown in Fig. 3-65A to locate approximately the electrical zero, and as shown in Fig. 3-65B for precise alignment in the same vicinity.

Torque and Control Differential Generators. Here, the approximate electrical zero is obtained with the setup shown in Fig. 3-66A, and the precise location with the setup shown in Fig. 3-66B.

When a pair of synchros is used in a precise application, it is sometimes possible to select the electrical zero by redefining terminal designations so that the random error curves subtract. By this technique, the system error can be made less than the error of the individual units.

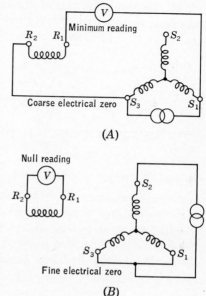

Fig. 3-65. Locating electrical zero on a control transformer.

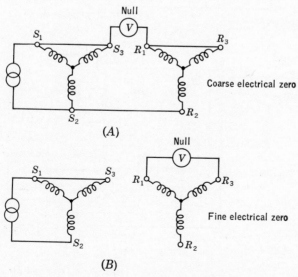

Fig. 3-66. Locating electrical zero on a differential generator.

3-33. Zeroing Multispeed Systems. The procedure for zeroing a two-speed system varies, depending on whether the gear ratio is even or odd. For an odd ratio, both the fine and coarse synchro transmitters and control transformers are zeroed independently, exactly as described above.

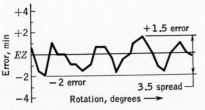

FIG. 3-67. Typical synchro error curve.

For an even gear ratio with a stick-off voltage added the procedure becomes slightly more complicated. The fine and coarse synchro transmitters and the fine control transformer are zeroed independently in the normal manner, but the stick-off voltage is added to the output of the coarse control-transformer rotor before it can be zeroed. This is done by approximately zeroing the coarse control transformer, adding the stick-off voltage, and then rezeroing.

3-34. Measuring Synchro Errors. The static accuracy of control synchros is defined in terms of deviation from the idealized performance

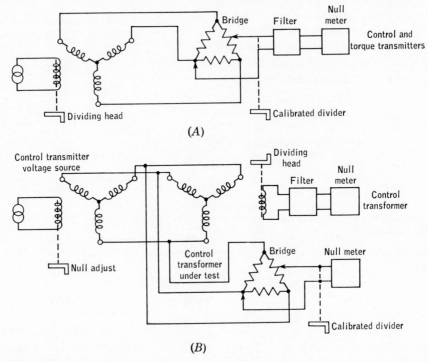

FIG. 3-68. Test setups for control and torque transmitters (*A*) and for control transformers (*B*).

equations given previously. For example, if a transmitter is rotated through a given angle, certain voltages are generated across the windings. The difference between these and the theoretical voltages results in an error, which is expressed in angular units. This is usually given as maximum error spread, or maximum error from electrical zero. Note the typical error curve shown in Fig. 3-67. Here the error spread is 3.5', while the maximum error from electrical zero is 2'. Error spread, then,

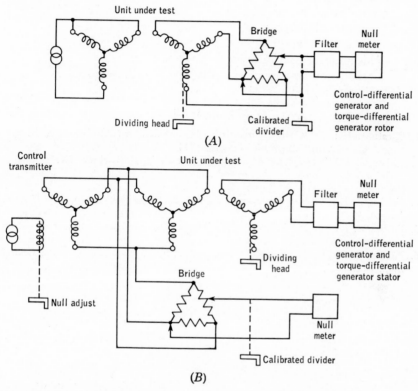

(A)

(B)

Fig. 3-69. Test setups for control and torque-differential generator rotors (A) and for stators (B).

is the algebraic sum of the individual maximum errors. The spread is seldom exactly twice the error from electrical zero, because the synchro curve is asymmetrical, including a high-frequency component and two lower frequency components. Maximum spread can be approximated as 1.5 times the maximum error.

The standard means of determining this error curve is by the proportional voltage method in which the synchro is connected to an accurate voltage dividing bridge. A balanced delta network, whose one arm comprises a voltage divider, is connected to the terminals of the synchro under test.   The divider arm is designed to have a resistance ratio R, defined by

$$R = 0.5 - \sqrt{3\!/\!2} \cot (\theta + 60) \tag{3-51}$$

The arm is calibrated in terms of an errorless synchro at rotor angle θ. Figure 3-68 shows the circuits for testing control and torque transmitters and control transformers, while Fig. 3-69 shows the circuits for testing control and torque differential generators.

An accurate dividing head turns the synchro rotor until a null is reached. Then the angular difference between the dividing head and the calibrated voltage divider is plotted through a complete synchro rotor revolution. This yields an error curve similar to that shown in Fig. 3-67.

Note that combinations of synchros can be calibrated as systems to ensure minimum error.

REFERENCES

1. Chestnut, H.: Electrical Accuracy of Selsyn Generator-control-transformer System, *Trans. AIEE*, vol. 65, pp. 570–576, 1946.
2. Weiss, G. H.: Linear Lumped Parameter Analysis of Synchros, IX, Effects of Angular Velocity on a Simple Control System, *NAVORD Rept.* 3633, U.S. Naval Ordnance Laboratory, White Oak, Md., Feb. 8, 1954.
3. Kadish, J. E.: These Seven Steps Design a Tach-stabilized Servo, *Control Eng.*, August, 1955.
4. Barber, B. T.: How to Design Speed Switching Circuits Using Nonlinear Elements, *Control Eng.*, November, 1954.
5. Barber, B. T.: How to Design Discontinuous Speed Switching Circuits, *Control Eng.*, December, 1954.

Chapter 4

RESOLVERS AND INDUCTION POTENTIOMETERS

4-1. Introduction. A line of induction-type components, including sine-cosine generators or resolvers and induction potentiometers, is available to the control-system designer. While these are analogous to resistance potentiometers, they have many advantages in function and performance over the resistive components. However, the induction units are more expensive, operate only on alternating current and usually require more complex auxiliary equipment for maximum precision. Table 4-1 compares the important characteristics of resistive and inductive units.

TABLE 4-1. RESISTIVE VERSUS INDUCTION COMPONENTS

Reliability. Induction components are more reliable, particularly under extreme operating conditions.

Complexity. More auxiliary equipment is usually required in high-accuracy induction component systems.

Cost. Approximately the same for both types of the same quality.

Resolution. Infinite for induction units. Resistive components are subject to resolution except in slide-wire construction.

Radio Noise. Negligible in induction components.

Isolation. Unlike resistive components, induction units have complete input-output isolation.

Scaling. In resistive units scaling can be readily adjusted by trimming resistors. However, the inductive device can include voltage step-up.

Voltage Variation with Frequency and Temperature. Resistive components can operate at frequencies down to direct current, vary little with temperature change, and are insensitive to input voltage variations.

Impedance. Ratio of input to output impedance in inductive components facilitates the excitation and loading of these units.

The induction-type component is essentially a rotating transformer (Fig. 4-1) similar in appearance to a miniature wound-rotor induction motor. One or more rotor (or stator) windings are excited by alternating current, and useful output voltages are induced in the windings on the stator (or rotor). These output voltages are functions of the input shaft angle and are scaled to the input voltage. It can be considered a mutual inductance that varies with angular position and has a precisely controlled calibration curve.

4-2. Reliability. One of the advantages of this type of component (in comparison with resistive devices) is an improved life expectancy. Standard induction components are rated at 1,200 hr at 1,500 rpm for a total of over one hundred million cycles. The improved reliability is derived principally from the fact that induction components do not require a wiper arm. The only sliding electrical contacts are on the rotor slip rings.

Induction components are free from contact bounce, wire hopping, and have smooth stepless output leading to infinite resolution. Since output

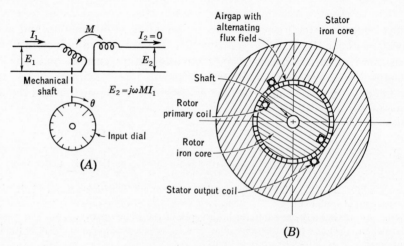

Fig. 4-1. Electrical and mechanical schematic of typical induction components. E_1, E_2 = input and output voltages, respectively; I_1, I_2 = input and output currents, respectively; M = mutual inductance between input and output coils, variable with shaft position.

voltage is obtained from a magnetic field, it is not affected by length of service. No radio interference is generated.

4-3. Electrical Characteristics. The transformer nature of induction components permits the isolation of input and output circuits. This is useful when voltages are to be added or subtracted, since special isolating transformers are not required and there is a free choice of ground points. Ground-point selection is important because electronic amplifiers are often used with these components.

The possibility of voltage step-up within the component simplifies signal scaling in computer circuits. Also, the magnetic cores of the induction units serve as an electrostatic shield between the input and output windings. These windings are buried in partially closed slots on the stator and rotor. Winding capacitance to ground is of the order of a few hundred micromicrofarads.

The voltage variation with shaft position is a function of the primary winding distribution (which generates the airgap flux) and the secondary-winding distribution. Skew is usually used to smooth the gradient changes resulting from the discontinuous nature of the coil arrangement in the slots. Skew also reduces the cogging effects from reluctance forces on the teeth.

There is no simple relation between the input and output impedances of an induction component. The input impedance of a lightly loaded unit is determined principally by airgap reactance (or main flux, as in any choke or inductive unit). Output impedance is determined by the resistances and leakages of the windings, and by the internal impedances of the voltage sources feeding the primary. Generally, output impedance is a function of shaft position because of the varying coupled impedance between the primary and secondary coils.

Variable output impedance is undesirable since it results in a changing output characteristic with load. This is in addition to the scaling change that occurs even when loading a constant output impedance. Where accuracies of a fraction of 1 per cent are required, the load impedance may have to exceed the output impedance by a factor of 1,000 or more. To minimize the loading problem, manufacturers often prescribe standard loads that the user must specify to achieve maximum accuracy. These loads may correspond to the input impedance of some standard electronic amplifier often used with induction units, or some other often used load. Dummy loading is sometimes required to meet manufacturers' specifications. In precise applications, cable capacitance must be included as part of the effective load.

Although computer and control circuits usually operate at some low audio frequency or on direct current, the high order of precision often requires the same attention to stray capacitances, grounding, and pickup that is necessary at radio frequencies.

Many induction components have the input and output coils arranged so that output impedance is independent of shaft position. Other induction components have dummy windings that reduce the variation in output impedance by a factor of 2 or 3. But these dummy windings must be located so that extraneous voltages are not introduced into the output.

Improved uniformity of output impedance results in freedom from loading error and a frequent savings in electronic isolation amplifiers. Often components can be directly loaded on the output of an induction unit and scaling can be adjusted with a trimming network.

4-4. Phase-shift Compensation.   In a-c systems, control and computation are performed by combining and operating on a-c voltages (or currents) that are usually in phase at some reference phase angle (usually 0° or 180° out-of-phase).   Thus, the amplitudes of the line-frequency sine wave can be added and subtracted directly, as can the voltages in a d-c system.   Any phase shift (away from the reference phase) will result in an inaccuracy, since vector and algebraic sums are no longer equal. In addition, high-performance closed-loop systems are critically responsive to such phase shifts and can cease functioning if the shift is excessive.

In miniature components, the resistance of the primary windings and the core loss combine to give normal phase shifts of ten or more degrees. This is inconvenient, since all components that operate together must be adjusted to the same phase shift.   Small changes in temperature can also cause appreciable phase-shift changes.

There are several methods of maintaining zero phase shift.   The user can purchase a set of induction components, and trim, scale, and compensate by means of networks and temperature and frequency-sensitive elements.   This is the best approach where size is important, but it is difficult to obtain optimum performance.   Where standard sized components are used and bulk is not a factor, reliable nonelectronic systems have been found practical.   For good performance over wide ranges of temperature and frequency, tube and transistor input amplifiers are available that incorporate adjustments for scaling, phasing, and compensation.   These amplifiers also provide isolation.

In these systems, the amplifiers are designed to give stable operation by means of heavy negative feedback.   Variations in amplifier-component combinations are caused almost entirely by manufacturing variations in the inductive components.   For this reason, adjusting resistors are best placed inside the cap of the rotating component.   Then the amplifiers or rotating components can be replaced without rescaling or rephasing the circuit.

Figure 4-2 shows some of the basic error characteristics of induction components.   In (A) the phase shift varies with temperature as a result of changes in the primary copper resistance.   In (B) the output error varies with shaft position.   The high-frequency pattern is caused by the slot openings and winding harmonics.   The low-frequency wave results from poor machining or rotor distortion, such as the elliptical rotor shape shown in (C).   In (D) the mutual inductance varies with input voltage. This introduces a variation in magnitude and phase of the output voltage.

4-5. Residual Voltage.   In addition to the useful output voltage, induction components develop residual output voltages as a result of electrical and mechanical dissymmetries in their construction.   Residual voltage consists of harmonics generated by the nonlinear iron and quadrature resulting from apparent short circuits in the iron circuit.

The harmonics increase sharply with increasing voltage (Fig. 4-3) and determine the maximum allowable voltage that can be imposed on a system. Because of this voltage limitation, little heat is developed in

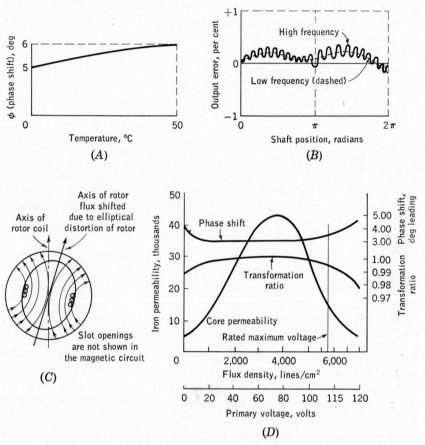

(A)

(B)

(C)

(D)

Fig. 4-2. Induction component errors. (A) Variation in phase shift with temperature; (B) variation in output error with shaft position; (C) errors shown in (B) result from distorted rotor shape; (D) variation in transformation ratio and phase with input excitation.

precision induction elements. Residual voltage can be measured by the equivalent minutes of angular displacement from the null required to generate an equal rms voltage. An alternate measure is the ratio of rms residual to the maximum useful output.

The quadrature voltage is 90° out of time phase with the useful output. It is caused by nonuniform conductivity in the electromagnetic circuit such as develops from smearing of the laminated core steel during grinding of the airgap surfaces. Quadrature is especially difficult to cope with since it is not readily filtered and cannot be canceled by rotating the shaft.

Because of these quadrature and harmonic components, there is a minimum residual or noise voltage at the null points. Since high-performance closed-loop systems use high-gain, easily saturated amplifiers, the residual voltage must be minimized by care in circuit wiring and by the use of high-quality components.

Residual voltage control is one of the most difficult manufacturing problems. Several techniques are available for quadrature and harmonic compensation such as the quadrature rejection circuit shown in Fig. 4-4. But these are either bulky and expensive or unreliable. In particular,

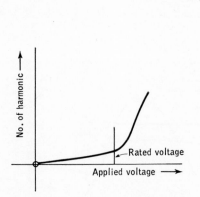

FIG. 4-3. Increase in harmonics with ap- FIG. 4-4 Circuit for bucking out sec-
plied voltage.   ondary quadrature.

harmonic filters must be used with caution since they introduce excessive time delays that exert an unstabilizing influence on a servo.

In addition to the generation of harmonics, iron nonlinearity causes other undesirable features. The variation of core permeability (Fig. 4-2D) with flux density causes the internal coupling coefficients of the induction component to change with supply voltage. This introduces scaling errors and causes the null points to shift with supply voltage. The first effect can be reduced by the use of compensating amplifiers. Both effects can be minimized by using high-permeability core materials such as Allegheny Ludlum's Mumetal or Carpenter's Hymu (Fig. 4-5). These core materials are expensive, and since they are strain-sensitive, add to the handling difficulties. With a knowledge of the core-permeability data, performance characteristics can be predicted by using an equivalent circuit.

As with all precision components, induction components require high-quality mechanical construction. Their accuracy depends on the flux

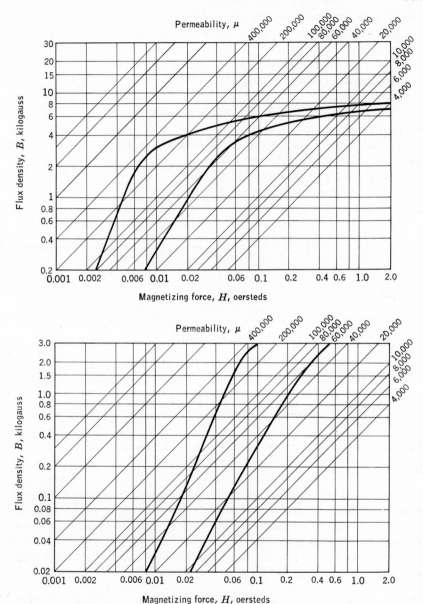

FIG. 4-5. Direct-current magnetization and permeability curves for Mumetal. Upper curve is for high flux densities and lower curve is for low flux densities. (*Courtesy of Allegheny Ludlum Steel Corp.*)

distribution in an airgap that may be 0.005 in. or smaller. Care in seating the mounting surface, accurate alignment, and freedom from shaft runout and eccentricity are necessary to obtain satisfactory performance.

These basic electrical and mechanical concepts apply to both induction resolvers and potentiometers.

4-6. Resolvers.[1,*] Problems such as the rotation of coordinates, solution of triangles for angles and sides, addition of angles, transformation between rectangular and polar coordinates, and the resolution, composition, or addition of vectors can be solved with electrical resolvers. They can also be used for angle transmission where high accuracies are required. Double sets of transmitters and receivers are not required.

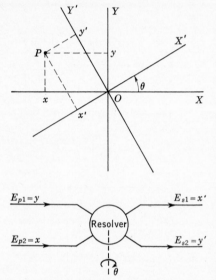

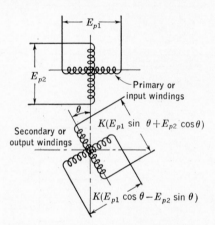

FIG. 4-6. Winding arrangement and defining trigonometric relations for an induction resolver.

FIG. 4-7. Rotating coordinates with a resolver.

The induction resolver is a special case of the induction-type component and consists of a rotor and stator, each with two independent windings. The axes of these windings are 90° apart. The secondary or output voltages are sine and cosine functions of the angle of shaft rotation. Figure 4-6 shows the winding details and the following equations express resolver performance.

$$E_{s2} = K(E_{p1} \sin \theta + E_{p2} \cos \theta) \qquad (4\text{-}1)$$

$$E_{s1} = K(E_{p1} \cos \theta - E_{p2} \sin \theta) \qquad (4\text{-}2)$$

Compared to alternate devices for the solution of trigonometric problems, these induction units are unusually compact. For example,

* References, indicated in the text by superscript figures, are listed at the end of the chapter.

in problems of vector composition and coordinate rotation the induction resolver is equivalent to two separate card-type sine-cosine generators, each with two inputs.

4-7. How Resolvers Are Used.   Figure 4-7 shows a resolver solving the problem of rotating coordinate axes.   The coordinates of point P are given as x and y in terms of the perpendicular X and Y axes.   Equations of analytic geometry give the new coordinates x' and y' of P with respect to the X' and Y' axes as

$$x' = x \cos \theta + y \sin \theta \tag{4-3}$$
$$y' = -x \sin \theta + y \cos \theta \tag{4-4}$$

where θ is the counterclockwise rotation of the new axes from the original orientation.   These equations are identical with Eqs. (4-1) and (4-2)

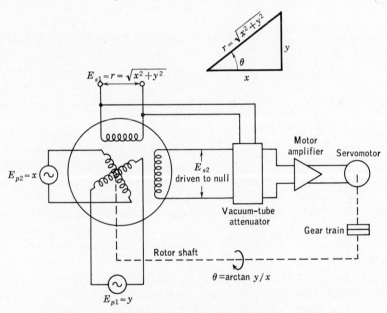

FIG. 4-8. Transforming from rectangular to polar coordinates.

relating the output and input resolver voltages, so that a direct solution of the problem is obtained from the output voltages.

Figure 4-8 shows how a resolver can be used to transform from rectangular to polar coordinates.   The rotor voltages set up mutually perpendicular flux fields in the airgap of the resolver.   The rotor is positioned by the servomotor so that E_{s2} is a null value, which signifies perpendicularity of the corresponding stator winding to the resultant airgap flux.   The other stator winding will then be oriented directly along the resultant flux axis, and its output will be a measure of the flux magnitude.   Voltage E_{s1} will correspond to the magnitude of the resultant of the two input voltages, while the resolver shaft angle indicates its vector orientation on polar coordinates.

The torque developed in the resolver servo for small deflections from

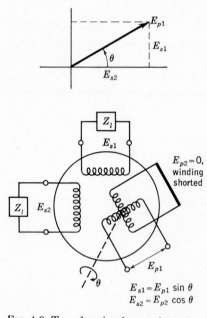

null position is proportional to the product of the voltage gradient of the error-measuring winding and the gain of the amplifier.   The voltage gradient in turn varies with the air-gap flux or with E_{s1}.   Thus, for constant amplifier gain, servo stiffness (restoring torque per degree deflection) varies with E_{s1}.   As E_{s1} ranges from near zero to its maximum rated value, servo performance may change from sluggish and inaccurate at one extreme to actual instability resulting from excessive stiffness at the other.   This undesirable situation can be corrected by inserting a vacuum-tube attenuator in the servo loop.   This is a form of amplifier incorporating a variable-mu tube to which E_{s1}, rectified, is applied as negative d-c bias.   Increasing E_{s1} reduces over-all amplifier gain,

$$E_{s1} = E_{p1} \sin \theta$$
$$E_{s2} = E_{p2} \cos \theta$$

FIG. 4-9. Transforming from polar coordinates to rectangular coordinates.

roughly maintaining constant servo stiffness.   Relatively inaccurate systems need not include this component.

Figure 4-9 shows the reverse situation of transforming polar coordinates into rectangular, by resolution of an applied voltage E_{p1} into components E_{s1} and E_{s2}.   Note that the unused primary winding is short-circuited.

4-8. Resolver Inputs.   Three principal types of inputs are used: sine-wave voltages of the same electrical phase; sine-wave voltages shifted 90° apart; and irregular waveshapes, usually of the sawtooth or square-wave variety.

With the first and most important input, the output voltages remain fixed in electrical phase shift and their magnitudes vary in accordance with Eqs. (4-1) and (4-2).   For the second and third types of operation, the output voltages can also be determined by these equations if the instantaneous values of the voltages are taken into consideration.

With two inputs 90° apart in electrical phase, each of the two rotor output voltages remain constant in amplitude, independent of rotor angular position.   However, the phase of the voltages varies continuously with rotor angular position. The phase shift between the two output voltages remains fixed at 90°. In this mode of operation, the equations expressing resolver performance are

$$E_{s1} = E_{p1}\underline{/\theta}$$ (4-5)
$$E_{s2} = E_{p1}\underline{/\theta} + 90$$

Where irregular waveshapes are used, resolver operation falls into two classes. In-phase square waves or flat-topped sine waves are used in some computing applications. If the two input waveshapes are the same, the performance is adequately described by Eqs. (4-1) and (4-2). This is usually the case.

Sawtooth waveshapes are often used in radar sweep applications. In a simple application, a sweep voltage is applied to one stator, and the two output voltages from the rotor windings are the same sweep voltage with

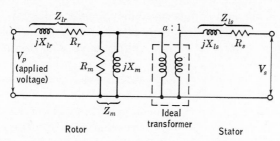

FIG. 4-10. Equivalent circuit of uncompensated resolver.

an amplitude proportional to the sine or cosine of the rotor angular position. If these two voltages are applied to the deflection plates, or coils of a cathode-ray tube, they cause a radial trace to be formed. The trace will assume the same angular position as the resolver rotor. This finds application in plan-position types of radar displays.

4-9. Equivalent Circuit. The resolver equivalent circuit is useful because variations in operating conditions act primarily to change the complex transformation ratio of maximum secondary voltage to primary voltage without appreciably affecting the essentially sinusoidal character of the output voltage variation with shaft angle. Furthermore, for balanced loads and low primary source impedance, the input and output impedances are independent of shaft position. Therefore, useful information can be obtained from the conventional transformer-type equivalent circuit corresponding to the four-terminal network formed by one primary and one secondary winding at maximum coupling. Figure 4-10 shows the basic uncompensated resolver equivalent circuit. In this position, neither of the windings couple the remaining two so those that are not shown can be ignored.

Often special data are required for special resolver applications. If a prototype unit is available, its equivalent circuit can be measured and the desired characteristics determined by calculation. When taking the measurements, a primary and secondary winding must be aligned for maximum mutual coupling. Because of the small size of these components, their leakage impedances are high and bridge-type measurements give more satisfactory results.

As shown later in Sec. 4-16, the equivalent-circuit constants can also be determined from manufacturer's data.

4-10. Transformation Ratio and Phase-angle Errors. As mentioned previously, frequency, temperature, secondary loading, and supply voltage changes affect the equivalent-circuit constants and cause corresponding changes in the transformation ratio and phase angle of a resolver. Circuit reactances vary directly with changes in supply frequency; winding copper resistance responds to ambient temperature variations; and changes in the iron core permeability with flux density cause jX_m to change with voltage. The leakage reactance and resistance of the resolver windings cause a drop in output voltage analogous to the regulation characteristics of a transformer.

The equivalent circuit also shows that the resolver nominal phase shift differs from zero, and in the smaller sizes can approach 4 or 5°.

Standardizing and temperature-compensating networks, together with rigid specifications of circuit impedances and loading, permit resolvers to be used for medium-accuracy computer work without the associated electronic equipment frequently needed in the more accurate applications. Here the equivalent circuit is useful in establishing circuit-component tolerances and the permissible variations in operating tolerances.

Standardization and compensation networks are usually incorporated in booster amplifiers. Boosters are high-gain amplifiers with adjustable negative feedback elements, easily adapted for standardizing the over-all gain and phase shift of the booster plus resolver combination. Usually the over-all phase shift is held accurately to zero degrees, with a transformation ratio of 1:1. Elements to compensate for variations in line voltage, frequency, and ambient temperature are usually included in the booster feedback system.

Boosters are also used as isolators to avoid loading computing devices that would normally feed the low-impedance primary windings of the resolver directly, and likewise to avoid resolver loading.

Two typical booster arrangements are shown in Figs. 4-11 and 4-12. These show excitation applied to only one resolver primary. Similar circuits would be required for exciting the other primary. Thus, a resolver with two input voltages requires two amplifier channels. These are frequently built on one chassis and sold as twin boosters. Since normally the secondaries are lightly loaded, no special secondary adjustments are necessary.   The effect of the load is included in the primary standardization.

The circuit of Fig. 4-11 uses two adjustable feedback loops.   In one of them R_p is set to be proportional to R_r, the resolver primary resistance. The fed-back voltage is then proportional to the drop across R_r and is

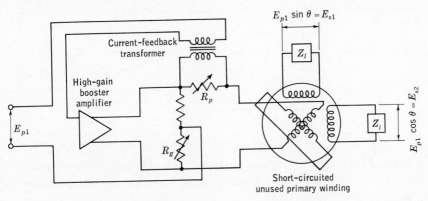

FIG. 4-11. Network-type booster compensation circuit. Z_l = standard secondary load; R_p, R_g = phase and gain attenuators; θ = rotor-shaft angle.

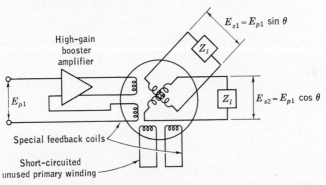

FIG. 4-12. Booster compensation system using special feedback windings. Z_l = standard secondary load; θ = rotor-shaft angle.

scaled by the current feedback amplifier so that the voltage across R_r is effectively canceled by the output of the amplifier.   The resolver appears to have no primary resistance and the over-all phase shift is zero.   The over-all gain is adjusted to a standard value by means of resistor R_g in the voltage feedback loop.   Resistance R_p (proportional to R_r) is made temperature-sensitive so that proper compensation takes place over a wide range of ambient temperatures.   The critical resistors in the compensation and standardization loops are located in the end cap of the resolver so that, when necessary, the booster amplifier can be replaced without subsequent circuit adjustment.

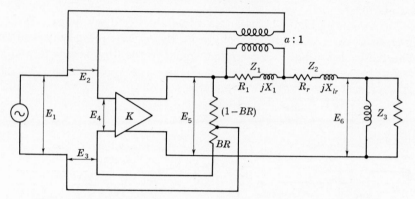

FIG. 4-13. Booster compensation system showing secondary winding.

4-11. Analysis of Booster Compensation System. To derive the fundamental relationships for this system, consider the circuit shown in Fig. 4-13. In this diagram

E_1 = input voltage
E_2 = fed-back voltage proportional to drop across Z_1
E_3 = fed-back voltage from voltage divider
E_4 = input voltage to amplifier
E_5 = output voltage from amplifier
E_6 = output voltage to load
Z_1 = impedance of current feedback element
Z_2 = resolver rotor impedance
Z_3 = load and stator impedance
R = resistance of voltage feedback resistor
B = fraction of R in feedback loop

The object is to obtain zero phase shift and a specified magnitude ratio between the input voltage E_1 and the output to the load E_6. From visual inspection of the circuit

$$E_1 + BE_5 + \frac{E_5}{Z_T} Z_1 a = E_4 \tag{4-6}$$

where $Z_T = Z_1 + Z_2 + Z_3$

$$E_1 + E_5 \left(B + \frac{Z_1 a}{Z_T} \right) = E_4 = \frac{E_5}{K} \tag{4-7}$$

$$\frac{E_5}{E_1} = \frac{-1}{B + Z_1 a/Z_T - 1/K} \tag{4-8}$$

$$\frac{E_6}{E_1} = \frac{1}{B + Z_1 a/Z_T - 1/K} \frac{Z_3}{Z_T} \tag{4-9}$$

Assume that K is very large so that $1/K$ is negligible. Then

$$\frac{E_6}{E_1} = \frac{-Z_3}{aZ_1 + BZ_T} \tag{4-10}$$

$$= \frac{-Z_3}{aZ_1 + BZ_1 + BZ_2 + BZ_3} \tag{4-11}$$

To obtain zero phase shift, independence of the permeability and loss characteristics of Z_3, and an adjustable magnitude ratio, let

$$aZ_1 + BZ_1 + BZ_2 = 0 \tag{4-12}$$

then

$$Z_1 = -Z_2 \frac{B}{a + B} \tag{4-13}$$

and

$$\frac{E_6}{E_1} = \frac{-Z_3}{BZ_3} = \frac{-1}{B} \tag{4-14}$$

Thus the magnitude ratio can be adjusted to the desired value by setting the voltage divider to the position indicated by B as determined from Eq. (4-14). Since Z_2 is fixed, and B depends on the desired magnitude ratio, zero phase shift can be obtained by adjusting Z_1 or a in accordance with Eq. (4-13).

4-12. Booster System with Compensator Winding Resolver. The booster technique shown in Fig. 4-12 is most commonly used. Special

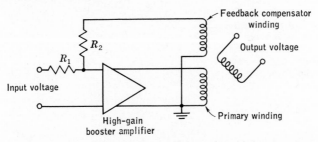

FIG. 4-14. Simplified schematic of compensator winding resolver-amplifier assembly.

feedback coils are wound in intimate proximity to the resolver primary windings so that the coefficient of coupling is practically unity. The output voltage from this winding is very nearly in phase with the rotor output voltage. It remains in phase despite changes in temperature and frequency, since the effects of primary copper loss are reflected equally in both the feedback and rotor windings. Resolvers of this type have their primaries wound on the stator so that extra slip rings are not required for the feedback windings.

To analyze the performance of this system, refer to the schematic of the amplifier-resolver assembly shown in Fig. 4-14. If the booster gain is very high, the feedback compensator winding develops a voltage that is almost equal to R_1/R_2 times the input voltage. And since the feedback winding is intimately coupled with the primary winding, its output voltage is essentially a measure of primary flux. Then the feedback amplifier delivers a primary voltage of the correct magnitude and phase to generate a flux field corresponding to the voltage applied at the input to the booster.

Thus assuming perfect coupling between the compensator and primary windings, the total flux field generated by the primary corresponds

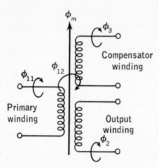

exactly to the applied voltage, thereby preventing phase shift caused by primary resistance and its corresponding temperature error. Although this compensating technique is sufficiently accurate to be widely used, a detailed study points up certain errors.

Figure 4-15 shows an elementary schematic of the coil arrangements in a compensator winding resolver, with maximum coupling between the primary and secondary windings. This reveals the various leakage and mutual fluxes occurring in a resolver. From this schematic it is possible to formulate an equivalent electrical circuit in which the individual flux linkages are replaced by circuit reactances (Fig. 4-16). On the basis of this equivalent circuit it is possible to determine the accuracy of the compensator winding method of resolver compensation.

FIG. 4-15. Flux linkage pattern in compensator winding resolver. ϕ_{11} = flux common only to primary winding; ϕ_{12} = flux common only to primary and compensator windings; ϕ_2 = flux common only to the output or secondary winding; ϕ_3 = flux common only to compensator winding; ϕ_m = flux common to all three windings; $\phi_{11} + \phi_{12} + \phi_m$ = total flux created by excitation of the primary winding.

Assume that both the secondary and compensator windings are unloaded. Also, because of the feedback circuit and the high-gain amplifier, it can be assumed that the compensator voltage is identical to the input voltage in phase, magnitude (except for a proportionality factor), and waveshape.

To determine the output voltage from the resolver secondary winding (at maximum coupling) it is necessary to work backward from the compensator output. Thus from the equivalent circuit,

$$K = \frac{V_\text{output winding}}{V_\text{compensator}} = \frac{a_2}{a_1} \frac{Z_m}{Z_m + jX_{l12}} \tag{4-15}$$

And if the resolver has a negligible core-loss factor so that Z_m equals jX_m, then

$$K = \frac{a_2}{a_1} \frac{X_m}{X_m + X_{l12}} \tag{4-16}$$

Equation (4-16) shows that a zero phase shift has been achieved, which, within the limits of the assumed equivalent circuit, is independent of temperature and frequency. However, at very high frequencies, stray capacities modify this expression.

Even assuming negligible core loss, a source of error results from the different nature of the X_m and X_{l12} reactances. Because the flux corresponding to X_m crosses a relatively small airgap (measured in thousandths of an inch) and has a substantial part of its reluctance in the nonlinear iron, while the flux corresponding to X_{l12} is essentially generated

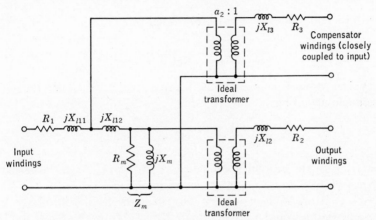

FIG. 4-16. Equivalent circuit for compensator winding resolver.

across the leakage airgaps, the ratio K will vary with the applied voltage in a similar manner to the variation of iron permeability with flux density. However, by using high-nickel alloy steels, it is possible to minimize this effect and limit it to a few hundredths of 1 per cent. (The compensator winding method of phase compensation nullifies this effect in relation to the phase of the output voltage.)

Now consider the effect when the core loss is not assumed negligible. The phase shift can be determined as the phase angle of

$$\frac{Z_m}{Z_m + jX_{l12}}$$

Establish an expression for Z_m. Let Z_m consist of jX_m, in parallel with R_m equals QX_m. Then

$$Z_m = \frac{jX_m Q}{Q + j} \tag{4-17}$$

Let θ_m equal the phase angle of Z_m. Then θ_m can be determined from

$$\theta_m = \frac{1}{\pi} - \arctan\frac{1}{Q} \tag{4-18}$$

And the phase angle of the output θ_0 is

$$\theta_0 = -\arctan \frac{X_{l12}}{Q(X_m + X_{l12})} \tag{4-19}$$

Let

$$\frac{X_{l12}}{X_m} = \tau \tag{4-20}$$

Then the output phase angle is

$$\theta_0 = -\arctan \frac{\tau}{Q(1 + \tau)} \tag{4-21}$$

which for small angles is very closely equal to

$$\theta_0 = -\frac{\tau}{Q(1 + \tau)} \tag{4-22}$$

In a typical resolver, Q might equal 8 and τ equal 0.10.   Then the output phase angle would be

$$\theta_0 = \frac{0.1}{(8)(1.1)} = -0.65° = -39.0'$$

Referring to the amplifier schematic of Fig. 4-14, it can be seen that the phase shift can be brought to zero by adding a capacitor across the feedback resistor.   When properly adjusted, the feedback voltage from the compensator would lead the input by 39', while the phase angle of the secondary output voltage would be zero.

In this circuit, the booster amplifier should have a net loop-voltage gain of 60 to 80 db.   Tests of typical units indicate that the ratio of the voltage delivered by the feedback winding to that delivered by the rotor does not vary by more than about ± 0.05 per cent, and that the electrical phase shift is constant to within 1' or less over a temperature range from -55 to $+85°C$.   When used with a suitable booster amplifier, the ratio of resolver rotor output to amplifier input has a similar stability.   These results are based on no-load operation.

Using a booster has little effect on such factors as residual voltage, axis alignment, or angular accuracy.   Its primary function is to preserve the transformation ratio and phase shift over the allowable range of operating conditions.   Only in the case of booster-compensated units are accurate transformation ratio and phase specifications guaranteed by the manufacturer.   But the user can obtain high accuracy for the boosterless types by the careful use of network standardization methods. This technique is shown in Sec. 4-16.

4-13. Resolver-winding Design Factors.   Resolver windings are designed to give an output voltage from the secondary windings that is as close as possible to a sinusoidal function of shaft position.   This is achieved by varying the arrangement of coils in each slot, and the number of turns in each coil, on both the rotor and stator.   The design is optimized within these limits.

There are two phases to the problem: first, to design the primary windings to develop as sinusoidal airgap flux as possible, and second, to design the secondary windings to discriminate sharply against the remaining harmonics in the airgap flux.

Figure 4-17 illustrates the discriminatory characteristic.   It shows in an elementary fashion how a coil of a definite peripheral span around the airgap corresponding to 0.8 pole pitches will not pick up the fifth harmonic, but will pick up most of the fundamental.   Thus in any position the net flux linked by the coil is zero with respect to the fifth harmonic component.   But at maximum coupling the coil links about 95 per cent of the maximum fundamental flux component.

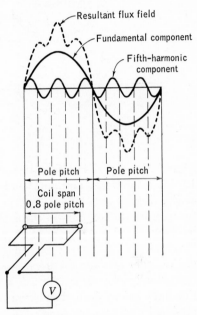

Although a pitch of 0.8 was used in the above example, it may not be possible to achieve this because of practical limitations on the number of slots.   However, the principle holds that pitch adjustment helps minimize sensitivity to specific harmonics and to groups of harmonics. It is the ratio of harmonic to fundamental output that determines the errors, so that although shortening the coil pitch reduces the fundamental flux, it improves the ratio.

FIG. 4-17. Flux pattern in resolver airgap showing effect of coil span on harmonic pickup.

Another way of obtaining the same result is to add the outputs of several coils in series, so that the sums of the fundamental components tend to add, while the harmonics tend to cancel.   A final adjustment involves setting the turns of the separate adding series coils to yield the minimum per cent harmonic.

Just as the above techniques reduce the sensitivity of the output to harmonics in the airgap flux, similar adjustments on the primary flux generating coils reduce the per cent of harmonics in the airgap flux. Final winding design requires that the primary and secondary together generate a minimum of those harmonic components to which the secondary is sensitive.

It has been determined that the optimum resolver winding is a sinusoidally distributed winding, in which the distribution in turns of the windings in the slots varies sinusoidally around the airgap periphery. These windings generate (primary) or pick up (secondary) only slot harmonics. A slot harmonic is defined as $ks \pm 1$, where k equals 1, 2, 3, . . . , and s equals the number of slots. Thus a sinusoidally distributed rotor with 12 slots develops harmonics of the order 11 and 13, 23 and 25, etc.

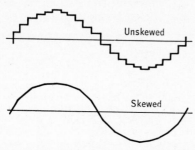

Similarly, the number of stator slots can be chosen to avoid picking up the rotor slot harmonics. Although perfect insensitivity to rotor harmonics is impossible, it is possible to design the stator so that it is only sensitive to high-order rotor slot harmonics. This helps, since the magnitude of developed harmonic output varies as the inverse square of the order of the harmonic. Thus a 20-slot stator picks up harmonics of order

Fig. 4-18. Steps show slot harmonics on skewed and unskewed resolvers.

19 and 21, 39 and 41, 59 and 61, etc. The last pair (59 and 61) are also 12 slot rotor harmonics and will be transmitted to the output.

Skewing can minimize even these slot harmonics, and final errors result from the inability of the skew to cancel both the 59 and 61 harmonics (Fig. 4-18). A compromise will minimize the net effect of the two harmonics. The errors caused by harmonics in a 12–20 resolver are of the order of a hundredth of a per cent.

Normally the skew is much greater than that required to minimize slot harmonics, since skewing also tends to even out dissymmetries and nonideal performance conditions.

4-14. Resolver Frequency Response.[2] Resolvers are designed primarily for 60- and 400-cps carrier-frequency operation. However, special units developed for wideband operation are suitable for use over a 100-kc bandwidth. The latter are used primarily with irregular waveshapes such as radar sweep voltages and high-frequency phase shifters.

The frequency response from the stator to the rotor is similar to that of a transformer with a high leakage reactance (Fig. 4-19). At low frequencies the response drops off at 6 db/octave. As noted from the equivalent circuit, the corner frequency, usually in the vicinity of 10 to 30 cps, is determined by the stator d-c resistance and the stator inductance. At this point the response is 3 db down. At high frequencies, the distributed capacity of the rotor resonates with the leakage reactance to give a peak in the response. This occurs at about 30 kc in a typical resolver and can result in as much as 10 to 15 db rise in response. When irregular waveshapes are used, this rise in response can produce ringing. But this can be prevented by connecting a damping resistor across the rotor.

Where compensating windings are used, the stator to feedback-winding response is similar to that for the stator to rotor, except at high frequencies. The lower leakage reactance to the feedback winding results in a much higher frequency response. For most types, the response is essentially flat to well above 100 kc. This simplifies the design of the booster amplifier. To achieve this high-frequency response in the resolvers with approximately unity ratio between the stator and feedback winding, corresponding terminals of these two windings should be operated at the same a-c potential. This minimizes the capacity effects between windings.

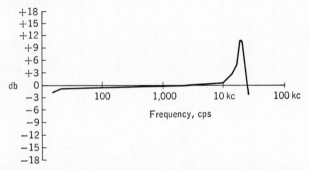

FIG. 4-19. Typical resolver frequency response.   (*Courtesy of Reeves Instrument Corp.*)

In low-frequency applications, the frequency response of the rotor and feedback winding are almost identical. When used with a suitable booster, the response can be made flat to as low a frequency as is desired, even below 0.1 cps, limited only by the loop gain of the amplifier circuit and the maximum current rating of the resolver.

4-15. Resolver Application Factors.   In accordance with the general discussion of induction components, the following precautions must be observed in resolver applications:

1. All secondary windings must be terminated in the load specified by the manufacturer whether they are actively used or not. Dummy loading may be called for.

2. The primary windings must be excited from balanced low-impedance voltage sources. If one primary is unused, it must be short-circuited.

3. All windings, used or otherwise, must be grounded in accordance with good practice in radio-frequency circuits. Manufacturers usually specify these ground points.

Often only one primary or one secondary is required in an application. Under this condition, axis alignment specifications and performance

TABLE 4-2. RESOLVER ERRORS

Error	Definition	Magnitude in precision units	Causes of error	Factors influencing error
Axis misalignment........	Deviation of winding axes from perpendicularity	2 to 3½′ of arc	Nonuniformity of magnetic circuit	Error varies with changes in iron permeability resulting from changing applied voltage
Phase error (booster unit).	Deviation from nominal phase shift (usually 0°)	2 to 3½′ of electrical angle	Inaccurate standardization; primary winding resistance*	Variation in iron permeability with supply voltage; changing primary winding resistance resulting from temperature variation
T.R. error (booster unit)...	Deviation from nominal T.R. (usually unity)	0.06 to 0.10 per cent	Inaccurate standardization; primary leakage reactance*	Variation in iron permeability with supply voltage
Quadrature residual voltage	Fundamental frequency residual, 90° out of time phase with useful output; expressed in per cent of maximum resolver output voltage	0.06 to 0.10 per cent	Nonuniform electrical conductivity of laminated iron stacks	Substantially independent of operating conditions
Harmonic residual voltage	Harmonic frequencies present in resolver output; expressed in per cent of maximum resolver output voltage	0.06 to 0.10 per cent	Nonlinear properties of iron; saturation effects	Goes down sharply with reduced applied voltages; substantially independent of temperature
Angular accuracy error...	Deviation of resolver output from a true sine function of shaft position†	0.02 to 0.10 per cent	Nonideal winding distribution; inaccurate skew	Substantially independent of operating conditions

* These sources of error may be nullified by proper booster compensation.
† Angle is measured from a null position. Output voltage exactly 90° from the null is taken as the maximum value of the reference sine wave. Error is expressed as per cent of the maximum (90°) output.

specifications of the unused winding can be waived. For this reason, manufacturers usually classify their production line output according to the number of available precision primary and secondary windings per component, thereby reducing production rejects.

The limiting factor in performance, whether the unit is compensated or not, is residual voltage, which determines the final sensitivity and accuracy of these components. Harmonic and quadrature voltages that appear at the null position must be kept below the level of allowable accuracy. Those components of quadrature not resulting from a phase shift differential between the separate primary windings cannot be eliminated by adjusting the primary standardization circuits.

Table 4-2 summarizes the common resolver errors.

All other factors being equal, resolver accuracy increases with increasing size, although some of the smallest components may be the most accurate available since they are the newest. Although the same accuracy specifications may be applied by a manufacturer to several units of a line of different sizes, the larger ones are probably more conservatively rated and are usually less sensitive to departures from standard conditions. This is true mainly because the relative leakage impedance is smaller for the larger units, and they are more rigid mechanically.

4-16. Typical Resolver Calculations. To show how equivalent-circuit techniques can be used to predict resolver performance and to standardize a boosterless unit, determine the following items based on manufacturer's data for a commercially available unit.

1. Establish the equivalent circuit by calculation.

2. Calculate the resolver transmission (output voltage ratio and phase shift) for 60 cycles from the equivalent-circuit constants.

3. Calculate resolver transmission from the equivalent-circuit constants for 400 cycles. (This should check with manufacturer's data for the 400-cycle unit.)

4. Design a standardizing network that will give zero phase shift and a specified output voltage ratio.

5. Determine influence of temperature and frequency variations on resolver transmission, and consider compensating techniques.

The commercial unit selected for this sample calculation is the Bendix Pygmy Autosyn Resolver with the following manufacturer's specifications.

Input voltage to rotor.............. 26 volts, 400 cycles, single-phase
Input impedance........................... 900 + j2,200 ohms
Rotor resistance (dc)................................. 560 ohms
Stator output voltage.............. 11.8 volts at maximum coupling
Stator resistance....................................... 165 ohms
Phase shift (rotor to stator)................................. 12°
Plus additional redundant data

1. *Calculate equivalent-circuit constants.* Referring to Fig. 4-20, the ratio of output voltage to input voltage is

$$\frac{Z_m}{Z_m + Z_{lr}} \frac{1}{a}$$

The phase shift is equal to the phase angle of Z_m minus the phase angle of Z_m plus Z_{lr}. But Z_m plus Z_{lr} constitute the input impedance which is given in the manufacturer's specifications as 900 plus $j2,200$ ohms. Thus by calculation, the magnitude of the input impedance is 2,370 at an angle of 67.7°. The phase shift is also given as 12°, so that the phase angle of Z_m is 67.7 plus 12, or 79.7°. The Q_m, or ratio R_m/X_m, is equal to tangent 79.7, or 5.5.

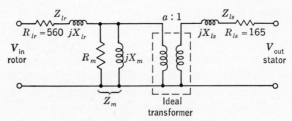

Fig. 4-20. Resolver equivalent circuit.

For convenience, Z_m can be converted to an equivalent series representation. This gives a circuit consisting of jX'_m and R'_m in series, where

$$\frac{X'_m}{R'_m} = Q_m \tag{4-23}$$

R'_m is equal to the input resistance minus the d-c rotor resistance. The input resistance can be obtained from the specified input impedance, so that

$$R'_m = 900 - 560 = 340 \text{ ohms}$$

And, from Eq. (4-23),

$$X'_m = Q_m R'_m = 5.5(340) = 1,870 \text{ ohms}$$

The reactance jX_{lr} can be calculated as the difference between the input reactance and X'_m, or

$$jX_{lr} = 2,200 - 1,870 = 330$$

This series circuit can now be converted to the corresponding parallel circuit by the formulas

$$X_m = X'_m \frac{1 + Q_m{}^2}{Q_m{}^2} = j1,930 \text{ ohms} \tag{4-24}$$

$$R_m = X'_m \frac{1 + Q_m{}^2}{Q_m} = 10,700 \text{ ohms} \tag{4-25}$$

With the constants calculated up to this point, the equivalent circuit takes the form shown in Fig. 4-21. Still to be determined are a and X_{ls}.

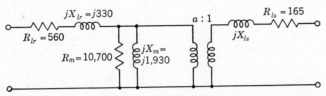

FIG. 4-21. Equivalent circuit with constants partially determined.

Since the output voltage is 11.8 volts, a can be calculated from the following formula.

$$V_{out} = V_{in} \frac{Z_m}{Z_m + Z_{lr}} \frac{1}{a} \qquad (4\text{-}26)$$

$$a = 1.76$$

In the absence of specialized data on the stator leakage reactance, assume that it bears the same ratio to the magnetizing reactance (as seen from the stator) as does the rotor leakage reactance. Thus

$$X_{ls} = \frac{X_m}{a^2} \frac{X_{lr}}{X_m} = \frac{X_{lr}}{a^2} \qquad (4\text{-}27)$$

$$X_{ls} = (0.568)^2(330) = 106.5 \text{ ohms}$$

This gives the final equivalent circuit shown in Fig. 4-22.

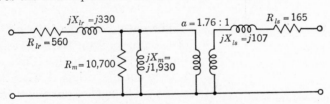

FIG. 4-22. Final equivalent circuit.

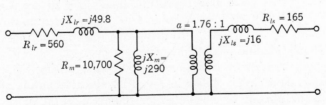

FIG. 4-23. Equivalent circuit for 60-cycle operation.

2. *Calculate resolver transmission for 60 cycles.* For 60-cycle operation, all the reactances in the equivalent circuit must be multiplied by the ratio 60/400. This gives the circuit shown in Fig. 4-23.

To simplify calculation with little loss in accuracy, the 10,700-ohm core-loss resistor can be neglected. Then

$$\frac{V_{out}}{V_{in}} = \frac{jX_{lr}}{R_{lr} + jX_{lr} + jX_m} \frac{1}{a} \qquad (4\text{-}28)$$

$$\frac{V_{out}}{V_{in}} = \frac{j290}{560 + j49.8 + j290} \frac{1}{1.76} = 0.251\underline{/58.7°}$$

Clearly this resolver is not intended for 60-cycle operation since the attenuation and phase shift are both very high and extremely temperature-sensitive.

In cases such as this, where the core-loss resistor can be neglected without materially affecting accuracy, the simple circle nomogram shown in Fig. 4-24 is handy for determining temperature sensitivity. The circle is constructed with a diameter representing V_{out} when the input primary resistance is zero. The vertical axis carries a linear scale of $1/Q_{in}$ with a value of one at an angle θ of 45°, where

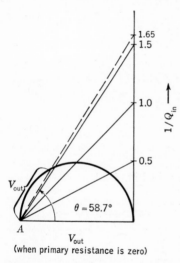

$$\frac{1}{Q_{in}} = \frac{\text{input primary resistance}}{\text{input reactance}}$$

$$= \frac{R_{lr}}{X_{lr} - X_m}$$

V_{out}
(when primary resistance is zero)

FIG. 4-24. Nomogram for determining temperature sensitivity of resolver when core-loss resistor can be neglected. For sample resolver on 60-cycle operation $1/Q_{in} = 560/(49.8 + 290) = 1.65$.

The output voltage for a given value of $1/Q_{in}$ has a magnitude represented by the intersection of a line connecting the $1/Q_{in}$ value and origin A with the semicircle. The angle θ represents the phase angle. Thus if a $\pm 50°C$ change in temperature causes a ± 20 per cent variation in $1/Q_{in}$, the nomogram can be used to determine the effect of this variation on the attenuation and phase shift of the output.

3. *Calculate resolver transmission for 400 cycles.* Using the constants for the equivalent circuit shown in Fig. 4-22, the attenuation and phase shift of the output can be calculated for 400-cycle operation.

Using Thévenin's theorem, express Z_m as an equivalent series impedance.

$$Z'_m = \frac{(10,700)j1,930}{10,700 + j1,930} = 1,900\underline{/79.8°}$$

and converting to the complex form

$$Z'_m = 1{,}900(\cos 79.8 + j \sin 79.8) = 337 + j1{,}870$$

Then determine the source impedance, where

$$\text{Source impedance} = \frac{Z_{lr}Z'_m}{Z_{lr} + Z'_m}$$

where $Z_{lr} = 560 + j330 = 649\underline{/30.6°}$

and $Z_{lr} + Z_m = 2{,}370\underline{/67.8°}$

so that

$$\text{Source impedance} = \frac{(649)(1{,}900)\underline{/110.4}}{2{,}370\underline{/67.8}} = 522\underline{/42.6°}$$

By taking into account the turns ratio

$$\frac{\text{Source impedance}}{a^2} = \left(\frac{1}{1.76}\right)^2 522\underline{/42.6} = 124.3 + j114.2$$

Thus the source impedance as seen at the output of the secondary is

Source impedance$_{\text{out}}$ = $124.5 + j114.2 + 165 + j107 = 289 + j221$

The no-load output voltage is the ratio of the equivalent series impedance Z'_m to the input impedance, where

$$\text{Input impedance} = Z'_m + Z_{lr} = 2{,}370\underline{/67.8°}$$

$$V_{\text{out}}(\text{no load}) = \frac{1{,}900\underline{/79.8}}{2{,}370\underline{/67.8}} \left(\frac{1}{1.76}\right) = 0.455\underline{/12.0°} \text{ leading}$$

Thus output attenuation is 0.455 and the phase angle is 12°. Note that the phase angle agrees with that specified by the manufacturer for 400-cycle operation.

As a check it is also possible to calculate the equivalent-circuit output by approximate methods.

$$\text{Phase shift} = \arctan \frac{560}{1{,}930} = 16.2°$$

$$\text{Attenuation} = \frac{1{,}930}{2{,}260} \left(\frac{1}{1.76}\right) = 0.486$$

Therefore the approximate no-load output voltage is

$$V_{\text{out}}(\text{no-load}) \cong 0.486\underline{/16.2°}$$

The poor correlation in phase shift is caused by the relatively high resistance values found in small components such as the sample unit. However, this approximation technique can be used for rapid estimates of performance.

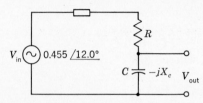

FIG. 4-25. Resolver standardizing network. Source impedance as seen at output = 289 + j221.

4. *Design a standardizing network for 400-cycle operation.* For purposes of illustration assume that the phase shift must be brought to zero and the over-all attenuation to 0.460. This can be accomplished by adding an RC network across the resolver secondary, as shown in Fig. 4-25. The problem is to select the proper values of R and X_c.

By observation, the ratio of voltage out to voltage in under load can be expressed by

$$\left. \frac{V_{out}}{V_{in}} \right]_{\substack{under \\ load}} = 0.455\underline{/12.0} \; \frac{-jX_c}{(289 + R) + j(221 - X_c)}$$

Thus for zero phase shift

$$\arctan \frac{X_c - 221}{289 + R} = 78°$$

$$\tan 78° = 4.7$$

$$X_c = 1{,}581 + 4.7R \qquad (4\text{-}29)$$

To simplify the analysis, realizing that there will be only light loads on the resolver, approximations can be used to determine the effect of the load on the output magnitude.

The phase angle can be set at zero by satisfying Eq. (4-29), while the output magnitude change is approximately equal to

$$\frac{221}{221 - X_c}$$

which constitutes an increase in output.

At this point, X_c can be selected to maintain an over-all attenuation of 0.460. The desired per unit increase in output is

$$\frac{0.460}{0.455} = \frac{0.455 - 0.005}{0.455} = 1 + \frac{5}{455} = 1 + 0.011$$

Therefore

$$0.011 = \frac{221}{221 - X_c}$$

and

$$X_c \cong \frac{221}{0.011} = 20{,}100 \text{ ohms}$$

so that at 400 cycles

$$C = 0.0199 \; \mu\text{f}$$

and from Eq. (4-29)

$$R = 3{,}940 \text{ ohms}$$

A circuit consisting of these components arranged as shown in Fig. 4-25 will give the required attenuation and zero phase shift.

5. *Determine effect of temperature and frequency.* If the resistor R in the output circuit is temperature-sensitive (that is, it is made of a material having the same temperature coefficient as the resolver windings), the phase-shift variations resulting from ambient temperature changes will tend to cancel.

Without this correction circuit, a 50°C change in temperature will change the primary resistance by 20 per cent, with a corresponding variation in phase shift; 20 per cent of 12° is about 2.4°. Higher temperatures have a greater effect. In a critical compensation problem, exact temperature compensation is obtained by carefully adjusting the variation of R with temperature.

Frequency shifts have little effect on attenuation in this circuit, but will produce roughly the same effect on phase as does temperature variation. That is, a 20 per cent change in frequency will cause a 20 per cent change in phase shift for either the primary or load circuits. However, in contrast to the temperature effect, phase changes caused by the inductive primary circuit will add rather than subtract. This causes the circuit to be particularly sensitive, and if phase is to be controlled, frequency must be controlled also.

Attenuation increases with increasing temperature, but at a relatively lower order than phase shift. However, the circuit in Fig. 4-25 has no provision for attenuation compensation.

In larger units, the attenuation error may be so small that it can be neglected. But if precise attenuation control is required in the above circuit, the primary resistance and the sum of R and the secondary resistance must be compensated to maintain constant value through the use of negative temperature-coefficient resistors.

4-17. Induction Potentiometers.[3] Induction potentiometers are precision signal transformers with transformation ratios that can be varied continuously between fixed minus and plus limits by rotating the shaft. These transformation ratios closely approximate linear functions of angular displacement. The units are available as alternatives to linear resistance potentiometers in applications requiring the special features of induction-type components.

Usually, a single primary winding is excited and a voltage proportional to the shaft setting is developed in a single secondary. Although most units are built for infinite rotation, performance is most accurate when operation is restricted to a band centered about a null position of the output winding. Figure 4-1 shows the magnetic circuit and winding configuration in simplified form.

The linear variation of output voltage is obtained by the suitable distribution of primary and secondary windings.   But since the linear function is nonperiodic, a typical induction unit has angular performance limitations, as shown in Fig. 4-26.   This particular potentiometer has four coils; however, two are dummies, used to increase accuracy by improving the uniformity of the input and output impedance with shaft position.

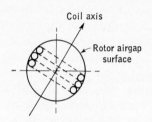

Coil axis
Rotor airgap surface

Figure 4-27 shows a typical winding distribution and flux pattern.   The primary-winding distribution establishes the airgap flux pattern, while the secondary distribution determines the variation in output flux linkages (and output voltage) with rotor shaft position in accordance with the fundamental laws of electromagnetic induction.

For a given performance, there may be many satisfactory combinations of primary and secondary windings.   A

Flux-pattern amplitude alternates at line frequency

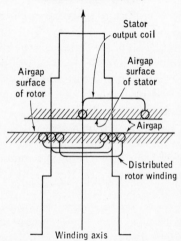

Stator output coil

Airgap surface of stator

Airgap surface of rotor

Airgap

Distributed rotor winding

Winding axis

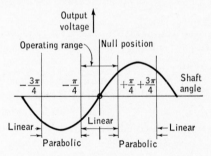

FIG. 4-26. Output voltage vs. shaft angle for typical potentiometer.

FIG. 4-27. Typical winding distribution and corresponding flux pattern.

choice depends on such factors as relative accuracy of the individual combination, availability of standard laminations, winding efficiency, and comparative insensitivity to nonideal conditions.

Similar to other induction components, potentiometer performance is governed by the relationship between the airgap flux fields and the output coil.   Thus any departure from the required winding configuration and/or the ideal airgap introduces errors.   Three major error sources are nonideal winding distribution; nonuniform airgap reluctance, partially a result of slot openings; and machining variations and nonuniform magnetic permeability.   These affect performance as shown in Fig. 4-2.

Besides accurate shaping of the output voltage vs. shaft angle, proper gain and phase scaling are necessary with an induction potentiometer. For example, a linear potentiometer must not only be precisely linear, but the slope and phase shift of the output characteristic must also be closely controlled. Phase shift should be independent of shaft position.

Whereas scaling in a resistive potentiometer is readily accomplished by means of external trimming resistors, in induction units the inductive input impedance and phase shift lend complications. Furthermore, the induction potentiometer needs compensation for variations in temperature, frequency, and supply voltage.

The equivalent circuit (Fig. 4-28) can again be used for calculating scaling and phase angle, and for predicting the effects of changing temperature, frequency, and applied voltage. The following formulas,

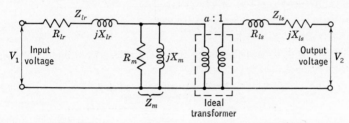

FIG. 4-28. Equivalent circuit of induction potentiometer defining its characteristics at maximum coupling.

based on the equivalent circuit, are useful in making estimates of induction potentiometer performance. They assume low leakage impedance and low core loss.

$$V_2(\text{open circuit}) = \frac{V_1}{a} \frac{X_m}{X_{lr} + X_m} \tag{4-30}$$

$$\text{Phase shift (open circuit)} = \frac{R_{lr}}{jX_{lr} + jX_m} \tag{4-31}$$

$$\text{Output impedance} = (R_{ls} + jX_{ls}) + \frac{1}{a^2}(R_{lr} + jX_{lr}) \tag{4-32}$$

4-18. Standardization and Compensation. Elements inserted in either the primary or secondary circuits can establish an exact scale factor and phase shift. Suitable temperature- or frequency-sensitive components can be included to compensate for variations in those quantities. Thus the designer need compute only approximate parameters, and establish the general nature of the compensation, since final adjustment is always made under test. Furthermore, since output voltage varies in a fixed manner with shaft position, test adjustment can be made at any shaft angle to standard phase and gain corresponding to that angle. The angle of maximum output (maximum rated angle) is frequently used.

To compensate for dissymmetry in the output for positive and negative angles, the average of the output voltages at the extreme positive and negative positions is often standardized.

Figures 4-29 and 4-30 show typical standardization and compensation circuits. The network shown in Figure 4-29 adjusts phase shift to zero and accurately sets the transformation ratio. It is moderately sensitive to fluctuations in carrier frequency, especially in the smaller sizes. But

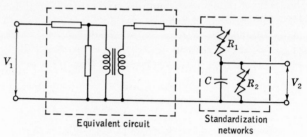

Equivalent circuit   Standardization networks

FIG. 4-29. Standardization network on secondary side. V_1 = input voltage; V_2 = output voltage.

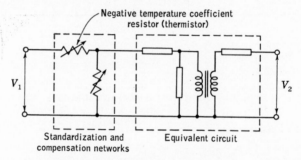

Negative temperature coefficient resistor (thermistor)

Standardization and   Equivalent circuit
compensation networks

FIG. 4-30. Standardization network on primary side.

temperature compensation can be obtained by making R_1 and R_2 temperature-sensitive. The arrangement shown in Fig. 4-30 will give zero phase shift, but is relatively sensitive to carrier-frequency shifts.

For maximum flexibility and accuracy, booster units are used with induction potentiometers. The techniques of booster application are similar to those used with resolvers, and equivalent networks and booster amplifiers are satisfactory.

While necessary for maximum accuracy, booster systems are complex and costly. Consequently for medium accuracies (0.25 to 0.50 per cent) designers often use a hybrid approach. Induction potentiometers, standardized and compensated by means of temperature- and frequency-sensitive networks, can use simple cathode followers for isolation. Sometimes, isolation amplifiers are omitted entirely and rescaling is accomplished with networks to correct for loading.

4-19. Design and Application. In practice, more than one input and output coil are required to get optimum performance. A permanently short-circuited quadrature winding, at right angles to the primary, compensates for most of the error resulting from nonideal airgap geometry. By bucking out stray flux at right angles to the excitation axis, this quadrature winding minimizes the effect of dissymmetries, reducing airgap uniformity tolerances required for a given accuracy by a factor of 5 to 10.

The shorted quadrature winding also minimizes the variation in output impedance with angular rotation. Such a winding can reduce the ratio of maximum to minimum output impedance from about 10:1 to about 3:2. It is this variation in output impedance that reduces the accuracy

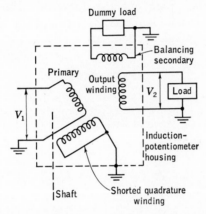

FIG. 4-31. Schematic diagram of precision induction potentiometer with balance and compensating windings.

of both loaded resistance and loaded induction potentiometers. Notwithstanding the use of the quadrature winding, the induction potentiometer is not to be heavily loaded, and is most accurate when terminated in accordance with manufacturer's specifications. Nonstandard loading not only changes scaling, but also distorts the performance curve.

An additional dummy secondary, terminated in a standard load, is also used in most induction potentiometers to maintain constant primary impedance and input current with shaft rotation. Figure 4-31 shows a schematic of an induction potentiometer with dummy windings.

In the application of precision potentiometers, the mechanical mounting and driving members must have a precision commensurate with the required electrical accuracy. The restricted usable angle of the induction potentiometer has both advantages and disadvantages. Since the complete angular motion is obtained in less than one revolution, high ratio gearing is required between the potentiometer and its drive motor.

Backlash must be low, particularly on the low-speed end. On the other hand, an induction potentiometer can move rapidly between its limits of operation, resulting in a fast-acting control with little generation of radio noise.

Because continuous rotation is possible, limit stops are not required. But for applications requiring only limited rotation, the induction potentiometer can be simplified mechanically and appreciably shortened, by using pigtails and limit stops in lieu of slip rings. When used as pickoff units (as with gyroscopes), jewel bearings can be used, or better yet, the rotor can be attached to the moving member and the stator mounted on the reference frame.

4-20. Induction-potentiometer Calculations. In general, induction component calculations parallel those discussed in the resolver section. The derivation of booster compensating techniques and performance calculations using the equivalent circuit are similar to the analogous resolver calculations.

REFERENCES

1. Davis, S. A.: Application Factors for Electrical Resolvers, *Elec. Mfg.*, March, 1953.
2. "Resolver Handbook," Reeves Instrument Corp., 1954.
3. Davis, S. A.: Induction Potentiometer as an Angular Position Indicator, *Prod. Eng.*, August, 1954, p. 138.

Chapter 5

TACHOMETERS

5-1. Introduction. A tachometer is a rotating electromagnetic component that generates an electrical output proportional to shaft speed. In automatic control systems tachometers perform two principal functions: closed-loop stabilization and computation. Examples of the computation function include the use of tachometers in speed control, or for the integration of electrical signals.

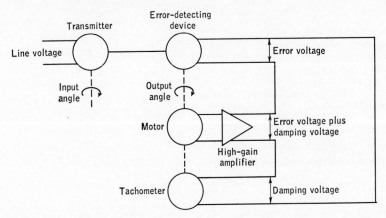

FIG. 5-1. Conventional position servo using a tachometer for velocity damping.

Figure 5-1 shows a tachometer used for velocity damping in a conventional position servo system. In this application, load is remotely positioned in accordance with the angular input to a transmitter. The tachometer and motor are mechanically connected to the output shaft of the error-detecting device, with the tachometer supplying damping proportional to shaft speed. An error voltage, proportional to the difference between the input and output angles, plus the speed-sensitive tachometer voltage are applied to the motor through a high-gain amplifier. The damping voltage introduces a corrective torque on the load shaft somewhat in advance of the undamped error. This improves system stability.

189

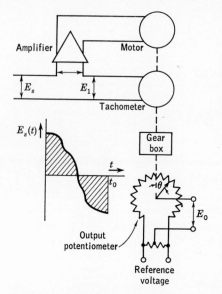

Application of the tachometer as an integrator is illustrated in Fig. 5-2. The input voltage to be integrated, $E_s(t)$, is a function of time. The output voltage E_O is proportional to the time integral of $E_s(t)$ from time t equals 0 to t_O or

$$E_O \alpha \int_0^{t_o} E_s(t) \, dt \qquad (5\text{-}1)$$

Thus E_O is proportional to the cross-sectioned area between those time limits under the curve representing $E_s(t)$. For integrations the tachometer output is equated continuously to E_s. This is achieved by applying the difference in those signals to a high-gain servo amplifier which powers the tachometer-drive motor. Any deviation produces a corrective modification in tachometer speed. The total angular rotation of the tachometer during an integration operation is transmitted by a gear reducer to the output potentiometer.

Fig. 5-2. Simplified schematic of tachometer integrator circuit. E_s = signal voltage; E_1 = tachometer voltage; E_O = output voltage; K = tachometer voltage per rpm; N = tachometer rpm; $\epsilon = E_s - E_1$; θ = total angular rotation of generator.

The following equations show that the potentiometer output is proportional to the integral of $E_s(t)$:

$$E_1 = KN \qquad (5\text{-}2)$$

and

$$\int_0^{t_o} E_s(t) \, dt = \int_0^{t_o} KN \, dt = K \int_0^{t_o} N \, dt \qquad (5\text{-}3)$$

but

$$\int_0^{t_o} N \, dt$$

is proportional to the total angular rotation of the output potentiometer and, therefore, proportional to E_O so that Eq. (5-1) applies.

The circuits of Fig. 5-1 and 5-2 can be used in either a-c or d-c applications by the selection of the appropriate system components.

For integration, or computation in general, maximum quality is required since the accuracy of the operation depends directly on the approximation to ideal performance of the tachometer. On the other hand, a damping tachometer need not be especially accurate, but must be essentially free from noise and extraneous effects. Linearity errors of the order of several per cent can usually be tolerated.

The liberal linearity specifications for damping generators permits the designer to achieve a high output gradient with improved signal-to-noise ratio. Computing tachometers with their tight linearity requirements, on the other hand, must rely on the utmost manufacturing precision, and on the quality of standardization and compensation to achieve a suitable signal-to-noise ratio.

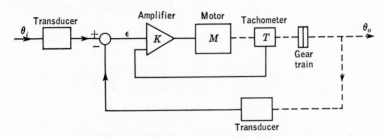

FIG. 5-3. Tachometer-stabilized servomechanism.

In a linear servomechanism, tachometer damping is the exact analytical equivalent of viscous drag on the motor shaft (Fig. 5-3). Varying the percentage of tachometer feedback in effect varies the damping factor D of the system. The open-loop transfer function of a servomotor coupled to a load is given by

$$\frac{\theta_0}{E} = \frac{K/D}{p(1 + pJ/D)} \tag{5-4}$$

where θ_0 = angular position of load shaft
J = system inertia
D = damping factor
K = stiffness or torque gradient of load shaft
J/D = time constant (usually minimized for closed-loop stability)

The ratio K/D is known as the velocity constant and is an inverse measure of the tracking error with uniform output velocity. For a high-velocity constant, D cannot be excessive. Therefore, to achieve satisfactory stability (minimum J/D) a low inertia is desirable. Since the tachometer is inherently a high-speed device, it can add considerable inertia if care is not taken in tachometer design. With tachometer feedback, the effective time constant becomes

$$\frac{J_m + J_T}{D_m + D_T} \tag{5-5}$$

where J_m = motor inertia
J_T = reflected tachometer inertia
D_m = motor viscous-friction damping
D_T = effective equivalent tachometer damping

If J_T is much greater than J_m, the tachometer may contribute no net benefit to performance.

The salient features of tachometer damping in comparison with viscous-friction damping are revealed when nonlinearity is encountered. Because of motor-amplifier saturation, the available control power is limited. Thus, viscous-friction damping reduces the system rating during extremes of operation by subtracting torque directly from the motor shaft. On the other hand, tachometer inertia reduces the maximum acceleration of which a servomotor is capable. Tachometer damping is frequently superior to ordinary network damping in systems where static friction is present, since the relative gain at zero speed (static positioning) can be made extremely high for comparable stability.

5-2. Types of Tachometers. The variety of speed-measuring devices is endless and possibly in specialized control applications very unusual techniques may find use. However, this coverage will be limited to those techniques that have found more or less common usage in automatic control systems. This limitation is normally established by accuracy requirements and the ease with which the output signal can be converted to a usable form.

The types of speed-measuring devices that are most commonly used in control systems are given below.

A-C Induction Tachometers. For use in a-c control systems. These devices are noted for high accuracy and excellent reliability.

D-C Tachometers. For use in d-c control systems. The best obtainable accuracy is about $\frac{1}{4}$ per cent, and unreliability is a handicap.

Other devices are not as important or widely used as those mentioned above, but will be treated briefly.

A-C Bridge Circuits. Although the adjustment and the control of tolerance is difficult, these devices are small and can be used to save space in special applications.

D-C Bridge Circuits. Widely used in d-c speed-regulating systems. They are efficient and compact.

A-C and D-C Operational Circuits. The output of these devices only approximates a linear relationship; however, they are useful in rough computation problems, and for derivative stabilization.

Capacitor Tachometers. Units are compact and accurate but suffer from poor waveform, high ripple, and poor low-speed performance.

Drag-torque Tachometers. Useful where maximum flexibility is required since input is completely isolated from output. The accuracy is medium.

Permanent-magnet Alternators. These devices are used with a rectifying circuit in unidirectional speed control. Performance is poor at low speeds; however, high output units are available with excellent linearity.

5-3. Tachometer Performance Criteria. Regardless of the type, each of the speed-measuring devices listed above has certain basic accuracy considerations. The points of importance under steady-state operating conditions are given below. Although all the items do not apply to every type of speed-measuring device, they may influence the selection of a tachometer for a specific application and should be considered when standardizing and compensating a unit.

Tachometer Linearity. Variation of output voltage from a linear relation with speed.

Output Waveform. Influenced by harmonics, ripple, and phase angle.

Stability of Output with Time. Instability is caused by the aging of parts, shifts in the magnetic circuit, and brush wear.

Stability of Output with Temperature. Depends on the temperature sensitivity of the magnetic properties of the iron and the resistivity of the windings. Also, changing mechanical dimensions because of thermal expansion.

Effect of Normal Variations in Input Voltage and Frequency. Results in inaccuracies if saturation curves are nonlinear or if permeability varies with flux density.

Zero-speed Output Signal. Caused by harmonic or fundamental residual in the zero-speed output of a-c units.

Generation of Radio Noise. Caused by sliding contacts on commutator, arcing, or ripple.

Phase Shift. In a-c systems, signals can only be handled algebraically when they are exactly in phase.

Acceleration Errors. During acceleration additional generated voltages occur and time lags are introduced that modify the accuracy of the output.

Although accuracy is usually the most important factor in selecting a tachometer, the required driving torque of the tachometer inertia, and its effect on automatic control system operation, reliability, and the size of the tachometer and any associated equipment, are also important considerations. The relative influence of each of these factors should be balanced against one another in selecting a tachometer for a particular application.

5-4. A-C Induction-generator Tachometers. The induction tachometer is similar in appearance to a two-phase induction motor. However, the tachometer is excited on only one phase, and a voltage of line frequency approximately proportional to the speed of shaft rotation is generated on the unexcited or output phase. Its advantages lie in its unique adaptability to a-c control systems and in the high-quality output obtainable with careful design. Possessing a ruggedness comparable to that of a squirrel-cage motor, a drag-cup tachometer can generate a clean signal of high accuracy, free of radio-frequency noise and magnetic slot ripple.

The ideal unit has the following characteristics when a sinusoidal excitation is applied to the main winding: the output voltage is proportional to shaft speed; at any speed the output voltage is proportional to input voltage; the phase of the output with respect to the input at any speed is either 0 or 180°, depending on the direction of shaft rotation; and the output does not contain any residual voltages.

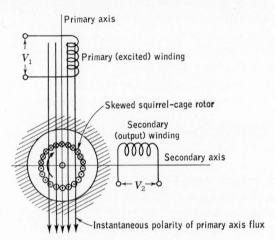

Primary axis

V_1 Primary (excited) winding

Skewed squirrel-cage rotor

Secondary (output) winding

Secondary axis

V_2

Instantaneous polarity of primary axis flux

$\otimes$ = Current or voltage vector directed inward
$\odot$ = Current or voltage vector directed outward
V_1 = Complex voltage applied to primary winding
V_2 = Complex voltage obtained from output winding

FIG. 5-4. Schematic diagram of squirrel-cage induction tachometer.

A schematic representation of an induction tachometer is shown in Fig. 5-4. Excitation is applied to the primary stator winding. The secondary winding is located 90 electrical degrees from the primary winding, and delivers the output voltage. The rotor is shown as a squirrel-cage type. In precision units a drag-cup rotor construction is employed.

As a simplifying assumption the rotor-bar inductance is neglected. This is a legitimate approximation for well-designed tachometers. The bar currents resulting from rotation will therefore be in phase with the generated voltage due to rotation, and a flux field is produced by the rotor along the secondary axis. If the primary axis flux pulsates sinusoidally, a sinusoidal voltage of the same frequency, fixed phase, and proportional to rotational speed is generated in the secondary winding. This represents tachometer action.

Stator leakage reactance and resistance, core losses, and rotor-bar inductance, which were neglected in this description, cause actual tachometer performance to vary from this ideal. These items introduce nonlinearity and a shift in the output phase with increasing generator speed.

5-5. Factors Preventing Ideal Performance. There are three principal types of errors that prevent the ideal performance of an induction generator. These are listed in Table 5-1 as residual voltage at zero speed, nonlinearity, and voltage gradient and phase-angle errors at low speeds.

TABLE 5-1. PRINCIPAL INDUCTION-GENERATOR ERRORS

Type of error	Components of errors	Sources of error voltage	External conditions affecting errors
Residual voltage at zero speed	Fundamental frequency voltage independent of rotor position: in-phase,* quadrature†	Unsymmetrical magnetic circuit. Nonuniformity of magnetic material. Irregular machining of airgap surfaces	Primary voltage, temperature, strained housing caused by careless installation
	Fundamental frequency voltage varying with rotor position: in-phase,* quadrature†	Nonuniformity of drag cup caused by nonhomogeneity of material and irregular machining	Relatively independent of external conditions
	Harmonic frequency	Excessive flux density causing saturation. Nonuniform permeability of magnetic material due to mechanical strain and directional properties	Primary voltage, frequency
Nonlinearity	In-phase voltage* Quadrature voltage†	Leakage reactance and resistance of primary winding causing reduction in primary flux with increasing speed. Rotor leakage also causes nonlinearity, but effect is negligible in drag cup	Relatively independent of external conditions
Voltage gradient and phase-angle errors at low speeds	Gradient Phase angle	Inaccurate standardization of phase angle and gradient by manufacturer. Deviation from conditions under which standardization was performed	Temperature, primary voltage, frequency

* In-phase error voltage is fundamental frequency error in time phase with the rotational voltage at low speed.

† Quadrature error voltage is fundamental frequency error voltage in time quadrature with the rotational voltage at low speeds.

As shown in Fig. 5-5, mechanical and magnetic dissymmetries distort the flux paths so that even at zero speed an output voltage is developed. The departure from the ideal geometry of the tachometer, in the form of an out-of-round rotor, causes undesirable coupling between the primary and secondary stator windings. This results in an output or residual voltage being induced in the secondary winding even though the rotor is stationary. This zero-speed output voltage exerts a deleterious effect on system performance, and tachometer manufacturers make every effort to minimize it.

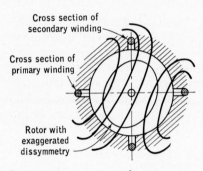

Cross section of secondary winding

Cross section of primary winding

Rotor with exaggerated dissymmetry

Fig. 5-5. An out-of-round rotor causes undesirable coupling between the stator windings.

Residual voltage can be conveniently divided into individual components, with each component contributing its characteristic disturbance to a control system (Table 5-1). Thus, residual voltage resulting from rotor dissymmetry (which varies with rotor position) is considered separately from residual voltage resulting from stator dissymmetry (which is independent of rotor position). As the rotor dissymmetry moves under successive stator poles, the coupling between stator phases varies periodically so that the frequency of repetition per rotor revolution equals the number of stator poles. In contrast, the coupling between stator phases caused by stator dissymmetry is independent of rotor position, and appears as a constant voltage of mutual induction. The variable and fixed residual components as a function of rotor angular position are shown in Fig. 5-6.

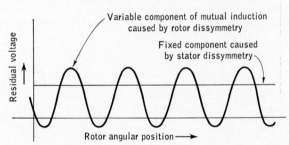

Variable component of mutual induction caused by rotor dissymmetry

Fixed component caused by stator dissymmetry

Residual voltage

Rotor angular position ⟶

Fig. 5-6. Variable and fixed components of residual voltage.

Residual voltage components are minimized by using precision manufacturing techniques and close assembly tolerances in addition to special trimming procedures that are applied during the various stages of assembly and test. Drag-cup rotors yield maximum uniformity. Cup uniformity is maintained by carefully controlling the material with regard to grain structure, by stress relieving after annealing and during assembly, and by boring out of solid stock where highest uniformity is required. In lower-accuracy units the drag cups are drawn. To maintain dimensional stability, all mating parts consist of materials having matching temperature coefficients. Cups are made from noncorroding materials, since 15 millionths of an inch corrosion in a cup of 15-mil wall thickness will cause a 0.1 per cent change in cup resistance and approximately the same change in tachometer output. The external frame is usually made of stainless steel with sufficient strength to prevent distortion of the laminated-iron stacks in manufacturing or handling.

The material selected for the drag cup must necessarily involve a compromise between temperature sensitivity and high conductivity. Where cups of pure copper or aluminum are chosen, machinability and softness are problems affecting manufacture. Where low inertia is important and resistance variation with temperature is not (as in a damping tachometer), aluminum cups are used. In high-precision devices such as are used in integrating applications, materials with low-temperature coefficients are specified, for example, manganin and Advance. However, these latter materials have such high resistivity that the output gradient is low. To increase the output signal, a large number of output turns are necessary, thereby increasing the output impedance. Careful and expensive manufacturing techniques are required to keep the signal-to-noise ratio at a suitable level.

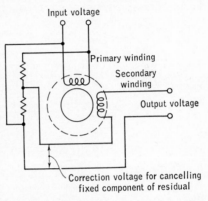

Fig. 5-7. Simple network for canceling fixed residual component.

In correcting for drag-cup dissymmetry, a notch or other intentionally introduced dissymmetry may be added. If properly located and of the correct magnitude, the added dissymmetry will cancel the existing dissymmetry. Similar procedures are applied to the stator, where stator teeth can be filed to introduce dissymmetry.

There are various methods of compensating for fixed coupling resulting from unsymmetrical stator shapes. One method is to connect the input and output with a network consisting of variable resistors and capacitors. Figure 5-7 shows one example of a simple network used for canceling the fixed residual component. Another technique is intentionally to place a slot on the laminated core where the entire core is mounted on a bolt through its center. This is shown in Fig. 5-8. The core can then be rotated, placing an adjustable stator dissymmetry in the circuit. Properly positioning the core will give minimum fixed coupling between stator input and output windings.

One type has the input windings on the outer laminated stator structure and the output windings on the laminated center core. With this arrangement, coupling is minimized by locking the center core in the best relative position. Still another design places the wound rotor in the center inside the cup. While this type of unit is cheaper and has a more stable structure, concentrating the windings at the center requires a larger-diameter cup with a resultant increase in inertia.

Depending on its phase angle, the fundamental frequency residual may appear to the external system as an apparent rotational voltage, or as an out-of-phase component tending to cause amplifier saturation. Time harmonics resulting from magnetic circuit nonlinearity tend also to

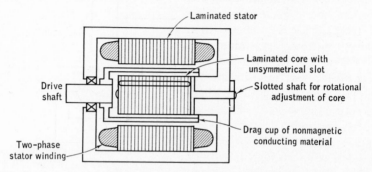

Fig. 5-8. Stator coupling can be adjusted to minimum by rotating slotted center core.

saturate high-gain amplifiers. Filters are generally not convenient for the elimination of harmonics, since their characteristics frequently change sharply with change in line frequency. They also introduce stability problems in closed-loop systems.

In addition to residual voltage, the induction tachometer is subject to two other types of errors: nonlinearity, and gradient and phase-angle errors. These are most easily defined in terms of the fundamental equation for tachometer speed-sensitive or rotational output voltage. This is in contrast to the residual output which exists independent of rotation.

Generator output voltage can be determined from the following relationship derived later in the chapter:

$$\frac{V_2}{V_1} = \frac{Av}{1 + Bv^2} \tag{5-6}$$

where V_1 = applied voltage on primary winding
  V_2 = rotational voltage induced in secondary winding (V_1 and V_2 are fundamental frequency components)
  A = complex tachometer gradient

B = complex nonlinearity coefficient

$$v = \frac{\text{actual rpm, } N}{\text{synchronous rpm, } N_s} = \frac{NP}{120f}$$

$$N_s = \frac{120f}{P}$$

P = number of tachometer poles

f = line frequency

At low speed v is small, making the Bv^2 term negligible. Then for practical purposes the right-hand side of Eq. (5-6) is Av, and the voltage output V_2 is proportional to speed for constant primary excitation. At synchronous speed A is the output voltage per volt input, neglecting Bv^2. It is known as the generator gradient and is the initial slope or gradient line (Fig. 5-9). When A is a real number, the output voltage and input voltage are in phase. This is a desirable condition, since the tachometer generator is normally used with other system components, and proper system operation occurs when all the a-c voltages are in phase.

In an as-manufactured condition, the value of A for most units will vary considerably. To adjust A to a standard real value, either the manufacturer or the user must add suitable networks to the primary or secondary circuit. Temperature compensation is also frequently included in these networks.

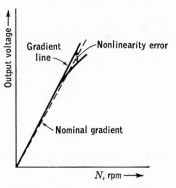

FIG. 5-9. Tachometer gradient characteristic.

Thus, gradient and phase angle errors are introduced by any condition which tends to make A deviate from a standard real value.

The Bv^2 term introduces curvature in the output-voltage curve (Fig. 5-9). The value of B depends on the leakage impedance of the primary winding. It is usually small enough to be neglected, except in the most exacting applications, if the speed is kept under about one-third synchronous speed.

In high-quality units a nominal gradient is set by the manufacturer for minimum nonlinear error over maximum velocity range. This gradient is determined from laboratory measurements on typical samples. The nominal gradient line intersects the actual output curve at approximately $\sqrt{3}/2$ times the maximum speed.

5-6. Equivalent-circuit Analysis. A more rigorous treatment of the performance characteristics of induction tachometers can be obtained from calculations based upon the equivalent circuit of Fig. 5-10, as derived in Ref. 6. There is a direct correspondence between the elements in the equivalent circuit and the elements in an induction tachometer so that the effect of variations in each can be observed. Thus variations in frequency will cause a shift in reactance parameters, and if rpm is held constant the ratio of actual speed to synchronous speed v will vary. Similarly, temperature variations will cause the circuit resistances to change in a known manner. If the equivalent-circuit constants are known, all the performance characteristics of the tachometer, including

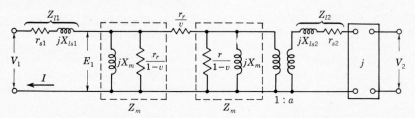

Fig. 5-10. Complete equivalent circuit of an induction-generator tachometer.

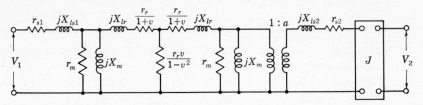

Fig. 5-11. Simplified equivalent circuit for drag-cup construction. Rotor leakage X_{lr} and core loss r_m are considered negligible.

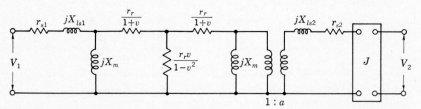

Fig. 5-12. Equivalent circuit for $T - \pi$ transformation.

its input and output impedances, can be determined. Using this information, temperature compensation and equalizer networks can be designed where required.

The complete equivalent circuit for an induction generator is shown in Fig. 5-10 (Symbol designations are given in Table 5-2.) By using the drag-cup-type construction the rotor leakage and core loss can be assumed to be negligible. This follows since the conductive drag cup is not surrounded by a mass of iron that could cause rotor leakage. Also, the large airgap results in low flux per ampere-turn excitation, and relatively low core losses. With these assumptions, the equivalent circuit can be reduced to the simplified version shown in Fig. 5-11. In turn, Fig. 5-12 is derived by means of a T-π transformation on the three rotor resistance elements that constitute the interphase coupling.

TABLE 5-2. SYMBOL DESIGNATIONS

V_1 = applied voltage on primary winding, nonlinearity neglected (B equals 0)

V_2 = secondary output voltage

E_1 = effective primary voltage which is generating airgap flux

K = complex constant representing effect of rotor on primary voltage

a = ratio of secondary effective turns to primary effective turns

I = primary current from constant-current source

r_{s1} = resistance of primary winding

r_{s2} = resistance of secondary winding

r_a = phase shift adjusting resistor

X_{ls1} = leakage reactance of primary winding

X_{ls2} = leakage reactance of secondary winding

r_r = equivalent drag-cup resistance

r_m = core loss

X_{lr} = rotor leakage

X_m = shunting impedance of primary winding

Z'_{in} = input impedance of primary winding

Z'_{out} = output impedance of secondary winding

Z_1 = secondary load impedance

Z_{l1} = impedance of primary winding

Z_{l2} = impedance of secondary winding

Z_m = impedance of $r_r/(1 - v)$ and jx_m in parallel

v = ratio of actual speed to synchronous speed

The object of the following is to derive a simple method of calculating the complex circuit of Fig. 5-12 and to establish convenient approximations for practical tachometers. Initially assume that the secondary is open-circuited (a legitimate assumption, say, when feeding the grid of a tube) and that Z_1 equals 0. Determine the ratio of V_2/E_1 by inspection.

$$\frac{V_2}{E_1} = \frac{jaZ_m}{r_r/v + Z_m} \tag{5-7}$$

Solving for Z_m, the networks included in the dotted boxes of Fig. 5-12

$$Z_m = X_m \frac{[\alpha/(1 - v)]j}{\alpha/(1 - v) + j}$$

where $\alpha = \dfrac{r_r}{X_m}$

Simplifying,

$$\frac{Z_m}{X_m} = \alpha \frac{1 - v + j\alpha}{\alpha^2 + (1 - v)^2} \tag{5-8}$$

Substitute Eq. (5-8) in Eq. (5-7) to determine V_2/E_1 in terms of a, v, and α.

$$\frac{V_2}{E_1} = \frac{jav}{1 - j\alpha} = Kav \tag{5-9}$$

where K is the complex constant of proportionality that determines the effect of rotor coupling on the voltage induced in the secondary. V_2/E_1 varies linearly with v. If the ratio V_2/E_1 or K is plotted as a function of α, for av equals 1, the nomogram shown in Fig. 5-13 is obtained. This is a useful device in determining induction-generator performance and in calculating compensating networks. Examples including the use of the nomogram are covered later.

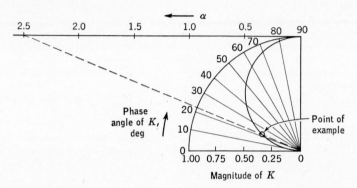

FIG. 5-13. Nomogram for determining the effect of rotor coupling on the voltage induced in the secondary. Example: $r_r = 1,000$ ohms; $X_m = 400$ ohms; $r_r/X_m = \alpha = 2.5$; $K = 0.372\underline{/21.8°}$.

The next step is to determine the ratio E_1/V_1 as a function of v to complete the performance equation. To determine this ratio, first derive an expression for Z_{in}, the total impedance across which E_1 acts.

$$Z_{in} = \frac{Z_m(r_r/v + Z_m)}{r_r/v + 2Z_m}$$

which can be expressed in the form

$$\frac{Z_{in}}{X_m} = \frac{\alpha/(1 - j\alpha)}{1 - [v^2/(1 - j\alpha)]} \tag{5-10}$$

The nonlinear characteristics of the tachometer are caused by variations of Z_{in} with speed. To calculate the nonlinearity, determine a general expression for the per cent change in Z_{in} as a function of v.

At very low speeds, v^2 is small and can be neglected so that Eq. (5-10) can be expressed as

$$\frac{Z_{in}}{X_m}\bigg]_{\substack{low \\ speed}} = \frac{\alpha}{1 - j\alpha}$$

The per unit change in Z_{in}, $\Delta Z_{\text{in}}/Z_{\text{in}}$, can be determined by

$$\frac{Z_{\text{in}}/X_m]_{\substack{\text{low} \\ \text{speed}}} - Z_{\text{in}}/X_m}{Z_{\text{in}}/X_m]_{\substack{\text{low} \\ \text{speed}}}} = \frac{[\alpha/(1 - j\alpha)] - \left[\dfrac{\alpha/(1 - j\alpha)}{1 - (v^2/[1 - j\alpha])} \right]}{\alpha/(1 - j\alpha)}$$

or

$$\frac{\Delta Z_{\text{in}}}{Z_{\text{n}}} = \frac{-v^2}{(1 - j\alpha)^2 - v^2} = \frac{-(v/[1 - j\alpha])^2}{1 - (v/[1 - j\alpha])^2} \qquad (5\text{-}11)$$

This can be expressed approximately as

$$\frac{\Delta Z_{\text{in}}}{Z_{\text{in}}} = -\left(\frac{v}{1 - j\alpha} \right)^2 \qquad (5\text{-}12)$$

Thus, tachometer nonlinearity depends on the parameter $(v/[1 - j\alpha])^2$ as expressed by Eq. (5-11).

The next step is to derive an expression relating the per unit change in E_1/V_1 to $\Delta Z_{\text{in}}/Z_{\text{in}}$. For this condition Z_{l1} is included and no longer assumed to be zero. Thus

$$\frac{E_1}{V_1} = \frac{Z_{\text{in}}}{Z_{l1} + Z_{\text{in}}} \qquad (5\text{-}13)$$

Differentiating E_1/V_1 with respect to Z_{in}

$$\frac{\Delta(E_1/V_1)}{\Delta Z_{\text{in}}} = \frac{Z_{l1}}{(Z_{l1} + Z_{\text{in}})^2}$$

Multiplying each side by ΔZ_{in} and dividing each side by E_1/V_1, the following expression is obtained

$$\frac{\Delta(E_1/V_1)}{E_1/V_1} = \frac{Z_{l1}}{Z_{l1} + Z_{\text{in}}} \frac{\Delta Z_{\text{in}}}{Z_{\text{in}}} \qquad (5\text{-}14)$$

In this equation $\Delta Z_{\text{in}}/Z_{\text{in}}$ is equivalent to the per unit change in Z_{in} so that

$$\frac{\Delta(E_1/V_1)}{E_1/V_1} = \frac{Z_{l1}}{Z'_{\text{in}}} \frac{\Delta Z_{\text{in}}}{Z_{\text{in}}} \qquad (5\text{-}15)$$

where $\dfrac{\Delta(E_1/V_1)}{E_1/V_1}$ = per unit change in E_1/V_1

$Z'_{\text{in}} = Z_{l1} + Z_{\text{in}}$

By substituting Eqs. (5-10) and (5-12) in Eq. (5-15) and neglecting the v^2 term as being negligible $\Delta(E_1/V_1)/(E_1/V_1)$ or the per unit error in linearity can be expressed by

$$\frac{\Delta(E_1/V_1)}{E_1/V_1} = \frac{-v^2\tau}{\tau(1 - j\alpha)^2 + \alpha(1 - j\alpha)} \qquad (5\text{-}16)$$

where $\tau = \dfrac{Z_{l1}}{X_m}$

For a tachometer operating with an open-circuited secondary, this equation establishes the total per unit error in linearity.   With the error varying with the square of the speed, operation is highly linear in the lower speed ranges.

In addition to a linear proportionality between the input voltage and output voltage, and between speed and output voltage, the relative phase angle of the input and output is also important.   Since these components operate in closed-loop systems, the output is usually required to be exactly in phase or exactly 180° out-of-phase with respect to the input. While this condition may not exist in a standard as-purchased unit, compensation in the form of series resistance in the primary circuit can be added for in-phase adjustment.

To determine the proper compensating series resistance, the over-all function relating input V_1 to output V_2 must be obtained.   By substituting in Eq. (5-13)

$$\frac{E_1}{V_1} = \frac{\alpha}{\alpha + \tau(1 - j\alpha)} \tag{5-17}$$

The over-all tachometer performance can be expressed by

$$\frac{V_2}{V_1} = \frac{V_2}{E_1}\frac{E_1}{V_1}$$

or substituting Eqs. (5-9) and (5-17)

$$\frac{V_2}{V_1} = \frac{jav}{1 - j\alpha}\frac{\alpha}{\alpha + \tau(1 - j\alpha)}$$

or

$$\frac{V_2}{V_1} = \frac{jav\alpha}{\alpha + \tau - 2j\alpha\tau - j\alpha^2 - \alpha^2\tau} \tag{5-18}$$

To permit the calculation of the compensating resistance, express τ as a complex number

$$\tau = \tau_r + j\tau_x \tag{5-19}$$

where $\tau_x = \dfrac{X_{ls1}}{X_m}$

$\tau_r = \dfrac{r_a + r_{s1}}{X_m}$

r_a = compensating resistance

Substituting Eq. (5-19) in Eq. (5-18),

$$\frac{V_2}{V_1} = \frac{jav\alpha}{\alpha + \tau_r + j\tau_x - j\alpha\tau_r + 2\alpha\tau_x - j\alpha^2 - \alpha^2\tau_r - j\alpha^2\tau_x} \tag{5-20}$$

Since the numerator of this equation has a phase angle of 90° leading, for the output to be in phase with the input, the denominator must have an equal phase angle.   To realize this condition, the real terms in the denominator must equal zero or

$$\alpha + \tau_r + 2\alpha\tau_x - \alpha^2\tau_r = 0$$

Solving for τ_r,

$$\tau_r = \frac{1 + 2\tau_x}{\alpha^2 - 1}$$

and

$$r_a = \frac{X_m\alpha(1 + 2\tau_x)}{\alpha^2 - 1} - r_{s1} \qquad (5\text{-}21)$$

As a useful relation in calculating the parameters of an equivalent circuit for a practical tachometer, determine tachometer output as a function of current input. This relation will be useful later. From the equivalent circuit

$$\frac{V_2}{I} = Z_{in}\frac{V_2}{E_1} \qquad (5\text{-}22)$$

Substituting Eqs. (5-9) and (5-10) in Eq. (5-22), the following expression is obtained

$$\frac{V_2}{I} = \frac{javX_m\alpha}{(1 - j\alpha)^2 - v^2}$$

for low speeds v^2 is negligible so that

$$\frac{V_2}{I}\bigg]_{\substack{\text{low}\\\text{speed}}} = \frac{javX_m\alpha}{(1 - j\alpha)^2} \qquad (5\text{-}23)$$

5-7. Typical Equivalent-circuit Calculations. To demonstrate the usefulness of the derived relationships, the following example covers the calculation of the equivalent-circuit constants using the data normally supplied by a tachometer manufacturer. The given information includes:

$V_1 = 115$ volts
$f = 400$ cps
$I = 0.073$ amp (stall)
$p = 5.4$ watts (stall)
Gradient $= 3.1v/1,000$ rpm at $-5°$ phase angle
Maximum speed for linear output $= 5,400$ rpm

The vector diagram relating these given facts is shown in Fig. 5-14. First determine the power factor and in turn the angle θ by which I lags V_1.

$$\text{Power factor} = \cos\theta = \frac{P}{V_1 I}$$

$$\cos\theta = \frac{5.4}{(115)(0.073)} = 0.643$$

$$\theta = 50°$$

The phase shift from I to V_2 with the output leads properly polarized is

$$\theta' = 50 + 175 = 225°$$

The value of α can be calculated from the basic formula Eq. (5-23) since the denominator $(1 - j\alpha)^2$ must contribute the proper phase angle to give a total phase shift of 225°.

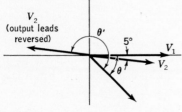

$$90 + 2 \arctan \alpha = 225$$
$$\arctan \alpha = 67.5$$
$$\alpha = 2.42$$

Fig. 5-14. Vector diagram relating given information about induction tachometer performance.

Measure the input and output impedance of the tachometer

$$Z'_{\text{in}} = 1{,}575 \text{ ohms}$$
$$Z'_{\text{out}} = 2{,}200 \text{ ohms}$$

and determine the ratio of secondary effective turns to primary effective turns a. Remember that impedance varies as the square of the turns.

$$a = \sqrt{\frac{Z'_{\text{out}}}{Z'_{\text{in}}}} = \sqrt{\frac{2{,}200}{1{,}575}} = 1.18$$

Since the unit has four poles, the synchronous speed is

$$N_s = \frac{120f}{P} = \frac{120(400)}{4}$$
$$N_s = 12{,}000 \text{ rpm}$$

At a speed of 1,000 rpm, v equals $\frac{1}{12}$ and the output voltage V_2 equals 3.1 from given information. Using Eq. (5-9), determine E_1.

$$\frac{V_2}{E_1} = \frac{jav}{1 - j\alpha}$$
$$E_1 = \frac{V_2(1 - j\alpha)}{jav} = \frac{j3.1(1 - j2.42)}{1.18(\frac{1}{12})}$$

(Sign changed from minus to plus because of polarity of output leads.)

$$E_1 = 82.5\underline{/22.5}$$

The value of E_1 can also be determined by using the nomogram of Fig. 5-13. From the nomogram the value of K is $0.384\underline{/-22.5}$. Then

$$\frac{V_2}{E_1} = avK$$
$$E_1 = \frac{V_2}{avK} = \frac{3.1}{1.18(\frac{1}{12})(0.384\underline{/-22.5})}$$
$$E_1 = 82.5\underline{/22.5}, \text{ which checks first calculation.}$$

From Eq. (5-23) calculate X_m. (Include effect of output lead reversal.)

$$\frac{V_2}{I} = \frac{javX_m\alpha}{(1 - j\alpha)^2}$$

$$\frac{3.1\underline{/-5}}{0.073\underline{/-50}} = \frac{-j(1.18)(\frac{1}{2})(2.42)X_m}{(1 - j2.42)^2}$$

Solving, $\qquad\qquad X_m = 1{,}220$ ohms

and since $\qquad\qquad \alpha = \dfrac{r_r}{X_m}$

then $\qquad r_r = \alpha X_m = 2.42(1{,}220) = 2{,}960$ ohms

Now determine the leakage impedance r_{s1} and X_{ls1} from the parameters that have already been calculated (Fig. 5-15). The equivalent input

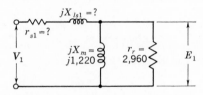

Fig. 5-15. Partially complete equivalent circuit for low speeds.

circuit at low speeds (v is negligible) is

$$\frac{E_1}{V_1} = \frac{jr_rX_m}{(r_{s1}r_r - X_{ls1}X_m) + j(r_rX_{ls1} + r_{s1}X_m + r_rX_m)} \tag{5-24}$$

and from previously calculated data

$$\frac{E_1}{V_1} = \frac{82.5\underline{/22.5}}{115\underline{/0}} = 0.719\underline{/22.5} \tag{5-25}$$

In Eq. (5-24) normalize by dividing numerator and denominator by $X_m{}^2$ and substitute

$$\frac{r_{s1}}{X_m} = \tau_r$$

and $\qquad\qquad \dfrac{X_{ls1}}{X_m} = \tau_x$

This gives

$$\frac{E_1}{V_1} = \frac{j\alpha}{(\tau_r\alpha - \tau_x) + j(\tau_x\alpha + \tau_r + \alpha)} \tag{5-26}$$

To satisfy the relation expressed by Eq. (5-25), the denominator of Eq. (5-26) must contribute a phase angle of 67.5°. Thus,

$$\arctan \frac{\tau_x\alpha + \tau_r + \alpha}{\tau_r\alpha - \tau_x} = 67.5° \tag{5-27}$$

Determine the magnitude ratio for E_1/V_1 by obtaining the magnitude of each of the complex quantities of Eq. (5-26).

$$\frac{E_1}{V_1} = \frac{\alpha}{[(\tau_r\alpha - \tau_x)^2 + (\alpha\tau_x + \tau_r + \alpha)^2]^{1/2}}$$

Square both sides of this equation and substitute value of E_1/V_1 from Eq. (5-25).

$$0.517 = \frac{\alpha^2}{(\tau_r\alpha - \tau_x)^2 + (\alpha\tau_x + \tau_r + \alpha)^2}$$

Since α equals 2.42, solve for τ_r and τ_x. Substitute Eq. (5-27) in Eq. (5-26).

$$(\tau_r\alpha - \tau_x)\tan 67.5 = \alpha + \tau_r + \tau_x\alpha$$
$$0.517 = \frac{\alpha^2}{(\tau_r\alpha - \tau_x)^2(1 + \tan^2 67.5°)}$$
$$2.42\tau_r - \tau_x = 1.29 \tag{5-28}$$

Substitute Eq. (5-28) in Eq. (5-27)

$$\tau_x\alpha + \tau_r + \alpha = 1.29 \tan 67.5$$
$$\tau_r + 2.42\tau_x = 0.70 \tag{5-29}$$

Solve Eqs. (5-28) and (5-29) simultaneously for τ_r and τ_x.

$$\tau_r = 0.558$$
$$\tau_x = 0.0584$$

Therefore
$$r_{s1} = 0.558X_m = 680 \text{ ohms}$$
$$X_{ls1} = 0.0584X_m = 71.1 \text{ ohms}$$

Thus the final equivalent circuit is as shown in Fig. 5-16. As a rough check on the calculated circuit parameters, determine the calculated

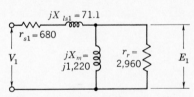

FIG. 5-16. Complete equivalent circuit.

power dissipation in the unit and compare with the measured stall power as specified in the given data. Power dissipation in the cup P_c can be expressed by

$$P_c = \frac{E_1^2}{r_r}$$
$$P_c = \frac{(82.5)^2}{2,960} = 2.3 \text{ watts}$$

Power dissipation in the series resistor P_r can be expressed by

$$P_r = I^2 r_{s1}$$
$$P_r = (0.073)^2\, 680 = 3.62$$

The total calculated power is P_c plus P_r, or 5.92 watts. This compares reasonably well with the measured stall power of 5.4 watts.

The final step is to calculate the nonlinearity error. From the given information, the maximum linear speed is 5,400 rpm so that

$$v = \frac{5,400}{12,000} = 0.45$$

From Eq. (5-12), the per unit change in Z_{in}, $\Delta Z_{in}/Z_{in}$, is

$$\frac{\Delta Z_{in}}{Z_{in}} = \frac{-v^2}{(1 - j\alpha)^2 - v^2} \qquad (5\text{-}12)$$

$$\frac{\Delta Z_{in}}{Z_{in}} = \frac{-(0.45)^2}{(1 - j2.42)^2 - (0.45)^2} = -0.0286\underline{/135}$$

The per unit change in the output gradient, $\Delta(E_1/V_1)/(E_1/V_1)$, can be calculated using Eq. (5-15)

$$\frac{\Delta(E_1/V_1)}{E_1/V_1} = \frac{Z_{l1}}{Z'_{in}}\frac{\Delta Z_{in}}{Z_{in}} \qquad (5\text{-}15)$$

The value of Z_{in} has been measured as 1,575 ohms at a phase angle of 50° corresponding to the phase angle between I and V_1 and Z_{l1} can be calculated from the relation

$$Z_{l1} = \tau X_m$$

where $\tau = \tau_r + j\tau_x$
or for a small value of τ_x

$$Z_{l1} = \tau_r X_m$$

Thus $\qquad \dfrac{\Delta(E_1/V_1)}{E_1/V_1} = \dfrac{(0.558)(1,220)}{1,575\underline{/50}}\,(-0.0286\underline{/135})$

$$\frac{\Delta(E_1/V_1)}{E_1/V_1} = 0.0123\underline{/-95}$$

This is about a 1.23 per cent shift in output and exactly in quadrature phase since the output was specified to be at a $-5°$ phase angle.

5-8. Standardization and Compensation. In addition to being useful for calculating the nonlinearity effects of tachometer performance, the equivalent circuit is also helpful in developing compensating and standardizing procedures. This method is useful either in the case of adjusting a nonstandard unit for application as an induction tachometer, or where a standardized and compensated unit is applied under other than specified conditions.

Often the application of a tachometer to a specific system involves being able to calculate or approximate such factors as the primary series resistance required to zero the output phase angle, the generator gradient, generator reaction to frequency fluctuations, and the effect of temperature variations on performance. The equivalent circuit is especially useful for such calculations.

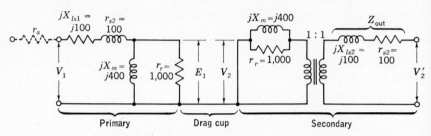

FIG. 5-17. Equivalent circuit for sample problem.   On open circuit $V_2 = V_2'$.

For example, assume that a two-phase four-pole 400-cps 115-volt drag-cup servomotor is to be evaluated for possible applications as an induction tachometer. The equivalent-circuit constants (Fig. 5-17), as determined by test and calculation, are as follows:

$$r_{s1} = r_{s2} = 100 \text{ ohms}$$
$$X_{ls1} = X_{ls2} = 100 \text{ ohms}$$
$$X_m = 400 \text{ ohms}$$
$$r_r = 1,000 \text{ ohms}$$
$$a = 1$$

The load impedance is considered infinite.   This condition applies if the output winding feeds the grid of a vacuum tube.

1. What value of series resistance is required in the main winding to zero the output phase?

Using Eq. (5-21), the compensating resistor has a value

$$r_a = \frac{X_m \alpha (1 + 2\tau_x)}{\alpha^2 - 1} - r_{s1} \qquad (5\text{-}21)$$

where $\alpha = \dfrac{r_r}{X_m} = \dfrac{1,000}{400} = 2.5$

$\tau_x = \dfrac{X_{ls1}}{X_m} = \dfrac{100}{400} = 0.25$

$r_a = \dfrac{400(2.5)(1.5)}{2.5^2 - 1} - 100 = 186 \text{ ohms}$

2. At what voltage should the primary winding be operated when the unit is used as a generator?

Although the component is rated at 115 volts when used as a motor, generator excitation voltage should be about 80 volts, thereby reducing core saturation and residual harmonics.

3. With the output phase adjusted to zero degrees by the addition of r_a, and the applied voltage 80 volts, what will be the output gradient?

To determine the ratio of V_2/V_1 for synchronous speed use Eq. (5-20).

$$\frac{V_2}{V_1} = \frac{jav\ \alpha}{\alpha + \tau_r + j\tau_x - j\alpha\tau_r + 2\alpha\tau_x - j\alpha^2 - \alpha^2\tau_r - j\alpha^2\tau_x} \quad (5\text{-}20)$$

where $v = 1$

$$\tau_r = \frac{186 + 100}{400} = 0.717$$

$$\tau_x = 0.25$$

$$\frac{V_2}{V_1} = \frac{j2.5}{[2.5 + 0.717 + 2(2.5)(0.25) - 2.5^2(0.717)]} + j[0.25 - 2.5(0.717) - (2.5)^2 - 0.717(2.5)^2]$$

Calculating the magnitude and phase angle of this relation gives the following result:

$$\frac{V_2}{V_1} = A = 0.224\underline{/0} \quad \text{volts/volt input}$$

In addition to giving the tachometer gradient A (neglecting nonlinearities) this also shows that the calculated compensating resistance r_a is correct since the over-all phase shift is zero.

For V_1 equals 80 volts, tachometer output at synchronous speed is

$$V_2 = (0.224)(80)\underline{/0}$$
$$V_2 = 17.97\underline{/0}$$

Also of interest is the gradient expressed in volts per 1,000 rpm. The synchronous speed of a four-pole 400-cps unit is 12,000 rpm, so that

$$\text{Gradient} = \frac{17.97}{12} = 1.5 \text{ volts}/1,000 \text{ rpm}$$

4. If the frequency increases by 5 per cent because of poor regulation of the power supply, what will be the effect on the output gradient and phase angle?

For the increased frequency, all the reactances increase by 5 per cent.

$$X_{ls1} = X_{ls2} = 105 \text{ ohms}$$
$$X_m = 420 \text{ ohms}$$
$$\alpha = \frac{1,000}{420} = 2.38$$
$$\tau_r = \frac{286}{420} = 0.68$$
$$\tau_x = \frac{105}{420} = 0.25$$

As in part 3 calculate a new gradient using Eq. (5-20).

$$\frac{V_2}{V_1} = \frac{j2.38}{[2.38 + 0.68 + 2(2.38)(0.25) - (2.38)^2(0.717)]} \\ + j[0.25 - 2.38(0.68) - (2.38)^2 - 0.68(2.38)^2]$$

This gives a new gradient

$$A = 0.236\underline{/-2.2}$$
$$V_2 = 18.9\underline{/-2.2}$$

The synchronous speed corresponding to 420 cps is 12,600 rpm. The gradient in volts per 1,000 rpm is

$$\text{Gradient} = \frac{18.9}{12.6}\underline{/-2.2}$$
$$\text{Gradient} = 1.5\underline{/-2.2} \text{ volts/1,000 rpm}$$

In this case the frequency variation causes a lagging phase shift of $-2.2°$ but does not affect the magnitude of the gradient. Thus only phase-shift compensation is required. This can be calculated using the method shown in part 1 of this problem. With another component having different circuit constants, magnitude compensation might also be required.

5. At rated voltage and frequency, a transformer (which may be assumed ideal) is connected across the tachometer output to increase the gradient to 3 volts/1,000 rpm. The cable leading from the transformer to the load has a capacitance of 1,200 $\mu\mu$f. How much variation in gradient magnitude and phase is caused by the stray loading?

For appreciable loading the drop across the output impedance Z'_{out} must be taken into consideration where

$$Z'_{out} = r_{s2} + \frac{a^2 r_r}{1 + \alpha^2} + j\left(X_{ls2} + \frac{a^2 r_r \alpha}{1 + \alpha^2}\right)$$

For this problem

$$Z'_{out} = 100 + \frac{1,000}{1 + (2.5)^2} + j\left(100 + \frac{1,000(2.5)}{1 + (2.5)^2}\right)$$
$$Z'_{out} = 238 + j445$$

To increase the gradient from 1.5 volts per 1,000 rpm to 3.0 volts per 1,000 rpm, a transformer with a step-up turns ratio of 2 is required. Because of this ratio the apparent output impedance is

$$Z'_{out} \text{ apparent} = (\text{turns ratio})^2 Z'_{out}$$
$$= (2)^2(238 + j445)$$
$$= 952 + j1,780$$

The impedance of 1,200 μμf at 400 cps is $-j331,000$ ohms.

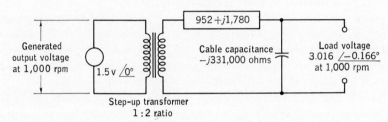

FIG. 5-18. Equivalent circuit showing effect of cable capacitance on the gradient.

The equivalent output circuit corresponding to rotation at 1,000 rpm is shown in Fig. 5-18. The voltage developed at the load per 1,000 rpm and consequently the gradient is

$$\text{Gradient} = \left[\frac{-j331,000}{(952 + j1,780) - j331,000}\right](2)(1.5)$$
$$\text{Gradient} = 3.016/\underline{-0.166} \text{ volts per 1,000 rpm}$$

The rise in output voltage from 3 to 3.016 volts is caused by the tendency of the cable capacitance to resonate with the inductance of the source. The effect of cable load on the magnitude and phase angle is appreciable and must be taken into account in precision applications.

6. Determine the torque required to drive this unit per 1,000 rpm.

The driving torque can be calculated approximately by using the following equation based on induction-motor theory:

$$T = \frac{V_1^2}{r_r} \frac{1,352}{N_s^2} \, 1,000 \text{ oz-in.}/1,000 \text{ rpm}$$
$$= \frac{80^2}{1,000} \frac{1,352}{(12,000)^2} \times 1,000$$
$$= 0.0578 \text{ oz-in.}/1,000 \text{ rpm}$$

This type of analytical approach can also be applied to the problem of temperature compensation. Temperature variations cause gradient problems through their effect on the winding resistances and the resistivity of the drag cup. These can be calculated in a similar manner to the effect of frequency change in part 4. Approximate compensation networks can then be devised.

Calculations using the equivalent circuit should be accurate to better than 10 per cent if the circuit parameters are carefully measured.

5-9. Quality and Tolerances of Induction Generators. Either mechanical limitations or an allowable nonlinearity establishes the maximum rotational speed of a component. Percentages of error are determined by the ratio of maximum error voltage to generated output voltage at the maximum speed. Thus quality is defined by the percentage of residual voltage, of nonlinearity, or of gradient error.

Commercially available tachometers can be divided into two classes according to precision. Those having inaccuracies greater than about 2 per cent are classed as low precision and find their greatest application as damping generators in servomechanisms. Those of higher accuracy are used in computer circuits and velocity-regulation systems.

The best tachometers available at this writing have accuracies on the order of 1 part in 2,000. Units of this precision are supplied with standardized output voltage-speed gradients and phase angles, and include temperature compensation.

Less accurate tachometers can be supplied as simple basic components, initially having broad tolerances and requiring adjustment and compensation by the user. These operations are performed through the addition of passive circuit elements, such as temperature-sensitive resistors, to the input and output circuits.

5-10. Application Notes. For maximum quality of performance, certain circuit design principles must be observed. Precision tachometer applications are tricky, and care is needed to avoid introducing errors.

Gear Mesh. To avoid gear chatter and instability in closed-loop systems, backlash between the tachometer and its driving motor must be reduced to a minimum. In integrator circuits, which require maximum precision, the motor and tachometer are placed on the same shaft.

Load Characteristics. Those design features which make for high tachometer accuracy, at the same time cause high output winding impedance. Normally, final factory adjustment of gradient and phase angle is performed with a standard load across the output terminals. In an instrument, stray cable capacitances can make the effective load substantially different from the apparent (standard) load, thereby disturbing the gradient.

Input Impedance. The drag-cup construction requires a large airgap, implying low input impedance, large exciting current, and high temperature. Lead impedance between the reference a-c lines and the tachometer terminals must be low so as not to disturb the voltage actually appearing across the primary winding. Also substantial warmup time may be required before characteristics stabilize.

Supply Voltage and Frequency. Deviations from rated value directly affect the magnetic-core flux density and consequently its permeability. Because of the directional properties of magnetic iron, the resultant flux axes may shift, introducing residual voltage. In addition, the change in machine parameters resulting from permeability variations has a direct influence on the output gradient and phase. The operating frequency can be shifted with little loss of accuracy through the use of external equalizer networks, but this requires complicated engineering design. Small changes in the nominal voltage and frequency ratings can be obtained by modifying the manufacturer's values of the standardizing elements.

Drag Torque. Induction tachometers develop a viscous drag proportional to rotational speed. This may introduce undesirable loss of effective torque in a servo. The system designer should be sure his motor can carry the tachometer load to the required speeds.

5-11. Acceleration Measurement with Induction Generators. The induction generator can also be used to measure acceleration if direct current is applied to the main winding instead of alternating current. Referring to Fig. 5-4, if the input is direct current, the quadrature flux along the secondary axis will also be direct current with a density proportional to speed. While the unit is operating at constant speed, the steady secondary d-c flux generates no output voltage. However, under rotor acceleration the secondary flux varies. The output is not alternating but rather is a smooth voltage with an amplitude proportional to acceleration.

The principal applications are the direct reading of acceleration, and servomechanism stabilization and performance improvement. Just as tachometer damping in a servo is dynamically analogous to viscous drag, acceleration damping is analogous to inertia. By proper adjustment, "negative inertia" can be designed into a system for increasing the speed of response.

5-12. D-C Tachometers. A d-c tachometer is essentially a small permanent magnet or separately excited generator. While any small d-c generator can be used in conjunction with a calibrated voltmeter to indicate speed, control-system applications require precise units with special attention to certain electrical and mechanical characteristics. Electrically a unit should deliver a noise-free output voltage that varies linearly with speed, and mechanically a unit should run smoothly, have low static and running drag, and low inertia.

A simple schematic of a d-c tachometer is shown in Fig. 5-19 together with the output emf as a function of angular displacement of the rotating armature.   In practice, the coils are actually buried in slots in the armature.   The individual winding turns are connected in series so that the

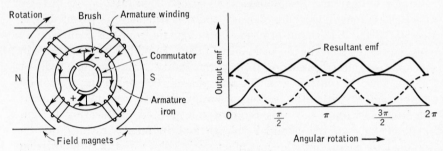

FIG. 5-19. Schematic of d-c tachometer with distributed winding.   Pulsation of output emf.

voltages add in any one coil.   Each coil is connected to the next coil and to one segment of a commutator.

The commutator serves as a rectifying switch.   All the armature coils to the right of the neutral axis are under the influence of the flux generated by the right-hand pole; while the left-hand coils are under the influence of the flux generated by the left-hand pole.   When a coil moves from under the north pole to under the south pole, the connections of the coil to the external circuit are reversed to achieve a direct voltage so that one brush is always positive and the other always negative.   This reversal or rectification is called commutation.   During reversal the brush simultaneously embraces more than one commutator segment, effectively short-circuiting some armature turns, and introducing circulating current (Fig. 5-20).   As will be discussed later, this current must be minimized to prevent main field distortion and consequent linearity errors.

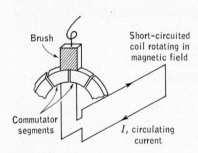

FIG. 5-20. Brush short-circuiting commutated coil.

In actual tachometers many coils are used.   These are distributed in such a manner that the ripple in the resultant emf (Fig. 5-19) is tolerable in speed-control applications.   This inherent ripple can cause definite amplitude saturation problems in critical closed-loop control systems.

In every case where a conductor is moving relative to a magnetic field, a voltage will be induced in the conductor equivalent to

$$e = Blv \times 10^{-8} \text{ volts} \qquad (5\text{-}30)$$

where B = flux density, gauss
  l = length of conductor, cm
  v = relative velocity of field and conductor, cm/sec

Thus in an elementary tachometer this represents the emf induced in each conductor. If the armature of the unit is wound with Z conductors, the total average emf is

$$E = \frac{P\phi ZN}{60a} \times 10^{-8} \qquad (5\text{-}31)$$

where P = number of poles
  ϕ = flux per pole, lines
  N = rpm
  a = number of parallel paths between positive and negative brushes
  E = total average emf, volts

An ideal d-c tachometer will have a gradient (variation of output voltage with speed) such as shown in Fig. 5-21. This can be expressed by

$$E = KN$$

where K is the gradient or constant of linear proportionality between the speed and voltage determined by the factors of Eq. (5-31). In actual tachometers, variations in K determine departures from the ideal linearity of a unit. Such factors as loading, eddy currents, and hysteresis can cause these variations in affecting the value of ϕ.

The other important factors that differentiate precision tachometers from standard d-c machines are functions of mechanical and electrical quality. Cogging is prevented by skewing the armature slots and tapering the pole-face contour; friction losses are reduced by limiting brush pressure, using high-quality antifriction bearings, and minimizing the commutator diameter; eddy currents are reduced by laminating the armature and poles; magnetic materials are selected for negligible hysteresis; fairly large airgap and linear magnetization range (large airgap reduces cogging and demagnetizing effects in permanent magnet units), high-resistance risers, and hard brushes are used to improve commutation; fine wire is used to obtain high signal-to-

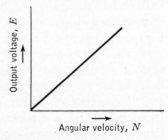

Fig. 5-21. Tachometer linear gradient.

noise ratio; and in general units are small (minimum inertia) with precision machining tolerances.

Tachometers with a linearity accuracy of better than 2 per cent are considered precision units, with the best available commercial d-c units having an accuracy of 0.25 per cent. This is about one-fifth the accuracy of high-quality a-c tachometers.

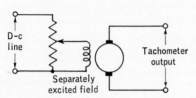

Fig. 5-22. Schematic of separately excited tachometer.

5-13. Separately Excited versus Permanent-magnet Excited Tachometers. In closed-loop systems where many components are operating in unison, line-voltage variations can introduce errors (unless the line voltage is closely regulated). To avoid the necessity for a precisely regulated line, a common practice is to include in every component the feature that its output will vary linearly with line voltage. Thus all null positions and computations will be unaffected by line fluctuations. Suitably designed separately excited tachometers (Fig. 5-22) operate well in this type system. Although more complex than the permanent-magnet generator, they afford maximum flexibility. Temperature compensation can be included in the field; compensating not only for variations in field copper resistance but also for changes in the characteristics of the magnetic material or the output resistance of the loaded armature. The field winding resistance is selected to draw rated field power on rated line voltage.

Permanent-magnet tachometers are compact, efficient, reliable, and have a high output gradient with a low temperature rise. However, they are not as readily compensated for ambient variations as are externally excited generators, and the output of a permanent-magnet tachometer does not possess the proportionality with the line-voltage feature. For this reason, they find widest use as stabilizing rather than computing

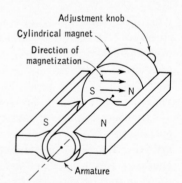

Fig. 5-23. Permanent-magnet tachometer with adjustable standardizing magnet.

devices. Temperature-sensitive magnetic shunts are often used that divert portions of the pole flux depending on temperature. There are a variety of special magnetic alloys that can be used for this purpose. One design of permanent-magnet tachometer (Fig. 5-23) has a cylindrical permanent magnet whose axis coincides with the motor-shaft axis.

Rotating this magnet adjusts the tachometer gradient. Many variations of this scheme are feasible.

Another problem encountered with permanent-magnet tachometers is that of demagnetization of the fields from a possible short circuit on the output windings. This can be prevented by purposely shorting the output during manufacture and demagnetizing the fields to the extent that further accidental short circuits during use will no longer affect the field strength. However, this is accomplished only at a sacrifice in output gradient.

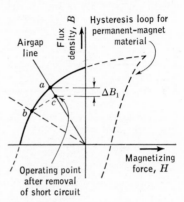

In Fig. 5-24 is shown a partial hysteresis loop for a typical field material. Operation will always occur along the airgap line, so that with no demagnetization the magnet will develop the flux density represented by point a. If the tachometer output is shorted during rotation to the extent that the material is demagnetized to point b, upon removal of the short the operating point will return to point c on the airgap line. This presetting during manufacture allows a similar short circuit to be applied accidentally during use without permanently affecting the magnetic material or tachometer gradient (the operating point will remain at c).

FIG. 5-24. Demagnetization characteristics of permanent-magnet tachometers.

In addition to the preliminary demagnetization during manufacture, the permanent field magnets must also be temperature stabilized by annealing above the maximum operating temperature after hardening. Care should be taken that the Curie point is not exceeded during annealing. Figure 5-25 shows curves indicating the resistance of various magnetic materials to temperature, impact, and stray fields.

5-14. Advantages of D-C Tachometers. Although d-c tachometers have been falling out of favor in the past few years, they have the following advantages compared to other types of speed-measuring devices:

1. Freedom from waveform and phase-shift problems.
2. Absence of residual output at zero speed.
3. Very high gradients in the smallest sizes (10 to 20 volts per 1,000 rpm). Tachometer gradients are limited by the size of the wire, the quality of the windings, and the output impedance of the tachometer which increases with an increase in the resistance of the windings.
4. Ease of temperature compensation in comparison with a-c tachometers.

5. Can be used with high-pass output filters to reduce servo velocity lags.

5-15. Disadvantages of D-C Tachometers.   Some of the reasons for the decreasing use of d-c tachometers are as follows:

1. Brush problems.   In all d-c machines the major problem is the brush contact to the rotor.   This is particularly troublesome in high-speed units.   To reduce brush vibration, the commutators are given the

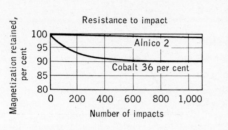

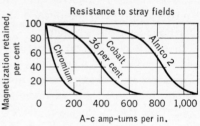

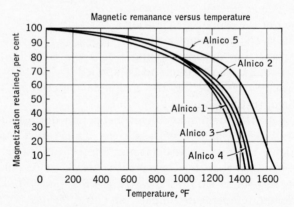

Fig. 5-25. Resistance of magnetic materials to impact, temperature, and stray fields.

best possible finish, concentricities are maintained to better than several tenths of a thousandth, and the rotors are accurately dynamically balanced.   These factors are important since vibration will increase brush wear and cause arcing by making and breaking the contact.   Brushes should be formed from a uniform high-resistance material to ensure uniform wear and help reduce commutating currents.   The brush holder should be accurately located and the closest fit specified that will permit free sliding of the brush.

Actually the brush problem is somewhat mitigated in d-c tachometers by low current drain and the small commutator diameter.   Also the voltages generated in the miniaturized components are not high (usually under 100 volts) even at maximum speed. One problem characteristic of tachometers is that the units must operate in both directions. This means that the brushes must be located exactly at the electrical neutral. While this will be discussed in more detail later, one method of improving commutation is to use narrow brushes that do not simultaneously short-circuit more than two adjacent commutator bars.

Regardless of the precautions that are taken, arcing will occur at points and the short-circuited commutated coil will develop current. This is particularly true at high altitudes where the arcing problem is accentuated because of certain ionization conditions. Likewise, moisture, temperature variations, and deposits of brush carbon on the commutator will adversely affect commutation, and periodic maintenance procedures should be set up to clean and check the brushes and commutator.

2. Generation of radio noise. Radio noise can be a source of interference to adjacent communication equipment. This noise develops from three sources: the generation of a high-frequency field because of pulsations in the commutated coil, a ripple generated by the finite winding distribution, and arcing at the brushes caused by commutation. Only the last item is important since the first two fields do not generate frequencies in the communications band, although it is conceivable that higher harmonics might cause trouble.

A filter is usually required to reduce the interference caused by the current flow at the sliding brush contact. Often a simple capacitor across the output terminals will perform satisfactorily, although where a tachometer must deliver appreciable current, an inductive element may

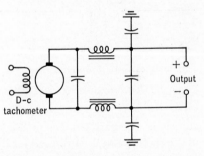

FIG. 5-26. Radio interference filter circuit for d-c tachometers.

be required. The capacitor size is determined experimentally and typical values will range from a few hundredths up to a tenth of a microfarad. Under any conditions, the best approach is to minimize radio interference before using a filter, and then to add a filter as required. Figure 5-26 shows a typical filter network.

3. Output ripple. A finite number of coils or commutator bars results in an output waveform having a definite inherent ripple. While this waveshape improves with an increasing number of rotor or armature coils, it is normally desirable to minimize the number of armature slots to reduce the cost of the armature-winding operation. Typical d-c tachometers have five or seven armature slots. As stated previously,

this pulsating output can cause amplifier saturation in closed-loop systems for velocity control.

4. Reduced use of d-c servomechanisms. Because of problems associated with drift and thermal effects in d-c amplifiers, d-c servomechanisms are gradually falling out of favor with designers. Since d-c tachometers are intimately associated with d-c servos, the number of applications of this component is decreasing. However, recent advances in d-c-controlled magnetic amplifiers have resulted in a renewed interest.

5. High torque requirements. The brush friction and hysteresis effects in d-c tachometers are influential in increasing the required driving torque.

5-16. Factors Affecting Ideal D-C Tachometer Performance. In addition to the disadvantages listed above, there are certain other factors that

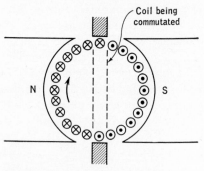

⊗ Indicates current flowing from paper

⊙ Indicates current flowing into paper

FIG. 5-27. Coil current reverses at instant of commutation.

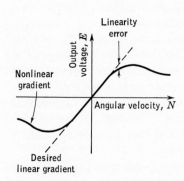

FIG. 5-28. Nonlinear tachometer gradient resulting from armature reaction.

can cause the performance of d-c tachometers to vary from ideal. Most of the factors can be corrected for by either proper design or compensation. Included are commutation problems, tachometer loading, temperature variations, and cogging.

The commutator reverses the connection of a coil to the external circuit at the instant the coil passes under another pole (Fig. 5-27). This essentially involves a change in the direction of flow of the coil current. When the coil is in the neutral plane during commutation, there is no generated emf; however, the inductive reactance of the coil is sufficient to oppose current reversal and reactance voltages are generated. This generates a bucking field that reacts on the main field during short circuit. The speed of the rotating machine determines the switching time of the current during the reversal and likewise the current magnitude, so that the net reaction opposing the main field increases as the square of the frequency or rotational speed. Figure 5-28 shows the effect of this bucking field on the tachometer gradient as speed increases. This represents one of the nonlinear effects associated with d-c tachometers.

Improved performance can be obtained by the use of commutating poles or interpoles (Fig. 5-29). These introduce a compensating emf in such a direction as to encourage the reversal of the current in the commutated coil. The winding arrangement of the interpoles must be adjusted for optimum performance, since excessive interpole volt-age can in itself interfere with commutation. Interpole correction increases with speed in the proper manner to compensate for the non-linear gradient droop shown in Fig. 5-28 and also performs well in both directions of rotation.

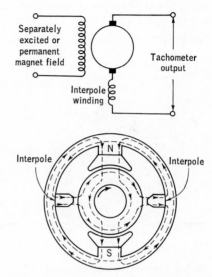

Tests performed on a small gener-ator of about 2 watts rating used as a tachometer showed that armature reaction caused about ±2 per cent variation in the linearity accuracy of the output gradient over a speed range of plus 9,000, through 0, to minus 9,000 rpm. The addition of interpoles brought the shape of the gradient under some measure of con-trol and enabled its linearity to be adjusted within about ±½ per cent.

FIG. 5-29. Tachometer schematics show-ing interpole winding and magnetic cir-cuits in interpole machine.

Another phenomenon associated with commutation results from the use of wide brushes that span several commutator segments. These brushes can short-circuit a group of coils, not all in the neutral region. An exact analysis of this action is very complex, involving the self- and mutual inductances of each coil. To minimize this problem and further to make commutation insensitive to slight shifts in brush position, narrow brushes and tapered pole pieces are used (Fig. 5-30). The tapered pole pieces cause a gradual thinning out of the flux in the interpole area so that exces-sive voltages caused by slight dissymmetries are not critical.

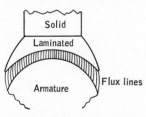

FIG. 5-30. Tapered pole con-struction.

When a d-c tachometer is subjected to loading, there is a reversal of current in the commutated coils that sets up a magnetic field in opposition to the main field. This armature reaction is similar to that caused by circulating currents in a short-circuited coil and introduces a nonlinear error that increases with speed. The result is nonlinear output gradient similar to that shown in Fig. 5-28.

The resultant magnetic field caused by the interaction of the main field and the field developed by armature reaction is shown in Fig. 5-31. The main field is strengthened at the trailing pole tips X and X' and weakened at the leading pole tips Y and Y'. In addition, the neutral axis has been shifted to coincide with the dotted axis, while the brushes are located on the no-load solid axis. As a result of this shift, the brushes short-circuit coils that are cutting the magnetic field and in which an active emf is being generated. Large currents will flow, causing brush arcing, and the tachometer will not develop its full output voltage. This condition is particularly serious in two-directional tachometer applications, since if the brushes are shifted to coincide with the electrical neutral in one direction of rotation, operation will be totally unsatisfactory when the unit is rotating in the other direction. Saturation at the trailing pole tips results in a net reduction in effective pole flux which further reduces tachometer output with increasing speed. Besides, the electrical neutral shifts with variations in load. This problem emphasizes the importance of operating precision d-c tachometers under the lightest possible load.

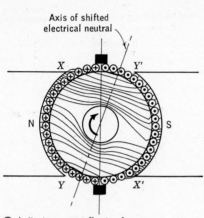

Axis of shifted electrical neutral

⊕ Indicates current flowing from paper
⊙ Indicates current flowing into paper

FIG. 5-31. Distorted magnetic field and electrical neutral shift caused by tachometer loading.

In addition to the commutating problems and reduction in output caused by the demagnetizing ampere-turns (armature reaction), the output voltage under a loaded condition is also reduced by the ohmic drop in the armature winding and by the brush drop. This can be expressed as follows:

$$V = E - IR - \Delta e \tag{5-32}$$

where V = loaded output voltage
$\qquad E$ = open-circuit output voltage
$\qquad IR$ = ohmic drop in armature winding
$\qquad \Delta e$ = brush drop (about 2 volts for more than negligible current)

With this condition the only way to obtain a linear gradient under load is to increase the field excitation as load increases. Although most tachometers are constant field separately excited or permanent-magnet units, it is conceivable that a small amount of series compounding could be used to correct for load variations.

Compensating winding buried in the pole faces, such as are used in large power generators to neutralize the effect of the demagnetizing ampere-turns, are uneconomical in small precision tachometers.

A third component of armature reaction that also reacts on the main field is generated by eddy currents circulating in the armature iron. These currents can be limited by careful lamination of the pole pieces in the armature.

Temperature variations as well as loading can cause gradient errors in a tachometer, since temperature changes in the magnetic circuit can cause the flux field to vary because of a shift in the magnetic properties of the iron or permanent magnet. Sometimes a magnetic shunt having a temperature-sensitive permeability can be installed for compensation. Temperature error is also important when a tachometer is subjected to a heavy load since the winding resistance is sensitive to temperature variation. It is also possible to compensate for this effect.

Cogging will prevent ideal tachometer performance. This results from the rotor slot openings and makes it difficult to achieve smooth operation and torque.

5-17. Design Factors in D-C Tachometers. There are certain design factors which if adhered to will assist in obtaining a unit that will give optimum performance.

Most precision tachometers are two-pole, two-brush units. This construction reduces the percentage of commutating fluxes, and, in the smaller sizes, there are more slots per pole resulting in smoother operation. In addition, the tolerances on the electrical neutral are broader and the cost of manufacturing is low. Where small units use few armature slots, a low-ripple output can be obtained by superimposing many coils per slot. Additional commutator segments permit the switching of sections of the coils. Not switching all the coils at once means less inductive reactance and a smoother output. High-speed operation also tends to minimize the ripple.

Proper armature slot skew and the use of a relatively large airgap and shaped pole pieces will minimize cogging. As shown in Fig. 5-32, the armature should be skewed at least one slot pitch. This will tend to even out the reluctance variations. Lower airgap densities will also reduce cogging and hysteresis drag torques. The ratio of airgap to slot opening is about $\frac{1}{3}$, so that large airgaps will range from 0.015 to 0.030 in. in small-size tachometers. The shaped pole pieces (Fig. 5-30) will prevent any abrupt changes in density around the gap.

The selection of armature diameter in a given frame size is dictated by the requirements of low inertia and sufficient space to contain an efficient stabilized field magnet. On the minimum diameter limit, there must be adequate provisions for a large number of turns and sufficient magnetic material to carry the field flux.

To obtain a high output gradient, wire sizes of No. 48 AWG and finer are used for the armature winding. Also high-resistance risers (Fig. 5-33) may be used to limit the commutated current.

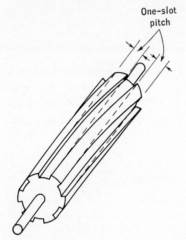

One-slot pitch

The drag torque should be kept low. At low speeds, this torque results from bearing friction, brush friction, and hysteresis loss, while at high speeds these units are subjected to windage and

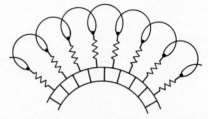

FIG. 5-32. Skew armature at least one slot pitch.

FIG. 5-33. High-resistance risers from commutator segments.

eddy-current drag plus an increased frictional component. Hysteresis and eddy-current drag can be minimized by using a good grade of laminated iron. The remaining drag depends on careful brush and brush holder design and the use of high-quality antifriction bearings. Tachometer speed is limited by the concentricity of the commutator, lightness of the brushes, and friction in the brush mounting.

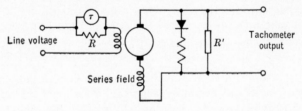

Line voltage R R' Tachometer output

Series field

FIG. 5-34. Methods of compensating d-c tachometers.

5-18. Compensation and Standardization of D-C Tachometers. Various devices and circuits can be incorporated with d-c tachometers to permit compensation and standardization. One of these devices is shown in Fig. 5-23 where an adjustable magnet is used to standardize the gradient of a permanent-magnet tachometer during manufacture.

Several other methods of compensation are shown in Fig. 5-34. The rectifier circuit across the output can be used to correct for slight unbalances in the two directions of rotation. The temperature-sensitive element R', also across the output, can be used to compensate for armature-resistance variation with temperature under loaded conditions. As mentioned previously, a series field can be used to compensate for load current by increasing field excitation in accordance with load increase.

The thermistor-resistor network in series with the field windings is selected to maintain the total field resistance constant regardless of temperature variation. Thermistors can be used in this application since they have a large negative temperature coefficient. Thus thermistor resistance decreases with temperature while the resistance of the copper field windings increases with temperature. The method of selecting the proper shunt network is shown in Fig. 5-35. Curve X represents the resistance variation of the windings with temperature. The network is selected to have a resistance-variation curve Y with a slope equal to curve X but negative in direction. The result of a series connection is represented by curve Z which indicates a constant total resistance regardless of temperature.

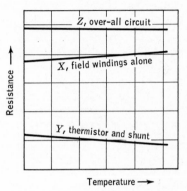

Fig. 5-35. Choose compensation network to give constant over-all resistance regardless of temperature.

5-19. Alternate Methods of Measuring Speed. In addition to the conventional a-c and d-c tachometers, there are other devices and circuits that can be used to obtain a voltage signal proportional to speed. Those to be discussed here are a-c and d-c bridge circuits, a-c and d-c operational circuits, permanent-magnet alternators, capacitor tachometers, and drag-torque tachometers. Most of these are not commonly applied in control system design because of inconvenient mechanical features, poor accuracy over all or part of the speed range, or such limitations as unidirectional operation.

5-20. A-C Bridge Circuits. Often the use of a tachometer can be avoided in applications where only crude accuracy for purposes of stabilization is required. The technique is to measure the input current to the motor and use the resultant signal as a speed factor. In a-c control systems a bridge network can be used to obtain this speed signal.

Unfortunately, most motors of the a-c induction type take a large exciting current that remains relatively unchanged with speed. Therefore, the component of the current that does change with speed is small. The use of a bridge circuit enables the measurement of this variable component by effectively canceling out the fixed component.

A typical a-c bridge network is shown in Fig. 5-36. Many other similar circuits are possible. The choke network consisting of L and R_L is designed to balance the motor inductance when the unit is stalled, so that the output across points X and Y is zero. However, any rotation of the motor will result in a signal being generated in the bridge output that can be used for damping or speed control.

This circuit suffers from a number of difficulties that limit its use. The choke that is used as part of the bridge balance must be a precise match for the servomotor over the entire amplifier bandpass and not merely at the carrier frequency. If this match is not achieved, there is a possibility of oscillation being set up because of positive feedback at some frequency

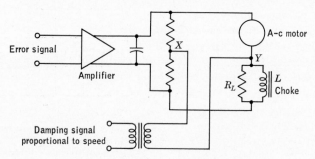

Fig. 5-36. Typical a-c bridge network.

where the mismatch of the inductance is sufficient to cause instability. This matching is difficult since essentially the motor and choke are different kinds of inductance.

Another undesirable feature of mismatched elements is the presence of appreciable harmonics in the bridge null. This condition is hard to counteract because harmonic filters can cause trouble from the point of view of stability of the amplifier loop. Also as the error level is raised, because of magnetic unbalance, a stall null signal appears. This stall signal is difficult to uncouple.

Because of the relatively low proportion of speed-sensitive current in small servomotors, this system is sensitive to shifts in temperature and line voltage. The loss in motor torque because of the additional bridge elements means that higher amplifier gain is required to maintain system performance.

The circuit is sensitive to the phase of rotation. Otherwise it would be useless in feedback-control systems where signal direction is as important as signal magnitude.

5-21. D-C Bridge Networks. The same principles that apply to a-c bridge circuits for stabilization can also be used in d-c systems where the absence of residual problems makes the situation simpler. D-c bridge circuits measure the motor counter emf which is directly proportional to speed for constant field excitation. There are a variety of techniques for doing this, one of which is shown in Fig. 5-37. In this circuit, the two sections of a voltage-dividing potentiometer R_1 and an armature resistor R_2 together with the motor armature form the four legs of a bridge. The circuit elements are selected so that bridge output is zero when the motor is stalled. As the motor starts to rotate, a voltage is developed that is proportional to speed and is polarity-sensitive.

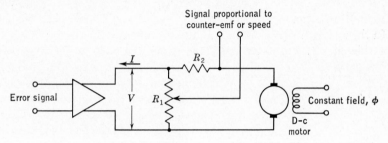

FIG. 5-37. Typical d-c bridge network.

The drop across R_1 is proportional to the driving voltage V while the drop across R_2 is proportional to the armature current. The bridge output is then proportional to the counter emf so that

$$v = K\phi Z'n \qquad (5\text{-}33)$$

or assuming that the field flux ϕ and the number of conductors Z' are constant then

$$v = K'n \qquad (5\text{-}34)$$

which is the desired result since the voltage signal is directly proportional to speed.

The approach indicated here is practical and widely used. This is in distinct contrast to the rather critical nature of the a-c bridge circuits discussed above.

5-22. A-C and D-C Operational Circuits. A unique way of measuring speed is based on the use of operational circuits for performing a differentiation of position. These circuits are simple derivative networks analogous to those used for introducing phase lead into servomechanisms.

In Fig. 5-38 are shown two operational circuits for use in d-c systems, while Fig. 5-39 shows an operational circuit for use in a suppressed carrier a-c system. The circuits of Figs. 5-38 and 5-39 perform in accordance with the relationship

$$E_2 = KE_1 + K' \frac{dE_1}{dt} \tag{5-35}$$

which shows that a term is obtained that is proportional to the rate of change of the input signal. However, these circuits only approximate a theoretical rate device since the network elements can only give an exponential response. The relation between the input and output voltages of the circuit shown in Fig. 5-38B can be approximately expressed by

$$E_2 = RC \frac{dE_1}{dt} \tag{5-36}$$

In the a-c circuit (Fig. 5-39) L and C are tuned to the carrier frequency. For this circuit, Eq. (5-35) only holds when the modulation frequency is

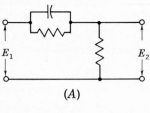

low compared with the carrier frequency. While these circuits can be accurately tuned and will maintain their setting over a wide temperature range, the detuning drift from changes in carrier frequency in excess of a few per cent is a serious limitation. The reduction in network output with frequency

(A)

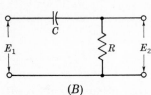

(B)

Fig. 5-38. Direct-current operational rate circuits.

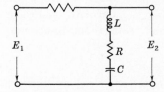

Fig. 5-39. Alternating-current operational rate circuit.

shift is not as objectionable as the output phase change, which interferes with the operation of phase-sensitive devices such as two-phase servomotors.

More complex networks including vacuum tubes can be used to obtain single or multiple integrals, higher derivatives, and other functions.

5-23. Permanent-magnet Alternators. These units are similar in operation to constant field synchronous generators and develop a highly linear output voltage of a frequency and phase variable with angular rate. They have occasional use in feedback-control systems, especially in high-speed unidirectional speed-control applications. They are suitable in systems requiring the synchronous rotation of more than one shaft. At very low speeds, the frequency becomes excessively low for convenient use.   The output is not sensitive in general to direction of rotation.   The variable-frequency feature restricts general use.   There are some applications where a permanent-magnet alternator is used to drive directly a synchronous or induction motor at a variable speed equal to alternator speed.

One means of using these devices is to rectify the output.   If high-performance diodes are used and the speed is kept high, the resultant ripple frequency can be canceled out by proper filtering.   Where a permanent-magnet alternator with a rectified output is used in bidirectional applications, some type of relay device that is sensitive to the direction of shaft rotation is used to reverse the d-c output with a reversal of the direction of rotation.

Errors in permanent-magnet alternators result from armature reaction caused by loading which generates an opposing flux to the flux of the main field, bucking fluxes caused by eddy currents in the laminations, and temperature variations.   As in d-c control components, there are certain inherent problems such as hysteresis and the nonlinearity of the magnetic iron.   In accurately calibrated permanent-magnet equipment, any short circuiting or heavy loading of the output can introduce a demagnetizing effect and disturb the calibration of the magnet.   Carefully aged magnets, stabilized in alternating magnetic fields, should be used in these critical applications.   If unregulated line voltage is a control-system problem, then a separately excited field may be required for the alternator.

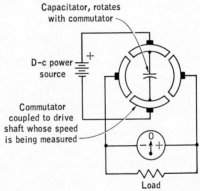

Fig. 5-40.   Schematic of capacitor tachometer.

These units have the reliability advantage of conventional a-c tachometers since no sliding contacts (brushes) are required.   Over a wide speed range, a linearity accuracy of 0.1 per cent can be obtained with little difficulty.

5-24. Capacitor Tachometers.   These units are accurate, simple, and reliable d-c tachometers.   As shown in Fig. 5-40, the capacitive tachometer operates on the principle of charging and discharging a capacitor from a d-c source with the output polarity dependent on the direction of rotation.   During each charging cycle the capacitor is given an opportunity to charge up to full voltage.   During the discharge cycle, the capacitor is permitted to give a full discharge.   Rotational speed is limited by the time constants of the charge and discharge circuits.   When charge time starts to become of the same order as the available switching time and the time constant of the circuit, the output becomes a nonlinear function of speed.

In Fig. 5-41 is shown the relation between tachometer output and speed. Current pulses and average current are plotted for two speeds, A and $2A$ rpm. Since the entire operation of the unit is based on these pulses, excessive radio interference is generated. Also, at low speeds filtering must be excessive to obtain an output voltage that is sufficiently smooth for control applications. Like the permanent-magnet alternator, the use of this component is limited by the low-frequency output at low speeds.

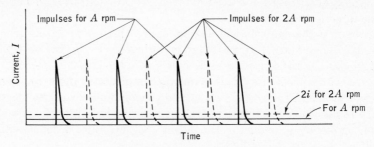

FIG. 5-41. Output waveform of capacitor tachometer.

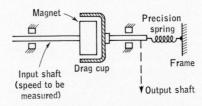

FIG. 5-42. Basic features of drag-torque tachometer.

Other characteristics of this component make it suitable for certain control-system applications: it is reversible, highly linear outputs can be obtained, the output is scaled to line-voltage variations, and it can be made independent of temperature variations. In addition, appreciable load current can be taken directly from the unit and used to operate a relay or some other control device.

5-25. Drag-torque Tachometers. These units can be obtained in many physical forms, all of which incorporate the basic features shown in Fig. 5-42. The rotating input shaft plus magnet produce an eddy current torque on the drag cup causing it to deflect against its spring. By using a precision wound spring, this deflection can be made proportional to shaft speed.

With a low torque potentiometer or an induction pickup unit on the deflected shaft, an output signal of any convenient scaling and frequency can be selected. This freedom of choice is important in control applications. Drag-torque tachometers are difficult to temperature-compensate because of variations in the drag cup, the spring, and the permanent magnet. Low-friction bearings are required for accurate operation. Accuracies of 0.25 per cent have been achieved by careful design.

REFERENCES

1. Vickers, H.: An Induction Generator Used with the All-electric Automatic Pilot for Airplanes, *Trans. AIEE*, vol. 57, pt. I, pp. 182–185, 1948.
2. Frazier, R. H.: Analysis of the Drag Cup AC Tachometer by Means of 2-Phase Symmetrical Components, *Trans. AIEE*, vol. 70, pt. II, pp. 1,894–1,906, 1951.
3. Burian, K.: Analysis of Induction Tachometer Generators, *AIEE* conference paper, presented at Winter General Meeting, 1953.
4. Stain, W. A.: The Determination of Rotor Inductance and Resistance of a Drag Cup Servomotor, *AIEE* conference paper, presented at Southern District Meeting, 1953
5. Tai Nien Feng: How to Calculate the Performance of AC Drag Cup Tachometers, *Control Eng.*, June, 1958, p. 90.
6. Chang, S. S. L.: The Equivalent Circuit of the Capacitor Motor, *Trans. AIEE*, vol. 66, pp. 631–640, 1947.

Chapter 6

A-C SERVOMOTORS

6-1. Introduction. The actuator requirements for a-c instrument servomechanisms are most satisfactorily met by the two-phase motor, connected as shown in Fig. 6-1. The main field is continuously excited to give high torque per control field watt. The windings are usually identical and equally rated. (However, where control power is at a premium, and load power low, the main field may be rated at two to three

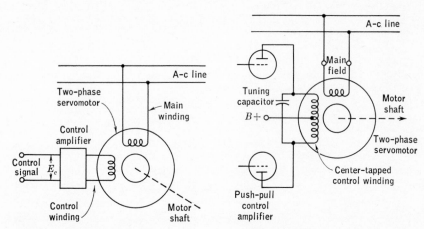

Fig. 6-1. Conventional operation of two-phase servomotor.

Fig. 6-2. Plate-to-plate operation of two-phase servomotor.

times the control field.) Motor torque at stall is proportional to applied control voltage, with direction determined by the polarity. The fixed-voltage main field is excited from the supply source, sometimes shifted in phase to achieve quadrature with the variable control voltage. Some servomotors are designed with a high-impedance center-tapped winding that can be fed directly from push-pull tubes with a somewhat higher dielectric stress to ground (Fig. 6-2).

In feedback-control systems, the most satisfactory general-purpose actuator is a motor having linear characteristics that can be analyzed in a

234

simple mathematical manner. Such a motor is characterized by the following features:

1. Stall torque is proportional to control voltage.
2. Torque for any control voltage decreases at a definite uniform rate with speed.

A linear motor with the torque characteristics of Fig. 6-3 is readily analyzed using differential equations or operational methods.

The balanced two-phase servomotor is essentially a two-phase induction motor with the parameters adjusted to approximate linear performance. Figure 6-4, curve A, shows the speed-torque characteristic of a conventional induction motor. This performance curve in no way resembles the

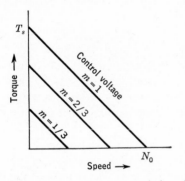

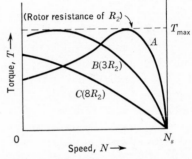

Fig. 6-3. Speed-torque characteristics of ideal servomotor.

Fig. 6-4. Speed-torque characteristics of induction motors with various values of rotor resistance.

desired characteristic. However, by increasing rotor resistance the characteristic is properly modified, as described in Fig. 6-4, curves B and C. Unfortunately, a compromise is necessary in the degree of linearity that can be achieved. The straighter the speed-torque curve, the less stall torque available, which means less power delivered to the load, smaller initial accelerations, and ultimately sluggish servo response. Thus in most servomotors, a compromise is made so that maximum torque occurs between slips of 1.5 and 2. This gives reasonable linearity and stall torque, and yields approximately maximum reversing torque.

Two-phase servomotors are inherently high-speed, low-torque devices, heavily geared down to drive the load. Because of their high speed, the stored kinetic energy of the rotor is high, and acts to prevent rapid changes in speed. For this reason, servomotors are designed for minimum inertia and maximum torque, resulting in a characteristic large length-to-diameter ratio for the rotor. Within limits, the torque-to-speed ratio can be improved by increasing the number of poles.

To achieve fastest response, the servomotor is designed for a maximum ratio of stall torque to rotor inertia (theoretical stall acceleration). Inertia varies as the fourth power of rotor diameter; developed output torque varies as the square of diameter. Servomotors, therefore, are distinguished by relatively small-diameter rotors for their frame size. Similarly, small servomotors have much higher torque-to-inertia ratios than do large servomotors. Theoretical stall accelerations of up to 50,000 radians/sec^2 are feasible in the small frame sizes.

To minimize rotor kinetic energy, servomotors are wound with as many poles as possible, so that they operate at low speeds (synchronous speed is inversely proportional to the number of poles). Increasing the number of poles should also (theoretically) provide a corresponding torque increase, consequently maintaining power output. However, the percentage torque gain is never as large as the speed reduction due to reduced efficiency. Thus motors with many poles operate at lower speeds, but are not as efficient in developing output power to drive a load.

Servomotors have small airgaps. If the number of poles is increased, winding inductance decreases, and losses go up. It is necessary to minimize the airgap to build up the inductance. Small servomotors may have airgaps as small as 0.001 in. Consequently manufacturing tolerances are critical, and coefficients of expansion must be carefully matched in all mating parts. Manufacturing processes designed to protect the motor over extreme environmental conditions also require close control.

Although two-phase servomotors are available in a variety of configurations, the most popular type uses a squirrel-cage rotor with a low ratio of rotor-to-frame diameter and high rotor resistance. This type gives the best over-all performance and is especially efficient in converting input watts to shaft torque. For specific applications, there are other rotor and stator configurations that have certain advantages in performance, construction, or cost. These include drag-cup motors, solid-iron rotors, closed stator slots, articulated stators, separate rotor and stator sections, and inverted motors. In addition, gearhead motors, motor-plus-damper combinations, motor-tachometer combinations, and completely packaged servomechanisms are also available.

The best motors available today are of the potted variety, possessing good mechanical rigidity and strength, and improved heat conduction in the windings. Advanced machining techniques and precision bearings have resulted in servomotors with as many as eight poles in frame sizes under 1 in. Noncorrosive high-nickel magnetic alloys are substituted for the usual silicon steel to prevent corrosion in the narrow airgap. Class H insulations, such as Teflon and silicone varnishes and bearing greases, have resulted in motors capable of operating at ambient temperatures of 160°C and higher. Maximum performance per pound can be obtained at these temperatures.

Because most a-c servomotors are used in military applications, standardization attempts have been spearheaded by the Bureau of Ordnance and the SAE, mostly in the 400-cps model. Bureau of Ordnance drawings are available to qualified manufacturers, and there are many reliable sources. In addition to standard models, there is a large demand for special motors with peculiar mechanical or electrical characteristics, so that many manufacturers specialize in this field.

Two-phase a-c motors are available in sizes up to 1 hp. Above this size they are much too inefficient and d-c motors or clutch actuators must be used. The majority of units are under 100 watts in size. Above 10 watts, most two-phase servomotors are cooled by a separate motor-driven blower included in the same housing as the control motor. A motor in a 10-watt frame will deliver about 2.5 times this output with blower cooling. However, at high altitudes, especially above 50,000 ft, blower cooling is ineffective.

Because of their ruggedness and reliability, freedom from radio noise, and the simplicity of their driving circuits (compared with the demodulator or d-c amplifier drift problems encountered with d-c motors), a-c servomotors are widely used, particularly in instrument servos where the load is negligible. At the present time size is the important factor, and motors are available down to $\frac{1}{2}$ in. outside diameter.

6-2. Two-phase Motor Theory. The two-phase induction motor consists of two input windings (coils fitted into slots in the laminated-iron stator structure) spaced 90 electrical degrees apart. Under balanced operation, the windings are excited with equal voltages, 90° apart in time phase. The motor currents generate magnetic fields in the airgap, which are also in space and time quadrature. The two component fields can be combined vectorially yielding a resultant field of fixed magnitude rotating at synchronous speed N_s, where

$$N_s = \frac{120f}{p}$$

f = frequency
p = number of poles

Thus a two-pole, 60-cps winding causes the resultant field to rotate at (120)(60)/2 or, 3,600 rpm, and a four-pole 400-cps winding at (120)(400)/4, or 12,000 rpm. Figure 6-5 shows how this rotating field develops in a two-pole machine. A series of nine instants during one cycle are taken. The instantaneous magnetomotive forces produced by phases A and B, at right angles mechanically, are shown as pulsating vectors. By combining the vectors for corresponding instants, a sequence of equally spaced, fixed-amplitude magnetomotive forces are obtained as resultants. This rotating flux field induces a voltage in the rotor conductors, whose magnitude is proportional to their relative speed. The rotor voltages in turn cause currents, which result in a torque being developed by interaction of the current-carrying conductors and the rotating field. This "drags" the rotor along after the synchronous rotating field. Since the rotor must develop sufficient torque to overcome windage, friction, and certain parasitic torques, it cannot reach synchronous speed.

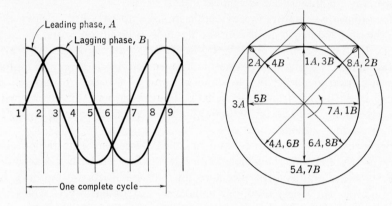

FIG. 6-5. Vectorial representation of induction-motor performance.

The difference between actual and synchronous speed is defined by a parameter known as *slip*, where

$$\text{Slip} = \frac{\text{synchronous speed} - \text{actual speed}}{\text{synchronous speed}} \tag{6-1}$$

Thus, in a four-pole 60-cps motor with a synchronous speed of 1,800 rpm and a no-load operating speed of 1,500 rpm, the slip is

$$\text{Slip} = \frac{1,800 - 1,500}{1,800} = 0.167 = 16.7 \text{ per cent}$$

In servomotors the no-load speed is approximately five-sixths synchronous speed, corresponding to a slip of one-sixth.

As external load is applied, rotor speed falls (or slip increases) to the point where sufficient current is generated in the slipping rotor to produce the torque to drive the external load.

6-3. Performance Characteristics of Two-phase Motors. Figure 6-6 shows the static characteristics of a typical high-performance servomotor. The first curve, A, shows the variation of torque with speed for rated phase voltage and varying load. It is nearly linear, corresponding to the idealized curves of Fig. 6-3. As indicated, the negative slope is achieved by using a high-resistance rotor. The negative slope indicates internal damping, which can be considered as viscous friction in the motor. This damping is measured by the negative slope of the speed-torque curve. The linearity assumption is satisfactory over a speed range not much in excess of one-half synchronous. Thus

$$D = \frac{T_s - T_n}{N} \qquad (6\text{-}2)$$

where T_s = torque at stall

D = damping coefficient, slope of speed-torque curve, dyne-cm/ radian/sec

T_n = output torque at shaft speed N

The damping in some other speed range is the slope of the speed-torque curve in the region in question,

$$D = \frac{T_1 - T_2}{N_2 - N_1} \qquad (6\text{-}3)$$

where $T_{1,2}$ and $N_{1,2}$ are corresponding values of torque and speed.

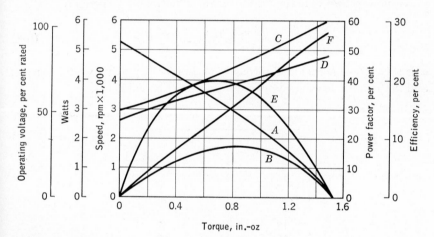

Fig. 6-6. Characteristics of a typical high-performance servomotor. (*Courtesy of Kearfott Co., Inc.*)

The power output curve (Fig. 6-6), curve B, has a parabolic shape and normally peaks at approximately one-half of no-load speed. Power input, curve C, and power factor, curve D, are plotted with rated voltage on both phases, as the load varies from no-load to stall. By comparing power input and output, an efficiency curve E is determined. The efficiency curve is not significant in determining the operating point of very small instrument motors. The final curve, F in Fig. 6-6, shows the variation in stall torque with control voltage, as fixed phase voltage is held constant. The curve is linear and constitutes a measure of motor stiffness K, where

$$K = \frac{T_s}{V_c}$$

A basic servomotor function is to develop torque with a minimum of input wattage. The quality of the electrical design can be established by the relationship between torque and watts. However, a high torque per watt characteristic is often achieved through the use of very close tolerances and expensive manufacturing techniques. Lower torque efficiencies may often be suitable, with a consequent reduction in cost. Since the speed-torque curve is almost straight in the normal operating range, and since input power is a maximum at stall, it is sufficient in studying the relationship between torque and power to examine the relation between torque and watts, as expressed below for stall conditions and balanced two-phase excitation. The quantity P_{rf} can be represented by $\eta_s P_{in}$, when P_{in} is the total stall input watts to the motor (twice the phase power) and η_s is the "stall torque efficiency." Therefore

$$T_s = \frac{1{,}352}{N_s} \eta_s P_{in} = \frac{1{,}352}{N_s} P_{rf} \qquad (6\text{-}4)$$

η_s is the ratio of actual stall torque to theoretically maximum stall torque, and is the basis for the comparison presented in Table 6-1.

TABLE 6-1. TYPICAL VALUES OF η_s IN WELL-DESIGNED MOTORS

Size	Poles	η_s, per cent
60 cycles:		
11	2	19
15	2	43
18	2	47
18	4	27
23	4	64
400 cycles:		
8	6	24
9	6	35
10	4	53
11	6	54
11	4	57
15	8	54
15	4	66
18	8	57
18	4	74
23	8	74
23	4	90

Since N_s varies inversely with p, T_s can be increased by increasing p without increasing P_{in}. However, as p increases, the efficiency of the magnetic circuit decreases, and heavier losses are developed. This decreases η_s. In practice, maximum torque is obtained by using the number of poles corresponding to the maximum product $\eta_s p$. The efficiency of power transfer to the rotor η_s increases as the airgap decreases.

The effect of line frequency may also be studied by examining the basic torque formula. Since synchronous speed increases with frequency, the stall torque of a 60-cycle motor is higher than that of a 400-cycle motor. This difference is not as great as indicated by Eq. (6-4), however, since η_s decreases with frequency because of increased exciting current. This is particularly noticeable in small frame sizes where 60-cycle motor performance is poor. Although increased carrier frequency can improve control system performance in many ways, the stall performance of a servomotor usually suffers.

Often servomotors are rated to operate under distinctly unbalanced conditions. That is, instead of applying equal power to both phases to secure balanced operation, the main phase may be intentionally over-energized to secure more output torque per control-field watt.[1,*] This minimizes the required output from the control amplifier. Section 6-4 treats unbalanced operation under stall conditions; the following sections handle the more complicated problem of unbalanced operation under running conditions.

6-4. Analysis of Unbalanced Operation under Stall Conditions. The stall analysis assumes (based on linear theory) that K is constant; stall torque varies as the product of the separate field voltages. Since phase power varies as the voltage squared, torque varies as the square root of the product of main and control power. Thus

$$T_s = k_t \sqrt{P_m P_c}$$

For balanced operation,

$$P_m = P_c = P$$
$$T_s = k_t P$$

By comparing with the formula for T_s under balanced conditions [Eq. (6-4)], k_t can be determined.

$$k_t = \frac{2,704}{N_s} \eta_s$$

Thus, the generalized unbalanced formula is

$$T_s = \frac{2,704}{N_s} \eta_s \sqrt{P_m P_c} \qquad (6-5)$$

Other useful expressions can be derived by comparing the stall torques that can be achieved with varying degrees of unbalance for a fixed total wattage to the motor. Let

$$P_m = P + \Delta P$$
$$P_c = P - \Delta P$$

Total input watts $= P_{\text{in}} = 2P$

T_{sb} = balanced stall torque
T_{su} = unbalanced stall torque

By substituting these relations in Eq. (6-5) for balanced and unbalanced operation, and by combining and simplifying these expressions, the following ratio is obtained:

$$\frac{T_{su}}{T_{sb}} = \sqrt{1 - \left(\frac{\Delta P}{P}\right)^2} \tag{6-6}$$

It is apparent from the plot of this function in Fig. 6-7 that considerable unbalances are tolerable before the stall torque falls off appreciably. In a similar manner, it is possible to determine the improvement in stall torque per control field watt due to the unbalanced mode of operation. Thus

$$\frac{T_{su}}{P_c} = \frac{2,704\eta_s}{N_s} \sqrt{\frac{1 + (\Delta P/P)}{1 - (\Delta P/P)}} \tag{6-7}$$

Figure 6-8 is a plot of this function. It is apparent that very high

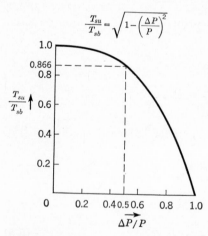

FIG. 6-7. Ratio of stall torques for unbalanced and balanced operation as a function of the degree of unbalance.

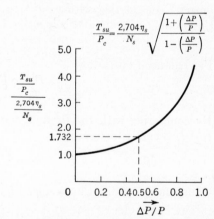

FIG. 6-8. Dimensionless curve relating stall torque per control-field watt under unbalanced power conditions to degree of unbalance.

torques per control field watt can be achieved in this manner. In specific instances, it is possible to decide how far to go in aiming for unbalanced operation by inspecting Figs. 6-7 and 6-8. Once the power adjustment in the two phases has been selected, the appropriate voltages can be determined by simple scaling. Where required, manufacturers will supply motors having special voltage and power ratings.

6-5. Characteristics of Actual (Nonidealized) Two-phase Servomotors. The previous discussion assumed the two-phase motor to be a linear actuating device and neglected nonlinearities that often provide the key

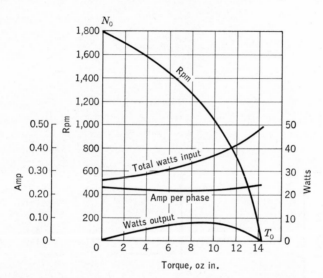

Fig. 6-9. Manufacturer's data for a typical servomotor. (*Courtesy of Diehl Manufacturing Co.*)

to more accurate design and the explanation of subtle phenomena. The ensuing sections show how a user can obtain the following information from the characteristics for balanced, rated conditions, normally furnished by a motor manufacturer in the form shown in Fig. 6-9:

1. Simple approximate expressions for the speed-torque characteristics as a function of slip

2. Expressions for the speed-torque characteristics corresponding to unbalanced operation

3. Equations for derived servomotor characteristics, such as power output, optimum gear ratio, damping characteristics, etc.

6-6. Analysis of Unbalanced Operation by Symmetrical Component Theory.[2] Except for certain stall conditions, the previous sections do not cover unbalanced operation (where control-field excitation is not equal

to main-field excitation).   Unbalanced operation may be analyzed by
the theory of symmetrical components, which states that unbalanced
applied voltages can be replaced by sets of balanced voltages, with the
resultant effect determined by summing the separate effects of the balanced systems.   Figure 6-10 shows an unbalanced set of voltages V_m
and V_c applied to the windings of a two-phase motor. V_c is expressed as
a fraction k of V_m, the balanced condition corresponding to k equals 1.
The unbalanced system can be represented by the sum of the two separate

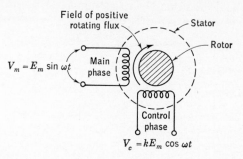

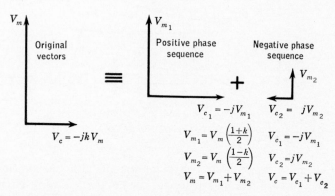

FIG. 6-10. Two-phase servomotor operating from unbalanced supply, and resolution
of unbalanced supply voltages into sum of two balanced sets.

balanced systems, so that the techniques and formulas derived for
balanced operation can be directly applied.   Since the phase sequence
of set 2 is opposite to both the original set and set 1, sets 1 and 2 are
referred to as positive and negative sequence systems, respectively.   The
negative sequence vector generates a rotating field in the induction motor
that corresponds exactly to the field generated by the positive sequence
vector, but rotating in the opposite direction.   If an induction motor is
going at slip s with respect to its normal field, then its slip with respect
to the negative rotating field is $2 - s$.   This must be considered in any
analysis of performance with negative sequence applied voltages.

6-7. Speed-Torque Curves for Nonidealized Operation. Figure 6-11 shows the condition of balanced operation of a servomotor with balanced sets of positive and negative sequence voltages of rated value separately applied.   The slip s for both sequences is always specified with respect

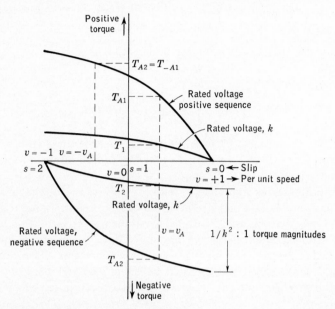

Fig. 6-11. Speed-torque curves for positive and negative sequence sets of balanced rated voltages, and k times rated values.

to the positive rotating field.   The speed-torque curves for k unequal to 1 can be readily derived from this figure.   Thus

$$V_{M1} = \frac{1 + k}{2} V_M$$

$$V_{M2} = \frac{1 - k}{2} V_M$$

Since V_{M1} and V_{M2} correspond to the balanced sequence voltages, the torque at any speed can be deduced from these values.   Substituting the parameter v equals speed per synchronous speed, or per unit speed for slip [v equals $1 - s$], determine the torques at $v = v_A$.

$$T_1 = \text{positive sequence torque} = \left(\frac{V_{M1}}{V_M}\right)^2 T_{A1}$$

$$T_2 = \text{negative sequence torque} = \left(\frac{V_{M2}}{V_M}\right)^2 T_{A2}$$

where T_{A1} and T_{A2} are the rated balanced positive and negative sequence torques.   Therefore, considering signs, the resultant torque is

$$T = T_1 - T_2 = \left(\frac{V_{M1}}{V_M}\right)^2 T_{A1} - \left(\frac{V_{M2}}{V_M}\right)^2 T_{A2}$$

$$T = \left(\frac{1+k}{2}\right)^2 T_{A1} - \left(\frac{1-k}{2}\right)^2 T_{A2}$$

where T = torque output of motor under unbalance k

By symmetry, $T_{A2} = T_{-A1}$, where T_{-A1} is the positive sequence torque at $v = v_{-A}$.   Thus

$$T = \left(\frac{1+k}{2}\right)^2 T_{A1} - \left(\frac{1-k}{2}\right)^2 T_{-A1} \qquad (6\text{-}8)$$

Thus, given the speed-torque curve for the speed range from v equals -1 to v equals $+1$, it is possible to plot the family of curves for unbalanced operations.

6-8. Infinite-series Approach.   While the above method for establishing performance is as exact as the usual design assumptions, it has the disadvantages that the speed-torque curves for negative rotation or negative v (not normally available as commercial data) are required, and that the method is largely graphical rather than analytical, often an inconvenience.   These disadvantages can be effectively overcome by representing the speed-torque curve by a series expansion in v.[3]   Thus,

$$T = T_0 + Dv + Mv^2 \qquad (6\text{-}9)$$

or on a per unit torque basis, with simplified nomenclature

$$t = 1 + dv + mv^2 \qquad (6\text{-}10)$$

where $t = \dfrac{T}{T_0}$

$d = \dfrac{D}{T_0}$

$m = \dfrac{M}{T_0}$

Limiting the expansion to three terms is suitable for most calculations, although with highly curved speed-torque curves, such as are not usually used in servomotors, an additional term may be required.

The coefficients of the second and third terms of Eqs. (6-9) and (6-10) can be established by the geometry of the balanced condition speed-torque curve.   Thus, in Fig. 6-12, where H measures the degree of curvature at the half no-load speed point $N_0/2$, the equation becomes

$$T = T_0 - \left(\frac{T_0 - 4H}{N_0}\right) N - \left(\frac{4H}{N_0{}^2}\right) N^2 \qquad (6\text{-}11)$$

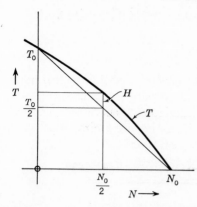

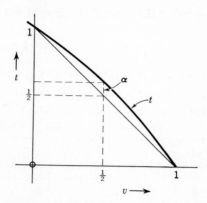

FIG. 6-12. H is a measure of the degree of curvature of actual speed-torque curve.

FIG. 6-13. Dimensionless speed-torque characteristic, where α is a measure of curvature.

While on a per unit basis, where α measures the degree of curvature at one-half of no-load speed (Fig. 6-13), the following relationships can be derived from Eq. (6-10).

$$\text{At } v = 0: \qquad 1 = 1$$
$$\text{At } v = \tfrac{1}{2}: \tfrac{1}{2} + \alpha = 1 + \frac{d}{2} + \frac{m}{4}$$
$$\text{At } v = 1: \qquad 0 = 1 + d + m$$

Solving the last two equations simultaneously yields

$$d = 4\alpha - 1$$
$$m = -4\alpha$$

so that
$$t = 1 + (4\alpha - 1)v - 4\alpha v^2 \qquad (6\text{-}12)$$

Thus, a knowledge of the stall torque, no-load speed, and the torque at one-half no-load speed establishes a suitable curve. Using the typical commercially available data from Fig. 6-9,

$$N_O = 1{,}790 \text{ rpm}$$
$$T_O = 14.2 \text{ oz-in.}$$
$$H = 11.0 - 7.2 = 3.8 \text{ oz-in.}$$
$$\alpha = H/T_O = 3.8/14.2 = 0.268$$

Substituting these values in the formula for the speed-torque curve, Eq. (6-11) gives

$$T = 14.2 - 14.2 \left(\frac{N}{N_O}\right)^2$$

or using the per unit basis, where t equals T/T_O and v equals N/N_O

$$t = 1 - v^2$$

By comparing this relationship with the general equation (6-10), notice that d equals approximately zero, and m equals -1. The calculated curve is shown plotted over the manufacturer's curve in Fig. 6-14. Better fits are achieved with smaller motors having a straighter speed-torque characteristic.

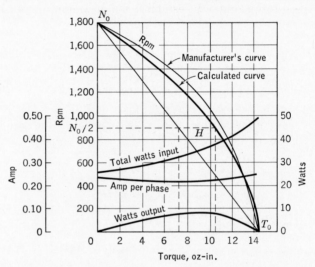

Fig. 6-14. Calculated speed-torque curve superimposed on performance curves of Fig. 6-9.

The speed for maximum power output and the magnitude of the maximum power output can also be determined from these series expansions. Multiplying Eq. (6-12) for torque by the speed v gives the power output. Power calculations based on the maximum power speed that is determined should be quite accurate since the power-speed characteristic is flat near its maximum.

$$p = tv = v + dv^2 + mv^3$$

where p is in arbitrary units. Next, differentiate this expression for power with respect to v.

$$\frac{dp}{dv} = 1 + 2dv + 3mv^2$$

Substitute suitable functions of the torque-curve parameters for d and

m and equate the derivative to zero.

$$12\alpha v^2 - 2(4\alpha - 1)v - 1 = 0$$

Solve this quadratic for its positive (useful) root.

$$v_{p\,max} = \frac{(4\alpha - 1) + \sqrt{16\alpha^2 + 4\alpha + 1}}{12} \tag{6-13}$$

where $v_{p\,max}$ = maximum power speed

Figure 6-15 is a plot of Eq. (6-13).   This can be applied to any reasonably straight speed-torque curve to establish the maximum-power point.

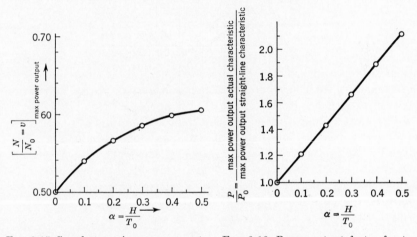

FIG. 6-15. Speed at maximum power output for two-phase servomotors.   FIG. 6-16. Power output factor for two-phase servomotors.

By substituting Eq. (6-13) in the expression for power, maximum power output can be determined.   Figure 6-16 shows the ratio of power output for a curved speed-torque characteristic, to the power corresponding to a straight line characteristic.   The latter power, P_O, can be calculated from

$$P_O = (1/5{,}408)N_OT_O \qquad \text{watts} \tag{6-14}$$

Then for small values of α, the maximum power corresponding to a curved characteristic P is related to P_O by the following expression.

$$P = P_O(1 + 2\alpha) \tag{6-15}$$

These curves can be used to determine the maximum power speed and the maximum power output for the motor having the characteristics shown in Fig. 6-14.   Referring to previous calculations, α was determined equal to 0.268.   From Fig. 6-15 v is 0.58 for an α of 0.268, so that the calculated speed for maximum power output is 1,140 rpm compared to the 1,170 read directly from the measured curve. Using Eq. (6-14), for a straight-line speed-torque curve, the output power is a maximum at $N_O/2$ and has the value

$$P_O = 4.96 \text{ watts}$$

To determine the calculated maximum output for the actual curved speed-torque characteristic, obtain the ratio P/P_O for α equal 0.268 from Fig. 6-16. Thus

$$\frac{P}{P_O} = 1.57 \qquad P = 4.69(1.57) = 7.35 \text{ watts}$$

compared to the 7.78 watts read from the measured curve. Although this speed-torque characteristic is more curved than most, the calculations supply sufficient data to correlate the above methods and actual performance. With straighter speed-torque curves, better correlation might be expected.

6-9. Speed-Torque Curves for Unbalanced Conditions. The speed-torque characteristics for unbalanced two-phase operation can be determined by applying symmetrical component theory. Using dimensionless voltages, the main field voltage is 1 and the control voltage is k. The torques corresponding to positive and negative sequences vary as the square of the corresponding sequence voltages. Designate the speed-torque characteristic due to control voltage k as

$$t_k = \left(\frac{1 + k}{2}\right)^2 t_v - \left(\frac{1 - k}{2}\right)^2 t_{-v}$$

where $t_v = 1 + dv + mv^2$
$t_{-v} = 1 - dv + mv^2$
Substituting yields

$$t_k = \left(\frac{1 + k}{2}\right)^2 (1 + dv + mv^2) - \left(\frac{1 - k}{2}\right)^2 (1 - dv + mv^2)$$

and simplifying gives

$$t_k = 2k + \frac{d}{2}(1 + k^2)v + 2kmv^2 \qquad (6\text{-}16)$$

where d and m can be established from the geometry of the balanced-condition speed-torque curve available from the manufacturer and k is the ratio of control voltage to main field voltage.

Several interesting characteristics of a servomotor can be determined from Eq. (6-16). For example, it is possible to examine the variation in zero-speed damping factor (coefficient of v, or initial slope of balanced speed-torque curve) as a function of control voltage k.

$$\frac{d}{2}(1 + k^2) = \text{damping factor} \tag{6-17}$$

Figure 6-17 shows a plot of the damping factor vs. k for v equals 0. Note that at very low control voltages (k near 0), the damping is one-half that expected under balanced conditions. And under these conditions, the usual destabilizing influences, such as backlash, resolution, resilience, etc., are most effective. The conservative positioning-servo-mechanism design rule is that effective motor damping for small signal

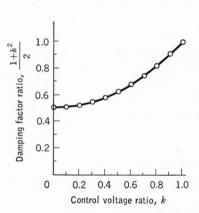

FIG. 6-17. Damping vs. control voltage for stall conditions.

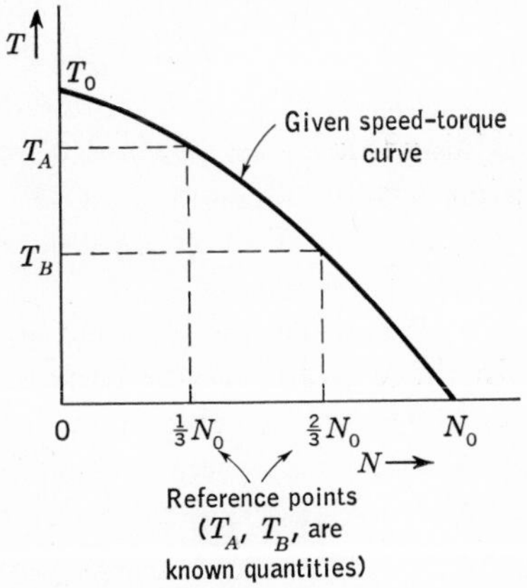

FIG. 6-18. Accuracy of curve-fitting technique can be improved by using an additional term.

stability is one-half the initial (zero-speed) slope of the normal speed-torque curve. This relationship is theoretically exact for any servomotor, and is not affected by the assumed quadratic representation of the speed-torque curve.

Servo gain is often expressed as the ratio of no-load speed to control voltage. This is a nonlinear relationship the nature of which can be determined by setting t_k equal to 0 in Eq. (6-16) and solving for v as a function of k.

$$mv^2 + vd\left(\frac{1 + k^2}{4k}\right) + 1 = 0 \tag{6-18}$$

Then for any given m and d, v can be solved for as a function of control voltage k.

There are additional applications of these techniques, all giving additional insight into motor performance beyond that supplied by the motor manufacturer. For example, by inserting a sinusoidal value for

k in the differential equation of a servomotor, the performance equations of a nonlinear motor can be obtained. An analytical expression can be developed for the reversing time of a motor driving an arbitrary load, in terms of m, d, and the characteristics of the load. Circle diagram and equivalent-circuit constants can be determined by applying the series expansion to the input current. This latter technique is also useful in establishing currents and impedances under unbalanced input conditions (for optimum driving-amplifier adjustment).

Where greater accuracy is required, the series approximation can be extended an additional term. Thus by using three points on a given speed-torque curve, as shown in Fig. 6-18, the following general expression is obtained:

$$T = T_O + C_1 N + C_2 N^2 + C_3 N^3$$

Dividing this by T_O to place it on a per unit basis and letting $N/N_O = v$ yields

$$\frac{T}{T_O} = 1 + \frac{C_1}{T_O} N_O v + \frac{C_2}{T_O} N_O^2 v^2 + \frac{C_3}{T_O} N_O^3 v^3$$

In this expression substitute

$$m_1 = \frac{C_1 N_O}{T_O}$$

$$m_2 = \frac{C_2 N_O^2}{T_O}$$

$$m_3 = \frac{C_3 N_O^3}{T_O}$$

$$t = \frac{T}{T_O}$$

$$t = 1 + m_1 v + m_2 v^2 + m_3 v^3 \tag{6-19}$$

Letting t equal 1, T_A/T_O, T_B/T_O, and 0 at v equal 0, $\frac{1}{3}$, $\frac{2}{3}$, and 1, respectively, yields a set of simultaneous equations readily solvable for m_1, m_2, and m_3 as follows:

$$m_1 = 9 \frac{T_A}{T_O} - 4.5 \frac{T_B}{T_O} - 5.5$$

$$m_2 = 9 - 18 \frac{T_B}{T_O} - 22.5 \frac{T_A}{T_O}$$

$$m_3 = -13.5 \frac{T_B}{T_O} + 13.5 \frac{T_A}{T_O} - 4.5$$

6-10. Equivalent-circuit Analysis of Two-phase Motor. In the analysis of a rotating machine by the equivalent-circuit method, a complex electromechanical structure (the rotating machine) is replaced by a

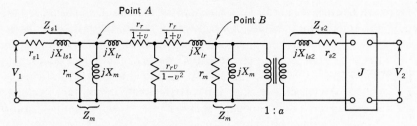

FIG. 6-19. General equivalent circuit for two-phase induction motor.

simple electrical network. Once the equivalent circuit is available, torque, current, power, and other items can be calculated without further reference to the actual machine. Equivalent-circuit constants can be predicted by the motor designer, or measured on actual machines.[4] The accuracy of equivalent-circuit calculations varies from 2 to 15 per cent, depending on the design and how accurately the circuit constants are known.

TABLE 6-2. EQUIVALENT-CIRCUIT SYMBOLS

V_1 = applied voltage on phase 1	Z_{s2} = stator impedance phase 2
V_2 = applied voltage on phase 2	r_m = core-loss resistance
a = ratio of phase 2 effective turns to phase 1 effective turns	X_m = core-loss reactance
	Z_m = core-loss impedance
r_{s1} = stator resistance phase 1	X_{lr} = rotor leakage
r_{s2} = stator resistance phase 2	r_r = effective rotor resistance
X_{ls1} = stator leakage reactance phase 1	v = ratio of actual speed to synchronous speed
X_{ls1} = stator leakage reactance phase 2	
Z_{s1} = stator impedance phase 1	

Figure 6-19 shows the equivalent circuit of a general two-phase induction motor, suitable for the analysis of either balanced or unbalanced operating conditions. The symbols used in this circuit are defined in Table 6-2. Assume that a voltage $-jaV_1$ is applied to phase 2 of this motor instead of voltage V_2. When this voltage is applied through the

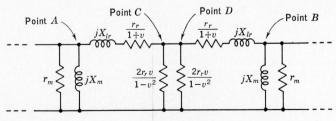

FIG. 6-20. To simplify equivalent circuit for balanced operating conditions, replace shunt resistance with two equal parallel resistances.

90° phase shifter, and scaled to suit the turns ratio a, both phases are energized equally and the motor is operating under balanced conditions. For this condition, points A and B are at the same potential. Break the shunt resistance into two parallel resistors, each having twice the combined resistance (Fig. 6-20). Points C and D are at the same potential by symmetry. Therefore, the general equivalent circuit can be separated at C and D, yielding the well-known simpler equivalent circuit for balanced two-phase motor operation shown in Fig. (6-21). Only one phase need be considered since both are identical. By substituting slip s for the per unit speed parameter v, the equivalent circuits of Fig. 6-22A and B can be obtained.

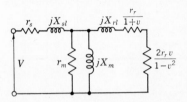

FIG. 6-21. Equivalent circuit for one phase of two-phase servomotor operating under balanced conditions.

In Fig. 6-22A, the power expended in resistor r_s is the stator copper loss, the power expended in resistor r_m is the core loss, and the power expended in r_r/s is the total power to the rotor P_{rf}. This total power to the rotor equals the sum of two powers: the rotor copper loss (resistor r_r), and the developed mechanical power [resistor $r_r(1 - s)/s$], Fig. 6-22B. Thus P_{rf} can be expressed as follows:

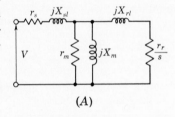

(A)

$$P_{rf} = mI_r^2 r_r + \frac{mI_r^2 r_r(1 - s)}{s} \quad (6\text{-}20)$$

where m = number of stator phases
$\quad I_r$ = rotor current
In turn

$$P_{\text{dev}} = mI_r^2 \left(\frac{r_r}{s} - r_r\right) = P_{rf}(1 - s)$$

$$(6\text{-}21)$$

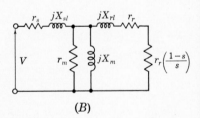

(B)

FIG. 6-22. Two forms of balanced equivalent circuits with relative speed expressed in terms of slip.

When $r_r(1 - s)/s$ equals (as s varies) the reflected source impedance seen from its terminals (V short-circuited), P_{dev} is maximum. And as pointed out previously, for a straight-line speed-torque curve corresponding to a very high rotor resistance, P_{dev} is maximum when $r_r(1 - s)/s$ is approximately equal to r_r. Thus rotor copper loss equals P_{dev} and only half the power to the rotor can be delivered as useful mechanical output. In addition, input power is reduced by stator and core losses before transfer to the rotor.

From Eq. (6-4), it can be seen that maximum torque is developed when r_r/s equals the reflected source impedance.

$$T = \frac{1,352}{N_s} P_{rf} \tag{6-4}$$

Slip at maximum torque increases proportionately with r_r.

The equivalent circuit is useful in determining the motor parameters for a maximum ratio of stall torque to stall input power.[5] At standstill, stall torque is proportional to the power dissipated in the rotor resistance r_r. The ratio of stall torque to stall input power, or torque per watt, depends on the fraction of total power dissipated in the rotor. The rotor resistance for maximum torque per watt may be determined analytically. It approximately equals the sum of rotor leakage X_{lr} and airgap reactance. The peak is broad, as can be seen from Fig. 6-23, where the shaded area represents the range of rotor resistance values for which the torque per watt efficiency is within 10 per cent of the maximum.

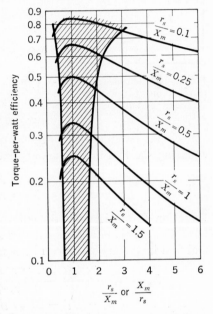

FIG. 6-23. Torque-per-watt efficiency vs. rotor resistance.

6-11. Equivalent-circuit Calculations. As indicated above, equivalent-circuit parameters can be measured in a laboratory, or they may be predicted analytically by the motor designer. Often a motor user may want to estimate equivalent-circuit parameters from the customary manufacturer's data, before buying and trying a motor. Equivalent circuit parameters can be approximated if the input data for the stall and no-load conditions are known.

Assume the stall input impedance Z_{sc} and the no-load impedance Z_{oc} are known. From these the approximate equivalent-circuit parameters can be determined. For simplicity, assume that the core loss r_m is negligible and rotor leakage reactance X_{lr} and the stator leakage reactance X_{ls} equal. These assumptions are satisfactory approximations for most instances. This yields the simplified equivalent circuit of Fig. 6-24, and the following relationships:

$$Z_r = r_r + jX_l \tag{6-22}$$
$$Z_s = r_s + jX_l \tag{6-23}$$

First obtain expressions for Z_{oc} and Z_{sc} by examining the equivalent circuit.

$$Z_{oc} = Z_s + jX_m \qquad (6\text{-}24)$$

$$Z_{sc} = Z_s + \frac{jX_m Z_r}{Z_r + jX_m} \qquad (6\text{-}25)$$

In the no-load condition, the rotor circuit is effectively open, yielding the simplified expression of Eq. (6-24). In the stall condition, slip equals 1, yielding Eq. (6-25).

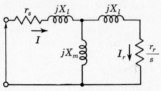

Equate the real and imaginary parts of Eqs. (6-24) and (6-25) to new unknowns as follows:

$$Z_{oc} = r_s + jX_l + jX_m = M + jN \qquad (6\text{-}26)$$

FIG. 6-24. Determine equivalent circuit parameters from stall and no-load performance data.

$$Z_{sc} = \frac{Z_s Z_r + jX_m(Z_s + Z_r)}{Z_r + jX_m} = P + jQ \qquad (6\text{-}27)$$

Since the object is to solve for the equivalent-circuit parameters of Fig. 6-24, Eq. (6-26) simplifies quite easily by equating the real and imaginary parts.

$$r_s = M \qquad (6\text{-}28)$$
$$X_l = N - X_m \qquad (6\text{-}29)$$

Equation (6-27) is more difficult to handle. However, by performing the following manipulations it can be converted into a form wherein the real and imaginary parts can be equated.

$$Z_{sc} = \frac{(r_s + jX_l)(r_r + jX_l) + jX_m(r_s + jX_l) + jX_m(r_r + jX_l)}{r_r + (jX_l + jX_m)}$$

$$P + jQ = \frac{(r_s r_r - X_l^2 - 2X_m X_l) + j[(X_m + X_l)(r_r + r_s)]}{r_r + j(X_l + X_m)}$$

Substituting Eqs. (6-28) and (6-29) yields

$$(r_r P + QN) + j(Qr_r + NP) = (Mr_r - X_l^2 - 2X_m X_l) + jN(r_r + M)$$

Equating the imaginary parts,

$$N(r_r + M) = Qr_r + NP$$

$$r_r = N\frac{M - P}{Q - N} \qquad (6\text{-}30)$$

Equating the real parts,

$$-r_r P + QN = -Mr_r + X_l^2 + 2X_l X_m$$

Rearrange and introduce a new variable F, where

$$F = [r_r(M - P) + QN] = X_l^2 + 2X_m X_l \qquad (6\text{-}31)$$

Substituting,

$$X_m = N - X_l$$
$$X_l^2 - 2X_lN + F = 0$$

Solving the quadratic for the positive root yields

$$X = N - \sqrt{N^2 - F}$$

and
$$X_m = \sqrt{N^2 - F} \qquad (6\text{-}32)$$

Summarizing the above equations yields all the desired equivalent-circuit parameters.

$$r_s = M \qquad\qquad X_l = N - X_m$$

$$r_r = N\,\frac{M - P}{Q - N} \qquad X_m = \sqrt{N^2 - F}$$

where $F = r_r(M - P) + QN$

$$Z_{oc} = M + jN$$
$$Z_{sc} = P + jQ$$

Sample Calculation. *Problem.* Determine the equivalent-circuit parameters for a Mark VII servomotor, given the following information from the manufacturer's catalog sheet.

AT STALL

Input voltage.............. 115 volts
Power factor................... 0.49
Input current............ 0.108 amp
Input power.............. 6.1 watts

AT NO LOAD

Input voltage.............. 115 volts
Power factor................... 0.26
Input current............ 0.100 amp
Input power.............. 3 watts

Solution. Using the technique described in the previous section, determine the input impedance at stall and no load.

Z_{sc} = input voltage/input current = $115/0.108$ = 1,065 ohms

Then with a power factor of 0.49

$$\text{arcos } 0.49 = 60.6°$$
$$\sin 60.6° = 0.87$$

and
$$Z_{sc} = 521 + j926 = P + jQ$$
$$P = 521$$
$$Q = 926$$

Under no-load conditions

$$Z_{oc} = 115/0.100 = 1,150 \text{ ohms}$$

Then with a power factor of 0.26

$$\arccos 0.26 = 74.9°$$
$$\sin 74.9° = 0.965$$

and
$$Z_{oc} = 298 + j1,100 = M + jN$$
$$M = r_s = 298$$
$$N = X_l + X_m = 1,100$$

Using Eqs. (6-30) to (6-32), determine the remaining parameters.

$$r_r = N \frac{M - P}{Q - N} = 1,100 \left(\frac{298 - 521}{926 - 1,100} \right) = 1,410 \text{ ohms}$$

$$F = r_r(M - P) + QN = 1,410(298 - 521) + (926)(1,100) = 706,000$$
$$X_m = \sqrt{N^2 - F} = \sqrt{(1,100)^2 - 706,000} = 710 \text{ ohms}$$
$$X_l = N - X_m = 1,100 - 710 = 390 \text{ ohms}$$

Figure 6-25 shows the completed equivalent circuit, including all parameters.

To check the accuracy of the above calculations, compute the stall torque and compare with the measured stall torque. First determine the rotor current, I_r.

$$I_r = I \left| \frac{jX_m}{r_r + j(X + X_m)} \right| = 0.108 \left| \frac{j710}{1,410 + j1,100} \right| = 0.0429 \text{ amp}$$

Then the power to the rotor per phase P_{rf} is

$$P_{rf} = I_r^2 r_r = (0.0429)^2 1,410 = 2.6 \text{ watts per phase}$$

and using Eq. (6-4) to determine the stall torque

$$T = \frac{1,352}{N_s} P_{rf}(\text{total}) = \frac{1,352}{6,000} (2)(2.6) = 1.170 \text{ oz-in.}$$

This compares with an actual stall torque of 1.52 oz-in., an error of 23 per cent. This is satisfactory considering the roughness of the approximations.

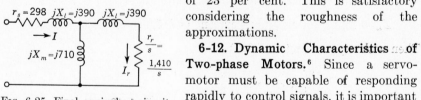

FIG. 6-25. Final equivalent-circuit parameters.

6-12. Dynamic Characteristics of Two-phase Motors.[6] Since a servomotor must be capable of responding rapidly to control signals, it is important to supplement the static characteristics with information on dynamic performance. Assuming a linear relation between torque and control phase voltages, the following represent the principal figures used in comparing the dynamic performance of two-phase motors.

Torque constant $K = T_s/V_c$, dyne-cm/volt
Velocity constant $K_v = K/D$, radians/sec/volt
Acceleration constant $K_a = K/J$, radians/sec²/volt
Natural or mechanical time constant $\tau = J/D$, sec
Torque-to-inertia ratio $\alpha = T_s/J$, radians/sec²

The torque-to-inertia ratio α defines the maximum acceleration that a motor at zero speed can accurately track. This ratio is a figure of merit when load inertia is negligible, as is often the case in instrument servos. If the load inertia is appreciable, and an output gear ratio is selected that matches motor inertia to load inertia for maximum acceleration, then the ratio of stall torque to effective motor-shaft inertia is one-half this figure of merit.

The motor time constant τ is comparable with the L/R time constant of an RL network. It is an inverse measure of the maximum frequency component of the control signal that the servo can accurately follow. The velocity constant K_v is an effective amplification factor. When an amplifier is used to drive the control winding, K can be effectively increased to very high values. With a servo error signal E applied to an amplifier, the servomotor in the linear region assumes the velocity KE/D (where K includes the amplifier gain). Conversely, if it is known that the servo must track an input velocity ω, then the consequent error is $\omega D/K$.

To determine the system characteristics of a servomotor, consider it as a black box with control voltage as an input and shaft rotation as an output. The differential equation of the system is

$$T = KV_c = J\frac{d^2\theta}{dt^2} + D\frac{d\theta}{dt}$$

When a step input of voltage is applied to this motor, the transient solution of this differential equation is

$$\frac{d\theta}{dt} = K_v V_c(1 - e^{-Dt/J}) \tag{6-33}$$

which is the well-known exponential response of a single time-constant system to a step input. From the differential equation, by operational methods, the transfer function of the motor may be derived

$$KG(p) = \frac{K_v}{p(\tau p + 1)} \tag{6-34}$$

This transfer function indicates that phase shift cannot exceed 180° at any frequency. Because of secondary time constants, experimental data

do not support this conclusion, and a more complex transfer function
is required to better describe motor performance.

$$KG(p) = \frac{K_v}{p(\tau p + 1)(cp + 1)} \tag{6-35}$$

This transfer function includes a second motor time constant c in addition to the mechanical time constant. In accordance with Brown[7] this

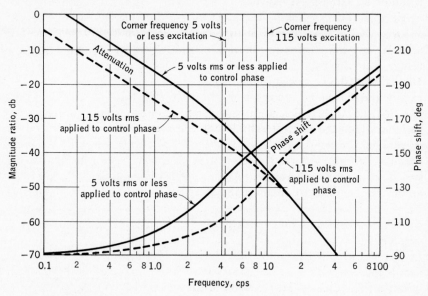

FIG. 6-26. Specifications and constants for Mark VII servomotor. (*Courtesy of
Kearfott Co., Inc.*)

SPECIFICATIONS		CONSTANTS	
	Control voltage	5 volts or less	115 volts
Frequency......... 400 cps	K.............	950 dyne-cm/volt	950 dyne-cm/volt
Rotor inertia....... 3.3 g-cm²	K_v.............	12 radians/sec/volt	4.9 radians/sec/volt
Stall torque........ 1.45 in.-oz	τ.............	0.038 sec	0.016 sec
No-load speed...... 5,000 rpm	D.............	79 dyne-cm/radian/sec	192 dyne-cm/radian/sec
Connected series...	L/R...........	0.0007 sec	0.0007 sec

is taken as the electrical time constant and when evaluated as L/R
yields the calculated frequency response plot of Fig. 6-26 for a Mark VII
servomotor. The specifications and constants for this motor are given
in Fig. 6-26. As expected, the calculated phase shift now approaches
270°. For practical purposes the electrical time constant is often ignored,
since it rarely influences performance at lower frequencies. Its principal effect is on system stability. For the specific motor considered
here, it is theoretically estimated to have a reciprocal angular frequency
of over 200 cps.

6-13. Servomotor Driving Circuits.[1] Since motor impedance varies considerably with speed, it is impossible to secure a universal match between the servomotor and its driver amplifier. Therefore, an optimum adjustment is established with the motor at stall. To secure unity power factor for motor impedance, the control winding is generally tuned by a parallel capacitor. While this introduces an additional inductive time delay in the loop, this delay normally occurs at such a high frequency that it does not introduce problems.

To minimize amplifier output impedance, negative feedback is used. With low output impedance the motor can be operated over a considerable speed range without appreciably disturbing the voltage balance required for satisfactory performance. In contrast, high output impedance can be quite harmful. For example, if a control winding is driven from a high source impedance, for a fixed error signal applied to the amplifier the increased motor impedance at high speeds results in a corresponding increase in control-winding voltage. This yields a higher torque than would be indicated by the desired straight-line speed-torque curve, and results in a typical change of shape as shown in Fig. 6-27.

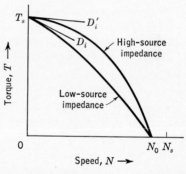

FIG. 6-27. Effect of control-source impedance on shape of speed-torque curve. D_i = initial or low-speed damping-coefficient slope, low-source impedance; D_i' = initial or low-speed damping-coefficient slope, high-source impedance.

This "effective" speed-torque curve is nonlinear, underdamped, and means poor servo stability. Effective damping can be considerably reduced or even made negative by increasing the control-source impedance. Actually, the change in shape of the speed-torque curve indicates the tendency of a servomotor to operate on single phase (with zero control volts). High source impedance often occurs when using magnetic-amplifier circuits and half-wave circuits to drive the control winding of a motor.

6-14. Single-phasing Criterion.[2] Single phasing is a loose term applied to servomotors that continue to run with zero voltage on the control phase winding. This occurs when the zero-speed internal damping is zero or negative. Although motors that single phase are often usable in servomechanisms where adequate damping is provided by other means, this characteristic is generally undesirable in small general-purpose servomotors that are used mainly in relatively simple systems.

As discussed previously, the prevention of single phasing (increase in internal damping) by using a high-resistance rotor that generates a straight-line speed-torque characteristic results in a reduction in motor efficiency. This is of little consequence in small instrument servomotors, but can become important in larger units.

The tendency of a servomotor to single phase depends on the nature of the control-winding driving circuit as well as on rotor resistance. The following driving-circuit conditions are listed in order of increased tendency to single phase: condition 1 is least likely and condition 3 is most likely.

1. Control winding energized from a voltage source having negligible internal resistance.

2. Control winding energized from a voltage source having high internal resistance.

3. Control winding shunted by a tuning capacitor and energized from a voltage source having high internal resistance.

Condition 2 is the most common criterion for single phasing of small servomotors. The test is run by disconnecting the control winding (corresponding to an infinite source impedance) while the motor is operating at no load, at which time the motor should stop. If high internal damping is generated by the main field, the motor will stop quickly, while the motor will coast to a stop under the influence of friction if there is zero damping. Stopping time is an inverse measure of damping. A motor with no single-phasing tendency during this test can still single phase if a tuning capacitor (such as is typically used to achieve unity power factor at stall) remains connected across the control phase after the phase is disconnected from the line.

Larger servomotors are often not subjected to the severe criterion of condition 2. A large motor that single phases violently when its control field is open can still demonstrate excellent damping when the control phase is short-circuited. In using such a motor it is imperative that the driving amplifier have low output impedance, a condition that can be achieved with generous feedback. Increased motor efficiency makes this well worthwhile.

It has been shown previously that under balanced operating conditions the damping at stall is a function of the magnitude of the control field voltage. At zero control voltage stall damping is one-half the value corresponding to rated control voltage. Thus if damping under rated conditions is zero or negative, it will also be zero or negative for zero control voltage. This establishes the single-phasing criterion for operation from a low-impedance source.

The motor design factor that determines single phasing is the rotor resistance. By applying Thévenin's theorem to the balanced two-phase motor equivalent circuit of Fig. 6-28, the simpler form of Fig. 6-29 is obtained.   In these diagrams

V_m = main field voltage

Z_c = external impedance in the control-winding circuit

Y_m = magnetizing admittance

$$V_a = -\frac{jV_c}{a} \frac{1}{1 + Y_m(r_s + jX_{sl}) + \dfrac{Z_c}{a^2}}$$

$$V_b = \frac{V_m}{1 + Y_m(r_s + jX_{sl})}$$

Thus with zero control phase voltage (V_c equals 0) a motor develops negative torque (positive damping) at all speeds only if

$$r_r > |Z_a| \tag{6-36}$$

where Z_a is the Thévenin's theorem source impedance as indicated in Fig. 6-29.   A motor will not single phase if its parameters satisfy the criterion expressed by Eq. (6-36) while operated in a balanced condition.

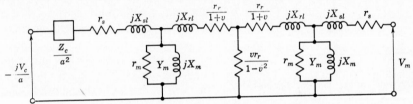

FIG. 6-28. Equivalent circuit form for determining single-phasing criterion.

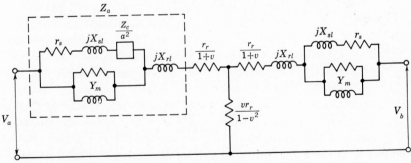

FIG. 6-29. Servomotor will not single-phase if r_r is greater than Z_a.

Next consider the case where the control winding is excited from an infinite impedance source, assuming tentatively that the main winding is excited from a similar source.   In this "balanced" condition the single-phasing criterion applies as before, with the modification that rotor resistance must exceed the Thévenin's theorem source impedance with the primary excitation source replaced by an open circuit.

Now reexamine the assumption that the primary excitation is derived from an infinite impedance source. Actually the only effect of this source impedance is to vary the voltage applied to the main winding as a function of the winding impedance or speed. By this reasoning it can be seen that the assumption of infinite main field source impedance is unnecessary, and the conclusions are still valid with finite impedance. This reasoning can also be extended to the case where the control winding is shunted by a tuning capacitor.

To determine the single-phasing criterion for the unbalanced condition of an infinite impedance source driving the control winding and a finite impedance source driving the main winding, consider the equivalent circuit of Fig. 6-30. Since there is no control-winding voltage, there is only a single-phase field pulsating in space. This pulsating field is equivalent to two opposite fields, each rotating at synchronous speed. Rotor slip with respect to the positive field is s, and with respect to the negative field is $2 - s$. The upper mesh of the equivalent circuit corresponds to the positive field and may be used to calculate the positive component of torque, while the lower mesh corresponds similarly to the negative rotating field.

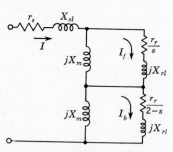

FIG. 6-30. Equivalent circuit for deriving more general single-phasing criterion under conditions of unbalanced source impedance.

The object is to determine whether the total torque is positive or negative for slow speeds. If positive, the motor will accelerate and single phase; if negative, the motor will be damped to a stop.

Torque can be calculated if the power dissipated in the rotor resistance is known as demonstrated by Eq. (6-4).

$$T_s = \frac{1,352}{N_s} P_{rf} \qquad (6\text{-}4)$$

The power to the rotor resistance can be determined by calculating the mesh impedances and currents flowing through r_r/s and $r_r/(2 - s)$. To simplify the derivation, replace s by $1 - v$, where v is per cent speed.

$$Z_f = \frac{jX_m[r_r/(1 - v) + jX_{rl}]}{r_r/(1 - v) + j(X_{rl} + X_m)}$$

$$Z_b = \frac{jX_m[r_r/(1 + v) + jX_{rl}]}{r_r/(1 + v) + j(X_{rl} + X_m)}$$

Now determine currents I_f and I_b.

$$I_f = \frac{jX_m}{r_r/(1 - v) + j(X_{rl} + X_m)}$$

$$I_b = \frac{jX_m}{r_r/(1 + v) + j(X_{rl} + X_m)}$$

and the power dissipated in the rotor resistances

$$I_f^2 \frac{r_r}{1 - v} = \frac{X_m^2 r_r}{[r_r/(1 - v)]^2 + (X_{rl} + X_m)^2} \frac{1}{1 - v}$$

$$I_b^2 \frac{r_r}{1 + v} = \frac{X_m^2 r_r}{[r_r/(1 + v)]^2 + (X_{rl} + X_m)^2} \frac{1}{1 + v}$$

Using Eq. (6-4), determine the positive and negative torques

$$T_f \propto \frac{X_m^2 r_r (1 + v)}{r_r^2 (1 + v)^2 + (X_{rl} + X_m)^2}$$

$$T_b \propto \frac{X_m^2 r_r (1 - v)}{r_r^2 (1 - v)^2 + (X_{rl} + X_m)^2}$$

Rearranging and assuming that v is small yields

$$T_f \cong \frac{[X_m/(X_{rl} + X_m)]^2 r_r (1 + v)}{1 + [r_r/(X_{rl} + X_m)]^2 (1 + 2v)}$$

$$T_b \cong \frac{[X_m/(X_{rl} + X_m)]^2 r_r (1 - v)}{1 + [r_r/(X_{rl} + X_m)]^2 (1 - 2v)}$$

Since the total torque is the difference between the torques generated by the forward field and the backward field, a motor will not single phase when T_b exceeds T_f.

$$T_b - T_f = h\left[\frac{1 - v}{1 + g(1 - 2v)} - \frac{1 + v}{1 + g(1 + 2v)}\right]$$

where $h = r_r \left(\frac{X_m}{X_{rl} + X_m}\right)^2$

$$g = \left(\frac{r_r}{X_{rl} + X_m}\right)^2$$

Letting $m = \frac{2g}{1 + g}$

and $n = \frac{h}{1 + g}$

rearranging and simplifying yields

$$T_\Delta = T_b - T_f = h(2v)(m - 1)$$

For T_Δ to be positive, m must be greater than 1.   Thus

$$m = \frac{2g}{1 + g} > 1$$
$$2g > g + 1$$
$$g > 1$$

where
$$g = \left(\frac{r_r}{X_{rl} + X_m}\right)^2$$

Therefore, the single-phasing criterion is

$$r_r > X_{rl} + X_m \tag{6-37}$$

Or, in other words, the rotor resistance must be greater than the sum of the rotor leakage and mutual inductance if the motor is not to single phase.

6-15. Phase Shifting of Main Field Voltage.[8]   In a-c servomechanisms, it is frequently necessary to shift the phase of the voltage on the motor main field winding with respect to the line.   There is no simple means of maintaining this exact phase shift at all speeds.   However, the two-capacitor method shown in Fig. 6-31 gives good results for small instrument servomotors when adjusted with the motor stalled.   In contrast with the single-capacitor method discussed below, using two capacitors permits simultaneous adjustment of both voltage magnitude and phase on the main winding.   The equations for establishing capacitor values, together with the equations for determining capacitor voltage are listed in the table in Fig. 6-31.   The following two examples show the use of this technique.

Example 1.   The Bureau of Ordnance Mark VII, 400-cps 115-volt servomotor has a rated current of 0.110 amp at stall and a power factor of 0.5.   Determine C_1 and C_2 and their voltage ratings if a 90° phase shift and unity magnitude ratio are to be achieved from a 115-volt line.

Solution.   Referring to Fig. 6-31, use Eqs. (7) for 400 cps:

$$C_1 = 397.8 \frac{(0.5)(0.110)}{115} = 0.190 \ \mu\text{f}$$

$$C_2 = 397.8(0.110) \frac{(\sqrt{1 - 0.5^2} - 0.5)}{115} = 0.139 \ \mu\text{f}$$

and the capacitor voltage equations to determine their voltage ratings

$$V_{C1} = 115(1 + 1)^{1/2} = 162 \text{ volts}$$
$$V_{C2} = 115 \text{ volts}$$

Example 2.   For a variation in the way these equations can be used, assume that a 90° phase shift is to be obtained with the motor discussed

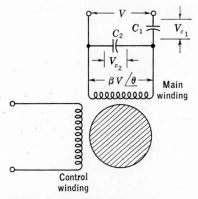

FIG. 6-31. Two-capacitor method of phase shifting main field excitation. Winding power factor $= P_f$; rated main-winding voltage $= V$; rated main-winding current $= I$.

General Form: Any phase shift and any magnitude ratio

$$(1) \quad C_1 = \frac{BP_fI}{\omega V} \csc \theta$$

$$(2) \quad C_2 = I \frac{(\cos \theta - B)P_f + \sin \theta \sqrt{1 - P_f^2}}{\omega V \sin \theta}$$

Special Form: For 90° phase shift and any magnitude ratio

$$(3) \quad C_1 = \frac{BP_fI}{\omega V} \qquad (4) \quad C_2 = I \frac{\sqrt{1 - P_f^2} - BP_f}{\omega V}$$

Special Form: For 90° phase shift and unity voltage ratio

$$(5) \quad C_1 = \frac{P_fI}{\omega V} \qquad (6) \quad C_2 = I \frac{\sqrt{1 - P_f^2} - P_f}{V}$$

Special Form: Eqs. (5) and (6) for 60 and 400 cycles

(7)	60 cps	400 cps
C_1, μfd	$2{,}652 \dfrac{P_fI}{V}$	$397.8 \dfrac{P_fI}{V}$
C_2, μfd	$2{,}652I \dfrac{\sqrt{1 - P_f^2} - P_f}{V}$	$397.8I \dfrac{\sqrt{1 - P_f^2} - P_f}{V}$

Capacitor Voltage Ratings:

Across capacitor C_1 $V_{C1} = V(1 + B^2 - 2B \cos \theta)^{\frac{1}{2}}$
Across capacitor C_2 $V_{C2} = BV$

in Example 1 without using C_2 (in other words, C_2 equals zero). Determine the voltage impressed on the main motor winding under this condition.

Solution. Setting Eq. (4) in Fig. 6-31 equal to zero,

$$0 = \sqrt{1 - P_f^2} - BP_f$$

Then B can be expressed by

$$B = \frac{\sqrt{1 - P_f{}^2}}{P_f}$$

and where P_f equals 0.5, the motor must be designed to accept 200 volts on its main winding.

The single capacitor plus resistor phase-shifting technique uses the configuration shown in Fig. 6-32. Assume that the windings are identical and that the problem is to shift the main winding line voltage 90° while maintaining the voltage magnitude at the motor.

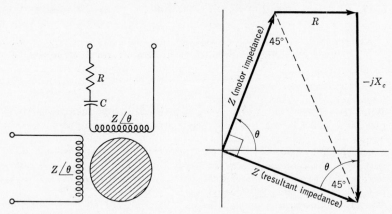

FIG. 6-32. Single capacitor plus resistor configuration.

FIG. 6-33. Vector diagram of main phase.

The vector diagram of Fig. 6-33 shows the geometric relations. The fundamental relationships are

$$\frac{R}{X_c} = \tan(\theta - 45)$$
$$X_c = Z \cos \theta + Z \sin \theta$$

Therefore the value of the phase-shifting capacitor can be calculated from

$$X_c = Z(\sin \theta + \cos \theta) \tag{6-38}$$

where Z is the motor impedance and θ is the motor phase angle.

In turn, the value of resistor R can be determined.

$$\frac{R}{X_c} = \tan(\theta - 45) = \frac{\sin \theta - \cos \theta}{\sin \theta + \cos \theta}$$
$$\frac{R}{X_c} = \frac{\sin \theta - \cos \theta}{X_c/Z}$$

and
$$R = Z(\sin \theta - \cos \theta) \tag{6-39}$$

Notice that this approach does not work for θ less than 45° since R must be less than zero, an unrealizable case.

6-16. Selecting a Motor and Gear-train Combination. A servomotor usually drives its load through a gear train. The motor must be capable of driving against the frictional load (including its own internal damping) and accelerating the effective inertia at a rapid enough rate to follow suitably the input signal to the servomechanism. Thus, the motor and gear train must be selected with previous knowledge of the load and the tracking requirements. The gear train acts like an impedance-matching transformer; optimizing the power transfer to the load.

6-17. Choosing the Motor-load Gear Ratio. Gear-ratio determination will be considered for three conditions: for linear systems the optimum

TABLE 6-3. COMMON SITUATIONS IN GEAR-RATIO SELECTION

1. When the reference signal varies at a relatively constant speed, the gear ratio should permit following at this speed.
2. When the reference signal experiences sudden increments (high acceleration) the gear ratio should be selected to achieve maximum torque to inertia ratio at the output.
3. Where static accuracy or slow smooth following is a principal consideration, the gear ratio should amplify motor torque so that the output torque is capable of maintaining the error within allowable limits. This gear ratio is usually inefficient in terms of power transfer to the load.
4. When there are special requirements such as the ability to maintain simultaneously a specified velocity and acceleration, or the need for rapid reversal, or the requirement of minimum time to come up to speed or a maximum allowable braking time.
5. When a specified friction load is to be carried at a given speed (either a constant friction or a linear speed-varying drag).

ratios for the typical situations of Table 6-3 can be determined from simple mathematical relationships based on an equivalent-circuit analysis. For nonlinear circuit elements, the optimum ratio must be determined graphically. And finally, for negligible load, the motor-load matching function is unimportant, and the ratio can be related to system gain, or stiffness.

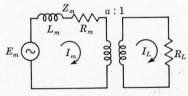

FIG. 6-34. Equivalent circuit for condition of maximum dissipative load velocity under steady conditions.

6-18. Optimum Gear Ratio in Linear Systems.[9] For linear motor and load the equivalent-circuit analysis can be used to determine the optimum gear ratio. Figures 6-34 to 6-36 show three simplified circuits that can be used for this purpose.

Tooth resilience (including backlash) and tooth elasticity are assumed negligible.

Figure 6-34 is used in deriving the gear ratio for maximum steady-state velocity of a friction load. Since the equivalent-circuit approach is used, electrical symbols are substituted for mechanical symbols. These correspond as follows:

$E \equiv T$ = torque at shaft
$L \equiv J$ = gear inertia
$R \equiv D$ = friction drag on shaft
$I \equiv$ load velocity
$a \equiv n_1/n_2$ = reciprocal gear ratio (less than 1)
$Z \equiv$ electrical impedance of L and R in series

The steady-state drop across the inductance L_m is zero (input gear inertia does not affect system performance at constant angular velocity).

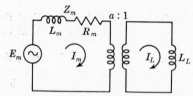

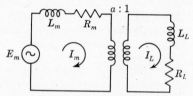

FIG. 6-35. Circuit for condition of maximum initial load acceleration.

FIG. 6-36. Circuit for condition of minimum required motor torque to attain a specified load velocity and load acceleration.

Thus load velocity can be expressed by

$$I_L = \frac{aE_m}{R_m + a^2R_L} \tag{6-40}$$

To optimize the gear ratio, differentiate I_L with respect to a and equate to zero. This yields

$$a = \sqrt{\frac{R_m}{R_L}} \tag{6-41}$$

Thus the optimum ratio equals the square root of the ratio of motor friction to load friction. This is analogous to matching electrical resistances.

Figure 6-35 shows the equivalent circuit of a gear train coupled to an inertial load. The object is to determine the gear ratio for maximum load acceleration. Assume zero initial velocity (I_m equals zero), and a suddenly applied torque E_m.

For this condition, motor torque can be expressed approximately by the equation

$$E_m \cong (I_m + a^2 L_L) \frac{dI_m}{dt} \qquad (6\text{-}42)$$

and load acceleration A_L is

$$A_L = \frac{I_L}{dt} = a \frac{I_m}{dt} \qquad (6\text{-}43)$$

Combining Eqs. (6-42) and (6-43), differentiating A_L with respect to a, and equating to zero gives

$$a = \sqrt{\frac{L_m}{L_L}} \qquad (6\text{-}44)$$

Thus the optimum ratio for this condition equals the square root of the ratio of motor to load inertias.

Figure 6-36 shows the equivalent circuit of a gear train driving a load consisting of both inertia and friction. The object is to determine the gear ratio that requires minimum motor torque to achieve simultaneously a specified load velocity and load acceleration. The given quantities are the motor and load frictional drag, R_m and R_L, the motor and load inertia, L_m and L_L, the specified load velocity, I_L, and specified load acceleration, dI_L/dt. Following a procedure similar to that of the previous two cases yields

$$a = \sqrt{\frac{R_m I_L + L_m \dfrac{dI_L}{dt}}{R_L I_L + I_L \dfrac{dI_L}{dt}}} \qquad (6\text{-}45)$$

which is the optimum gear ratio.

Optimum Gear Ratio Using Graphical Technique.[1,10] Under unusual load conditions or with nonlinear motor characteristics, optimum gear ratio can be best determined by using the following graphical technique.

Unless the load is negligible, simultaneous figures of load velocity and acceleration are usually specified. If calculations are made at the low-speed or load shaft for a gear ratio n, then this is expressible as a required load power:

$$P_L = v \left[(J_L + n^2 J_m) \frac{dv}{dt} + (F_L + n^2 v D) \right] \qquad (6\text{-}46)$$

where v = load velocity
J_L = load inertia
J_m = motor inertia
$\dfrac{dv}{dt}$ = load acceleration
F_L = load friction
$n^2 v D$ = motor friction
D = motor damping coefficient

Because of reflected motor damping and inertia, the total power requirement is a function of gear ratio. The following steps establish whether a given motor can supply the above P_L (and at the same time determine the optimum gear ratio). For a series of gear ratios, the motor operating at nv will drive the load at the required rate v. From the motor speed-torque curve, the motor torque T corresponding to speed v is determined. Then motor power is

$$P_m = \frac{1}{1,352} NT \qquad (6\text{-}47)$$

where N = rpm (corresponding to nv)

T = torque, oz-in.

P_m = power, watts

If the curves of motor power P_m and load power P_L are plotted together vs. gear ratio (Fig. 6-37), the capacity of the motor to drive the load is

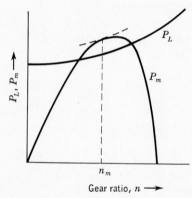

Fig. 6-37. Graphical method of determining optimum gear ratio.

apparent. A range of suitable gear ratios is also established. For best performance, the selected gear ratio should give a maximum factor of safety or ratio of P_m to P_L. This ideal ratio n_m occurs within the overlapping portion of the curves.

The foregoing procedure does not include the effect of gear-train inertia, which may sometimes be significant. If gear-train inertia is significant, first determine an optimum n_m approximately by the above graphical procedure. Then using the techniques of Sec. 6-19, select the number of stages and the individual stage ratios for the required over-all ratio n_m, and calculate equivalent gear-train inertia J_g referred to the load shaft. With gear-train inertia included, Eq. (6-46) becomes

$$P_L = v \left[(J_L + J_g + n^2 J_m) \frac{dv}{dt} + (F_L + n^2 v D) \right] \qquad (6\text{-}48)$$

Using Eq. (6-48), plot another P_L curve on Fig. 6-37 and determine a new optimum n_m. In almost all systems this is sufficient, although the procedure can be repeated with the new n_m if necessary.

6-19. Gear-ratio Selection with Negligible Load. When the load is negligible, gear ratio may be related to any combination of the following factors:

1. Adequate speed and/or acceleration of the load
2. Required value of loop gain
3. Sufficient output torque to overcome friction easily, ensuring smooth
following and adequate static accuracy

6-20. Choosing Number of Stages and Stage Ratios. The effective
gear-train inertia for a given over-all ratio between driving element and
load can be minimized by the proper choice of the individual stage ratios.
(Over-all gear ratio is determined as discussed above.) Since gear inertia
varies as the fourth power of diameter, the first stage or two usually use
small gears, and therefore have relatively low ratios. The slower gears
beyond the second stage contribute little to effective inertia.

For most servomechanism gear trains, satisfactory calculations can
be made by assuming identical pinions throughout, and uniform materials
and face widths. Inertias of shafts, bear-
ing races, and other small parts are
neglected.

**6-21. Stage Ratios by Equivalent-cir-
cuit Analysis.** The equivalent circuit may
be used to determine the stage ratios for
minimum gear-train inertia. Resilience,
backlash, gear friction, and other residual
effects are assumed negligible. The equivalent circuit then takes the relatively simple form of Fig. 6-38. This approximate

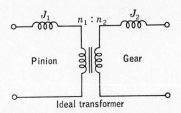

FIG. 6-38. Equivalent circuit for
ideal gear train including effects
of gear inertia.

equivalent circuit is actually suitable for the dynamic analysis of most
closed-loop systems. Gear inertia can be related to the inertia of the
mating pinion by using the following expression. Subscripts 1 and 2 refer
to pinion and gear, respectively.

$$J_2 = \left(\frac{n_2}{n_1}\right)^4 \left(\frac{\rho_2}{\rho_1}\right) \left(\frac{W_2}{W_1}\right) J_1 \tag{6-49}$$

where J = gear inertia
n = number of gear teeth
ρ = density of gear material
W = gear-face width

Figure 6-39 shows a two-stage gear train with finite inertia in the separate stages, and its equivalent circuit. The problem is to choose stage
ratios a_1 and a_2 which minimize train inertia reflected back to the motor
shaft, for an over-all ratio a.

For simplicity it is assumed that the same gear materials and face
widths are used throughout, and that shafts, clamps, and other miscellaneous hardware contribute negligible inertia. These assumptions are

not essential, however.   The equivalent-circuit approach applies to the most general situation.

Proceeding from Eq. (6-49), assuming two identical pinions, it can be shown that a_1 is approximately

$$a_1 = \sqrt[6]{\frac{a^2}{2}} \tag{6-50}$$

For minimum reflected inertia in a two-stage gear train, the first stage ratio should bear this relation to the over-all gear ratio.

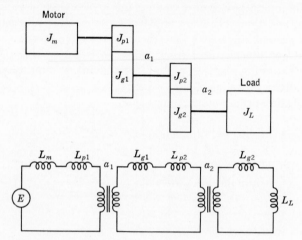

FIG. 6-39. Two-stage gear train and its equivalent circuit.

From the first stage ratio, calculate the ratio of gear-train inertia to motor pinion inertia.

$$\frac{L_T'}{L_p} = 1 + \frac{3}{(2a)^{\frac{2}{3}}} + \sqrt[3]{\frac{a^2}{2}} \tag{6-51}$$

where L_T' = gear train inertia as seen at motor shaft

This represents the inertia of a two-stage gear train.   For comparison, the ratio of total inertia to motor pinion inertia for a single stage having the same over-all ratio can be expressed by

$$\frac{L_T'}{L_p} = \frac{1}{a^2} + 1 \tag{6-52}$$

For a specific value of total ratio a equals $\frac{1}{27}$, Eqs. (6-51) and (6-52) give a relative total gearing inertia for the one- and two-stage trains of $27(2)^{\frac{2}{3}}$. Thus the use of multiple stages results in decidedly lower gearing inertia. However, there are other factors to be considered such as manufacturing tolerances, space limitations, and cost.

This above analysis has been extended to any given number of stages. The results are conveniently available in curves and a nomogram which follow.

6-22. Number of Stages and Ratios from Curves and a Nomogram. Applying the procedure and assumptions of the preceding section, the curves of Fig. 6-40[11] are obtained. These suggest the optimum number of stages for a given over-all gear ratio, and give the ratio of gear train to motor pinion inertias for optimum individual stage ratios.

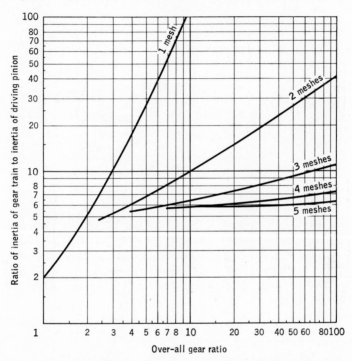

FIG. 6-40. Curves for determining optimum number of gear stages. (*Courtesy of Reeves Instrument Corp.*)

For example, for an over-all ratio of 11, four stages are close to optimum and the ratio of reflected train inertia to driving pinion inertia is 5.8.

Figure 6-41 shows four sets of curves that can be used to determine the number of gear meshes and the individual mesh ratios for minimum total gear-train inertia reflected to the driving shaft.[9,12] These curves cover over-all ratios ranging from 1.60 to 1,000. For example, if the over-all gear ratio is again 11, refer to Fig. 6-41*B*. For four stages as noted above, the approximate mesh ratios for minimum inertia are: first mesh, 1.51; second mesh, 1.63; third mesh, 1.86; fourth mesh, 2.36. Or, if the over-all ratio is 75, Figure 6-41*C*, the approximate mesh ratios

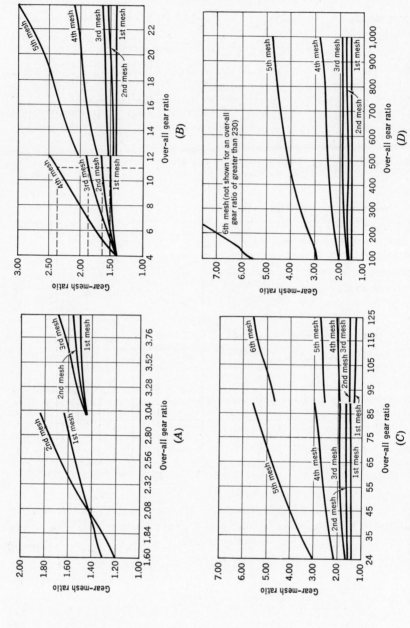

FIG. 6-41. Optimum number of gear stages and the individual mesh ratios for minimum reflected moment of inertia.

for five stages are: first mesh, 1.55; second mesh, 1.65; third mesh, 2.00; fourth mesh, 2.77; fifth mesh, 5.20.

These values can be adjusted to give feasible gear ratios and the closest approximation to the over-all ratio. For simplicity or economy, fewer gear stages are usually specified for a given over-all ratio than would be indicated by Fig. 6-41. In this case the nomogram of Fig. 6-42[11] is a useful auxiliary tool, specifying the individual stage ratios for minimum reflected inertia for any given number of stages. This nomogram is conveniently used in conjunction with Fig. 6-40. It also assumes identical pinions and negligible shaft inertias.

As indicated above, the appropriate number of stages for an over-all gear ratio of 75 is five. However, for simplicity of the mechanical setup and conservation of space, a four-mesh system can be used with only a small increase in reflected inertia. Assume this condition.

Referring to the nomogram, place a straight edge through the point representing the total number of stages (four), and the over-all gear ratio on the right-hand scale (75:1). From the left-hand scale it can be seen that the gear ratio of the first stage is 1.72 (compared to 1.55 as obtained above for five stages). Round this off to 1.75 and determine the remaining gear ratio, 75/1.75 equals about 43. Repeat this process using 43 as the over-all ratio and 3 as the number of stages to determine the second-stage ratio. The other stage ratios are found in a similar manner.

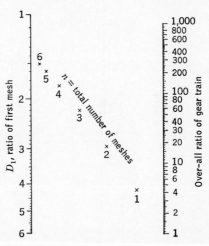

FIG. 6-42. Nomogram for approximating the optimum ratio for each gear mesh when number of gear stages and over-all gear ratio are specified. Assumptions: (1) All driving gears have the same pitch diameter. (2) All gears are solid cylinders of constant dimensions; inertia of shafts, clamps, and hubs is considered negligible.

To check the increase in inertia resulting from the use of four instead of five stages, refer to Fig. 6-40. The ratio of gear-train inertia to pinion inertia for five stages is 6.2, and for four stages is 7.1.

6-23. Minimizing the Inertia of Power Gear Trains. In power gear trains, or in applications where gear strength is a design factor due to shock loads, gear size must increase at the low-speed, high-torque meshes. It is suggested that the reader refer to Ref. 13 for a thorough treatment of the techniques used in minimizing inertia in power gear trains.

6-24. Selecting a Typical Gear Train. The following uses the preceding techniques in the solution of a typical gear train selection application.

Problem. Assume that a servomotor having the characteristics shown in Fig. 6-43 (Servomechanisms, Inc., Model No. 60E1-7) must drive a load of the following specifications.

Load speed..........................	50 rpm
Load inertia........................	500 g-cm²
Load acceleration required while operating at 50 rpm..........	100 radians/sec²
Load friction........................	3 oz-in.

Determine the required gear ratio, the number of stages, the stage ratios, and the gear train inertia.

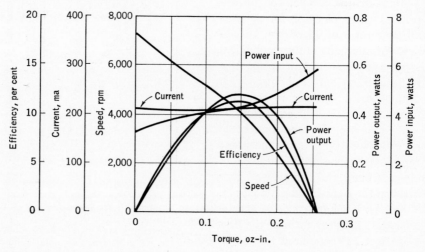

FIG. 6-43. Motor characteristic curves. Motor inertia = 1.0 g-cm². (*Courtesy of Servomechanisms, Inc.*)

Solution. First determine the over-all gear ratio by using the graphical method as shown in Fig. 6-37. Calculate load power and motor power vs. gear ratio by selecting several gear ratios and using the motor performance curves and the load requirements.

As expressed in Eq. (6-46), load power consists of two parts: that required to overcome total system friction, and that required to accelerate total system inertia. First determine the inertial power P_{Li}.

$$P_{Li} = v(J_L + n^2 J_m)\alpha$$

where v = load speed

$J_L + n^2 J_m = J_T$ = total inertia referred to load shaft

α = load acceleration at speed v

$J_T\alpha$ = load torque = T

Thus
$$P_{Li} = \frac{Tv}{1,352} \text{ watts}$$

where torque is in ounce-inches and speed in rpm.

From the load specifications, P_{Li} can be calculated by using the following tabulation:

Gear ratio	Total inertia, J_T	Torque, T, dyne-cm	Torque, T, oz-in.	Load inertial power, P_{Li}, watts
20	900	90,000	1.30	0.048
40	2,100	210,000	3.02	0.11
60	4,100	410,000	5.9	0.22
80	6,900	690,000	9.9	0.37
100	10,500	1,050,000	15.1	0.56

Assuming that motor damping is included with the motor speed-torque characteristics, the dissipative load power (frictional) can be calculated from

$$P_{Lf} = vF_L$$

and is constant for a constant speed.

Then motor power vs. gear ratio, and total load power vs. gear ratio can be calculated from the following tabulat on:

Gear ratio	Motor speed, rpm	Motor torque, oz-in.	Motor power, watts	Frictional load power, P_{Lf}, watts	Inertial load power, P_{Li}, watts	Total load power, P_L, watts
20	1,000	0.23	0.17	0.11	0.048	0.16
40	2,000	0.21	0.31	0.11	0.11	0.22
60	3,000	0.18	0.40	0.11	0.22	0.33
80	4,000	0.15	0.44	0.11	0.37	0.48
100	5,000	0.10	0.37	0.11	0.56	0.67

The power vs. gear-ratio values are plotted in Fig. 6.44. Since the motor-power curve overlaps the required load-power curve a maximum amount between 30 and 60, any gear ratio in this range will give suitable performance margin. Tentatively use a ratio of 40:1.

Taking a pinion inertia of 0.02 g-cm,[2] establish the effective inertia of the gear train. According to Fig. 6-41C, the optimum number of stages for an over-all ratio of 40 is five. But in the interest of economy and reduced complexity, this train will be designed with three stages. Using the nomogram (Fig. 6-42), the three-stage ratios are as follows. (Since this is a low power system, it is satisfactory to assume identical pinions and similar materials throughout.)

First stage.................. 2.1:1, or say 2:1
Second stage............... 3.1:1, or say 3:1
Third stage............... $(^{4}\%_{6})$:1, or say 6:1

With a final over-all ratio for the three stages of 36:1.

To make sure that the added inertia of the gear train will not upset the system, determine this inertia from the configuration shown in Fig. 6-45.

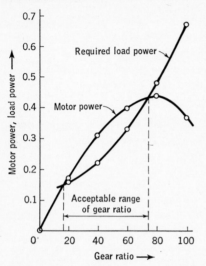

The gear-train inertia as seen at the motor shaft can be calculated as follows:

$$J_{\text{eff}} = J_P - \frac{2^4 J_P}{2^2} - \frac{3^4 J_P}{6^2} - \frac{6^4 J_P}{36^2}$$
$$- \frac{J_P}{2^2} - \frac{J_P}{6^2}$$

$$J_{\text{eff}} = \frac{307}{36} J_P = 8.53 J_P$$

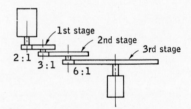

FIG. 6-44. Graphically optimizing the gear ratio.

FIG. 6-45. Gear-train configuration.

Then the gear-train inertia is 8.53 times the 0.02 g-cm² of the pinion, or 0.1706 g-cm².

Now recompute the required load power for the selected ratio as a check.

Motor inertia.......................... 1 g-cm²
Gear inertia (at motor shaft)........... 0.17 g-cm²
Total inertia at motor shaft........... 1.17 g-cm²

Then the total inertia as seen at the load is

$$500 + (1.17)(36)^2 = 2{,}020 \text{ g-cm}^2$$

and the torque required to accelerate the load at the load is

$$2{,}020(100) = 2.02 \times 10^5 \text{ dyne-cm} = 2.9 \text{ oz-in.}$$

Then the total power required to accelerate the load and overcome load friction is

$$\frac{(2.9 + 3)50}{1,352} = 0.194 \text{ watt}$$

The motor speed is 50(36), or 1,800 rpm. At this speed the motor develops 0.28 watt. This leaves a margin of

$$\frac{0.28}{0.19} = 1.47$$

or 47 per cent to handle the bearing and gear friction, and the normal tolerances on the motor.

6-25. Heating Problems in Two-phase Motors.[1] The servomotor manufacturer specifies a temperature rise for a given operating condition. That temperature rise, together with the safe operating limits of the insulation, lubricants, and other materials in the motor, establishes the maximum safe ambient temperature. Of the many special conditions for which the manufacturer may state the rise, some typical ones are:

1. The motor temperature rise at stall, when mounted on a black anodized aluminum plate of specified dimensions
2. The motor in still air, unmounted and stalled
3. The motor at stall when under a stated duty cycle
4. The motor running at maximum power output

The information furnished by the manufacturer must be considered in the light of the user's specific application. The servomechanism duty cycle must be considered. Is the servo continually slewing with both fields fully energized, or is it tracking slowly with negligible control field power? Motor ambient temperature can be seriously affected if the motor is near other servomotors or hot electronic equipment. Good air circulation from a blower can reduce motor-temperature rise by as much as 50 per cent, permitting double the output in a given frame size.

Many large servomotors are equipped with built-in fans for forced circulation. However, this cooling means is ineffective in the rarefied air of high altitudes above 50,000 ft. For normal operation in ambient temperatures up to 71°C, motors mounted on aluminum plates and operating at stall have stall input powers that vary with frame size. Typical values are

Size	Watts
8	3
10	6
15	12
18	20
23	30

These are standard Bureau of Ordnance frame sizes in which the diameter in tenths of an inch is approximately equal to the numerical frame designation.   Note that the ratio of watts to diameter squared (watts per square inch of surface) is almost constant.

6-26. Slot Effect and Bearing Friction.[6]   Slot effect, or minimum breakaway voltage V_{se}, is usually defined as the minimum variable-phase voltage that will just cause a motor to rotate when rated voltage is applied to the fixed phase.   This slot-effect test actually lumps together the bearing friction with the true slot lock which is due to magnetic attraction caused by nonuniformity in the magnetic field around the airgap.   To perform this test, the voltage applied to the variable phase is gradually increased until the shaft starts to rotate.   Slot effect can be defined as a torque by using the following expression.

$$T_{se} = \frac{T_{(rated)}}{V_{c(rated)}} V_{se} = KV_{se} \qquad \text{dyne-cm} \qquad (6\text{-}53)$$

Bearing friction is normally lumped in the slot-effect test described above, but can be separated by measuring the minimum voltage V_f that will just keep the motor running when applied equally and simultaneously (but in time quadrature) to both phases of the motor. The true slot lock, which is approximately proportional to the square of the fixed phase voltage, is thus made negligible.   The circuit shown in Fig. 6-46 can be used to measure bearing friction.   The applied voltage is gradually decreased, while the variable capacitor C is tuned so that the two phases are 90° out-of-phase.   The voltage at which

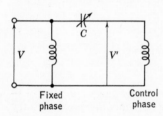

FIG. 6-46. Test arrangement for determining motor bearing friction.

the rotor stops turning is the friction voltage.   This friction torque is proportional to the product of V_f and V_f', so that if the friction value is required in terms of torque rather than voltage, the following relationship can be used.

$$T_f = \frac{V_f V_f'}{V_{rated} V_{rated}'} T_s \qquad (6\text{-}54)$$

Both slot effect and bearing friction degrade system performance.   They cause system insensitivity since the error-detecting device must develop sufficient error voltage through the amplifier to provide the minimum breakaway voltage.

6-27. Effects of Skew.   Skewing the rotor of a squirrel-cage motor has a similar effect to that of distributing a winding.   Thus, rotor sensitivity to the various stator harmonics that are generated as a result of the nonideal distribution of the stator windings may be varied by varying the skew. Sometimes skew is used to cancel a particular harmonic such as the third or fifth, while at other times the skew represents a compromise among the various harmonics, perhaps minimizing a significant group. Too much skew has the effect of increasing rotor leakage reactance, and to some extent bar resistance, reducing output torque. Small skews used to eliminate a specific higher-order harmonic are very difficult to control in production.

In small two-phase servomotors the third harmonic is apt to be the most troublesome, and the rotor is often designed with a skew of two poles (a wavelength) of the third harmonic. As an example consider a 16-slot stator wound for use in a two-phase, eight-pole servomotor. The third harmonic has 3 by 7, or 24 poles in 360°, corresponding to 15° per pole. To eliminate completely third harmonic effects, the skew should be 2 by 15, or 30°.

If a low skew angle was used (much less than 30°), the third harmonic would generate induction torques exactly as a 24-pole machine. This torque opposes normal motor torque, its principal effect being to reduce no load speed. Thus, low skew rotors are used whose no-load speed is about one-third less than conventional rotors, effectively providing increased damping for good performance in servomechanisms.

Finally, no skew or incorrect skew can emphasize those harmonics that can lock in with corresponding stator harmonics at standstill, causing slot effect and reducing sensitivity by increasing the control voltage required to start the motor. Because so many harmonics contribute to slot effect, it is impossible to find one skew angle that will eliminate slot effect entirely.

6-28. Variety of Mechanical Designs.[14] As pointed out previously, the most popular type of general-purpose two-phase servomotor uses a low-inertia, high-resistance squirrel-cage construction specifically designed for servo use. But for specific applications, some of the types discussed below are superior to the squirrel-cage motor.

In the drag-cup motor, the rotor conductors are formed into a drag cup of conducting material rotating in the airgap (Fig. 6-47). The slotted rotor laminations are replaced by a set of stationary iron-ring laminations that provide a low-reluctance path for the magnetic flux. This type motor is noted for uniformity of developed torque with rotor angular position, freedom from cogging and slot effects, and low bearing friction resulting from the absence of radial airgap forces on the nonmagnetic rotor. However, the requirement for relatively large airgaps has resulted in low torque per watt efficiency in the smaller sizes of drag-cup units. Thus they are used primarily where uniform torque and minimum bearing friction are necessary.

As a compromise between the high performance of the squirrel-cage motor and the uniformity of the drag-cup unit, some small servomotors use rotors of pure unlaminated iron. Although the over-all torque per watt input may be 20 per cent less for the solid rotor than for the squirrel cage, these units are sometimes used to obtain smooth performance, low control starting voltage, and reduced manufacturing costs.

Other varieties of mechanical designs include: closed stator slots, with stator coils machine-wound from the outside to reduce winding costs; articulated stators, another way to permit the use of machine-wound coils on a separable stator; separate rotor and stator sections, so that the

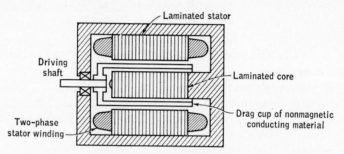

Fig. 6-47. Cross section of drag-cup two-phase servomotor.

rotor and stator can be designed into a user's equipment; and inverted motors, where the rotor assembly rotates around the outside diameter of the stator.

Two-phase servomotors are also available packaged with other system components. For example, units containing a motor, gear train, control transformer, and resistance potentiometers are available as packaged assemblies. Plug-in connectors are used wherever possible. Other varieties of packaged components include standard motor-gearhead combinations, motor-plus-damper combinations (including adjustable eddy-current or mechanical damping in sizes down to 1 in.), and motor-generator combinations for tachometer stabilization.

REFERENCES

1. Davis, S. A., and J. Spector: Application Factors for Two-phase Servo Motors, *Elec. Mfg.*, June, 1955.
2. Koopman, R. J. W.: Operating Characteristics of 2-Phase Servomotors, *Trans. AIEE*, vol. 68, pp. 319–329, 1949. (See discussion of this paper by S. S. L. Chang.)
3. Davis, S. A.: Output Characteristics of Two-phase Servomotors, *Elect. Mfg.*, July, 1956.
4. Liwschitz-Garik, M.: "Electric Machinery," vol. II, AC Machines, D. Van Nostrand Company, Inc., Princeton, N.J., 1946.

5. Weiss, G.: Induction Torque- and Servo-motor Design, *Power App. and Systems*, *AIEE*, October, 1955, pp. 809–815.

6. Brown, R. N.: Motors for High Performance Servo Systems, presented at IRE regional meeting, Johns Hopkins University, September, 1953.

7. Brown, L. O.: Transfer Function for a Two-phase Induction Servo Motor, *Trans. AIEE*, vol. 70, part 2, pp. 1890–1893, 1951.

8. Davis, S. A.: Two-capacitor Method of Phase Shifting, *Control Eng.*, January, 1956, p. 71.

9. Davis, S. A.: Mechanical Components for Automatic Control, *Prod. Eng.*, September, 1954.

10. Carrick, L. N.: Optimum Gear Train Ratios for Instrument Servomechanisms, *Prod. Eng.*, July, 1951.

11. Design of Servo Gear Trains to Minimize Reflected Inertia, Reeves Instrument Corp., RIC039-1C-7-53.

12. Burgess, E. G., Jr.: Designing Gear Trains for Minimum Inertia, "Annual Handbook of Product Design for 1954," p. E14.

13. Petersen, D. P.: Predicting Minimum-inertia Power Gear Trains, *Machine Design*, June, 1954.

14. Davis, S. A.: Rotating Components for Automatic Control, *Prod. Eng.*, November, 1953, pp. 129–160.

Chapter 7

D-C CONTROL MOTORS

7-1. Introduction. Direct-current machines of the series, shunt, compound, or externally excited variety are widely used in closed-loop control systems, particularly for the control of speed and torque. They range in size from a few watts, driven by vacuum-tube amplifiers, to several hundred horsepower, driven by Ward Leonard generators or rotating amplifiers. In all cases, control is achieved by varying either the field excitation or armature current, or both.

In the smaller sizes, d-c servomotors have been primarily used in aircraft control systems, where weight and space limitations require motors to deliver maximum power per unit volume. They are often used for intermittent duty, or where unusually high starting torques are required. Their speed-torque characteristics (except for the series motor) are similar to those of two-phase a-c servomotors.

7-2. Advantages and Limitations of D-C Control Motors. The advantages of d-c control motors when compared with a-c motors are:

1. Direct-current motors can deliver a high output from a small frame size since there are no slip losses as in an a-c motor.

2. Usually a d-c motor can be driven from a smaller control amplifier than an equal-rating a-c motor.

3. Direct-current motor circuitry permits the use of particularly simple stabilizing techniques.

4. Residual voltages are usually negligible in dc motor circuits.

5. Direct-current motors are more efficient than a-c motors in applications requiring variable speed.

6. Certain designs of d-c motors do not require input power under no-signal conditions. (In contrast, a-c motors always require main field power.) This makes the d-c motor ideal for applications involving long periods of standby and intermittent high output.

7. Direct-current motors can be easily controlled to give variable speed and special speed-torque characteristics at high efficiency.

8. Direct-current motors can be used as d-c tachometers as well as motors.

9. Direct-current motors obviously adapt themselves to d-c systems such as d-c analog computers, d-c supplies, etc.

10. Direct-current motors are applicable to particularly high or low speeds, above the synchronous speed of an a-c machine, for example, or below the speed for efficient a-c operation (where too many a-c motor poles may be required).

The disadvantages are:

1. Direct-current vacuum-tube servo amplifiers drift (gradually develop an output for zero input), and, therefore, require a zeroing adjustment or a relatively unreliable chopper-type drift balancing circuit.

2. Direct-current motors have commutators that require periodic maintenance checks to ensure reliable brush performance, usually not feasible where many miniature control motors are used in a complex assembly. Probably these brushes represent the greatest single preventive to the more widespread use of small d-c motors.

3. A secondary objection is the radio interference generated by the brushes. Special filters and shielding are often required to reduce this interference to a satisfactory level.

4. Commutator and brushes occupy a large percentage of available motor volume in the small sizes, and substantially increase motor friction.

5. Isolation and impedance matching difficulties mitigate against the use of d-c circuits (and motors).

6. The use of the induction-type electrical resolver (for which there is no completely satisfactory d-c equivalent) by the military has promoted the development of a-c systems in preference to d-c systems (and therefore motors).

7. The high field strengths used in d-c machines increase cogging and therefore decrease small signal sensitivity. This is further accentuated by brush friction.

8. In field control circuits, hysteresis, nonlinearity, and highly inductive input circuits add to the stabilization problem.

9. Units with strong permanent magnet fields develop high drag due to rotor hysteresis losses.

These disadvantages constitute a relative rather than an absolute index of reliability. For many applications, d-c motor life is completely satisfactory (being limited as noted above by brush life). Direct-current motors have been built to withstand rigid military environmental specifications for humidity, salt spray, altitude, and temperature range, in addition to shock and vibration.

7-3. D-C Motor Theory.[1,2,*] The performance of a d-c machine can be described in terms of the fundamental laws of electromagnetic theory.

* References, indicated in the text by superscript figures, are listed at the end of the chapter.

These are the laws relating current, magnetic field strength and torque, and field strength, velocity, and developed voltage.

Torque is developed by the action of a magnetic field on current-carrying conductors distributed around the periphery of an armature. Refer to the simple case of a single conductor in a magnetic field shown in Fig. 7-1. There will be a force exerted on this conductor proportional to the product of the field strength in the vicinity of the conductor, the current through the conductor, and the length of the conductor. In electrical machines, the conductors are usually so arranged

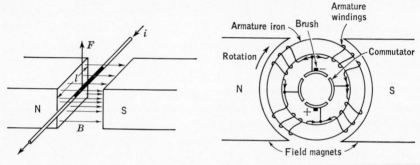

FIG. 7-1. Force on a single conductor in a magnetic field.   FIG. 7-2. Basic structure of a d-c machine.

that the flux density in the airgap is normal to the length of the conductor. For this case the force is

$$F = \frac{Bil}{10} \quad \text{dynes} \tag{7-1}$$

where B = flux density in lines per square centimeter, gauss
    i = current in conductor, amp
    l = effective length of the conductor, cm

The torque developed can be determined by examining the basic structure of a d-c machine (Fig. 7-2). The conductors, arranged as coils, are distributed around the periphery of the armature. The individual coils are interconnected to form a completely closed winding, or sometimes several completely closed windings. The ends of the coils are connected in an orderly fashion to the separate bars or contact points of the commutator.

During rotation, the commutator behaves like a multiposition switch whose poles are the brushes connecting to the external circuit. Rotation causes a switching action which continually connects the coils so that all the armature conductors lying under the north pole carry currents flowing in one direction, while those lying under the south pole carry currents in the reverse direction. The commutator reverses the current in each armature coil at that instant when it passes through the neutral axis or when it leaves the influence of the north pole field and enters the influence of the south pole field, or vice versa.

The force produced on each armature conductor is additive so that the total torque produced by the armature is

$$T = 7.37 \times 10^{-9}\, ZBilr \text{ lb-ft} \tag{7-2}$$

where B = gap density, lines per square inch
  i = armature amperes per path
  Z = number of active torque-producing conductors
  l = active length of one conductor, in.
  r = average lever arm of a conductor, in.

Note that all items except B and i in Eq. (7-2) depend only on the design of the machine. In addition

$$B = \frac{\phi}{A}$$

where A is the area of the airgap per pole in square inches and ϕ is the total pole flux in maxwells. Then Eq. (7-2) can be rewritten

$$T = \phi i K$$

where K is a constant of the machine.

Thus torque delivered by a d-c motor depends directly on the airgap flux and armature current. As stated previously, control is achieved by varying either the field excitation (airgap flux) or the armature current.

7-4. Counter Electromotive Force. As a result of the torque, the motor will rotate. Superimposed on the conditions just described, a voltage is induced in the individual armature conductors as a result of their rotation in the magnetic field. This voltage is in a direction opposing the flow of current and is referred to as a counter electromotive force. It limits the current flowing in the motor armature.

The counter emf V_g generated in the motor windings can be calculated from the following formula.

$$V_g = \phi Z'N \tag{7-3}$$

where $Z' = \dfrac{Zp_1}{10^8 p_2(60)}$
  N = rpm
  p_1 = number of poles
  p_2 = number of parallel armature paths

When the motor armature is at rest, the counter emf is zero and the motor armature current i_a equals V_a/R_a, where V_a is the voltage impressed on the armature and R_a is the armature resistance. When the armature is rotating under steady-state conditions, the current is also limited by the counter emf and equals

$$i_a = \frac{V_a - V_g}{R_a} \tag{7-4}$$

The mechanical power P in watts developed by the motor armature can be expressed by

$$P = V_g i_a = V_a i_a - i_a^2 R_a \qquad \text{watts} \tag{7-5}$$

or $\qquad P = \phi Z' i_a N$

The equations derived above form the basis for computations on all the special varieties of d-c machines. Their simplicity and directness suggest the clear connection between fundamental laws and performance, with a minimum of derived intermediate corollaries required for clear understanding. The principal limitations to the accuracy of these formulas result from secondary nonlinearities, such as the effects of commutation, armature reaction on the saturation of the pole tips, and brush drop as a function of armature speed and current.

7-5. Commutation and Special Compensating Windings.[2,3]   The problems associated with commutation present the most difficulty to the d-c motor designer. The theory of commutation is not nearly as well developed as is the remainder of the design features, and most of the unpredictability in the performance of d-c machines relates to this area. The problem has been emphasized in aircraft servomotors where the high-altitude rarefied atmosphere interferes with the switching action. It must be realized that switching with a commutator requires the same provisions for arc suppression and timing that are commonly considered in other contactor devices. However, because of the difficulty of hermetic sealing and the high relative speed between contacts, the commutation problem is much more severe than in relay design.

Special windings for improving commutation are used on d-c machines, but, because of the additional complexity and expense, they are only included in large machines where poor commutation would be intolerable. Among these are commutating poles or interpoles to assist commutation, and compensating windings to cancel out the deleterious effects of armature reaction. These two features together cancel the armature field and introduce a controlled commutating field.

When a motor is under load, the armature generates a magnetomotive force which influences the magnitude and distribution of the resultant field flux. The commutator and the position of the brushes on it determine the magnetic behavior of the armature winding, the brush axis determining the position of the magnetic axis of the armature winding. Figure 7-3 shows that the armature flux or cross flux strengthens the flux density on one-half of the pole and weakens the other half. Since, because of saturation, one pole half is weakened more than the other pole half is strengthened, this results in a net reduction in main flux. The armature magnetomotive force causes a displacement of the neutral zone.

In a motor, the neutral zone is displaced in a direction opposite to rotation. This disturbs the commutating action since the neutral axis is perpendicular to the pole axis only at no load. This can be corrected by shifting the brushes from the neutral axis, but this increases armature reaction (decreasing the net main flux) and is intolerable in servomotors which must be capable of bidirectional operation.

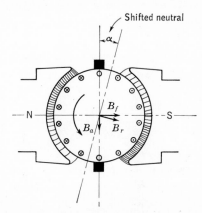

FIG. 7-3. Distorted magnetic field and shifted neutral caused by armature reaction.

To obtain good commutation, commutating poles or interpoles are used to produce the necessary commutating field (Fig. 7-4). The interpole axis is perpendicular to the pole axis,

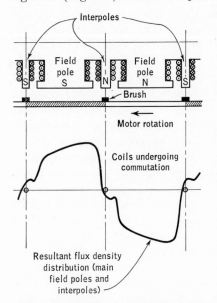

FIG. 7-4. Interpole windings and resultant flux-density distribution.

while the interpole field opposes the armature field, completely canceling it out in the neutral zone. Actually the interpole field must be stronger than the armature field, for, in addition to canceling the field, it must induce an emf in the short-circuited coil (resulting from brush contacting two adjacent commutator bars) which opposes the emf of self-induction and the voltage drop under the brushes.

But interpoles cancel the armature cross flux only in the commutation zone and do not affect the nonuniform distribution of flux in the poles. Where machines are subject to sudden heavy loads and rapid reversal, a compensating winding is used to suppress the armature field. Complete suppression of the armature field is possible only by using a winding distributed over the whole pole surface. For this reason, the compensating winding is placed in the pole shoe as near the surface as possible (Fig. 7-5). To be effective, the armature and compensating windings must be connected in series so that conductors of each lying within the same pole pitch carry the same current in opposing directions.

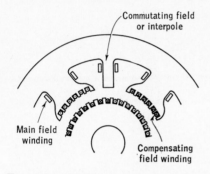

FIG. 7-5. Direct-current-machine magnetic structure including interpoles and compensating windings.

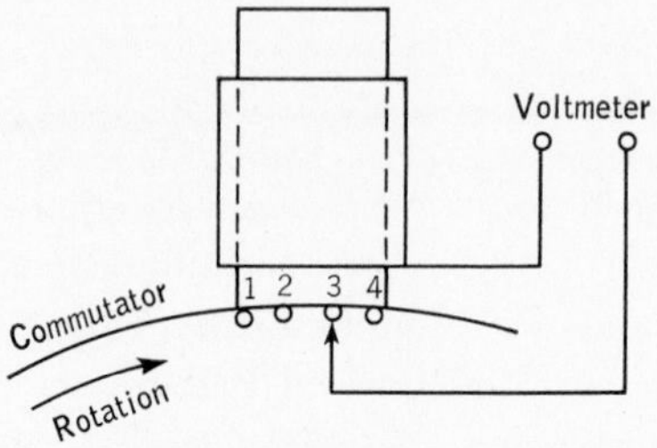

FIG. 7-6. Arrangement for measuring brush voltage drop.

A compensating winding will suppress the magnetomotive force of those armature conductors that lie under pole shoes. The remaining magnetomotive force (about 30 per cent) as well as the emf of self-induction, and the voltage drop under the brushes, must be suppressed by the interpoles.

A brush curve represents the voltage drop between the brush and commutator for different points on the commutator. This drop is usually measured at four points (Fig. 7-6). This curve gives an indication of the shape of the commutating curve (and the effectiveness of the corrective windings) since the voltage drop is greater where the current density is greater. Figure 7-7 shows three different shapes of brush curves.

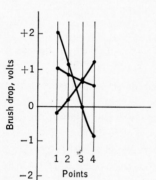

FIG. 7-7. Variety of brush voltage drop curves obtained using test setup of Fig. 7-6.

7-6. Types of D-C Control Motors.[4] The principal varieties of d-c motors used in servomechanism applications are the series motor, the separately excited shunt motor, and the permanent-magnet motor. The following sections treat these motors in detail, with specific reference to their performance specifications, dynamic characteristics, and areas of application. Special varieties with split or tapped fields are covered because of their importance in control applications.

7-7. General Relations for Separately Excited Shunt Machines.[5]
When looked at externally, the d-c motor is a simple device. For
machines represented by the schematic of Fig. 7-8 the following equations
apply.

$$V_a = V_g + i_a R_a + L_a \frac{di_a}{dt} \tag{7-6}$$

$$V_f = i_f R_f + L_f \frac{di_f}{dt} \tag{7-7}$$

$$V_g = K_D \phi \omega \tag{7-8}$$

$$T = K_D \phi i_a \tag{7-9}$$

where L_a = armature inductance
$\quad V_f$ = applied field voltage
$\quad i_f$ = field current
$\quad R_f$ = field resistance
$\quad L_f$ = field inductance
$\quad \omega$ = angular velocity
$\quad K_D$ = proportionality constant

These are fundamental equations. The counter emf V_g has been discussed previously, and opposes V_a, the applied armature voltage. In
the steady-state condition, the inductive
voltages of Eqs. (7-6) and (7-7) vanish.
In most servomotors, the armature inductance is negligible, so that Eq. (7-6)
reduces to

$$V_a = V_g + i_a R_a \tag{7-10}$$

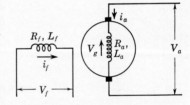

FIG. 7-8. Schematic of separately
excited shunt machine.

which is much simpler to handle analytically. However, the field inductance is
not negligible, and normally constitutes one of the principal time delays
in a motor.

Equation (7-8) merely states that the generated voltage (counter emf)
is proportional to the product of flux and speed. Equation (7-9) likewise expresses the familiar law relating to torque on a conductor in a
magnetic field. Note that for a consistent set of units, the constants of
proportionality in Eqs. (7-8) and (7-9) are equal.

The accuracy of these equations is limited by nonlinearities and by
nonideal geometry, resulting in unintentional coupling between circuits.
In high-quality servomotors, the effects of the latter factor can be neglected. However, the various nonlinear relationships cause significant
inaccuracies. For example, the carbon brushes in the armature circuit
do not follow Ohm's law. Except at very low currents, the armature
brushes contribute a constant voltage drop of about 1 volt per brush,

rather than the current-proportional drop that is normally expected. However, in well-designed motors, the total brush resistance is small compared to the over-all circuit resistance, and for all practical purposes, this source of nonlinearity can be neglected.

But the principal nonlinearities, relating to the characteristics of the iron, cannot be neglected. Airgap flux is related to field current by a magnetization curve such as is shown in Fig. 7-9. This indicates the flux variation as a function of increasing and decreasing field current. There are hysteresis effects, and the ascending and descending curves do not coincide. If magnetic-circuit operation is kept below the knee of the saturation curve, this curve can be closely approximated by a straight line, with negligible hysteresis. Then the nonlinearity will be significant only in special modes of application.

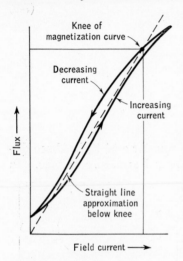

FIG. 7-9. Magnetization curve indicating nonlinearities resulting from iron magnetic characteristics.

In any case, if a strong fixed field that thoroughly saturates the magnetic circuit is applied to the motor, these nonlinearities do not influence performance. Actually, the field of a highly saturated d-c machine remains quite constant, notwithstanding the demagnetizing tendency of armature reaction. This is especially true if the fixed excitation is provided by a permanent magnet with very low incremental permeability. The reduction in flux of the fixed-excitation main poles due to cross-magnetization resulting from armature reaction is usually less than 10 per cent and is ignored in motors used in feedback-control systems.

On the other hand, if a motor is controlled by varying field excitation, magnetic nonlinearity is a significant factor. The hysteresis that may occur after a wide amplitude transient acts very much like backlash in a gear train, tending to cause instability. During normal operation, when the control signals are relatively small, the nonlinear effect is not as significant. The series motor, discussed below, is inherently nonlinear and, since the varying armature current also passes through the field, the resulting variation in field excitation makes this motor susceptible to magnetic-circuit nonlinearities.

7-8. Armature-excited Shunt Machines. The transfer function of a d-c servomotor varies with the way it is connected. The armature-excited unit represents one method of connection, the method that gives the most nearly ideal linear performance.

In this mode of operation, the field is excited by a constant field current or by a permanent magnet. The flux, ϕ, can be considered constant, so that Eqs. (7-8) and (7-9) become

$$V_g = K'_D \omega \qquad (7\text{-}11)$$
$$T = K'_D i_a \qquad (7\text{-}12)$$

where
$$K'_D = K_D \phi$$

Thus the fundamental equation for the armature circuit is

$$V_a = K'_D \omega + \frac{R_a}{K'_D} T + \frac{L_a}{K'_D} \frac{dT}{dt} \qquad (7\text{-}13)$$

To be evaluated, this equation must be combined with the equations of motion since it involves three variables—impressed voltage, torque, and velocity—all functions of time.

Before evaluating this equation, consider the limiting case when the applied voltage is a constant and the rate of change of torque is zero. This condition corresponds to the steady-state speed-torque characteristics that are normally given for a servomotor. Considering T as the independent variable in Eq. (7-13), solving for T when dT/dt is zero gives

$$T = \frac{K'_D}{R_a} (V_a - K'_D \omega) \qquad (7\text{-}14)$$

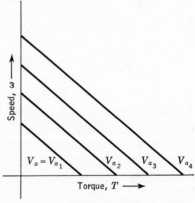

Fig. 7-10. Family of straight-line speed-torque curves for an armature-excited shunt machine. $T = \dfrac{K'_D}{R_a} (V_a - K'_D \omega)$.

This equation corresponds to the family of straight-line speed-torque curves of Fig. 7-10. This shows the individual speed-torque curves for various values of control signal, in this case impressed armature voltage.

The constants K'_D and K'_D/R_a can be estimated from the speed-torque curves normally provided by the servomotor manufacturer. Thus, given the stall torque (ω equals 0) at rated armature voltage V_a,

$$\frac{K'_D}{R_a} = \frac{T}{V_a} \qquad (7\text{-}15)$$

And at the free running speed, where torque is zero,

$$K'_D = \frac{V_a}{\omega} \qquad (7\text{-}16)$$

Returning to the evaluation of the complete mesh equation, Eq. (7-13), the equation of motion of the mechanical system is given by

$$T = J\left(\frac{d\omega}{dt}\right) + f_v\omega \tag{7-17}$$

J and f_v are the inertia and viscous friction associated with the mechanical characteristics of the motor plus load. Thus, f_v does not include any intrinsic motor electrical damping. Actually it is this electrical damping that is to be evaluated; in Eq. (7-17) it is included in T, which is a function of ω. Differentiating with respect to time, and combining with Eq. (7-13) gives

$$J\frac{L_a d^3c}{R_a\,dt^3} + \left(J + \frac{L_a}{R_a}f_v\right)\frac{d^2c}{dt^2} + \left(f_v + \frac{K_D'^2}{R_a}\right)\frac{dc}{dt} = \frac{V_a K_D'}{R_a} \tag{7-18}$$

where c = angular *position* of output shaft

Rewriting this equation in terms of the differential operator p gives

$$\frac{c}{V_a} = \frac{K_D'/R_a}{p\left[J\dfrac{L_a}{R_a}p^2 + p\left(J + \dfrac{L_a}{R_a}f_v\right) + \left(f_v + \dfrac{K_D'^2}{R_a}\right)\right]} \tag{7-19}$$

Equation (7-19) represents the basic transfer function for this method of motor connection and can be used in any linear analysis of a servo-mechanism incorporating this motor. It is a higher-order equation than the normal transfer function representing a servomotor because of the third-order term resulting from the armature inductance term L_a. Thus the L_a term contributes to the phase shift or time delay in this motor and makes the servo stabilization problem more difficult. Fortunately this term is usually small and can often be neglected, at least for a first approximation. For negligible armature inductance the relationship is much simpler.

$$\frac{c}{V_a} = \frac{K_D'/R_a}{p\left[Jp + \left(f_v + \dfrac{K_D'^2}{R_a}\right)\right]} \tag{7-20}$$

This expression is very similar to the transfer function of a two-phase a-c servomotor. Added to the mechanical damping f_v, there is an electrical viscous damping term $K_D'^2/R_a$ which contributes additional damping. In most control systems, this additive damping term is much larger than the friction damping term. This is especially true in instrument servos operating characteristically under very light load. Note that the term $K_D'^2/R_a$ is in reality the slope of the static speed-torque curves of

Fig. 7-10. Thus, to determine the magnitude of this term, it is only necessary to measure the slope of the speed-torque curve.

7-9. Permanent-magnet Motors. Armature-excited permanent-magnet motors have increased in popularity with the development of powerful permanent-magnet materials such as the Alnicos. Since no field coils are required, these motors are rugged and relatively inexpensive. The permanent-magnet field generally operates in the saturated region to minimize the effects of armature reaction. The principal difficulty with these motors is the demagnetizing effect of the armature current during heavy current transients, so that the permanent magnets must be stabilized in the same manner as the field magnets of d-c tachometers (see Chap. 5). Magnet stabilization means that the fields operate below their maximum strength. Permanent-magnet motors are designed to withstand full excitation reversal with no significant reduction in their magnetic properties.

Compared to the separately excited shunt motor, the permanent-magnet unit has about the same or slightly better efficiency and similar performance. Usually the permanent-magnet motor has a straighter speed-torque curve, and better low-speed damping. With the large magnetizing forces and the low incremental permeability of the magnets, permanent-magnet motors are less sensitive to armature reaction than wound-field machines.

Their efficiency and performance characteristics are opening up applications for permanent-magnet motors in the fractional horsepower field, as well as ensuring their established place in the millihorsepower range.

7-10. Field-driven Shunt Machines. Field control, with constant armature current and the control signal applied to the field winding, is used when a system is operated from vacuum tubes or thyratrons, and the armature current is too great to be handled by tubes of a convenient or economical size. The power required for field control is only a fraction of the power required for armature control. In general, the time constant of the field circuit L_f/R_f is large compared with the armature-circuit time constant. Consequently, field control does not give as rapid response as armature control. Also, as previously discussed, motor performance under field control is not as linear as under armature control.

The basic equations for this type motor can be written if operation is confined to the linear region of the magnetization curve. Constant armature current is necessary for the linear operation of a field-excited motor, which is equivalent to saying that the armature is excited from a very high-resistance source. The source resistance must be so high that the counter emf V_g does not affect the magnitude of the armature current. Stated another way, V_g and $L_a(di_a/dt)$ are negligible compared to the voltage drop across the armature resistance, i_aR_a.

Combining the following equations,

$$V_a = i_a R_a \tag{7-21}$$

$$V_f = i_f R_f + L_f \frac{di_f}{dt} \tag{7-22}$$

$$V_g = K_D'' i_f \omega \tag{7-23}$$

$$T = K_D'' i_f i_a \tag{7-24}$$

$$T = J \frac{d^2 c}{dt^2} + f_v \frac{dc}{dt} \tag{7-25}$$

gives the transfer function

$$\frac{c}{V_f} = \frac{K_D'' V_a / R_a R_f}{p^3 \dfrac{L_f}{R_f} J + p^2 \left(J + \dfrac{L_f}{R_f} f_v\right) + p f_v} \tag{7-26}$$

Equation (7-26) can be compared with the transfer function for the armature-excited unit [Eq. (7-20)]. Note that there is no equivalent electrical damping term, so that all damping must be derived from mechanical friction of the motor and load. Also the field inductance and time constant are not negligible, and a third-order transfer function results. While it can be analyzed by conventional servo methods, this third-order transfer function increases the problem of servo-loop stabilization.

The performance features of a field-driven d-c motor can be summarized as follows:

1. Constant armature current is necessary for linear operation.

2. The back emf must be small compared with the armature resistance drop.

3. Field inductance is not negligible, and a third-order transfer function results.

4. There is no equivalent viscous damping introduced by the electric circuit.

7-11. Series-connected Motors. This connection is used where high starting torques are required, and linearity is relatively unimportant. It is a popular motor for relay-type feedback-control systems, and the split-field series motor of Fig. 7-11 can be reversed with simply a single-pole two-position relay. This ease of reversibility is traded for a slight loss in efficiency.

The approach used above for the shunt motor can be adapted to the series motor, but, because of the extremely nonlinear performance of this type motor, the analysis is necessarily very approximate and has only qualitative value. To derive this approximate, but useful, relationship, the equations can be set up and assumptions introduced where necessary.

Assuming a linear magnetization curve, the equations for a series motor are as follows:

$$V = i(R_f + R_a) + (L_a + L_f)\frac{di}{dt} + V_g \qquad (7\text{-}27)$$

$$V_g = K_D''i\omega \qquad (7\text{-}28)$$

$$T = K_D''i^2 \qquad (7\text{-}29)$$

In these equations, V is applied in series with the armature and field, and i is their common current (Fig. 7-12). When the above equations are combined in the same manner as the equations for the previous motor connections, a decidedly nonlinear differential equation is obtained.

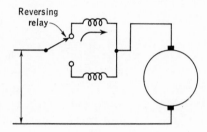

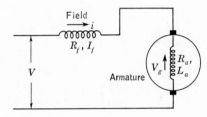

FIG. 7-11. Split-field relay-reversed series motor.

FIG. 7-12. Equivalent circuit schematic of series motor.

The conditions of linear operation that must be assumed to develop a useful answer state that:

1. The steady-state speed-torque curve is a straight line.
2. The speed-torque curves are parallel and uniformly spaced for equal increments of input signal.

Thus assumptions must be made in the above equations that are equivalent to these two requirements.

Assume that over a given and useful region of the normal speed-torque curve for a series motor (Fig. 7-13), this curve can be approximated by a straight line. But, as shown in Fig. 7-14, the steady-state torque-speed and torque-current characteristics of a typical series motor are decidedly nonlinear so that the selection of constants is predicated on achieving a good approximation only in the region of interest.

$$T = K_1 i \qquad \text{(generated torque)} \qquad (7\text{-}30)$$

$$T = K_2 \omega + K_3 \qquad \text{(torque as a function of speed)} \qquad (7\text{-}31)$$

Substituting Eq. (7-30) in Eq. (7-27) gives

$$V = \frac{T}{K_1}(R_f + R_a) + (L_a + L_f)\frac{1}{K_1}\frac{dT}{dt} + V_g \qquad (7\text{-}32)$$

For steady-state operation, dT/dt equals zero and Eq. (7-32) becomes

$$T = \frac{K_1}{R_a + R_f} (V - V_g) \tag{7-33}$$

For linear performance, $K_3 = K_1 i$. Substitute Eq. (7-31) in Eq. (7-33). Thus

$$V_g = \frac{K_2}{K_1} (R_a + R_f)\omega \tag{7-34}$$

The assumptions of linear performance yield as a corollary the linearity of generated voltage with velocity. Hence, Eq. (7-32) becomes

$$\frac{V K_1}{R_a + R_f} = T + \frac{L_a + L_f}{R_a + R_f} \frac{dT}{dt} - K_2\omega \tag{7-35}$$

Substituting for T from the equations of motion and simplifying gives the following transfer function:

$$\frac{c}{V} = \frac{K_1/(R_a + R_f)}{\left(\dfrac{L_a + L_f}{R_a + R_f}\right) Jp^3 + p^2\left[f_v\left(\dfrac{L_a + L_f}{R_a + R_f}\right) + J\right] + p(f_v - K_2)} \tag{7-36}$$

Note that the slope K_2 of the speed-torque curve is usually negative, so that the additional damping is positive and directly additive to f_v, the mechanical viscous friction.

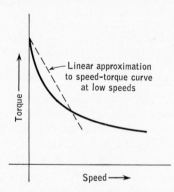

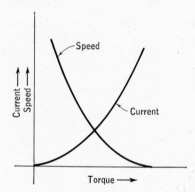

Fig. 7-13. Curved speed-torque characteristic of series motor and linear approximation over a small region.

Fig. 7-14. Steady-state torque-speed and torque-current characteristics of a series motor.

Thus, for small changes in speed where essentially linear operation can be assumed, series motor performance is generally described by a third-order transfer function. The restricted region of analysis indicates that the transfer function must be used with care, since generally only a qualitative result can be obtained.

7-12. Methods of Exciting Small D-C Control Motors.[6] Small d-c control motors are usually excited by one of the amplifying devices listed in Table 7-1. Because of the ease of incorporating stabilization circuits with the d-c amplifier-motor combinations, many of these control circuits

TABLE 7-1. WAYS TO EXCITE SMALL D-C MOTORS

Method	Remarks
Relay	Light, compact, simple, with high power amplification. Limited life and noise generation are principal disadvantages. Mercury relays can stand severe service, but cannot be used in all positions. By using "dithering" circuits, continuous control can be approximated.
Thyratrons	Handle less current than relays. Not as suitable as relays for low-voltage motors because of drop across thyratron. Longer life than relays. Thyratron circuits often require d-c supplies or transformers, relatively bulky items.
Vacuum tubes	Smoothest control. Simplest with field-excited motors where relatively large amounts of motor output can be controlled with small vacuum tubes. Less efficient than thyratrons where large amounts of power must be controlled.
Semiconductors	Compact and efficient. Smooth control. May be used as a conventional amplifier, switching element (equivalent to mechanical relays), or as a solid-state equivalent to the thyraton as a controlled junction rectifier.

can include stabilization features. Direct-current motor stabilization circuits will be treated in detail in the next section.

The most suitable control circuit depends to some extent on required motor excitation. Is the motor to be controlled by feeding a separately excited shunt field, or the motor armature? A permanent-magnet motor obviously requires armature excitation, while a series motor simultaneously excites both armature and field. The following discusses circuits suitable for any of these types.

Figure 7-15 shows a simple motor-control circuit for field excitation. There is quiescent direct current in the halves of the tapped winding, but

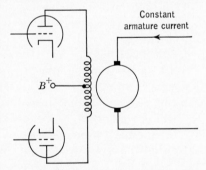

FIG. 7-15. Vacuum-tube-excited, split-field, separately excited motor.

the physical arrangement of the field coils is such that no net magnetic field is produced in the motor. A signal that makes one grid more positive than the other produces an unbalance in the separate halves of the field coils.   This results in a net magnetic field so that the motor develops torque and rotates.   The quiescent field current causes additional heating as a result of field winding copper loss but, since field power is only a fraction of motor power, losses from this source are not serious. Unfortunately, the quiescent currents do not improve linearity (as is sometimes the case in push-pull circuitry), since at balance there is no net ampere turns and, therefore, absolutely zero core flux.   The hysteresis and linearity are the same as for single-ended operation.

The armature should be excited from a constant-current source.   If several similar motors are used in a system, the effect of constant-current operation can be roughly approximated by connecting the armatures in series across the line.   Otherwise a resistor must be used in series with the source.

Circuits of this type are practical for exciting small servomotors, since field power is normally about 10 per cent of motor power and easily within the range of hard vacuum tubes.   As shown here, there may be an appreciable delay in field-current build-up during transients, but current-feedback circuits (that produce output currents rather than voltages) can easily be incorporated in the amplifier.   For example, a pentode output tube yields a current rather than a voltage response with a consequent increase in motor response speed.   As in all circuits calling for plate operation of the motor, the field windings must be capable of withstanding the B+ voltage continuously without insulation breakdown.

Figure 7-16 shows the schematic, performance curves, and speed vs. field current for various torque values for a commercially available split-field motor controlled by triodes.   The motor operates on a normal field current of 6 ma, but will start under no load with a field current of 1 ma.   The armature is separately and continuously excited through a 28.5-ohm series resistor from a 27-volt d-c source.   The field assembly consists of two independent 10,000-ohm windings, encapsulated in plastic.

With an electronic amplifier (as shown), the motor provides practically noiseless, variable-speed, reversible operation.   It has a low inertia rotating element for fast response, and delivers a maximum of $\frac{1}{500}$ hp. Typical characteristic curves are shown in Fig. 7-16B.

The unusual torque increase at low speeds shown in Fig. 7-16C indicates that the motor is not operating under ideal conditions.   The armature is not being supplied from a constant-current source in spite of the series resistor, and at low speeds the decreased V_g causes a rise in armature current and the consequent torque increase.

The same motor can be supplied with a single field winding, of any specified value up to 20,000 ohms.   Thus other control techniques are applicable to the same basic motor.

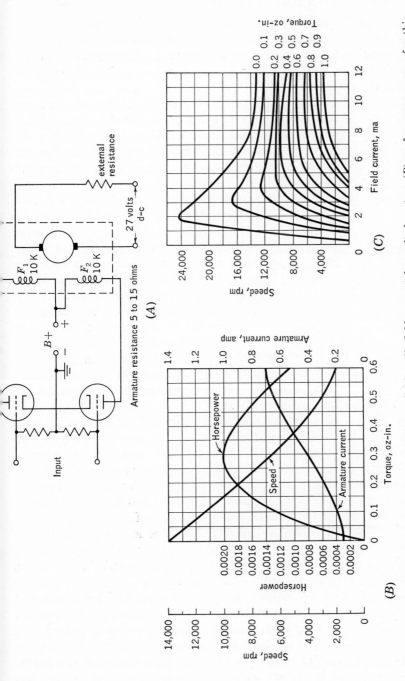

FIG. 7-16. (A) Control circuit for commercially available split-field separately excited motor; (B) performance curves for this motor; (C) speed vs. field current for various torque values. *Note:* Maximum field current in either winding 12 ma. Normal operation: Approximately 6 ma max. in both windings for zero speed. Full output in either rotation; 6 ma differential current. (*Courtesy of Holzer-Cabot Motor Div.*)

Figure 7-17 shows a thyratron control circuit for a split-field series motor, including a demodulator for converting from an a-c control signal to the d-c signal required to operate the motor.   The a-c signal is of the same time phase as the a-c thyratron plate voltage.   Depending on the sense of the error, one or the other thyratron will carry the greater current, thereby establishing the direction of rotation.   At null the motor currents in the two fields are equal, and there is no net torque.

This circuit results in reduced motor efficiency because of the distorted voltage applied to the motor.   Some reduction in distortion can be achieved by using a full-wave circuit.   These generally need two additional thyratrons.

The thyratron circuit differs from the vacuum-tube circuit of Fig. 7-15, in that the thyratron functions primarily as a switch for connecting the motor armature to the line.   This makes it more difficult to introduce current feedback, or to operate from a high-impedance source.   If this type unit is driven from a current rather than a voltage source, the transfer function simplifies and the third-degree equation in the denominator reduces to a second-degree equation.   However, even with this limitation, circuits such as are shown in Fig. 7-17 perform satisfactorily.

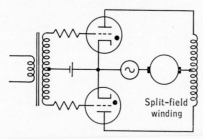

FIG. 7-17. Thyratron control circuit for split-field series motor.

There are a wide variety of thyratron control circuits for different modes of control described in the literature.   Thus, as required, suitable thyratron grid-control circuits can be actuated by alternating current, direct current, saturable-core reactors, and other phase-shift elements. Depending on the excitation circuit preceding the thyratron grids, either a smooth continuous control or an on-off type of control can be achieved. Thyratrons exhibit the switching characteristics of relays and, in addition, have the following advantages: they have longer life because of the absence of sparking and mechanical contact wear; they can be driven at higher frequencies; and they can rectify as well as switch.   However, like relays, they generate radio interference.

Relay-controlled d-c motors are quite common, and many compact airborne servomechanisms use this combination as the actuator element. Roughly speaking, relay control is analogous to on-off thyratron control, and analogous circuits exist for both.   The circuit of Fig. 7-18A is quite similar to the thyratron circuit of Fig. 7-17.   As mentioned previously, this arrangement is convenient because of its easy reversibility from a single-pole two-position switch.   The normal spark-suppression circuits are not included in Fig. 7-18*A*. The disadvantage of the split-field series motor is that it has twice the series-field copper loss of the conventional series motor (which unfortunately is not easily reversible), since only one-half the field winding is active at one time. This is equivalent to doubling the field resistance. Figure 7-18*B* shows a vacuum-tube circuit equivalent to the relay circuit of Fig. 7-18*A*.

Figure 7-19 shows an armature-excited, fixed-field, relay-controlled motor. The designation of the two relays as CW (clockwise) and CCW

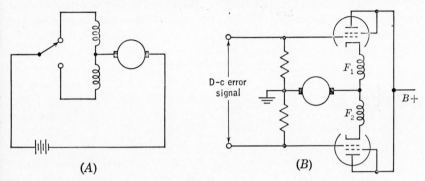

FIG. 7-18. (*A*) Split-field relay-controlled series motor; (*B*) vacuum-tube equivalent to circuit shown in (*A*).

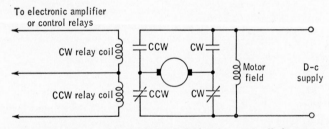

FIG. 7-19. Armature-excited, fixed-field, relay-controlled motor.

(counterclockwise) corresponds to the assumed direction of motor rotation when the particular relay is energized. Each relay is a two-position two-pole unit, with one contact normally open and the other normally closed. For the condition shown in the diagram, neither relay is energized and there is no voltage applied to the motor armature. This means that there is no steady heat loss under quiescent conditions. Energizing either relay will connect the motor across the d-c line with one polarity or the other.

The relays themselves can be driven by smaller sensitive relays that serve as "preamplifiers," or they may be driven by vacuum tubes or thyratrons from circuits similar to those used for motor control. In effect, energizing a relay coil is dynamically analogous to driving a motor field, a solenoid, or any other inductive d-c load, and approximately the same considerations apply.   Unfortunately, each relay introduces additional time delay and nonlinear phase shift, contributing to the problem of closed-loop stability.   Components sometimes used in conjunction with relay control circuits for d-c motors include demodulators or phase-sensitive detectors, drift-compensated d-c amplifier preamplifiers, etc. Since the field of a d-c motor is inductive, suitable filters must be included to suppress noise superimposed on the d-c signal.

7-13. Stabilization Circuits for D-C Machines.[3]   Direct-current servomechanisms are easier to stabilize or to adjust for specialized characteristics than are a-c servomechanisms.   This is because the d-c stabilizing

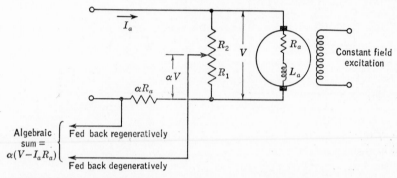

FIG. 7-20. Static-network technique for generating a speed-sensitive stabilizing voltage. $R_1 + R_2$ = high-resistance potentiometer; αR_a = low-value series resistor.

$$\frac{R_1}{R_1 R_2} = \alpha$$

$$V = I_a R_a + V_g = I_a R_a + C\frac{n}{60}$$

$$n = \frac{60}{C}(V - I_a R_a)$$

elements are more nearly ideal than the corresponding a-c elements: lead networks using resistors and capacitors in a d-c servomechanism require corresponding carrier-tuned RLC networks in an a-c servomechanism.   The characteristics of these a-c networks can be defined in elementary terms only for signal frequencies that are low with respect to the carrier frequency (about 10 per cent maximum), and for carrier frequencies that exactly equal the tuned network frequency.   Also, d-c tachometer feedback is not complicated by residual voltage problems.

In addition to these conventional stabilization techniques, d-c motors exhibit appreciably greater intrinsic motor damping than do a-c machines. And fortunately, this greater damping does not coincide with low motor efficiency as it does in a-c servomotors.   Thus, even relatively large d-c servomotors with high efficiencies often have a straight speed-torque characteristic, while a similar characteristic in an a-c machine would indicate very low efficiency.

Besides the more or less conventional damping techniques, there are a variety of methods peculiar to d-c motors. Figure 7-20 shows a common technique for generating a "tachometer" or speed-sensitive voltage for use in feedback stabilization. This method is convenient and can be easily adjusted by using an external line resistor αR_a, where α is a fraction that establishes the permissible heat dissipated in the line resistor. This fraction should be small, not only to minimize waste heat, but also to

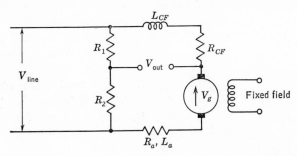

FIG. 7-21. Alternate network arrangement for generating a speed-sensitive voltage. L_{CF} = inductance of motor compensating field; R_{CF} = resistance of motor compensating field; R_a = armature resistance including commutator voltage drop; R_1, R_2 = high resistances, whose ratio is adjusted to yield zero output at zero speed.

$$V_{\text{out}} = \frac{R_1}{R_1 + R_2} V_g \qquad \text{at balanced condition}$$

$$\text{Balance criterion:} \frac{R_1}{R_2} = \frac{R_{CF}}{R_a} = \frac{L_{CF}}{L_a}$$

avoid seriously affecting the performance characteristics of the motor. After α is selected, the across-the-line potentiometer, R_1 plus R_2, can be set and locked in the position that gives zero output when the motor is stalled.

Although this scheme is usable and practical, it suffers because of sensitivity to armature resistance. Armature heating, which changes winding resistance, as well as variations in brush-contact resistance, result in an output at zero speed with a consequent zero offset or servo nulling error. However, the lower the ratio of armature $i_a R_a$ drop to rated motor voltage, the smaller the error. Also, this circuit is not ideal under transient conditions since the balance does not take into consideration the inductive reactance of the armature. But even though this inductance causes a drop during transients, performance is usually adequate since L_a is usually quite small.

An alternate, but similar, circuit for developing a speed-sensitive voltage is shown in Fig. 7-21. By numerical techniques presented elsewhere in this chapter, it is possible to estimate V_g rather accurately from the manufacturer's data and to calculate V_{out} at a given speed.

The motor winding is tapped at the armature brush (a convenient point to bring out an extra connection) so that the inductance of the commutating field, L_{CF}, is available as a balancing element. The exact balance conditions for both the static and dynamic conditions can be obtained by adjusting R_{CF} and the ratio of R_1 to R_2.

Since torque is proportional to current in armature or field-excited machines, current feedback represents acceleration if the load on the motor is primarily inertial. However, as seen from the speed-torque characteristics in the vicinity of the operating speed, motor damping must be considered part of the load. For example, a shunt motor with armature excitation has relatively low damping in the vicinity of zero speed.

Another and perhaps better way to secure acceleration control is to differentiate a speed-sensitive voltage with an RC network. The speed-sensitive voltage can be obtained either from a tachometer or from one of the circuits shown in Figs. 7-20 and 7-21. Sometimes differentiation is performed by taking the voltage output of a transformer, which is a measure of the rate of change of primary current.

7-14. Typical D-C Motor Calculations. To demonstrate the application of some of the previously derived relations, calculate the following from the manufacturer's data for a typical d-c servomotor:

> Motor losses
> Theoretical stall torque
> Theoretical stall acceleration
> Damping constant
> Time constant
> Transfer function

The motor used is the Barber-Colman Co. permanent-magnet d-c motor, Type EYLM 70001. The performance characteristics of this motor are shown by the curves of Fig. 7-22, and as listed in Table 7-2. Outline

TABLE 7-2. TYPICAL PERMANENT-MAGNET MOTOR CHARACTERISTICS

Voltage...	26 volts direct current
Current at rated output................................	0.75 amp
Rated output..	15 mhp
Speed at rated output................................	6,800 rpm
Duty cycle based on 125°F rise and 200°F ambient.........	Continuous
Rotation...	Reversible
Weight...	0.44 lb
Moment of inertia (WK^2).............................	4.52×10^{-3} lb-in.^{2}

dimensions are shown in Fig. 7-23. These calculations only apply in the region where current and torque are proportional, since for higher torques nonlinearity may be encountered due to the demagnetizing effect of armature reaction.

From the curves of Fig. 7-22, a torque of 0.25 lb-in. corresponds to a current of 1.1 amp and a speed of 5,200 rpm. As a second point, take

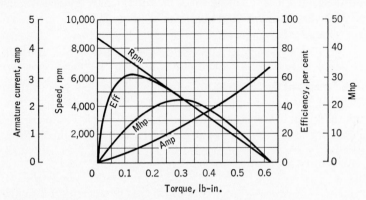

Fig. 7-22. Performance curves for motor used in sample calculation. See Table 7-2 for motor specifications. (*Courtesy of Barber-Colman Co.*)

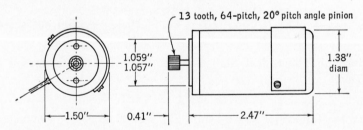

Fig. 7-23. Outline dimensions of motor described in Fig. 7-22.

the no-load condition where the speed is 8,700 rpm and the armature current i_a is negligible. To facilitate the use of these data, the following expressions can be derived:

$$V_g = \phi Z'N = \frac{CN}{60} \tag{7-37}$$

where N = speed, rpm
$C = 60\phi Z'$

and

$$T = 1.41 C i_a \tag{7-38}$$

$$N = \frac{V - i_a R_a}{C} 60 \tag{7-39}$$

In the no-load condition, the $i_a R_a$ term in Eq. (7-39) is negligible, so that this equation becomes

$$N = \frac{60V}{C}$$

and
$$C = \frac{60V}{N} = \frac{60(26)}{8,700} = 0.179$$

where the applied motor voltage V is 26 volts. The armature resistance can be determined under stall conditions, where the armature current is 3.3 amp (Fig. 7-22).

$$R_a = \frac{V}{i_a} = \frac{26}{3.3} = 7.9 \text{ ohms}$$

Check Losses at 5,200 RPM. Determine the copper loss in the armature P_{Cu} and the power output of the motor P. The difference between the sum of P_{Cu} and P, and the total power input to the motor is the stray losses (brush friction, hysteresis and eddy-current losses in the armature, tooth ripple losses, etc.). If brush friction is known, it can be separated from the iron losses.

$$P_{Cu} = R_a(i_a)^2 = 7.9(1.1)^2 = 9.6 \text{ watts}$$
$$P = \frac{16}{1,352} (T)N = \frac{16(0.25)(5,200)}{1,352} = 15.4 \text{ watts}$$
$$P_{Cu} + P = 9.6 + 15.4 = 25 \text{ watts}$$
$$\text{Total input power} = P_T = Vi_a = 26(1.1) = 28.6 \text{ watts}$$
$$\text{Stray losses} = P_T - (P_{Cu} + P) = 3.6 \text{ watts}$$

Determine Theoretical Stall Torque. This can be calculated from Eq. (7-38).

$$T = 1.41(0.179)(3.3) = 0.83 \text{ lb-in.}$$

The actual stall torque as read from Fig. 7-22 (0.63 lb-in.) is less because of armature reaction.

The errors in this analysis are due to brush drop, armature reaction, and friction losses and hysteresis. Nevertheless, the results are accurate enough for most purposes. Unfortunately, manufacturers do not normally provide data on the inductive components, which are required for transient analysis.

Determine Theoretical Stall Acceleration. The stall-torque acceleration equals the stall torque divided by rotor inertia. Rotor inertia is available from Table 7-2.

$$J = 4.52(10^{-3})(16)(182) = 13.2 \text{ g-cm}^2$$
$$T = 0.63(16)(69,600) \cong 700,000 \text{ dyne-cm}$$
$$\alpha = \text{theoretical stall acceleration}$$
$$= \frac{T}{J} = \frac{700,000}{13.2} = 53,000 \text{ radians/sec}^2$$

Determine Damping Constant. The damping constant is equivalent to the slope of the speed-torque curve (a straight line in this case).

$$N_{\text{no load}} = \frac{8,700}{60} 2\pi = 913 \text{ radians/sec}$$

$$D = \text{damping constant} = \frac{T}{N_{\text{no load}}} = \frac{700,000}{913}$$
$$= 767 (\text{dyne})(\text{cm})(\text{sec})/\text{radian}$$

Determine Time Constant of Motor. The time constant is equal to the ratio of inertia to damping constant.

$$\text{Time constant} = \frac{J}{D} = \frac{13.2}{767} = 17.2 \text{ msec}$$

This is much smaller than the time constant of a comparable ac motor.

Determine Transfer Function. The transfer function was derived in Eq. (7-20) as

$$\frac{c}{V_a} = \frac{K'_D/R_a}{p\left[Jp + \left(f_v + \frac{K'^2_D}{R_a}\right)\right]}$$

Assume negligible mechanical friction. Then the time constant is

$$\frac{JR_a}{K'^2_D} = 17.2 \text{ msec}$$

giving $K'_D = 77.8$, and $K'_D/R_a = 9.85$,

$$\frac{c}{V_a} = \frac{9.85}{p(13.2p + 765)}$$

7-15. Comparison of Permanent-magnet Motor with A-C Motor. The relative features of a-c and d-c servomotors can be determined by comparing the motor described above with the Bureau of Ordnance Mark VII. Not only is the BuOrd motor larger in diameter (1.437 to 1.38 in.) but it also represents an optimum design resulting from the efforts of many competent designers over many years. At present, the Mark VII represents an optimum two-phase 400-cycle servomotor.

Table 7-3 compares certain characteristics of these two motors. Some things are immediately apparent. The d-c motor seems to give the best over-all performance. For the same frame size, d-c motor inertia is greater than a-c motor inertia, since the d-c motor requires a wound armature and commutator and consequently a bulkier rotor. The d-c motor does not require standby power, that is, there is no power drain for zero armature voltage; while there is a continuous power drain by the main phase of an a-c motor.

While the d-c machine is not designed to operate at high torque in the vicinity of stall, this is not a usual servo requirement except under intermittent conditions. The d-c motor has a much greater power output (about 6:1) for approximately the same motor losses, and a reserve power output for peak loads and intermittent conditions of about 9:1. This high efficiency in small frame sizes is a distinguishing feature of d-c motors.

TABLE 7-3. COMPARISON OF D-C AND A-C MOTORS

Characteristic	A-C motor Mark VII	D-C motor ELYM 70001	Remarks
Stall torque.......	1.45 oz-in.	10.1 oz-in.	D-c unit not designed for continuous stall operation
No-load speed.....	5,000 rpm	8,700 rpm	
Inertia..........	3.3 g-cm²	13.2 g-cm²	
Time constant....	17.1 msec	17.2 msec	
Theoretical stall acceleration.....	31,000 radians/sec²	53,000 radians/sec²	
Damping factor...	193 (dyne)(cm) (sec)/radian	767 (dyne)(cm) (sec)/radian	Calculated on basis of straight line between stall and no-load points
Power output at maximum efficiency	1.7 watts	11.2 watts	
Motor losses at maximum efficiency..........	6.7 watts	8.3 watts	This power corresponds to heating and temperature rise
Maximum power output..........	1.8 watts	16.4 watts	
Straightness of speed-torque curve..........	Good	Good	Curvature more noticeable in a-c motor characteristic

Regardless of the intrinsically high inertia of the d-c motor, it is capable of very high acceleration because of its large margin of torque over the a-c motor. This is a critical factor in systems with rapidly varying inputs.

7-16. Small D-C Motor Applications.[1] Small d-c motors are used where significant amounts of power must be efficiently controlled. They operate efficiently under variable-speed conditions and are capable of developing very high intermittent starting torques (particularly the series type). Motors are available for operation from battery sources, as well as from normal line voltages. Because they are often used for intermittent operation, their capacity for high output from small sizes is a decided advantage. For increased flexibility, d-c motors are also available with built-in clutches and brakes, gear trains, and speed governors.

Permanent-magnet motors are used for fan and blower drives, rapid transfer switches, electromechanical actuators, generators, and programming devices. Elementary control circuits that short armature terminals provide dynamic braking. The induced voltages and currents in the armature (from the strong permanent-magnet field) bring the unit to a

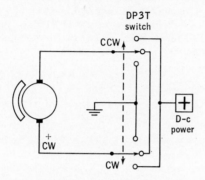

Fig. 7-24. Two-direction and braking-relay control circuit for permanent magnet motor.

rapid stop; for example, a typical motor will stop from 10,000 rpm in approximately 1,000 revolutions. Of course, the magnets must be stabilized to eliminate both long- and short-term demagnetizing effects that can result from full-speed reversal. A typical two-direction and braking relay control circuit for permanent-magnet motors is shown in Fig. 7-24. In this circuit, alternate polarity signals and a shorted armature connection correspond, respectively, to the two active and the neutral position of the relay. In most permanent-magnet control motors, brush life at sea level will exceed 1,000 hr at rated duty cycle. Also some units have tapered airgaps, which improve commutation by minimizing armature reaction effects.

Many permanent-magnet motors can be used as generators, with good linearity and low armature slot and commutator ripple over the operating range.

In ordering a d-c control motor from a manufacturer, the following items should be specified: operating voltage; speed; rated output power; duty cycle; life expectancy; ambient temperature; type of application; MIL, JAN, AN, USAF applicable specifications; special features (brake, integral r-f filter, gearhead, etc.); mounting and shaft requirements; and normal operating altitude.

REFERENCES

1. Liwschitz-Garik, M., and C. C. Whipple: "Electrical Machinery," vol. I, DC Machines, D. Van Nostrand Company, Inc., Princeton, N.J., 1946.
2. Langsdorf, A. S.: "Principles of Direct-current Machines," 6th ed., McGraw-Hill Book Company, Inc., New York, 1959.
3. Tustin, A.: "Direct Current Machines for Control Systems," The Macmillan Company, New York, 1952.
4. Blackburn, J. P.: "Components Handbook," vol. 17, MIT Radiation Laboratory Series, McGraw-Hill Book Company, Inc., New York, 1948.
5. Bruns, R. A., and R. M. Saunders: "Analysis of Feedback Control Systems," McGraw-Hill Book Company, Inc., New York, 1955.
6. Greenwood, I. A., Jr., J. V. Holdam, Jr., and D. MacRae, Jr.: "Electronic Instruments," vol. 21, MIT Radiation Laboratory Series, McGraw-Hill Book Company, Inc., New York, 1948.

Chapter 8

MISCELLANEOUS COMPONENTS

8-1. Introduction. In addition to the universally used components described in the preceding chapters, there are several less well-known induction and inductive pickoff devices intended for use in specialized applications. When properly applied, these latter components often permit substantial system simplification, so that a knowledge of their performance characteristics should be useful to the electromechanical system designer. Included in this chapter are descriptions of the Synchrotel, microsyn, E-shaped inductive pickoffs, Inductosyn, and Magnesyn.

8-2. The Synchrotel. The Synchrotel (developed by the Kollsman Instrument Corp.) is a novel synchro-type device that can function as a

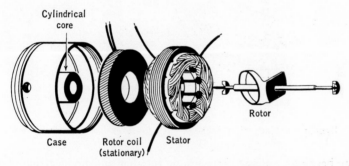

Fig. 8-1. Exploded view of Synchrotel. (*Courtesy of Kollsman Instrument Corp.*)

very low-torque control transformer or as an inductive pickoff. The low-inertia, low-friction movable element of the unit can be directly coupled to the most sensitive aircraft-type instrument to convert rotary instrument movement into a proportional electrical signal with a high degree of accuracy. A typical application might be to couple a Synchrotel to a low-torque gyro-gimbal shaft to permit angular-position transmission.

Figure 8-1 shows an exploded view of this device. A single-phase winding, corresponding to the rotor winding of a conventional synchro, is wound on a spool that slips over the cylindrical core portion of the case.

The case is constructed of a highly permeable magnetic material. The stator is a conventional polyphase synchro-type assembly that fits into the case next to the stationary rotor winding and surrounding the cylindrical core, but with a sufficiently large internal diameter to leave an annular space between the core and the stator teeth. The rotor consists of an oblique section of a hollow cylinder, attached at one end to the rotor shaft, so that the oblique section rotates in the annular clearance between the core and the stator teeth, and the shaft passes through the center of the hollow core. The rotor is made of aluminum for minimum mass, and the shaft terminates in instrument pivots that run in

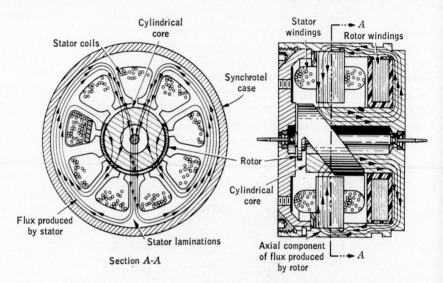

FIG. 8-2. Synchrotel magnetic structure.   (*Courtesy of Kollsman Instrument Corp.*)

sapphire bearings. Since there are no brushes and no electrical reaction at null, only sufficient positioning torque is required to overcome the friction of the jewel bearings.

In use, the stator windings are excited with alternating voltages that produce a resultant radial alternating flux (Fig. 8-2). The portion of this flux that links the single-turn loop of the rotor induces a current in this loop, which, in turn, produces an axial component of alternating flux in the cylindrical core. The flux in the core induces an alternating voltage in the output coil (rotor winding) with an amplitude that is a sinusoidal function of the relative positions of the rotor and of the stator radial flux.

Several design features lead to high angular resolution and accuracy with minimum positioning torque required from the prime mover:

1. Rotor mass and moment of inertia are held to an absolute minimum.

2. The jewel-bearing mounted rotor and the absence of brushes make static friction torque negligible when the unit is energized.

3. The rotor is effectively skewed with respect to the stator, minimizing the effects of the stator slots and rotor axial play on component accuracy.

4. All iron-to-iron airgaps are between stationary members, and are therefore relatively insensitive to radial play in rotor bearings.

5. Reaction torque at the null-voltage position is always zero. And with a properly sized capacitor across the output windings there is no perceptible electrical reaction for any rotor position.

Since rotor design substantially prevents tooth errors, the principal error that is a function of angular position has the form of a smooth sine wave with one cycle for 360° of shaft rotation.

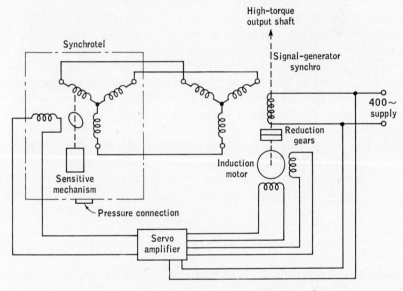

Fig. 8-3. Servo using Synchrotel as a control transformer.

8-3. The Synchrotel as a Control-transformer Synchro.

The Synchrotel is most frequently used in a servo system similar to that shown schematically in Fig. 8-3. A sensitive transducer transforms pressure information (pressure, altitude, air speed, etc.) into rotation of the Synchrotel rotor. The signal-generator synchro rotor is connected to the a-c supply and induces rotor-position-defining voltages in the three Y-connected stator windings. These voltages are fed to the Synchrotel stator, where a resultant field is established whose position is determined by the rotor position of the generator synchro. The rotor winding of the Synchrotel then yields a voltage that is a sinusoidal function of the difference between the angular positions of the Synchrotel rotor and the signal-generator rotor.   The amplified rotor voltage is impressed on the control phase of a two-phase servomotor and drives the signal generator to one of the two positions that will produce a null condition of the Synchrotel rotor.   In doing so, the rotor of the signal-generator synchro continually follows the rotor position of the Synchrotel.   This then is identical to a conventional synchro angle transmission system, except that the synchro control transformer is replaced by a Synchrotel.

The desired null position is selected by properly adjusting the amplifier phase-shift characteristic, and the relative phasing of the signal-generator rotor and the motor fixed phase.

8-4. The Synchrotel as an Inductive Pickoff.   Where it is desired to obtain a 180° a-c phase reversal for an extremely small angular motion, the Synchrotel is capable of generating a substantial volts per degree gradient with a low minimum signal level.   To secure an in-phase signal, a capacitor is usually connected across the Synchrotel rotor leads, the value of the capacitor depending on the load impedance.   There are no ambiguous points for 360° of rotor rotation so that the pickoff cannot "get lost."   Output voltage amplitude is proportional to the sine of the angle away from the null.   When a Synchrotel is used as an inductive pickoff in a follow-up system, a working accuracy of the order of minutes of arc can be obtained.

8-5. Synchrotel Electrical Characteristics.   The electrical characteristics of two Synchrotel models are given in Table 8-1.   When a Synchrotel is energized by a signal generator so that the maximum stator voltage is 9 volts line-to-line (see Fig. 8-4), the electrical characteristics will be as shown in the table.   For 400-cps duty, the output of the Synchrotel is usually shifted about 100° from the input of the signal generator.   This phase shift can be used to obtain the required quadrature at the servomotor.

If, however, it is desired that Synchrotel output be in phase with the input, a capacitor must be connected across the Synchrotel rotor winding.   If Synchrotel output feeds the grid of a tube, the capacitor should have a value of 0.1 μf.   But if the amplifier has a transformer input, an appropriate value of capacitance must be found by experiment.   The table lists the characteristics for a 0.1-μf capacitor and a high-impedance load.

8-6. Synchrotel Equivalent Circuit.   Since the Synchrotel is typically either at standstill or rotating very slowly, it may be regarded as a static device whose input-output coefficient of coupling is a function of angular position.   The reader will remember that a similar approach was taken in obtaining synchro equivalent circuits in Chap. 3.   In the interest of simplicity, the Synchrotel equivalent circuit is presented for the case of

TABLE 8-1. SYNCHROTEL CHARACTERISTICS*

Characteristic	Type 1269				Type 1849
				0.1 µf across secondary	
Frequency, cycles	400	60	1,000	400	400
Voltage input (line-to-line), volts	9.0†	9.0	9.0	9.0	9.0
Current, ma	110.5–149.5	185	80	130	175
Input, volt-ampere	0.99–1.35	1.66	0.72	1.17	1.58
Temperature rise, °C	14	23	6	14	21
Secondary voltage output:					
Rotor in max. position, volts	10.0–12.0	0.5	18.0	13–15	10–12
Rotor in null position, volts‡	0.15	0.15	0.15	0.15	0.05
Angular accuracy	±1°15'	±1°30'	±1°00'	±1°15'	±0°45'
Repeatability, deg	0.01	0.01	0.01	0.01	0.01
Secondary output impedance, ohms	$3{,}800 \pm 10\%$	$1{,}200 \pm 10\%$	$7{,}500 \pm 10\%$	$6{,}000 \pm 10\%$	$3{,}800 \pm 10\%$
D-c line-to-line resistance:					
Primary, ohms	$50 \pm 10\%$	$50 \pm 10\%$	$50 \pm 01\%$	$50 \pm 10\%$	$41 \pm 10\%$
Secondary, ohms	$670 \pm 10\%$	$670 \pm 10\%$	$670 \pm 10\%$	$670 \pm 10\%$	$670 \pm 10\%$
Phase shift (output lags input by approximately), deg	102	30	45	0	102
Rotor static torque, not over, g-cm	0.005	0.005	0.005	0.005	0.005
Weight of rotor, g	0.76	0.76	0.76	0.76	0.76
Weight of unit, g	87	87	87	87	108
Moment of inertia (of weight), g-cm²	0.11	0.11	0.11	0.11	0.11

* All data taken with test circuit shown in Fig. 8-4.
† May be increased to 16.0 volts for application where more output is required.
‡ Worst position (mostly quadrature fundamental).
Reproduced through courtesy of Kollsman Instrument Corp.

maximum coupling, i.e., the output is set for maximum. Under this condition, the magnitude and phase angle of the maximum output can be observed as a function of temperature or any other significant variable. The output at other shaft positions is a known (closely sinusoidal) function of the maximum output.

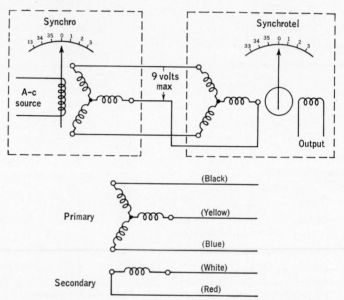

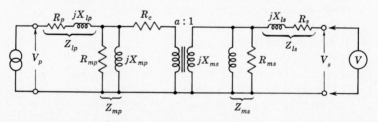

Fig. 8-4. Standard Synchrotel test circuit and internal wiring diagram.

Fig. 8-5. Synchrotel equivalent circuit corresponding to a condition of excitation applied from one leg of a three-phase stator to the other two legs joined together. The rotor is adjusted for maximum voltage to the output coil. R_p = primary resistance; X_{lp} = primary leakage reactance; X_{mp} = primary airgap reactance; R_{mp} = stator core-loss resistance; R_c = rotor resistance; a = primary-to-secondary turns ratio; X_{ms} = secondary airgap reactance; R_{ms} = output core-loss resistance; X_{ls} = secondary leakage reactance; R_s = secondary resistance.

Figure 8-5 shows the equivalent circuit of a Synchrotel. The presence of the rotor conducting ring provides an extra mesh linking the input and output circuits. The figure defines the parameters. Measurements are simple once the configuration is assumed. Since the equivalent circuit is a four-terminal network, it is necessary to assume a standard position where two stator leads at the same potential can be tied together. For uniformity, set the Synchrotel to electrical zero. Then turn the shaft 90° in a counterclockwise direction for maximum coupling to the output. Tie S_1S_3 together and energize with $\sqrt{3}/2$ times maximum rated line-to-line voltage. This applied voltage results in standard flux density in the Synchrotel magnetic circuit. The behavior of the Synchrotel for this standard position is typical of its behavior in any random position.

From this equivalent circuit it is possible to derive certain fundamental relations between the circuit parameters, the output voltage, and the reaction torque on the rotor. For example, capacitor loading of the Synchrotel is often used to improve the output gradient, and to reduce phase shift and reaction torque. The effect of capacitor loading is readily analyzed by the equivalent circuit. In addition, the effect of changes in frequency, temperature, component design parameters, etc., can be checked out very quickly.

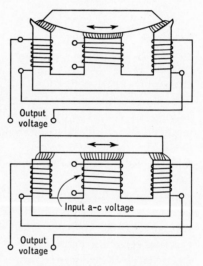

Fig. 8-6. Rotary- and linear-motion E-shaped inductive pickoffs.

8-7. E-shaped Inductive Pickoffs. Simple pickoff devices such as shown in Fig. 8-6 can be used where very low friction is required and the motion is limited to a small linear or angular range. These devices use E-shaped transformer laminations with windings on the three legs. Usually, the center coil is excited by an a-c voltage and the two outer coils connected so that the voltages induced in these coils cancel when the armature is in the center or null position.

When the armature is displaced from null, the flux generated in the center leg is no longer equally distributed between the two outer legs, increasing in the leg toward which the armature moves. As a result of the unbalanced flux in the leg, voltage is generated in the output coils approximately proportional to the magnitude of armature motion. As the armature passes through the null position, the output voltage undergoes a 180° phase reversal, a necessary condition for operation in a null-seeking servomechanism.

To achieve good linearity of output voltage with armature displacement, geometric tolerances must be closely controlled. High-permeability lamination material, such as Mumetal, minimizes nonlinearities and harmonics introduced by the iron. A similar result can be achieved by using a fairly large airgap, which, at the same time, reduces the pickoff's sensitivity to slight mechanical misalignments. By making the armature length equal to the distance between the center lines of the outer legs it is possible to minimize reluctance forces or torques exerted on the armature by the magnetic circuit, while still maintaining a reasonable range of linear motion. The reaction force on the armature is given by

$$F \propto I^2 \frac{dL}{ds} \tag{8-1}$$

where i = current flowing in center coil

$\dfrac{dL}{ds}$ = rate of change of self-inductance with mechanical displacement

It is apparent from Fig. 8-6 that, neglecting the iron portion of the magnetic circuit, the total reluctance as seen from the center leg is independent of armature position as long as the fringing flux paths are not modified by armature displacement. Thus for limited armature movement the fringing fluxes are unchanged, resulting in constant total reluctance, inductance independent of armature position, and zero reaction torque.

In a similar manner, the reluctance of the outer legs varies in linear fashion with armature displacement, a necessary condition if output voltage is to be a linear function of armature movement. Minimum reaction torque is particularly important when the pickoff is driven by a low-level transducer. However, when the transducer incorporates a restraining spring or its equivalent, any springlike pickoff reaction torque can be considered as part of the over-all spring constant and its effect included in the calibration of the system.

As in all inductive-type pickoffs, residual voltages appear in the output. These voltages consist of a component in phase with the normal generated output, a component in time quadrature, and harmonics generated as a result of iron nonlinearities. The in-phase residual voltages appearing at null can be canceled either by a network energized from the a-c supply and suitably coupled to the output winding or by shifting the armature zero position. The latter method, rezeroing the armature, is ideal for correcting for slight unbalances in magnetic assembly symmetry. Quadrature residual voltage, on the other hand, cannot be canceled by zero shifting, but requires network trimming procedures. Often a properly sized capacitor, connected from one or the other primary lead to the ungrounded output lead, will null the quadrature voltage. Harmonic residual voltages are minimized by keeping iron flux density low, by keeping the airgap large, and by using high-permeability nickel steels. Where necessary, harmonics can be eliminated by using a bandpass filter, adjusted to pass only fundamental frequency. However, a harmonic filter can introduce servo dynamic errors and care must be taken in its design. In general, residual voltages tend to reduce servo sensitivity, causing amplifier saturation and therefore reducing gain.

Pickoff sensitivity can be improved by reducing the airgap to a minimum and shortening the armature so that in the null position it just barely overlaps the two outer legs. But this impairs linearity and adds considerable reaction torque, making mechanical setup particularly critical.

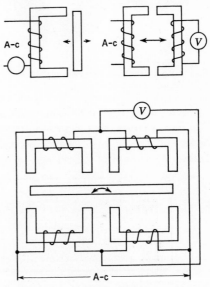

Figure 8-7 shows other types of inductive pickoffs whose operation depends on varying the airgap reluctance. In these devices, a distinct magnetic reaction force is exerted on the armature so that they can only be used where this reaction torque is not objectionable. Reaction force increases so rapidly with reduced airgap that it is possible to develop a snap action in an improperly designed device, such that the armature locks in the minimum airgap position.

FIG. 8-7. A variety of single-ended and double-ended inductive pickoffs.

8-8. The Inductosyn. The Inductosyn (developed and trademark registered by Farrand Controls, Inc.) can be used where precise positioning accuracies are required. The rotary- and linear-motion varieties of this device have accuracies of ± 5 sec of arc and ± 0.0001 in., respectively. This compares with an accuracy of $\pm \frac{1}{2}'$ of arc that can be obtained from a two-speed synchro system using the best possible gearing.

Physically, the Inductosyn consists of engraved patterns of conductors on thermally stable glass plates, forming a multipolar inductive structure. The necessary dimensional stability for a device of this high accuracy can only be achieved through a structure of this type. Because of the absence of magnetic material, carrier frequencies of the order of 10 to 100 kc are necessary for efficient coupling. Similarly, the large number of poles in the Inductosyn means that a conventional synchro system must be used as a "coarse" control to avoid ambiguities in positioning.

As an electrical data-transmission device, the rotary Inductosyn is similar to an electrical resolver having a single input winding and a pair of uncoupled output windings. However, the Inductosyn has a large number of poles, and a complete voltage cycle is produced for a rotation equal to the spacing between pole pairs. Rotary Inductosyns are normally built with 108, 128, and 144 poles, corresponding to 54-speed, 64-speed, and 72-speed resolvers. Thus, an Inductosyn transmitter behaves like a single-input high-precision resolver having a large number of poles, or else like a conventional two-pole resolver geared up by the above ratios. Some of the many useful arrangements of both rotary and linear Inductosyns exploit this electrical identity.

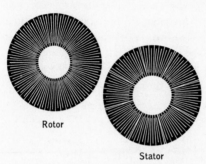

Rotor

Stator

FIG. 8-8. A 108-pole rotary Inductosyn. (*Courtesy of Farrand Controls, Inc.*)

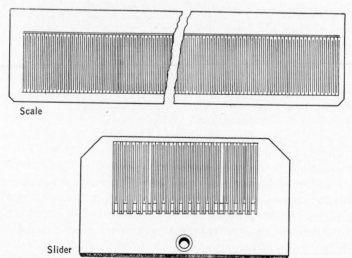

Scale

Slider

FIG. 8-9. Two halves of a linear Inductosyn.   (*Courtesy of Farrand Controls, Inc.*)

If two rotary Inductosyns are paired and their stationary (stator) coils coupled together, they may be used as transmitter and receiver for the transmission of angular data, in much the same way as a pair of resolvers. However, because of the large number of poles, a succession of ambiguous null points appear equal to one less than the number of pole pairs.

Figure 8-8 shows the rotor and stator for a 108-pole rotary Inductosyn. Note that the stator is divided into sectors. Successive sectors are arranged to be one-quarter cycle (90 electrical degrees) out-of-phase with each other; alternate sectors are connected in series to form the two separate output circuits. The slider and scale of a linear Inductosyn are shown in Fig. 8-9. The scale is analogous to the rotor, and the slider to the stator of the rotary type. While the individual linear scales are limited in length to about 10 in., greater distances can be measured

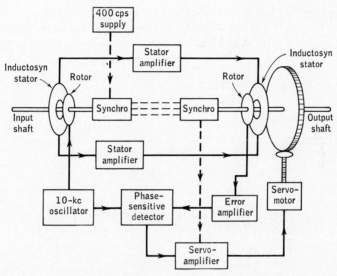

Fig. 8-10. Inductosyn angle-repeater system using standard synchros as coarse data elements.

by using several Inductosyns end to end. Both rotary and linear types are used in a similar manner in servo systems.

8-9. Inductosyn Applications. The Inductosyn was originally designed as a datum element for a shaft-repeating servo system such as the one shown in Fig. 8-10 using two 108-pole Inductosyns. In this case two standard synchros are used as coarse data elements. Often a conventional two-speed synchro system is used in conjunction with the Inductosyns, making effectively a three-speed Inductosyn system. The system shown here uses a 10-kc carrier frequency. Inductosyn output voltage is nearly proportional to frequency up to 100 kc, and because the output voltage at 10 kc is about $\frac{1}{200}$ of the input voltage, it is difficult to operate at lower carrier frequencies. The two stator amplifiers shown in the figure are necessary because of the low coupling between Inductosyn elements. With the amplifiers matched to within 0.1 per cent, accuracies of 5″ of arc can be obtained using 3¼-in.-diameter glass plates mounted directly to the shaft.

In another interesting basic circuit (Fig. 8-11) the Inductosyn can be used to form an electronic gear train. Here, a 108-pole Inductosyn is connected to a conventional resolver in a shaft-repeating servo system. Since the Inductosyn has 108 poles and the resolver only 2, the resolver turns 54 revolutions for one revolution of the Inductosyn. When the Inductosyn has 144 poles, the resolver makes one revolution for every 5° rotation of the Inductosyn. Then the resolver dial can be easily calibrated in degrees, minutes, and seconds.

In addition to the conventional servo system applications, the Inductosyn has found favor as a highly accurate position-measuring device in

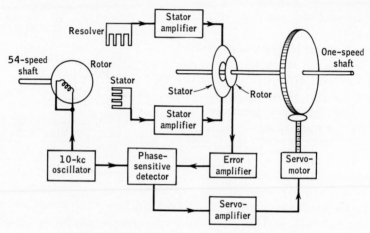

Fig. 8-11. Resolver-Inductosyn electronic gear train.

machine-tool numerical control systems. In these systems, numerical information representing work table or tool position is entered through selector switches, punched tape, or punched cards. The coded position information is then converted into a form compatible with the form used by the position transducer and applied as the input to a positioning servo. The linear Inductosyn is particularly well suited to this application since it is one of the few highly accurate linear transducers. It does have the disadvantage, though, that the coded input information must be converted into sine-cosine functions before it can be compared with the output of the position-measuring Inductosyn.

The error curves for an Inductosyn are approximately sinusoidal in shape with a half-amplitude of about 5″ of arc. Repeatability accuracy is of the order of 1″ of arc or 25 μin. Particular care must be taken in installing these devices to ensure proper operation and high accuracy.

8-10. The Magnesyn. The Magnesyn (trademark registered by the Bendix Aviation Corp.) is a rotary induction component consisting of a permanent-magnet rotor operating within a toroidally wound stator. Because they are low-power components, they are usually used to drive pointers or other indicators for the remote indication of angular position. Since they deliver a three-phase voltage similar to that of a conventional synchro, a Magnesyn can be used together with a synchro in an angle-repeating servo system, provided a suitable transformer is employed to match the Magnesyn phase voltages with the synchro phase voltages. Linear Magnesyns are also available, but the relatively high friction forces opposing the straight-line motion of the permanent magnet limit these devices to use as input-signal generators.

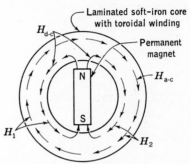

FIG. 8-12. Rotary Magnesyn magnetic circuit.

The Magnesyn is essentially a saturable reactor in which the unidirectional flux field produced by the permanent magnet is modified by the alternating flux field generated by applying alternating current to the toroidally wound core. The laminated core is made of a high-permeability square-loop magnetic material such as Hypersil or Deltamax. By passing a sufficiently large alternating current through the winding, the toroidal magnetic path will be alternately saturated and unsaturated twice each cycle. Biasing this with the unidirectional field of the permanent magnet produces a second-harmonic flux variation in the toroidal magnetic path.

Figure 8-12 shows this. The permanent magnet generates a magnetomotive force H_{dc} in each half of the annular core. Since the toroidal core is presumed to be symmetrical, H_{dc} will be equal in the two halves of the ring. In addition, at some specific instant, the alternating current will generate a clockwise magnetomotive force H_{ac} that is positive with respect to H_{dc} in one-half of the core and negative with respect to H_{dc} in the other half. Thus,

$$H_1 = H_{ac} - H_{dc} \tag{8-2}$$

and

$$H_2 = H_{ac} + H_{dc} \tag{8-3}$$

In turn magnetomotive force H_1 results in a flux density B_1 which consists of two components: (1) B_{ac}, common to both halves and varying at the same frequency as H_{ac}, and (2) B_x, which exists because of the presence of H_{dc} combined with H_{ac}. This can be expressed by

$$B_1 = B_{ac} - B_x \tag{8-4}$$

$$B_2 = B_{ac} + B_x \tag{8-5}$$

Combining Eqs. (8-4) and (8-5) to obtain B_{ac} and B_x yields

$$B_{ac} = \frac{B_1 + B_2}{2} \tag{8-6}$$

$$B_x = \frac{B_2 - B_1}{2} \tag{8-7}$$

Thus, there exists a second-harmonic flux density B_x varying at twice the frequency of the fundamental flux B_{ac}.

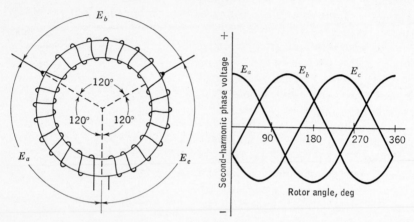

FIG. 8-13. Voltage distribution in Magnesyn.

FIG. 8-14. Variation of second-harmonic voltages in Magnesyn.

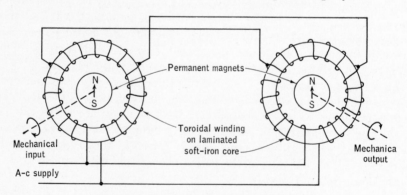

FIG. 8-15. Back-to-back rotary Magnesyns.

If now the toroidal winding is tapped at the 120° and 240° points, as shown in Fig. 8-13, then three-phase second-harmonic voltages will be generated that vary according to the curves of Fig. 8-14. Note that this voltage variation is identical to the voltage variation in a conventional synchro stator as the rotor is moved. Fundamental-frequency voltages are also present, but their magnitude does not vary with rotor angular position.

By connecting two Magnesyns back to back, as shown in Fig. 8-15, and displacing the permanent-magnet rotor of the transmitter with respect to the rotor of the receiver, currents will flow since the second-harmonic voltages at the coil taps are no longer equal. This produces a restoring torque that brings the receiver rotor into alignment.

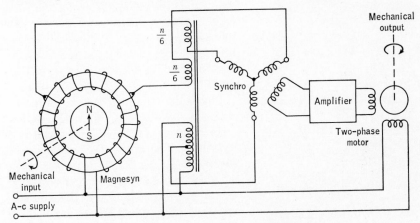

FIG. 8-16. Magnesyn-synchro angle-repeating servo.

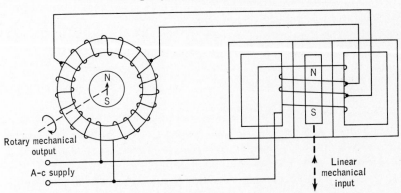

FIG. 8-17. Back-to-back rotary and linear Magnesyns.

A Magnesyn can also be used in place of the transmitting synchro in a synchro follow-up system (Fig. 8-16) if a suitable coupling transformer is used. This transformer must be designed so that the fundamental frequency component from the Magnesyn does not reach the secondary of the synchro. Of course, the reason that this is not necessary in a Magnesyn-to-Magnesyn system is that equal and opposite fundamental frequency voltages that cancel each other are produced by the two Magnesyns.

As pointed out previously, linear Magnesyns are also possible (Fig. 8-17). These use tapped coils as does the rotary unit and are analogous in every respect, except that high friction forces restrict their use to transmitting.

8-11. The Microsyn.   The name "microsyn" refers to the four-pole structure of Fig. 8-18.   Developed at MIT during World War II, this device has found wide usage in measurement and control applications requiring high accuracy and sensitivity over limited angular ranges.   Particularly suited to gyroscope systems, it has recently been applied to many other types of industrial as well as military equipment.

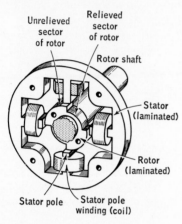

Physically, the microsyn consists of a four-pole stator and specially shaped rotor, both of laminated high-permeability steel.   The microsyn is analogous to a circular differential transformer, or to a variable-reluctance balanced-bridge signal generator similar to that described previously as an E-shaped pickoff. The balanced-bridge construction permits the microsyn to compensate for errors that might otherwise be introduced by mechanical dissymmetry.

Fig. 8-18. Microsyn schematic.

The important features of this device are:

1. High linearity over a limited angular range, including phase reversal at null.

2. Resolution of the order of 0.01°, concurrent with very high signal-to-noise ratios.

3. Low operating torque or friction because of the absence of slip rings or other mechanical restraints, and because of the balanced low-inertia rotor.   Undesirable electromagnetic reaction torques are negligible.

4. Desirable scale factors equivalent to high sensitivity.

5. Good reliability because of simplicity of mechanical construction. In many applications the microsyn rotor and stator elements are coupled directly to the parts whose relative motion is being measured.

The three basic microsyn types—signal generator, torque generator, and elastic-restraint generator—are described and illustrated in Table 8-2.   In each instance the microsyn coil configuration that provides the required function is indicated, together with a description of how the function is obtained.   Characteristic curves show how well the functions are performed.

Most often the microsyn is used as a position indicator or signal generator.   In this application it can be used in conjunction with Bourdon tubes, bellows, and various flowmeters and manometers to measure pressure, or with bimetallic elements and other temperature-sensitive devices to measure temperature. Linear and angular motion, density, humidity, viscosity, and other quantities can be measured and converted to an electrical signal by the signal generator.

Figures 8-19 to 8-21 show a variety of microsyn applications as suggested by the Boston Division of Minneapolis-Honeywell. In linear balancing systems of the telemetering type, the microsyn is ideal for such applications as measuring pressure, temperature, or flow. Figure 8-19 shows such a system. The low-voltage electrical line is trouble-free

TABLE 8-2. MICROSYN TYPES

SIGNAL GENERATOR

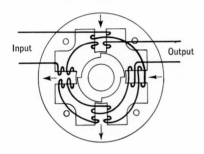

Description. Generates output voltage proportional to displacement angle over limited angular range. Negligible magnetic reaction torques. Excellent sensitivity and linearity, and low null voltage. Operates only on alternating current. Pickoff in very low-torque systems.

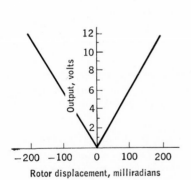

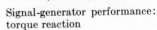

Signal-generator performance: in-phase signal output

Signal-generator performance: torque reaction

Theory. The signal generator primary in the null position, as a result of its symmetry, has no net output coupling with the output winding. However, should the rotor be turned from null, fluxes in the two opposing legs increase while fluxes in the remaining legs decrease, resulting in an unbalance, with a net voltage induced in the output winding. Under ideal conditions, the increase and decrease in flux of the pole groups cancel so that primary inductance is maintained constant. Therefore, there is no reaction torque.

TABLE 8-2. MICROSYN TYPES (*Continued*)

TORQUE GENERATOR

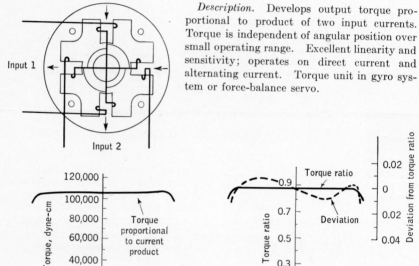

Description. Develops output torque proportional to product of two input currents. Torque is independent of angular position over small operating range. Excellent linearity and sensitivity; operates on direct current and alternating current. Torque unit in gyro system or force-balance servo.

Torque-generator performance: torque output

Torque-generator performance: torque output ratio

Theory. The torque generator has basically the same winding arrangement as the signal generator. For a linear signal generator, the variation in mutual inductance between primary and secondary is a linear function of angle. Since self-inductances of primary and secondary are constant according to the reasoning applied to the signal generator, then reaction torque is proportional to the product of the currents of input and output windings and the constant rate of change in mutual inductance with respect to angle. Thus, the torque generator develops a torque proportional to the product of its currents, and at the same time the torque is relatively independent of angular position over the range.

TABLE 8-2. MICROSYN TYPES (*Continued*)

ELASTIC-RESTRAINT GENERATOR

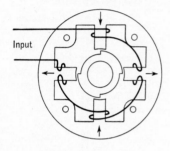

Description. Develops a spring-type restoring torque which varies as the square of the applied current. Moderate accuracy Relatively large leakage fluxes. Used as an "electrical spring."

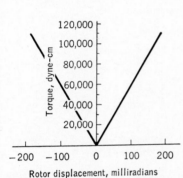

Elastic-restraint generator performance: torque output

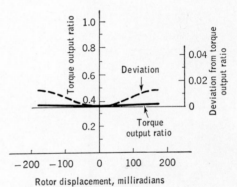

Elastic-restraint generator performance: torque output ratio

Theory. The arrangement of coils in the elastic-restraint generator is such as to give a linear variation of self-inductance. Departures from ideal performance are more pronounced in the elastic-restraint generator than in other applications. This unit is little used, since its function may usually be achieved with a torsion spring.

and safe and can conveniently be connected to a remote indicating point. System accuracy is subject only to the limitations of the primary sensing element. In its simplest application and where compactness and light weight are important, signal generator output can be fed directly to a torque generator.

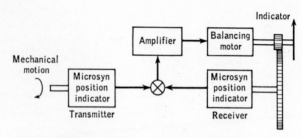

FIG. 8-19. Remote data transmission.

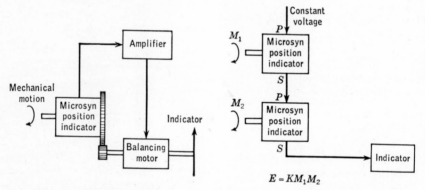

FIG. 8-20. Measurement of mechanical variables.

FIG. 8-21. Multiplication with two microsyns.

Figure 8-20 shows a microsyn incorporated in a self-balancing servo system providing torque and motion amplification. Such an arrangement finds application, for example, in viscosity determinations, micrometry, and for barometric pressure indication. Similar systems also find common military usage in gyro instruments for angular displacement and rate measurement, as well as in acceleration-measuring equipment.

Microsyns, by virtue of their high sensitivity and low-reaction torque, can be used for addition, subtraction, multiplication, or division of variable mechanical inputs. Figure 8-21 demonstrates a method of obtaining the product of two variables.

INDEX